THE LIVING HISTORY OF PAKISTAN

Judges & Generals in Pakistan

Volume-I

by

INAM R SEHRI

CONTEMPORARY HISTORY IS NOT
THAT WHAT HAS BEEN HAPPENING AROUND?
IT IS THE STATEMENT OF FACTS
ABOUT WHAT THE PEOPLE
CONSIDERED SIGNIFICANT

Grosvenor House
Publishing Limited

Re-Print   June 2017

The book cover picture is copyright to Inmagine Corp LLC

This book is published by
P H P Grosvenor House Publishing Ltd
28-30 High Street, Guildford, Surrey, GU1 3EL.
www.grosvenorhousepublishing.co.uk

A CIP record for this book
is available from the British Library

[All page with usual statements ending with]

ISBN 978-1-908596-62-8

For

SALIHA RAHIM
AND
SEHRIs

My partner & friends

(.... tolerating me since 33 years)

Other Books from

INAM R SEHRI

KHUDKUSHI
(on Suicide) [in Urdu] (1983)
{Details of historical perspective of 'Suicide' in various societies; & investigation techniques differentiating in Murder & Suicides}

WARDI KAY ANDAR AADMI
(Man in uniform) [in Urdu] (1984)
{Collection of short stories keeping a sensitive policeman in focus}

AURAT JARAIM KI DALDAL MEIN
(on Female Criminality) [in Urdu] (1985)
{Describing various theories and cultural taboos concerning Female Criminal Behaviour}

POLICE AWAM RABTAY
(on Police Public relationship) [in Urdu] (1986)
{Essays describing importance of mutual relationships}

DEHSHAT GARDI
(on Terrorism) [in Urdu] (1987)
{Various theories and essays differentiating between Freedom Fighting & Terrorism in Middle Eastern perspective}

QATL
(on Murder) [in Urdu] (1988)
{The first book written for Police students & Lawyers to explain techniques of investigation of (difficult) Murder cases}

SERVICE POLICING IN PAKISTAN
[in English] (1990)
{A dissertation type book on which basis the PM Benazir Bhutto, in 1990, had okayed the Commissionerate System of Policing in Pakistan. Taking Karachi as the pilot project, later, it was levied for all major cities and still going on as such}

SHADI

(on Marriages) [in Urdu]   (1998)

{A detailed exposition of Marriage explained in various religions, cultures, countries and special groups; much applauded & commented upon on PTV in 1998-99}

All the above books were published by Pakistan's number one publisher

SANG E MEEL PUBLICATIONS,
The Lower Mall LAHORE, Pakistan

And are always available with them in latest re-prints.

It's me; my Lord!

INAM R SEHRI

- Born in Lyallpur (Pakistan) in April 1948

- First degree from Government College Lyallpur (1969)

- Studied at Government College Lahore & got first Master's Degree from Punjab University Lahore (1971);

- Attachment with AJK Education Service (1973-1976)

- Central Superior Services (CSS) Exam passed (batch 1975)

- Civil Service Academy Lahore (joined 1976)

- National Police Academy Islamabad (joined 1977)

- LLB from BUZ University Multan (1981)

- Got Master's Degree from Exeter University of UK (1990)

- Regular Police Service: District Admin, Police College, National Police Academy, the Intelligence Bureau (IB), Federal Investigation Agency (FIA) [1977-1998] then migrated to the UK permanently.

Just spent a normal routine life; with hundreds of mentionable memoirs allegedly of bravery & glamour as every uniformed officer keeps, some times to smile at and next moment to repent upon but taking it just normal except one or two spills. During my tenure at IB HQ Islamabad I got chance to peep into the elite civil and military leadership of Pakistan then existing in governmental dossiers and database.

During my stay at FIA I was assigned to conduct special enquiries & investigations into some acutely sensitive matters like Motorway Scandal, sudden expansion and build-up of Sharif family's industrial empire, Nawaz Sharif's accounts in foreign countries; Alleged Financial Corruptions in Pakistan's Embassies in Far-Eastern Countries; Shahnawaz Bhutto's murder in Cannes (France); Land Scandals of CDA's Estate Directorate; Ittefaq Foundry's 'custom duty on scrap' scam,

Hudaibya Engineering & Hudaibya Paper Mills enquiries, Bhindara's Murree Brewery and tens more cases like that.

> [*Through these words I want to keep it on record that during the course of the above mentioned, (and also which cannot be mentioned due to space limits) investigations or enquiries, the then Prime Minister Benazir Bhutto, or Gen Naseerullah Babar the then Federal Interior Minister, or G Asghar Malik the then DG FIA, had never never issued direct instructions or implicit directions or wished me to distort facts or to go malafide for orchestrating a political edge or other intangible gains. Hats off to all of them!*]

I should feel proud that veracity and truthfulness of none of my enquiry or investigation could be challenged or proved false in NAB or Special Courts; yes, most of them were used to avail political compromises by Gen Musharraf's government. Most of the case files belonging to Sharif Family's concerns were either 'removed or got lost' by 'well wishers' of Nawaz Sharif and Ch Shuja'at Hussain from the FIA because in February 1997, PML government was once more in saddles and I was shunted away to the Railway Police.

These case files were 'lost' under the garb of their call up and transfers from FIA to 'Ehtesab Cell' and the process was manoeuvred by Saif ur Rehman, Nawaz Sharif's dearest Ehtesab Chief. The second part of that 'clean up Operation' was handled by the then PM's slave judge Malik Qayyum of the Lahore High Court. Under 'special order or arrangement' no other judge was able to hear any of the cases connected with Sharif family or their friends.

Researchers of contemporary history can dig out from the records at Lahore High Court pertaining to 1997, which would prove that:

- Not even a single case of aforementioned details was dealt with by any other judge of the High Court except J Malik Qayyum. All the above referred cases were invariably sent to J Malik's Bench.

- J Malik Qayyum was given a fairly junior or ad-hoc judge to sit with him on the Bench so that Justice Malik Qayyum's words could make out the whole judgment.

- All those cases, each having bank records to make a file of 700 to 1500 pages, were finished within three hearings in which, instead of sending a lawyer, a sub-inspector of FIA had appeared from prosecution to say that *'no witness to offer, my Lord'*.

- All the case files were used to be discussed at J Malik Qayyum's residence a night before where Ehtesab Cell's Hasan Waseem Afzal used to make out 'cardinal points' for the Court.

- All the above mentioned cases were examined, heard, concluded and judgments written between April to September 1997; six months were enough to do that cleansing job.

- Mostly the judgments were spread on 17-18 pages, carrying stereotyped paragraphs with a difference in the texts mostly on the first and the last pages only.

[*Not confirmed but an aged advocate of LHC named Ch Yaqoob used to make & type out the judgments for J Qayyum. J Malik Qayyum was otherwise, beyond doubt, competent to dictate judgments but Ch Yaqoob was assigned this job to do in urgency; used to be paid by Hasan Wasim Afzal from Ehtesab Cell's secret funds.*]

Some of those case files remained available with Gen Musharraf's regime. Those were the files which were sent to the Accountability Courts till mid 1996 to launch trial under due process and Ehtesab Cell could not do much about them. Three of them were used to negotiate and bring Nawaz Sharif to 'terms' in the first week of December 2000 when a Brigadier in uniform visited the former PM in the Attock Fort Jail for his 'escape' to Saudia. The same files were shown to Nawaz Sharif at the Islamabad Airport on 10th September 2007 to affect his repatriation to Saudia again.

Since ending 2007, the PML(N) has been vowing to bring forward or reopen NRO cases against their PPP counterparts and others trying to make fool of the people of Pakistan conveying that PML(N) leadership has been clean and no case against them exists in the NRO or NAB. It is not the whole truth; not even the half.

PML(N) cronies were able to remove or get lost the case files or to avail favourable judgments from LHC but I still keep copies of most of those cases; not to place them before the media but as my 'asset' because I had suffered a lot on that account, personally, financially & morally.

That's all, my dear countrymen.

Contents

My Apologies:

Mostly my published articles; so chapters may not be inter-related.

Each chapter is a different scenario.

'Judges & Generals in Pakistan' is a collection of essays, may be irritating for someones; explaining diverse scenarios. This book evaluates some varying news, editorials, opinions and criticisms on historical issues.

No misleading intelligence story, no distracting investigative report, no concocted interview and no feed from the 'concerned ones' yet everything seems innovative; no fiction in this book but simple narration of facts.

> *'It is the collection of tragedies and misgivings which are deliberately buried in suspicious darkness since decades. I've simply dig them out, collated and placed together for those who want to keep a track of their past;'* I simply presume.

You read your newspaper daily and regularly and many of you go through it thoroughly but you do not keep record of even important events. This book contains nothing but the news, editorials, opinions and criticisms on certain topics, of course, which have cogent references to your history, your representatives, your leaders, your ideal guides and not the least, your nation, your Pakistan.

People are also living on that part of earth, known as Pakistan, where:

- An army General takes over the country; promises with the nation in a telecast to hold general elections within 90 days but continues to rule for eleven years in the name of Islam.

- A chief justice writes a landmark judgment, a light tower for all generations to come, setting guidelines for induction and promotion of judges in the superior judiciary but lacked courage to impose the same judgment on his own person.

- The Supreme Court has held two opposing judgments in 1993 & 1997 for two opposing Prime Ministers dismissed on the same charges under the same Article 58(2)(b) of the Constitution.

- The two judges (out of 17) of the Supreme Court suddenly pass a judgment commanding their own Chief Justice not to function as Chief Justice.

- The Supreme Court rejects a law of direct legalized corruption (NRO) by one political party but deliberately and continuously ignores indirect legalized corruption through 'eating up bank loans and mark ups' by another key political party.

- The civil dictators and monarchs rule the country on turn by turn basis, through family successions but fooling and cheating their people with loud slogans and high banners of democracy.

- The Constitution is democratic by objective but under the constitutional provisions there cannot be elections in the political parties at any level, at any stage or at any place.

- There are tens of parties vowing to bring Islamic Code of Governance but they do not possess any written document to implement the same in practice because they do not have consensus.

- The Federal *Shariat* Court had been used as a cave to accommodate the 'punished and disgruntled' judges of the higher judiciary.

- The Islamic *Hudood* Laws are in vogue since 1979 but not a single male partner of rape has ever been stoned till today. Female partners are many times stoned and flogged.

I've purposefully started the military details after late 1973 to avoid mention of some of our military heroes like Gen Yahya Khan and Gen Tiger Niazi of East Pakistan fame. For the former, his Second in Command Gen Abdul Hameed had instructed the staff that:

> *'When boss conveys some orders after sun set, please recheck them all in the morning from me or his staff officer.'*

For the later, known facts have explicitly come on record that:

> *'He did not hesitate to maltreat the young women even in his office during office hours.'*

So I considered better to start with later events.

In Pakistan, an evergreen topic is always found alive in debating forums: Army rule or civil way of governance; which is better. The intelligentsia holds that both were looters. A few families have plundered the national wealth through civil dictatorial rule whereas some army Generals, though made less fortunes for their own but provided extensive opportunities to their *'helping jageerdars, political Generals, politico-industrialists, peer Syeds and bureaucrats'*.

The tragedy has been that the superior judiciary was always found standing by them all, through their compromising attitudes or cowardice or ineptness or sometimes under duress; of course, never for financial gains but occasionally for political slots.

The interference of army in government affairs had even started in the Qaid e Azam days. Just after formation of Pakistan, one General Akbar once dared to know from Qaid e Azam that *'why you have posted that man at this place and why you have not posted this man at that place.'* The great Qaid immediately went furious and gave a polite bull-shit to the General saying that:

> *'It is none of your business to bother about. It is civil government's domain.'*

In the developed nations, decisions about movements of the army for wars are invariably taken in Parliaments and Civil Secretariats. Sir Winston Churchil had once said that:

> *'War is too serious a matter to be left with the Generals.'*

The same General Akbar was subsequently found involved in a revolt against the 1ˢᵗ Prime Minister of Pakistan Liaqat Ali Khan. Thus the tussle between army and civil governments could find its routs as early as in 1951 onwards.

The judiciary always supported the army coup in Pakistan. But surely, the judiciary alone cannot be made to bear the burden of all our evils. Judicial decisions are not given in a vacuum. Realism has an overwhelming influence on court behaviour.

Borrowing phrases from a famous superior judgment that the *'doctrine of necessity'* can be made a double-edge sword if courts wanted to. Court decisions are *'reflections of the time'* and attempts at *'defining what's real'*. Realism results in verdicts after what judges *'see right in front of their eyes'*; such verdicts have little or nothing to do with Article 6 or 209 or whatever else is in the Constitution.

Tailpiece: "If you are neutral in situations of injustice, you have chosen the side of the oppressor." *Bishop Desmond Tutu* (1931-) [Nobel Prize for Peace 1984.]

(Inam R Sehri)
Manchester UK
30th December 2011

Scenario 1

HUMBLE SUBMISSIONS:

In the name of those:

"......unsung heroes who have suffered immeasurably for many years because they preferred right over wrong.......of the scores imprisoned and tortured, coerced and intimidated ...... Many chose unemployment and exile rather than to agree with perverted justice.

They paid a heavy price in health, livelihood and reputation and right to happiness ....but they took a stand for justice which those who had sworn to do so, refused to do."

Since the first day of schooling, all children of Pakistan are mostly briefed that their homeland was created by Mohammad Ali Jinnah on the basis of two nations - theory and for the propagation of Islam. It was true and remained so during its initial years of existence but study of the later developments proved that this piece of land was separated from the Indian subcontinent for exclusive rule and malicious usage by *Generals backed by Judiciary and Jagirdars*.

Since the first day of constitutional developments in Pakistan it was being envisaged that the general populace would be subjected to democratic rule but in practice all public institutions are being controlled by army Generals in the name of 'eradicating political corruption'; civil dictators in the name of 'democracy' and bureaucracy mainly consisting of serving or retired army officers, close relatives of first row politicians and Generals.

Since the first day of parliamentary history of Pakistan the federal and provincial assemblies are being used as debating forums only and legislation, got coined by ruling dictator families, is simply floated on the floors to have accents & stamps only.

Since the first day of its independence the Pakistani rulers are continuously betraying the people in the name of Islam; sometimes by introducing *Hadood* Ordinance (of 1979), sometimes by imposing *'Shriah'* law, sometimes by announcing that all penal codes would be revised in the light of Islamic injunctions and sometimes by establishing separate courts to hear these such cases. The irony of fate is that not even a single male has been finally convicted *under Hadood Ordinance* since its promulgation in 1979. [Yes; in a case of *Hadd,* one poor woman was punished under these laws and her co-accused male partner was set free]

AND the most unfortunate mention is that throughout the history of Pakistan, the higher echelons of judiciary, who were supposed to protect the constitution and democratic institutions always stood up to help the Generals & *Jagirdars* and upheld their unconstitutional acts. I'll beg to quote a wishfull thinking:

> *'This is not the country I opted for in the Referendum held in my home province of NWFP in 1947 and this is not the country I would like to die in. I badly want a Pakistan to defend, a nation I can belong to, fight for and die for'.*

This is what **Roedad Khan,** a former bureaucrat (remained posted as Federal Secretary Interior, too) has written in his book **Pakistan - *A DREAM GONE SOUR*:** [Oxford University Press (1997)]

Roedad Khan recalls the advice of Mr Jinnah to civil officers: *'to serve a government if it is formed according to the constitution. Public services deteriorated in Pakistan and a stage has now come wherein public servants have been reduced to the 'level of domestic servants'.*

But the governing principle for the Pakistani civil servants for the last two decades has been that *'if you are not with them [rulers], you are against them'* and the irony of fate is that the same has been going true for judiciary, too.

*Hazrat **Ali Bin Abu Talib (RAA),*** the fourth Caliph had told that:

> *'if the judicial system goes corrupt somewhere & justice becomes unapproachable for the public, that society is bound to perish'.*

In my humble (personal) opinion, the institution of judiciary in Pakistan has already broken down. There are so many occasions to mention, so many stories to be told and so many events to be analyzed that one may need thousands of pages for narration.

If I were in Pakistan, I would have been hanged on the charges of 'Contempt of Court' or 'Scandalizing the Courts' and thus I could not do this unpleasant job there. But the very basic question arises that in democratic societies whether a judge's judicial personality and characteristics, judge's ability to understand law in prevailing cultural or political scenarios; a particular judge's educational and professional knowledge, his mode of entry and rising to the superior positions or judge's decision making potential on merits and fearlessness or alleged political sympathy AND the judgments passed by the courts in some particular background of events can be analyzed, commented upon or dissected in writing or discussions in public media openly or not.

To find out answer to these questions, I shall take shelter of an <u>article written in August 1999 (as referred in the website of American Society of International Law) by a world known media lawyer</u> **Zahid Ebrahim** on the issue of 'scandalizing the court'. <u>This research was done by him in the backdrop of certain decisions taken by the Supreme Court of Pakistan in cases related to the subject of contempt of court involving some members of the parliament and a provincial assembly. Those wrong doers were members and office bearers of the then ruling party, too.</u>

The laws of contempt are primarily designed to balance the freedom of expression with the judiciary's quest to maintain its authority and safeguard public order. Broadly speaking, contempt of court falls into three general areas:

- violation of an order of a court,
- interference in the judicial process and
- Criticism of a judge, his judgment, or the institution of the judiciary.

More precisely the academics try to engulf the contemporary law of contempt where it seeks to prohibit the criticism of the judge, his judgment or the institution of the judiciary. One should understand that the law of contempt is a 'sacred cow' of the legal world. However, the description of this class of contempt is to be taken subject to one important qualification. That is: <u>Judges and Courts are alike open to criticism, and if reasonable argument and justification is offered against a judicial act as contrary to law or the public good, no court would treat that as contempt of Court</u>. [*The Queen v. Gray* (1900) 2 QB 36]

The extent of tolerance in implementation of contempt of court law had been cited by the courts in England much earlier. The issue had best been understood by the Queen's Bench, Appellate Division for England and Wales [Ref: *R. v. Metropolitan Police Commissioner, ex parte Blackburn* (1968) 2 QB 150] when it refused to hold a member of parliament in contempt for authoring an article in which he vigorously criticized a judgment of the Court of Appeal. The Queen's Bench ruled that:

3

'No criticism of a judgment, whatsoever vigorous, can amount to contempt of court providing it keeps within the limits of courtesy and good faith.'

It may not be out of place to mention here a world famous case of a Kenyan lawyer, Feroze Nawrojee, who was once charged for contempt of and scandalizing the court. The basis was a letter written by him when he got frustrated by an inordinate delay in deciding a motion to stay proceedings in a traffic case in which a prominent critic of the Kenyan Government had been killed. The protest note of Nawrojee carried an expression of anxiety over an inordinate delay in hearing. It is on record that the Kenyan High Court had concluded:

"The courts could not use their contempt power to suppress mere criticism of a judge or to vindicate the judge in his personal capacity, but rather could use it only to punish scurrilous abuse of a judge when necessary in the interests of justice......and a judge must scrupulously balance the need to maintain his or her authority with the right to freedom of speech"

Feroze Nawrojee was absolved of the contempt charges in the above cited case. (**Ref: *Republic v. Nawrojee, High Court of Kenya,*** Misc. Crim. App. No. 461 of 1990, unreported, as referred to in the Article IX Freedom of Expression Manual, 1993 p 182)

The law makers and jurists, while defining and protecting the laws on contempt of court, frame the phrases on the assumption that the judiciary is incapable of bowing to outside influences and immune from bias or prejudice. And this is a hard fact that in all societies, including Pakistan, the courts are reluctant to admit that they may be susceptible to political, economic and moral prejudices prevailing in their surrounds.

Moreover, the balance between freedom of expression and maintenance of public confidence in the judiciary has not been settled yet. For example, in the *Masroor Ahsan* case, the Supreme Court of Pakistan had dismissed a large number of contempt petitions, including one against the Prime Minister who had earlier accused the former Chief Justice of the Supreme Court of reviving 'horse trading' in the country by suspending a constitutional amendment and acquitted the alleged contemnors. Although, the contempt actions were dismissed, the Supreme Court of Pakistan had laid down strict rules that:

".....[it is only] fair comments about the general workings of [the] Court made in good faith, in public interest [and] in temperate

language...without impugning the integrity or impartiality of the judge [which] are protected." (**Ref: Masroor Ahsan & Others v. Ardeshir Cowasjee & Others PLD 1998 SC 823**)

There is a school of thought who still believes that the verdict in the Masroor Ahsan case was influenced by the political environment of the day and would have constituted contempt under the traditional law. But the others consider it a milestone because, while responding to criticism levelled at the Supreme Court of Pakistan for acquitting the legislators of the ruling party on contempt charges, the Chief Justice of the Supreme Court had remarked that:

" ..... the court was not bothered about criticism till the time it was according to law and in temperate language." (**Ref: The Dawn of 15th June 1999**)

Now let us take account of certain facts of recent history of Pakistan. After announcement of 20th March 1996 decision on the subject of appointment of judges by a full court, the then Prime Minister Ms Benazir Bhutto had declared it, on 28th March 1996 in the National Assembly session, as an effort to take away the inherent powers of democratically elected parliament. The next Prime Minister Nawaz Sharif and his companions, on 28th November 1997, practically insulted the judiciary, raided and ransacked the Supreme Court premises thus conveying the message that the superior courts should work under the directions of political bosses.

In the developed world, the media people have succeeded in convincing the judiciary to listen them and read their criticism if based on facts and evidence. In 1997, the European Court had accommodated the columnists and newsmen and tilted themselves in favour of freedom of expression through their decision in a case titled ***De Haes & Gijsels vs. Belgium.*** In this case, De Haes and Gijsels had published articles accusing four Belgian judges of bias. They were prosecuted for contempt of courts wherein the European Court ruled that:

"...... although Mr. De Haes & Mr. Gijsels' comments were without doubt severely critical, they nevertheless appear proportionate to the stir and indignation caused by the matters alleged in their articles. As to the journalists' polemical and even aggressive tone, which the court should not be taken to approve, it must be remembered that Article 10 protects not only the substance of the ideas or information expressed but also the form in which they are conveyed." (**Ref: De Haes & Gissels vs. Belgium, 25 [1997] EHRR 1**)

5

However, it must be acknowledged that the European Court were also influenced by the fact that De Haes and Gissels had offered to demonstrate the truth of their allegations with the help of the case files, though were denied this opportunity by the Belgian Courts.

In Pakistan, in the arena of recent developments on the subject, there is much room for both judiciary and politics to create better environment for the general public. All the foregone governments, both political and military sponsored, had failed to stick to the expected norms of respects for the judiciary and had used them as their subordinate offices. The regimes in succession had failed to provide autonomy and freedom for the superior courts and had always opted to twist their arms in favour of ruling politicians and army dictators.

The last word: though the offence of 'scandalizing the court' continues to be a hot debate all over the globe, but here in England, the last successful prosecution for scandalizing the court had been reported in 1931, as **David Pannick** maintained in his book **'Judges'**

> *'..... (that successful prosecutions tend to) inhibit journalists, who wrongly suspect that they have a legal obligation to speak respectfully and cautiously when discussing the judiciary."* (**Ref:** <u>David Pannick, Judges, Oxford University Press, 1987)</u>

In the words of the Chief Justice Aziz Ahmadi of India, a citizen cannot be expected to wait for the system to correct itself; he would be expected to take upon himself the task of enforcing the rights granted to him by the constitution.

There is a risk that Pakistan — which typifies what Gunnar Myrdal calls a *'soft state'* because it lacks social discipline, it is high on promises and low on delivery — will join those many countries in Africa and soon become one of the failed states. This risk draws closer every day.

As per wording of **Shahid Javed Burki** uttered from the World Bank desk during the 1990s:

> *" .... The country is now left with no viable institutions, including that of the judiciary and ...... we are in danger of losing Jinnah's legacy. Given the impact of change, Pakistan could cease to exist in its sovereign nation-state form. Approaching the twenty-first century, Pakistanis may at last find their elusive commonwealth, only it may not be the one envisaged by the nation's creators."*

It is time for our politicians, bureaucrats, academic scholars, army Generals and intellectuals to rise to the occasion and ensure that forecasts of pseudo-historians do not come true.

In the light of the whole discussion, I feel strength to write more details in the following pages while repeating the words of Roedad Khan again:

'The lesson is that when dykes of law and justice break, revolutions begin'. We may not be far off from that position.

Scenario 2

JUDICIARY IN 1954-73:

Draconian use of 'Doctrine of Necessity:

On 25th July 2003, two civil judges and a magistrate were killed by prisoners of the Sialkot District Jail while they were on an official visit to the jail premises accompanying a heavy contingent of the local police.

Why did they have to kill the judges?

Dr Farrukh Saleem, an Islamabad based analyst, rightly pointed out that *'.... It is important for the judiciary to peer into history for answers.'*

Here are some dates and events describing the judicial history of Pakistan; one can find out if the events are inter-connected and if some stuff is also available in between the lines.

On 21st September 1954, the Constituent Assembly amended the Government of India Act. The amendments precluded the Governor General from acting except on the advice of his ministers. All ministers were to be members of the Assembly at the time of their selection and continue to hold office only so long as they retained the confidence of the legislature.

Justice Munir, in Molvi Tamizuddin Khan's case, declared that the Assembly was not a sovereign body. He gave ruling that the Constitutional Assembly had *'lived in a fool's paradise if it was ever seized with the notion that it was the sovereign body of the state.'* The historians keep the opinion that when Justice Munir denied the existence of the Assembly's sovereignty, he, in fact, had destroyed Pakistan's constitutional basis. He did further harm when he did not indicate where sovereignty resided.

Through Special Reference No.1 of 1955, the then Governor General Ghulam Mohammad asked the Federal Court for an advisory ruling regarding his powers. Justice Munir, relying on Bracton's maxim 'that which is otherwise not lawful is made lawful by necessity', and on the Roman law maxim urged by Jennings, 'the well-being of the people is the supreme law' declared that:

'Subject to the condition of absoluteness, extremeness, and imminence, an act which would otherwise be illegal becomes legal if it is done bona fide under stress of necessity, the necessity being referable to an intention to preserve the Constitution, the state, or the society, and to prevent it from dissolution, and affirms....... that necessity knows no law... ....necessity makes lawful which otherwise is not lawful'. (**Ref: PLD 1955 FC240**)

Thus, because the Constituent Assembly was denied a judicial remedy, the Governor General's position seized the ultimate power of the state. It also followed from the court's decision on sovereignty that the Assembly could be dissolved by the Governor General for political purposes.

21st March 1955: Chief Justice Muhammad Munir of the Federal Court (the present Supreme Court) legalized the dissolution of the 1st Constituent Assembly. Justice A.R. Cornelius (a non-Muslim) of the Federal Court dissented. Cornelius opined that the Constituent Assembly was 'sovereign', the governor-general's dissolution was illegal and that 'Pakistan owed no duty to the Crown.'

31st March 1955: Despite objections from powerful political elements, the Governor General of Pakistan intended to have the constituent convention pass the constitution, as already drafted by the then central cabinet 'Constitution through Ordinance'.

16th May 1955: On 24th October 1954 the Governor-General of Pakistan, Ghulam Mohammad (GM), dissolved the Constituent Assembly and appointed a new Council of Ministers on the grounds that the said Assembly no longer represented the people of Pakistan. The fact was that the draft of the constitution was ready to be announced on 25th December 1954, but the governor general dismissed that assembly on 24th October 1954, to avoid the curtailment of his powers of dismissing the government of the elected prime-minister. Mr GM had more objections to the constitution which the Assembly was about to adopt.

The President of the Constituent Assembly, Maulvi Tamizuddin, appealed to the Chief Court of Sind at Karachi to restrain the new Council of Ministers from implementing the dissolution and to determine the validity of the appointment of the new Council under Section 223-A of the constitution. [*In those days, Pakistan comprised of two parts, West Pakistan & East Pakistan (Bagladesh after 1971) and Karachi was the capital of Pakistan. M Tamizuddin was from East Pakistan*] (**PLD 1955 Sindh 96**)

In response, members of the new Council of Ministers appealed to the court saying that it had no jurisdiction to deal with the dissolution of the Assembly and appointments of the ministers. They argued that Section 223-A of the constitution had never been validly enacted into the Constitution because it was never approved by the Governor-General, and therefore anything submitted under it was invalid. The Sindh Chief Court ruled in favour of Maulvi Tamizuddin and held that the Governor General's approval was not needed when the Constituent Assembly was acting only as a Constituent Assembly and not as the Federal Legislature. The Federation of Pakistan and the new Council of Ministers then appealed to the Supreme Court, the appeal was heard in March 1955. (Reference: *Federation of Pakistan v Maulvi Tamizuddin Khan*)

In the appeal hearing under Chief Justice Muhammad Munir, the court decided that the Constituent Assembly functioned as the 'Legislature of the Domain' and that the Governor-General's assent was necessary for all legislation to become law. Therefore, the Sindh Chief Court had no jurisdiction to overturn the Governor General's dissolution and Mr Ghulam Mohammad's step was held as valid.

However, the ground of which the court found in favour of the Federation of Pakistan called into question the validity of all legislation passed by the Assembly, not to mention the unconstitutionality of the Assembly itself since 1950. To solve this problem, the Governor-General had to invoke Emergency Powers to retrospectively validate the Acts of the Constituent Assembly. An appeal was filed against the Governor-General for invoking emergency powers and the then Chief Justice of Pakistan had to determine the constitutionality of invoking the Emergency Powers.

The Court held that in this case the Governor-General could not invoke emergency powers because in doing so he validated certain laws that had been invalid because he had not assented to them previously. Justice Munir also ruled that constitutional legislation could not be validated by the Governor General but had to be approved by the Legislature. Lack of the Constituent Assembly did not transfer the Legislature's powers to the Governor-General.

The Federal Court of Pakistan gave ruling that:

• The Governor General in certain circumstances had the power to dissolve the Constituent Assembly.

- The Governor-General had during the interim period the power 'under the common law of civil or state necessity' of retrospectively validating the laws listed in the Schedule to the Emergency Powers ordinance.

- The new Assembly (formed under the Constituent Convention Order 1955) would be valid and able to exercise all powers under the Indian Independence Act 1947.

In his verdict, CJP Ch Munir declared it was necessary to go beyond the constitution to what he claimed was the Common Law, to general legal maxims, and to English historical precedent. He relied on Bracton's maxim, *'that which is otherwise not lawful is made lawful by necessity'*, and the Roman law maxim urged by Jennings, *'the well-being of the people is the supreme law.'*

Justice Sajjad Ali Shah in his essay titled 'Blessings of Judicial Activism' published in DAWN on 26th September 2006 has explained the above facts with references given below:

*[In consequence of judgment of the Federal Court, 35 constitutional acts and many decisions under writ jurisdiction became invalid for want of assent of the Governor General. There was total confusion and chaos: the Governor-General issued an ordinance with retrospective effect to rectify the mistake. The Federal Court held in **Usif Patel's case** (PLD 1955 FC 387) that the Governor-General was not empowered to issue an ordinance for constitutional matters in the absence of the constituent assembly whatsoever.*

The Governor-General then made special reference to the Federal Court for guidance (PLD 1955 FC 435). The Federal Court allowed retrospective validation of invalid acts to be approved by a new constituent assembly directed to be elected. This judgment gave rise to the doctrine of state necessity, which is also called the law of necessity, later used by the courts to justify martial laws and the dismissal of constitutions.]

23rd March 1956: First Constitution of Pakistan declared. Major General Iskandar Mirza changed his portfolio from Governor General to the President of Pakistan.

28th October 1958: Chief Justice Muhammad Munir called Iskander Mirza's dissolution of the 2nd Constituent Assembly & abrogation of 1956's Constitution, a 'legalized illegality' meaning thereby that a victorious revolution and a successful coup d'etat is an internally recognized legal method of changing a constitutional government.

When Isikandar Mirza dissolved the parliament in 1958 and announced martial law, Justice Munir and the Supreme Court were readily available to place a judicial stamp of approval on what had taken place. Justice Munir had given the verdict that:

> 'It sometimes happens, however, that the Constitution and the national legal order under it is disrupted by an abrupt political change not within the contemplation of the constitution. Any such change is called a revolution, and its legal effect is not only the destruction of the existing constitution but also the validity of the national legal order ...
> ....For the purpose of the doctrine here explained, a change is, in law, a revolution if it annuls the constitution and the annulment is effective...Thus the essential condition to determine whether a constitution has been annulled is the efficacy of the change...Thus a victorious revolution, or a successful coup d'etat is an internally recognized legal method of changing a constitution.
>
> ...If what I have already stated is correct, then the revolution having been successful, it satisfies the test of efficacy and becomes a basic law-creating factor'.

The above extract has been taken from the decision announced by the Chief Justice of the Federal Court in the case titled *State v. Dosso (PLD 1958 SC 533)*. The constitutional petition was filed in the backdrop of proclamation of martial law issued by President Iskandar Mirza in the first week of October 1958, wherein:

• The Constitution of 23 March 1956 was abrogated.

• The Central and Provincial governments were dismissed.

• The Parliament and Provincial Assemblies were dissolved.

• All political parties were abolished.

• Until alternative arrangements were made, Pakistan remained under martial law's flag.

Gen Ayub Khan, Commander-in-Chief of Pakistan Army was accordingly appointed as the Chief Martial Law Administrator and all the armed forces of Pakistan placed under his command. Explaining the reasons for these steps the President, *interalia*, had observed:

> *'The constitution which was brought into being on 23 March 1956, after so many tribulations, is unworkable. It is full of dangerous compromises, that Pakistan will soon disintegrate internally if the inherent malaise is not removed. To rectify them, the country must first be taken to sanity by a peaceful revolution.'*

The learned Chief Justice went on to observe that if a revolution succeeds, it is a **legalised illegality**. The revolution itself becomes a law creating fact because thereafter its own legality is judged not by reference to the annulled constitution but by reference to its own success. For this view, reliance was placed on the writings of Hans Kelsen contained in his book General Theory of Law and State. The court held that the 1958 revolution satisfied the test of efficacy and had thus become a basic law creating fact. It was accordingly found that the Laws (Continuance in Force) Order 1958, however transitory or imperfect it might be, was a new legal order and had destroyed the old legal order, with the result that the validity of the laws and correctness of judicial decisions were to be determined with reference to that order and not the earlier legal order.

In nut shell Justice Munir's decision in Dosso case set the constitutional stage for Ayub Khan, the then Commander in Chief of the Pakistan Army, to take over the government from Iskandar Mirza. It would be remembered in the history that Gen Ayub Khan's take over (on 27th October 1958) took place just next day the Court's decision was announced.

> [*Upon retirement, Justice Munir had accepted a government job in Tokyo and then formally accepted a cabinet position under Gen Ayub Khan's government. The Governor General Iskandar Mirza was sent into exile, to UK.*]

14th April 1972: Interim Constitution of Pakistan was passed by the National Assembly and Martial Law was lifted.

[It may be remembered that the army had gone angry with Mr Bhutto till then because, when he became Martial Law Administrator, then President and then the Prime Minister, he had sent 22 serving Generals home. It was natural that 22 top families, their next generation in army, their relatives and associates all went upset and the PPP continuously suffered a lot since then.]

7th & 20th April 1972: The Supreme Court of Pakistan declared Yahya Khan's martial law to be illegal. The decision was announced four months after the departure of that army ruler.

Gen Yahya Khan was also a Commander in Chief of the Pakistan Army who imposed Martial Law in March 1969, after receiving a written letter from Gen Ayub Khan, the then President of Pakistan 'to do your duty to run the country'. He performed his duty by promulgating another martial law next day.

Gen Ayub Khan himself had violated his own constitution by handing over power to the Commander-in-Chief of the army, Gen Yahya Khan, instead of the National Assembly Speaker as was provided for the transfer of power in the constitution. Gen Yahya Khan abrogated the 1962 constitution of Ayub Khan and introduced the "Legal Framework Order" containing the rules relating to the holding of general elections and framing of the future constitution for Pakistani people.

Gen Yahya's rule ended on 20th December 1971 with the fall of Dacca.

In this case, commonly known as *Asma Jilani Case (PLD 1972 SC 139)*, on behalf of the military government, the law of necessity was pleaded but the Supreme Court rejected the plea and held that the commander of the armed forces was bound by oath to defend the constitution and had no power to dismiss the same as the constitution was the fundamental law of the country. This judgment was very bold with full manifestation of judicial activism as the doctrine of necessity was rejected; the doors of army rule were shut.

This was the judgment after which, when writing the new Constitution of 1973 an Article 6 was inserted in it to prevent the army from dismissing the Constitution and imposing martial law (but subsequent history of 1977 and 1999 proved that all this went in vain).

In *Asma Jilani vs The Government of Punjab and others,* on 7th April 1972, the Supreme Court of Pakistan declared that Gen Yahya Khan had usurped power that his action was not justified by the revolutionary legality doctrine and consequently his martial law was illegal. The court, after its detailed reasoning, came to the conclusion that:

'With the utmost respect, therefore, I would agree with the criticism that the learned Chief Justice Mohammad Munir not only misapplied the doctrine of Hans Kelsen, but also fell into error that it was a generally accepted doctrine of modern jurisprudence. Even the

14

disciples of Kelsen have hesitated to go far as Kelsen had gone...I am unable to resist the conclusion that Mohammad Munir erred both in interpreting Kelsen's theory and applying the same to the facts and circumstances of the case before him. The principle enunciated by him is wholly unsustainable.' (**Ref: PLD 1972 SC 139**)

Justice Yaqub Ali Khan concluded that the judgment in Tamizuddin Khan's case of 1955 and Dosso's case of 1958 had made *'a perfectly good country into a laughing stock, and converted the country into autocracy and eventually ...into military dictatorship'*. He pointedly criticized the abrogation of the 1956 constitution, observing that *'Iskandar Mirza and Ayub Khan committed treason, and destroyed the basis of representation between the two wings.'*

The decision was though bold but it cannot be forgotten that the Court declared Yahya Khan a usurper only after he had ceased to hold office while the other usurpers were dead.

Similarly once more, the SC tried to put up a brave face in the Haji Saifullah case by declaring Gen. Zia's dissolution of the National Assembly invalid; but, again, this was done only after the dictator's death [*making his son, Ejaz ul Haq, publicly boast in a moment of truth that had his father been alive the judgment could not have been delivered*]. (**Ref: *South Asia Tribune; 7-13 September 2003, Issue 58*)**

It may not be out of place to mention that constitutional package for 1973's constitution was drafted in the light of this judgment of the Supreme Court of Pakistan, which had opined in Asma Jilani case: *'As soon as the first opportunity arises, when the coercive apparatus falls from the hands of the usurper, he should be tried for high treason and suitably punished. This alone will serve as a deterrent to the adventurers'*.

Asma Jilani case indeed was the basis for the framers of the 1973 Constitution drafting not only the Article 6 dealing with high treason but also making a specific exception to the constitutional principle of non-retro-spectives of offences and punishments in the case of such high treason and desecration of the constitution. Acutely aware of the potential for mischief of Pakistan Army and its corrupt political partisans, such as those who eventually would endorse the 8th and 17th Amendments, the framers went on to include the Article 12(2) stating that any such offence would not fall under the Protection against Retroactive Punishment or indemnity granted by the parliament via Article 270. Article 12(2) states:

'Nothing in clause (I) or in Article 270 shall apply to any law making acts of abrogation or subversion of a Constitution in force in Pakistan at any time since the twenty third day of March one thousand nine hundred and fifty six, an offence.'

The academics noted that the ruling in Dosso's case, famous Justice Mohammad Munir's judgment (*that where a constitution and the national legal order under it is disrupted by an abrupt political change not within the contemplation of the constitution, such a change is called a revolution and its legal effect is not only the destruction of the existing constitution but also of the validity of the national legal order, irrespective of how and by whom such a change is brought about*) was held not to be good law. *Gen Yahya Khan was held to be an usurper and all the actions taken by him were found to be illegal and illegitimate.* In order to avoid the disastrous consequences of declaring all acts done during his rule, whether legislative or otherwise, to be of no legal effect; it was, however, held that those which were in the wider public interest could be skipped on the principle of condonation, notwithstanding their illegality or varied interpretations whatsoever.

10th April 1973: Pakistan got another constitution, still in vogue, if and when our civil & military dictators allow showing its twisted and distorted face; widely used as reference in media papers and courts but never respected by spirit.

Scenario 3

JUDICIARY IN 1977

Nusrat Bhutto Case:

It may be recalled that in 1976 Z A Bhutto announced general elections in the country and after the polls were held in early 1977 an agitation started alleging that the election had been rigged. There were large-scale demonstrations, law & order became worse and there was arson, loot and plunder. The parleys and negotiations between the ruling party and opposition failed although an understanding had been reached. At that juncture, Mr Bhutto introduced as Article 96-A in the Constitution to provide for a referendum for a vote of confidence for him. Under this provision it was said that:

> 'If at any time the Prime Minister considers it necessary to obtain a vote of confidence of the people of Pakistan through a referendum, he may advise the President to cause the matter to be referred to a referendum in accordance with law made by the Parliament of Pakistan in vogue whatsoever.'

The only disturbing element in this new article was that:

'Any dispute arising in connection with the counting of votes at a referendum shall be finally determined by the Referendum Commission or a member thereof authorized by it and no dispute arising in connection with referendum or the result thereof shall be raised or permitted to be raised before any Court or other authority whatsoever.'

In nut shell, the courts and their existence were negated altogether. No objection, no cry and no petition for its revision came up.

However, no referendum could take place because of the volatile situation in the country and this provision being time-specific ceased to be part of the Constitution in September 1977. Nevertheless, on presumption that there was no concluded agreement between the government and opposition parties, Gen Ziaul Haq, the then Chief of Army Staff, on 5th July 1977 imposed Martial Law and held the 1973 Constitution in abeyance.

[On 5th July 1977, Gen Ziaul Haq pronounced martial law. Sajjad Ali Shah (afterwards elevated as Chief Justice of Pakistan) was the Registrar

Supreme Court. He immediately rang up the Chief Justice, Yaqoob Ali Khan and told him that after martial law, Mr Bhutto and his cabinet members had been arrested. The CJP replied that the Law Ministry and the Establishment Division had already told him and that Gen Ziaul Haq was coming to see him as the Chief Martial Law Administrator at 11 AM. The CJP had also briefed him about the arrangements to be done. Gen Ziaul Haq came at 11 AM; the Registrar received and escorted him to the CJP's chambers. The Registrar Mr Sajjad Ali Shah left the two heads there and doors closed.

Soon after the then Federal Secretary Law, Abdul Haye Qureshi was called there. All the accompanying Generals were oozing outside after a hectic night. Two main things were decided between the two;

- Firstly: that in the communiqué for the nation, in respect of the Constitution neither the word 'abrogated' would be used nor 'suspended', it would be said as **'held in abeyance'**.

- Secondly: All the Chief Justices of the High Courts were made governors of the respective provinces. (After two years they were given confirmations if needed and promotions too.)

All it was a very calculated move to win the higher judiciary in favour of military rule that was why the decision of Nusrat Bhutto case was as Gen Ziaul Haq wanted.

19th September 1977: Chief Justice of Pakistan Yaquab Ali Khan admitted Begum Nusrat Bhutto's petition challenging the constitutionality of Zulfikar A Bhutto's detention. Bhutto was removed from the government and was arrested on 5th July 1977 as sitting Prime Minister. That day after promulgation of the Martial Law, Gen Ziaul Haq had suspended all democratic institutions.

22nd September 1977: Yaqub Ali Khan, the Chief Justice of Pakistan, was forced to retire because he had dared to accept Begum Nusrat Bhutto's petition for hearing.

The interesting fact was that the CJP Yaqoob Ali Khan, while accepting Nusrat Bhutto's petition, wrote an order on that *'the political prisoner Mr Bhutto should also be produced before the court'*. When Gen Ziaul Haq was told of such instructions of the Supreme Court, he immediately ordered to suspend whole of the superior judiciary and to bring Generals and Brigadiers instead to act as 'senior military courts'. Governor Punjab Justice Aslam Riaz Hussain immediately approached Gen Ziaul Haq and asked audience for few minutes. When Justice Aslam met the CMLA, the schemers of the said proposal; A K Brohi, Sharifuddin Pirzada and Gen K M Arif were also present. Justice Aslam dared to advise the CMLA to refrain from that act in the wake of possible revolt by the lawyer's community countrywide.

Gen Ziaul Haq thought for a while but how to deal with CJ Yaqoob Ali Khan's orders. A mid-way was worked out that the government should file a review petition on the grounds that *'by causing Mr Bhutto's presence in the Supreme Court, there is an apprehension of law & order situation associated with security risk.'* It was agreed. Review petition was got prepared and placed before the apex court next day.

The review petition was admitted, the apparent problem solved but the same evening it was, however, decided to replace the Chief justice of Pakistan Yaqoob Ali Khan also.

23rd September 1977: Sheikh Anwar-ul-Haq, an officer of Administrative Cadre, a person who lacked adequate judicial training, was appointed the Chief Justice of Pakistan.

> [Quoting **'Judicial Murder of a Prime Minister'** written by Tariq Aqil and appearing on 7th December 2004 at www.Chowk.com, it is a historical fact that the new Chief Justice took his oath of office along with other Supreme Court judges, Omitting the paragraph in the oath laid down in 1973 constitution whereby the supreme court judges swear to *"preserve, protect and defend the constitution"*. By this contrived deliberate manner the judges ceased to function as constitutional judges and were absolved from faith with the oath they had sworn earlier.]

10th November 1977: The imposition of the third Martial Law was challenged in *Nusrat Bhutto's case* (**PLD 1977 SC 657**) wherein, using fulcrum of 'ground realities and the objective conditions', the Supreme Court had declared the imposition of Martial Law as valid on the **doctrine of State necessity,** but the Court observed that the power of judicial review was available to it to examine the legality or otherwise of the actions of the government and particularly the Court would also see whether the necessity continued to exist or not.

Notwithstanding the above quoted judgment, a Provisional Constitution Order of 1981 was promulgated by Gen Ziaul Haq ousting the power and jurisdiction of the Superior Courts to judicially review actions of the Martial Law regime. In nut shell, the Supreme Court of Pakistan in

Begum Nusrat Bhutto case, unanimously validated imposition of martial law under the 'doctrine of necessity'.

In its judgment dismissing Begum Nusrat Bhutto's petition challenging detention of former Prime Minister Z A Bhutto and 10 others, the nine-member court headed by Chief Justice Anwar ul Haq remarked that:

> '....... after massive rigging of elections followed by complete breakdown of law and order situation, bringing the country on the brink of disaster, the imposition of martial law had become inevitable......... the court [Supreme Court of Pakistan] would like to state in clear terms that it had found it possible to validate the extra constitutional action of the Chief Martial Law Administrator (CMLA) not only for the reason that he stepped in to save the country at a time of grave national crisis and constitutional breakdown, but also because of the solemn pledge given by him that the period of constitutional deviation shall be as short as possible.'

> 'It is true that owing to the necessity of completing the process of accountability of holders of public offices, the holding of elections had to be postponed for the time being but the declared intention of the Chief Martial Law Administrator still remains the same namely, that he has stepped in for a temporary period and for the limited purpose of arranging free and fair elections so as to enable the country to return to a democratic way of life.

> In the presence of these unambiguous declarations, it would be highly unfair and uncharitable to attribute any other intention to the Chief Martial Law Administrator, and to insinuate that he has not assumed power for the purposes stated by him, or that he does not intend to restore democratic situations in terms of the 1973 constitution'. (**Ref: PLD 1977 SC 673-674**)

It may not be out of place to mention that before making formal announcement of the decision, the CJP Anwarul Haq had sent his draft to Gen Zia ul Haq Chief Martial Law Administrator for prior approval. On seeing the said draft, Gen Ziaul Haq immediately got furious and returned it with remarks that:

> '.......In the decision why the Chief Justice had not given him the authority to make changes in the Constitution. The said Chief Justice got his office of the Supreme Court opened in the same evening, made the desired changes in the draft and had immediately sent to Gen Ziaul Haq again for approval. That decision was read over next day and Mr

Z A Bhutto was hanged on the basis of the same decision. (Column by
Dr Safdar Mahmood: **Daily Jang London dated 5th July 2007**)

In an article captioned as '**Tale of a vitiated trial**' written by Fakhar
Zaman, sent to all media websites on **4th April 2000,** it was opined
that:

*'The real culprit responsible for impairing the image of the judiciary
was General Ziaul Haq, Chief Martial Law Administrator, assisted by
the two Chief Justices, Molvi Mushtaq Hussain and Anwar-ul-Haq,
who lent him their noble judicial positions in bringing the conspiracy
against the Prime Minister to fruition.*

*These were the two judges who also lent legality to the imposition
of martial law and prepared the ground for amendment of the
Constitution itself to help achieve the evil designs to the dictator. It was
with the blessings of these two that Zulfikar Ali Bhutto was removed
from the scene and a usurper was able to rule the country for eleven
long years and, in process, destroyed many of its valuable institutions.'*

The Supreme Court had also held that the facts in Begum Nusrat
Bhutto's case were distinguishable as the Constitution had not been
dismissed but only suspended and the intention was to restore it. What
an assessment and what was the foresightedness.

Going into more details, the said decision from the Supreme Court of
Pakistan titled **Begum Nusrat Bhutto V. The Chief of the Army Staff** and
Another (PLD 1977 SC 657 & 1977 (3) PSCR 1) was announced on a
petition by Begum Nusrat Bhutto, under Article 184 (3) of the 1973
Constitution of Pakistan, sought to challenge the detention of Mr.
Zulfikar Ali Bhutto, former Prime Minister of Pakistan, and the other
leaders of the Pakistan People's Party under Martial Law Order no. 12
of 1977 contending that the Chief of the Army Staff had no authority
under the 1973 Constitution to impose martial law in the country. It was
also contended that his intervention amounted to an act of treason in
terms of Article 6 of the Constitution; that as a consequence the
proclamation of martial law dated 5th July 1977 and other actions of
arrest and detention were all without lawful authority.

This petition was heard by a bench of nine judges of the Supreme Court
consisting of S. Anwar-ul-Haq, Chief Justice, Wahiduddin Ahmad,
Muhammad Afzal Cheema, Malik Muhammad Akram, Dorab Patel,
Qaisar Khan, Muhammad Haleem, G. Safdar Shah and Nasim Hasan
Shah.

The leading judgment was written by S. Anwar-ul-Haq, Chief Justice. His opinion was also agreed with by Justice Nasim Hasan Shah, who had stressed in a separate note that '....when the political leaders failed to steer the country out of a crisis, it is an inexcusable sin for the armed forces to sit as silent spectators. It is primarily, for this reason that the army, perforce had to intervene to save the country.'

On the issue of validity of Proclamation of Martial Law on 5th July 1977, it was held that:

> *In these circumstances neither the ratio decidendi of Dosso v. State nor that of Asma Jilani v. the Punjab Government is strictly applicable to the present case. The question next arises whether the above intervention was a step which could lawfully be taken? So far as this point is concerned, it is an admitted position that there is no provision in the constitution authorizing the army commander, even in the event of the break-down of the constitutional machinery, to intervene in the manner that he did.*

> *But Mr. Sharif-ud-Din Pirzada, the Attorney-General of Pakistan, submitted before us that since the country cannot be allowed to perish for the sake of the constitution, the intervention was justified on the doctrine of state necessity, while Mr Brohi contended that as the old legal order had been effectively replaced by a new legal order [leaving no vacuum], henceforth all questions of legality were answerable with reference to it.'*

The speech of Gen Ziaul Haq was repeatedly read in the apex Court that:

> '.... I was obliged to step in to fill in the vacuum created by the political leaders. I have accepted this challenge as a true soldier of Islam. My sole aim is to organize free and fair elections which would be held in October (1977) this year. Soon after the polls, power will be transferred to the elected representatives of the people....;

These words were included in the decision and the whole judgment was based on the sincerity and sacredness of this phrase.

> [*That was why Justice Nasim H Shah had to opine that in view of the break-down of the normal constitutional machinery and to fill the vacuum, the armed forces were obliged to take an extra- constitutional step. Martial law was imposed, in the picturesque words used in the written statement filed by Mr. Brohi, not "in order to disable the*

constitutional authority, but in order to provide a bridge to enable the country to return to the path of constitutional rule".]

The Judgment said that 'the question whether the conditions prevailing in Pakistan necessitated the above step (of imposing Martial Law) has to be answered by reference to the happenings from 7th March 1977 up to 5th July 1977 which reveal that the constitutional and moral authority of the National Assembly which had come into being as a result of the elections held on 7th March 1977, as well as the Federal and Provincial governments formed thereafter had been continuously and forcefully repudiated throughout the country over a prolonged period of nearly four months. With the result that the national life stood disrupted.

A situation had arisen for which the constitution provided no solution. The atmosphere was surcharged with the possibility of further violence, confusion and chaos. As the constitution itself could not measure up to the situation, the doctrine of state necessity became applicable for where the safety of the state and the welfare of the people are in imminent danger. Necessity justifies a departure from the ordinary principles of law. In these circumstances the step taken by the armed forces in imposing martial law stands validated, on the principle of state necessity, as urged by the learned Attorney General (Mr Sharifuddin Pirzada)'.

All the nine judges had unanimously declared that the petition challenging the army coup was liable to be dismissed.

J Malik Qayyum, in an interview published in daily *the 'Jang' dated 5th February 2006*, however, had pointed out that:

> *'The Supreme Court should have given 90 days period to Gen Ziaul Haq to go for general elections. [Gen Zia had originally announced such elections within 90 days; dates were also announced but then postponed for indefinite period in the name of Islamic rule.] Through this judgment a military coup was accepted as legal which was wrong. Though my father J Malik Akram was one of the judges on that bench of the SC but I, being a student of law, dare to differ with that opinion and the said judgment.'*

In nut shell; the Supreme Court had observed that *'the declared objectives of the imposition of Martial Law are to create conditions suitable for holding free and fair elections in terms of the 1973 constitution, which was not being abrogated, and only certain parts of which were being held in abeyance, namely, the parts dealing with the federal and provincial executives and legislatures.'*

The President of Pakistan was to continue to discharge his duties as heretofore under the same constitution. Soon after the polls, the power was to be transferred to the elected representatives of the people but, in the name of accountability of some politicians; elections were postponed.

Accountability of that military ruler, Gen Ziaul Haq, did not end till his plane was blown up in air on 17th August 1988. The dead body was not available from the crime scene. Some days later, certain Afghan *Mujahideen* offered his *'Janaza'* prayer at the side space of Faisal Mosque Islamabad and soon after Nawaz Sharif got built his tomb there.

Still the people believe that in that tomb only the fractured eye-glasses of Gen Ziaul Haq are buried, not any part of his body, because nothing could be found from the crash scene.

Scenario 4

JUDICIARY IN 1978:

Bhutto Hanged by biased Judges:

Zulfikar Ali Bhutto, during his tenure of premiership in 1970s had promoted one junior judge named Aslam Riaz Hussain J. who happened to be a close friend of the then Attorney General Yahya Bakhtiar (and known to be not a bright judge) while superseding seven judges, including one J Mushtaq Hussain (Known as Maulvi), to the rank of the Chief Justice of the Lahore High Court (LHC).

During the military rule of Gen Ziaul Haq, Justice Maulvi Mushtaq Hussain, was elevated to the slot of the Chief Justice. The fact is still available on record of the Ministry of Law that J Maulvi Mushtaq had then opted for proceeding to Switzerland on two years leave after he was superseded, but returned immediately after Gen Ziaul Haq had imposed martial law in July 1977.

On **11th November 1974**, an FIR was lodged at the Ichhra police station Lahore after the assassination of Nawab Mohammad Ahmed Khan Kasuri implicating former prime minister Zulfikar Ali Bhutto for conspiracy to murder his political opponent Ahmad Raza Kasuri, under Sections 120-B, 302, 109, 301 and 307 of the Pakistan Penal Code.

Ahmad Raza Kasuri MNA, son of the deceased, claimed in the FIR that he was the actual target. Ichhra police station had consigned the investigation against Mr Bhutto to record room in 1975, but again started investigations in 1977 when Gen Ziaul Haq ordered to re-open the said case after having detailed meetings with J Maulvi Mushtaq. It was sufficient to have an idea of Gen Ziaul Haq's cunningness against the PM Zulfikar Ali Bhutto because it is a normal police practice that investigations are always consigned to record when no further evidence is available.

On 3rd September 1977, the deposed PM Mr Bhutto was arrested, but much surprising for the General, ten days later he was granted bail by Justice K M A Samdani of the Lahore High Court, as the case did not hold any legal ground. The same day on 13th September Bhutto was released from jail; however, within three days his bail was cancelled.

On 16th September midnight, army commandos *'climbed like black cats over the walls of Al-Murtaza, knocking out all the guards before they could raise a cry, hammering their rifle butts at the front door till almost flew off its heavy hinges.'* This time he was arrested and hand-cuffed, for never to be released again, and despatched to Sukkur Jail straightaway.

The then Punjab government had also set up Justice Shafiur Rehman Commission on the complaint of Ahmed Raza Kasuri to un-earth real facts of Bhutto case but a report had not been made public.

When question of Z A Bhutto's trial surfaced, CJ LHC Maulvi Mushtaq managed to get skipped the stage of trial at Session Court level on the pretext of *'importance of the case as a former PM was being brought in the dock'*. It was otherwise mandatory by law that every murder case should have been tried by a District & Session Judge so that the respective high court could be moved by the aggrieved party for exercising appellant jurisdiction.

Z A Bhutto's was perhaps the only case in the history of Pakistan where the Lahore HC had acted in a murder case by degrading itself to the level of original jurisdiction. It was purposefully done because J Maulvi Mushtaq Hussain, who headed the bench which handed down the controversial death sentence at the end to Mr Bhutto, had harboured bias against the former prime minister.

A few lines from *'Daughter of the East' by (late) Benazir Bhutto* would give us the deep insight:

> *"The case against my father rested primarily on the confession of Masood Mahmood, the Director General of the Federal Security Force. Masood Mahmood was one of the public servants who were arrested soon after the coup and who we had been told was tortured to give false evidence against my father.*
>
> *After almost two months of detention by the military, Masood Mahmood had decided to become an <u>'approver'</u>, a witness who claims to be an accomplice in a crime and is pardoned on the promise that he will tell the 'truth' about the other participants.*
>
> *(Then) Masood Mahmood was claiming that my father ordered him to murder the politician Kasuri... There were no eye-witnesses to the attack. So much so that the FSF guns, which the 'confessing accused' claimed to have used in the murder attempt did not match the empty cartridges found at the scene.*

The witnesses were briefed on what they should say and favourable answers were deliberately whittled down. At the end of the trial, not one of the objections raised or the contradictions in the evidence pointed out by the defence consuls and which appeared in 706 pages of testimony [for Mr Bhutto's defence]".

General Arif had recorded the fact that it was Gen Ziaul Haq himself who came to the prosecution's help by granting pardon to the approver Masood Mahmud. Similar promises were reportedly made to the three other FSF officials also but they were hanged. As expected, J Maulvi Mushtaq and his full bench found Zulfikar Ali Bhutto guilty of murder and sentenced him to death on 18ᵗʰ March 1978.

A veteran western writer **Stanley Wolpert** writes in his celebrated book titled **'Zulfi Bhutto of Pakistan'** that:

"Expecting a fair trial from a person like Maulvi Mushtaq was very much unlikely. The whole nation witnessed in disgust how the judicial process was blatantly transgressed and the principles of justice and impartiality were trampled upon. The Acting Chief Justice Maulvi Mushtaq Hussain never so much as attempted to suppress or hide his personal animus. It never occurred to him that he should refuse himself from the trial [against Zulfi Bhutto]."

Barrister Aitzaz Ahsan, who was witness to the entire court proceedings in the Bhutto case, also held that the trial was very hostile. At one stage the hostility and hatred of J Maulvi Mushtaq went to such a high pitch that Mr Bhutto had inadvertently used guarded language against him. But Bhutto was sentimentally aroused to reflect his mind in that manner because the whole bench was biased and hurling hatred and sarcastic remarks at their former prime minister.

The judges on bench who found him guilty, especially J Mushtaq Hussain, were clearly motivated against Bhutto. The question of bias raised by Bhutto was the single most important aspect of the case which, if addressed honestly, could have changed the course of history.

Against J Mushtaq Hussain, Bhutto's stance was supported by several facts. A division bench of the LHC consisting of Justice K M A Samdani and Justice Mazharul Haq was already enquiring into a private complaint of Ahmed Raza Kasuri, whose father was killed. While the enquiry was going on, an incomplete *challan* was submitted in magistrate's court which was immediately forwarded to the respective District & Sessions Judge of Lahore.

Later on, J Maulvi Mushtaq Hussain transferred the case from the Court of Sessions to LHC the same day when Bhutto was re-arrested on 16th September 1977. Again, on the same day, the Chief Justice constituted a special bench of five judges presided over by himself, though a complete *challan* was not submitted till then and yet the trial was fixed for 24th September 1977.

In the statement submitted before the Supreme Court during the hearing of his appeal, Z A Bhutto had stated:

> *"It is indeed a mockery for this regime to pontificate on the independent character of the Chief Election Commissioner when it has brazenly merged the office of the Chief Election Commissioner and the Chief Justice of the Lahore High Court, under the control of the man who is known to be after my blood.*
>
> *There has been an encounter with J Mushtaq Hussain earlier; when he was pleased to hear my detention petition virtually 'in camera' inside the prison walls of Lahore Camp Jail. This was in January 1969. However, it was not he who released me from detention, but the government, which withdrew the detention order.*
>
> *Once again, when he (Mr Bhutto) became President, Maulvi Mushtaq Hussain met me in the Punjab House Rawalpindi. He gave blatant indications of his ambitions suggesting that, at this political juncture in the history of Pakistan, the new President would need a trustworthy man in the control of the judiciary.*
>
> *He was gravely dejected when his expectations were not met, when a few months later Sardar Muhammad Iqbal was appointed as the Chief Justice of the Lahore High Court by my government. He did not conceal his anger. He displayed his resentment in many ways. When following the Constitutional Amendment, Mr. Justice Aslam Riaz Hussain was appointed as the Chief Justice of Lahore HC; he interpreted this second suppression to be an intolerable insult."*

But lack of fairness was not restricted to the high court; it permeated the Supreme Court too which found the objections rose by Bhutto not worthy of consideration as if there was a pact between the judges.

In early 2011, a reference (no: 1/2011), to have a fact finding verdict from the Supreme Court of Pakistan after thirty years, was moved by the then PPP Law Minister Babar Awan. In that petition Mr Awan contended that Z A Bhutto had died in custody much before he was hanged and alleged that it was a case of custodial assassination.

Babar Awan regretted that the high court had kept pending an application of Mr Bhutto to be decided after the trial in which he had expressed his apprehensions of an unfair trial by the court. Mr Awan also read out different applications and letters written by Mr Bhutto like that of 5th October 1977, challenging the maintainability of the trial; another letter of the same date highlighting bias of J Maulvi Mushtaq; application of 5th November 1977 expressing that he had no expectation of a fair trial; letter of 25th February 1978 sent to the then Punjab Governor requesting him to transfer the case to another bench with much other material.

After admitting Babar Awan's reference, the Chief Justice Iftikhar M Chaudhry had nominated a special bench comprising 11 judges and preferred to hold day to day hearing. Justice (rtd) Tariq Mehmood, was asked to assist the court as *amicus curiae* (friend of the court) because he had personally witnessed the Bhutto trial in 1977-79.

Fauzia Wahab, Information Secretary of the PPP had opined at www. Bhutto.org & www.Sixhour.com that:

> *'An alive Bhutto was too dangerous. No chances could be taken. His strong roots in the people of Pakistan, his ability to turn foes into friends, his commanding stature in international politics made him a formidable figure in the complex polity of Pakistan. The generals knew that Zulfikar Ali Bhutto could not be defeated politically. His presence would be of constant threat for them.'*

Gen Ziaul Haq knew that support of the judiciary was crucial to accomplish his plans. Capital punishment through the military courts against him would raise protests of injustice the world over and could potentially backfire. Therefore, on the assumption of power, he cleverly inducted the chief justices of all provincial High Courts as Acting Governors of their provinces. J Maulvi Mushtaq, who nursed an animosity against Bhutto since long, was appointed as the Acting Chief Justice of the Lahore High Court. A vilification campaign against Zulfikar Ali Bhutto ensued.

The 're-filed case shortly after the coup' by Ahmed Raza Qasuri, (**Ref: Pakistan - A Modern History by Ian Talbot**) came in handy for the dictator. Although a High Court Inquiry under Justice Shafi-ur-Rahman had exonerated Mr Bhutto in this case, but Gen Ziaul Haq was bent upon getting rid of the living legend at all costs.

Much later; Dr J Nasim Hasan Shah, one of the signatories writing death obituary for Mr Bhutto, in a staggering press interview to the **daily 'Jang' on 23rd August 1996** had openly indicated the bias of the presiding judge of the trial court, J Maulvi Mushtaq, who had personal grudge against Mr Bhutto. An interesting aspect was that Justice Shah himself was an ad-hoc judge at the time of Bhutto's trial and was confirmed only when the desired decision was penned down and he had affixed his signatures on that sheet of unprecedented judicial murder. What a little price Justice Nasim H Shah got for his tyrannical act.

The former Chief Justice had no hesitation to affirm that J Maulvi Mushtaq should have avoided naming himself as a member of the trial bench to maintain dignity of the court in the principled tradition of justice. It was in this context that during the trial, J Maulvi Mushtaq had made uncalled for personal remarks provoking Bhutto to boycott the trial.

Dr J Nasim Hasan Shah had also admitted that never before in the judicial history of Pakistan any abettor was awarded capital punishment. Justice Shah quoted the actual wording that:

'During the hearing of the case, I asked Yayha Bakhtiar (Bhutto's lawyer) if he wanted to argue for remission of his punishment but he refused. Later this became a major issue in the review petition. In my personal view, Bhutto's punishment could have been reduced...'

Justice Nasim Hasan Shah when asked that if he could have given a dissenting note after all; said confidently that *'it could have been done but his lawyer's argument was that he didn't care about the punishment. We had some limitations and Yahya Bakhtiar had stubbornness, which annoyed us.'* Some historians hold that Bhutto's counsel had also contributed much towards Bhutto's capital punishment.

Justice Nasim H Shah further hinted that both Gen Ziaul Haq and Maulvi Mushtaq had fears that Bhutto's survival could be risky for them, so he should better be eliminated first and no chances taken. *'I am very sorry it had to be done'*; Justice Shah's words had reflected much about the military ruler's tyrannical mind and weakness of the judicial heads.

Furthermore, Justice Shah was not hesitating to tell that there was immense pressure on judges. He told that:

"Justice Haleem was apprised by the 'agencies' that his only son lived in Karachi and his life was in danger and he was very scared ....

'Basically what could the poor judges do in such circumstances?' There was one witness testimony after the other."

The world known jurists and legal experts had termed Bhutto's hanging as **'judicial murder'** including Ramsay Clarke, a former US Attorney General. T W Rajaratnam, a former judge of the Sri Lankan Supreme Appellate Court wrote a thought provoking book titled *'A judiciary in crisis?'* having Bhutto's trial stories. One Victoria Schofield said that:

'Those who were blinded by hope, optimism and trust in the judicial institutions of the country only saw that the military authorities had already made up their minds. The judicial process merely prolonged the agony and uncertainly. No one could honestly say that Zulfikar Ali Bhutto was sent to death for his alleged part in a murder; he was sent to death because in the political climate of Pakistan at the time, the people who had the power wanted him out of the way.'

I A Rehman (Referring to *the 'News' of 17th April 2011*) had rightly opined that soon after the coup of July 1977 Gen Ziaul Haq had started thinking of extending his reign beyond the 90 days he had promised at the outset. This meant staying in confrontation with Bhutto and the PPP for a long time and PPP could not be suppressed so long as Bhutto was around. The army junta had felt it when Bhutto received a stirring reception upon his arrival in Lahore in August 1977. Even ordinary villagers had perception that there was one vacant grave and if it was not occupied by Bhutto Gen Ziaul Haq would be laid down there.

Due to backing of Gen Ziaul Haq, Bhutto's trial was again maligned after dismissal of the review petition by the Supreme Court when a state sponsored public campaign was run in the media to strengthen Gen Ziaul Haq's hands and his resolve to execute Bhutto.

One could go through the newspaper headlines from those days: 'SC verdict supported'; 'Zia urged to implement SC order'; 'No clemency for Bhutto'; 'Court verdict must be implemented'; 'Bhutto deserves no mercy'. Moreover, Ahmed Raza Kasuri was not alone in declaring that *'if Pakistan has to live, then Bhutto has to go'*, astonishingly once PPP's Federal Law Minister Babar Awan was also there to lead processions carrying placards of **'Hang Bhutto'**.

The fact, however, remained that most Pakistanis did not accept the Bhutto verdict as just and that is why the PPP mustered consistent support of the general populace for the Bhutto family during the movement against General Ziaul Haq and in the elections held during 1988-2008 and even after.

If one goes through late **Bhutto's** book titled '**If I'm Assassinated**', one would find certain stunning facts about the inside thinking of J Maulvi Mushtaq, the so called Chief Justice. Once Z A Bhutto protested on conversion of his trial from open proceedings into an in camera trial for his defence. During the trial, one judge made the profound observation that '*We are trying you and not the public.*' On this illuminating remark, J Maulvi Mushtaq added '*but he wants publicity.*' What an irony; Mr Bhutto had observed.

Mr Bhutto was once informed in *Kot Lakhpat* jail that his request to address the court had been rejected. Since 9th January 1978, he was not being defended by lawyers. He had not heard the prosecution witnesses during his illness and absence from the court. He was insulted and humiliated by the court during the open trial for three months.

Contrarily, the prosecution versions had received the full blast of publicity but suddenly the trial was converted into a secret meeting. The dice was completely loaded against him but with all those tormenting handicaps, when he sought to address the closed court in defence of his life, he was not permitted. His request was turned down. Undoubtedly it was an ex parte judgement where the trial court had awarded the death sentence without hearing the defence of 'accused'.

Late Mr Bhutto once wrote that during trial the bench, in particular J Maulvi Mushtaq was always rude, abrasive and insulting to him. Quite opposite, J Maulvi Mushtaq was kind and soft towards the confessing co-accused (perhaps Masood Mehmood). He smiled at the bench for their rotten and partial minds. He enjoyed their rustic sense of humour at Bhutto's expense.

The approver, Masood Mehmood sometimes translated certain questions in Urdu and Punjabi for the bench whenever he thought that they were not able to follow the English. '<u>The taunts, the frowns and shouts were reserved only for Mr Bhutto; sympathetic and favourable commands used for him were "*shut up*," "*get up*" and "*take this man away until he regains his senses etc.*'</u>

Syed Afzal Haider, a prominent lawyer, living witness to the whole trial and a retired judge had placed all the court proceedings and documents in his book on Bhutto's court killing. First volume comprised of 1500 pages whereas the second volume is the analysis of the whole case in the light of previous court references.

Syed Afzal Haider has discussed in detail that Mr Bhutto was denied the right to be tried before a Session's Court. In his book, he mentioned the dates when Justice Anwarul Haq spoke against Bhutto during the trial of the case and made public speeches. Mr Haider also referred to a letter in his book in which Bhutto told J Anwarul Haq not to sit on his bench but who bothered. The most significant was the fact that in 1978 the Islamic provisions were ready and the law of *Qisas & Diyat* was in place.

Having been a member of the Council of Islamic Ideology for five terms and having seen the records, Mr Haider knew that the law was not allowed to be implemented because, according to Section 9, life sentence was given to the person who was found to be a conspirator. Gen Ziaul Haq had withheld the law while J Afzal Cheema was also involved in it.

Bhutto was simply denied the best lawyers. The lawyer from Sindh was sent back, the lawyer from Punjab was packed off, and so the trial was not fair. It was absolutely unfair. Mr Haider categorically told that J Mushtaq Hussain was a cruel, cold and highly callous man. He behaved very badly in the court being head of a full bench. He called Bhutto *'a bad Muslim'* and a *'compulsive liar'*. Of course, the God worked His justice and everybody saw how he [Maulvi Mushtaq] died. Residents of Model Town Lahore still remember his horrible death.

Aslam Riaz Hussain was also the sitting judge of the Supreme Court. Being his friend, once Mr Haider asked him why did he not participate in Bhutto's appeal trial; reply came that he was asked by the CJP Anwarul Haq to sit in this case but he told the latter that he would decide the case firstly on the question of bias, that J Maulvi Mushtaq Hussain was biased or not. The CJP Anwarul Haq said, *'No, I am sorry, you can't come.'* This decision was a predetermined conclusion. What prompted J Nasim Hasan Shah, God knows better.

Once Syed Afzal Haider was holding a seminar in Lahore on Bhutto's vicious trial, in which Rajaratnam, the Chief Justice of Sri Lanka and an author of a world known book on Bhutto, was also invited from Colombo. CJP Muhammad Afzal Zullah had called him and kept him in wrongful confinement in his chamber for seven hours because he did not want him to participate in the seminar on Bhutto trial. Such was Justice Zullah's prejudice, hatred and hostility against Mr Bhutto. He was released only when the convention was over.

In nut shell, aftermath of Bhutto trial is still continuing. The judgment is continuously being rejected by the bench, the bar, and the people of Pakistan and by all generations to come.

Scenario 5

JUDICIARY IN 1979:

Z A Bhutto's Judicial Murder:

In Pakistan, general elections were held on 7th March 1977. Pakistan Peoples Party (PPP) emerged as the victorious Party. At the behest of Gen Ziaul Haq, the then Chief of Army Staff (COAS), all the opposition parties in coalition, named themselves as Pakistan National Alliance (PNA), accused government of so-called rigging in the elections. PNA had started countrywide protests and processions against those election's results. These protests went so intensified that Bhutto had to call army in Lahore to apply 'partial Martial Law' to control law & order situation. The armed troops had taken control of the city.

The Martial Law was challenged in the Lahore High Court (LHC). The petition was accepted and heard. The CJ LHC Aslam Riaz Hussain gave verdict that there was no need of Army in the town so the Martial Law was declared unjustified. The PM Bhutto got angry over the decision. The PPP resorted to threats that CJ's house would be hit with grenade but nothing happened. Bhutto and the PPP had suffered a great loss of credibility due to that judgment.

Negotiations with PNA ultimately succeeded. An Agreement was reached amongst them on 8th June 1977 for holding fresh general elections on 8th October 1977.

On **5th July 1977**, the COAS Gen Ziaul Haq imposed Martial Law unilaterally. The National Assembly, the Senate and the Provincial Assemblies were dissolved and Constitution was held in abeyance. After declaring Martial Law in the country, Gen Ziaul Haq addressed a press conference on 14th July and claimed:

> "We have no intentions of any witch-hunting. ... The courts are still functioning and we have not stopped anyone going to the courts to take the politicians to task. Then why do they want me or the Military or the armed forces to hang a few politicians? Why should I? Isn't it as much of a concern of the public as it is mine? It should be done by them, if it is to be done."

Living Bhutto, it is said, was more dangerous for Gen Ziaul Haq's military rule. The fear of Zulfikar Ali Bhutto's return to power had forced Gen Ziaul Haq to take an extreme action of execution of Bhutto through judiciary though there are other explanations too. As the then Secretary Information of the PPP **Fauzia Wahab opined** that:

"Allegedly his strong roots in the people of Pakistan, his ability to turn foes into friends, his commanding stature in international politics made him a formidable figure in the complex polity of Pakistan. He was too strong to be tackled politically. His presence would be of constant threat for them ... (And)...the General knew that the support of the judiciary was crucial...... Therefore, on the assumption of power, he cleverly inducted the chief justices of all provincial High Courts as Acting Governors of their provinces.'

Gen Ziaul Haq's Military Junta established a dummy government of PNA with CMLA as President. Zulfikar Ali Bhutto, the sitting Prime Minister and the Chairman of PPP was arrested on the same day and then released on 28th July 1977. Mr Bhutto was re-arrested on 3rd September 1977 from his residence named Clifton in Karachi, on the charges of a fabricated murder case; then released on 13th September 1977 against a bail order issued by the Lahore High Court. Referring to the pages of *'Pakistan—- A Modern History' by Ian Talbot*:

'Ahmed Raza Qasuri came forward for Gen Zia although a High Court Inquiry under Justice Shafi-ur-Rahman had exonerated the former Prime Minister in this case. But the Army was bent upon to go ahead [to get rid of Zulfikar Ali Bhutto].'

After registration of the FIR on 11th November 1974, the federal government had appointed Justice Shafiur Rehman to hold a judicial inquiry into the matter. Referring to Mr A Sattar Najam Advocate, **the 'Dawn' of 8th April 2011** narrated that *'though Justice Rehman had ideological differences with Z.A. Bhutto and his party but even then he conducted a fair inquiry and declared him innocent.'*

Justice Shafi ur Rehman, who was later elevated to Supreme Court, was known for his impartiality. Then Mr Ahmad Raza Kasuri, the complainant, had also expressed his satisfaction over the judicial inquiry and the matter was settled down. All witnesses and evidences were recorded during the probe and its findings were never challenged. When Gen Ziaul Haq ousted the elected government of Z.A Bhutto on 5th July 1977 the murder case was reopened and the trial was commenced on 24th September 1977.

Mr Sattar Najam was perhaps Assistant Advocate General at that time and later, during Gen Ziaul Haq's regime fake cases were registered against him allegedly for forging case documents before the judicial inquiry. He had to flee Pakistan due to constant raids on his house and threats to his family on the instance of the military ruler. He came back to Pakistan in Benazir Bhutto's first rule in 1988 and was made Deputy Attorney General then raised to Advocate General of Punjab.

Gen Ziaul Haq had managed to remove the record of the judicial inquiry from all concerned forums, including the High Court. The concerned record was also stolen from his house when he was out of the country during Gen Ziaul Haq's rule. Mr Najam told that *'due to this attitude of Justice Mushtaq, his fellow judge Justice Gulbaz Khan had refused to sit on the bench but later he had to withdraw the decision,'* may be due to immense pressure from the military rulers.

Z A Bhutto was charged with conspiracy to murder Nawab Mohammed Ahmed Qasuri (father of Ahmad Raza Qasuri), the alleged target in an assault on his car.

[The background of this murder case was that on 11th November 1974 shortly after midnight, Ahmed Raza Qasuri, member of the National assembly and a bitter critic of ZAB and the Peoples Party was on his way home, with his family after attending a marriage ceremony in Shadman Colony Lahore. The stillness of the night was broken by the sound of gunfire; in a split second Nawab Mohammed Ahmed Khan sitting in the front seat received fatal injuries and was pronounced dead on arrival at the nearby United Christian Hospital. Shortly after Ahmed Raza Kasuri lodged a first information report (FIR) in police station Ichchra Lahore.

The assailants were unknown but Ahmed Raza managed to name Zulfuqar Ali Bhutto as the brain behind the murderous attack on his father. The logic behind the accusation was that Ahmed Raza had become a thorn for ZAB and his people's party as he was a member of the opposition, information secretary of the *Tehreek-i-Istiqlal* and a renowned critic of Bhutto and his policies. He added that in June 1974 Bhutto had threatened him on the floor of the National Assembly, *"You keep quiet! I have had enough of you! Absolute poison! I will not tolerate your nuisance any more."*]

Coming back to the history, 13th September's bail to Z A Bhutto was granted by Justice KMA Samdani of the Lahore High Court declaring that the case did not hold any legal ground. Gen Ziaul Haq had realized that odd situation but, as has been quoted in *'Zulfi Bhutto of Pakistan' by Stanley Wolpert*:

'.....from now on he (Gen Zia) would also have to take on the task of meeting out justice to his hated enemy by bringing him up for murder in his own reliable martial law court.......he (Zulfi) had been warned, upon his release from prison on 13th September that an order for his detention under some preventive law or martial law was being prepared. He (Zulfi) feared that Gen Ziaul Haq had now decided to perpetuate himself, and thought that if elections were postponed, there would be disastrous consequences for the country.'

So, as it could be expected from the courts in Pakistan that they always sided with the rulers, within three days Zulfikar Ali Bhutto's bail was cancelled. In the mid-night of 16th September, Z A Bhutto was again re-arrested from his residence at Karachi named *Al-Murtaza*, not in a respectable manner but through army commandoes by surrounding the hole campus by some & one platoon by jumping over the walls and striking the doors with heavy iron rods as if the former prime minister was a hardened criminal, possibly going to run away from the back door of his residence after hearing about the police. Astonishing it was.

This time he was arrested, for never to be released again, on basis of the same murder charges and was taken to the Sukkur Jail about 500 km away from Karachi.

Justice Samdani, who had released Z A Bhutto on bail was transferred back to the Sindh High Court. Another development is also on record that a courageous Chief Justice of Pakistan Yaqub Ali Khan was forced to retire by the 22nd of the same month, because three day earlier, he had admitted Begum Nusrat Bhutto's petition in the Supreme Court of Pakistan challenging the constitutionality of her husband's detention.

Justice Anwar-ul-Haq was announced as the new Chief Justice of Pakistan, who had no legal training and had entered the judicial service as an administrator but had the honour of being a personal friend of Gen Ziaul Haq. Gen Ziaul Haq had brought him there because he knew that any loophole in managing Z A Bhutto's trial could have jeopardized his grand scheme. This time Z A Bhutto was arrested under some military order putting behind the High Court's bail orders.

The trial of Zulfiqar Ali Bhutto and five other defendants commenced on 11th October 1977 in the Lahore High Court before a bench of following five judges (i) Maulvi Mushtaq Hussein as Chief Justice, (ii) Justice Zaki ud Din Pal (iii) Justice MSM Qureshi (iv) Justice Aftab Hussein and (v) Justice Gulbaz Khan. The public prosecutor was Ejaz Hussein Batalvi and ZA Bhutto was defended for part of the proceedings by D.M Awan, Ehsan Qadir Shah, and Enayatullah. By this time the military regime of Gen Zia ul Haq was in complete control of the country. All pillars of state including the judiciary and the executive had been made subservient to the whims and wishes of the military dictator.

How the judiciary were made to dance to the tune of the rulers .... See these paragraphs:

[The procedure adopted became a glittering piece of judicial history that Mr. Bhutto was denied trial at the sessions level which was (and still it is so) otherwise imperative to meet the ends of justice and was/is the established procedure in criminal jurisprudence. The main reason for holding a trial initially by a Sessions Judge is to provide the accused an opportunity to appeal before the High Court in the event of his conviction. It is a legal requirement in Pakistan.

Further, it enables two judges of the High Court to assess the reasoning adopted by the lower court. All that mandatory requirements were ignored and bypassed.

A Division Bench of the Lahore High Court was already inquiring into a private complaint of Ahmad Raza Kasuri about the incident of his father's murder (which later on exonerated Mr Bhutto of the charge of murder). The bench was also seized of the bail matter. An incomplete *challan* (prosecution report with details of evidences) was meanwhile submitted in the court of a magistrate of Lahore which was immediately forwarded to the Session Court.

The withdrawal of the matter from the lower court to the High court was decided without hearing the accused or his counsel, and confirmed the suspicion of bias.

The CJ Maulvi Mushtaq Hussain afterwards told a German diplomat on question of transferring the case, that *"Because no other judge would be able to control the accused"*. [Article *'Tale of a vitiated murder by Fakhar Zaman* is referred]

Professor F C Crone of Copenhagen, who had followed the proceedings of the case, had commented in *Asia Week of 5th May 1978* that *'the trial could not, by any standard, be characterized as fair. It appears that the coup generals see Bhutto's death—-his judicial murder—-as a logical necessity of removing a dangerous political enemy'.*

Referring to *'Judicial Murder of a Prime Minister* 'written by **Tariq Ali,** Gen Ziaul Haq's mind was already made up; he was determined to kill Bhutto. This is evident from the interview he gave to the media on 6th September 1977 in which he confirmed that he had personally ordered the arrest of Z A Bhutto and added:

> *"Mr. Bhutto was a Machiavelli of 1977. An evil genius running the country on more or less Gestapo lines, misusing funds, blackmailing people, detaining them and even perhaps ordering people to be killed."*

The Lahore High Court pronounced their judgment on **18th March 1978.** Bhutto was found guilty and sentenced to death. This unanimous decision stated that the prosecution had proved their case and that Zulfikar Ali Bhutto was a "compulsive liar". Gen Ziaul Haq had earlier stated in an interview to monthly *'Urdu Digest' on 15th September 1977* that:

> *'Bhutto is a cheat and a murderer and he would not be able to escape the severest punishment on the basis of the evidence already available'.*

The prosecution's star witness was Masood Mahmood, a shady character of dubious antecedents and a former Director General of Federal Security Force (FSF), on whose testimony the entire structure of case was built and finally proved to be the bedrock of the Government's case. The judges of the Lahore High Court were totally unconcerned and oblivious to the fact that Masood Mehmood made a confessional statement in order to save his own neck and thus should have been classified as:

- an unsatisfactory witness,

- an accomplice and a participant in the crime,

- he admitted his guilt three years after the crime was committed,

- he made his confessional statement a long time after he was arrested, detained and kept in solitary confinement,

- there were many other criminal charges against him, and

Allegedly the judicial process was blatantly transgressed and the principles of justice and impartiality were crushed. In the words of **Stanley Port** again:

"The Chief Justice Maulvi Mushtaq never so much as attempted to suppress or hide his personal animus. It never occurred to him that he should refuse himself from the trial."

Benazir Bhutto contended in his book titled *'Daughter of the East'* that:

"........The witnesses were briefed on what they should say. .... At the end of the trial, not one of the objections raised or the contradictions in the evidence pointed out by the defence appeared in the record 706 pages of testimony."

As expected, Justice Maulvi Mushtaq and his full bench found Zulfikar Ali Bhutto guilty of murder and sentenced him to death.

J Maulvi Mushraq was a known Bhutto hater and made no secret of his dislike and enmity with the former Prime Minister. Just *before the beginning of the trial, the constitution of the court was challenged* by Z A Bhutto on the grounds of appointment of J Maulvi Mushtaq as the Chief Election Commissioner by Gen Ziaul Haq. Z A Bhutto's appeal and rejoinder to the press alleged partisanship against Maulvi Mushtaq Hussein and labelled it a mockery of justice in combining the office of the Chief Election Commissioner and CJ LHC.

Z A Bhutto also pointed out the visible bias and vindictive nature of J Maulvi Mushtaq by bringing to light the fact that <u>Maulvi Mushtaq on the retirement of Justice Iqbal, had been superseded during Bhutto's rule</u> although he was the senior most judge of the Lahore High Court and since that day he had nurtured a grudge against Z A Bhutto. All the allegations were repeated in the application for transfer of the case on behalf of Z A Bhutto before the High Court and the Supreme Court of Pakistan. The High Court dismissed the appeal summarily on 9ᵗʰ October 1977.

Throughout the course of trial in the Lahore High Court, Justice Maulvi Mushtaq Hussain failed to disguise his contempt for Z A Bhutto and continued to spit venom in the form of rude, insulting and uncalled for remarks against him. While Z A Bhutto was placed behind the dock he was once given a chair with the enigmatic and uncalled for remarks by Justice Maulvi Mushtaq Hussain that *"We know you are used to a very comfortable life"*.

On one occasion J Maulvi Mushtaq even mentioned a 'hypothetical' case of judges being superseded for appointment of a Chief Justice. The jurists present there laughed because indeed the Chief Justice himself was the judge superseded during Bhutto's term as Prime Minister for which Mr Bhutto was being prosecuted not on the charge of Kasuri's murder.

J Maulvi Mushtaq also gave an *interview to the BBC* correspondent Mark Tulley. He spoke about common law traditions and that he was disappointed that Amnesty International did not send observers. The Chief Justice stated that the Bhutto's case was being heard by five judges although the law required only two. This was not only unusual but also against all judicial ethics for a judge to comment publicly on a case being tried in his own court. The Chief Justice completely forgot that the person most in need of an assurance that justice would be done was the accused Z A Bhutto himself.

On **25th March 1978**, Z A Bhutto lodged an appeal to the Supreme Court of Pakistan against his death sentence announced by the Lahore High Court. Z A Bhutto appealed to the Chief Justice Anwarul Haq to withdraw from the case as he had publicly criticized Bhutto and his Government. The Supreme Court bench consisted of nine Judges at the start.

This appeal was rejected by Chief Justice of the Supreme Court Anwar ul Haq as being *"unfounded and based on misunderstanding."* Hearing of the appeal continued from 20th May 1978 to 23rd December 1978.

6th February 1979: J Anwarul Haq, Chief Justice of Pakistan, delivered the decision and upheld LHC's death sentence by a ratio of 4:3. During the course of trial in the Supreme Court the number of Judges hearing the appeal was reduced to seven from nine. Justice Qaiser Khan retired on 30th July 1978 because his contract was not renewed as was done in the case of Justice Burhanuddin. Justice Wahidud Din stepped down after suffering a stroke on 20th November 1978 thus was removed from the panel. One Justice Malik Akram had played a decisive role while going against Mr Bhutto.

The three judges who voted for Z A Bhutto's acquittal were Justice Dorab Patel of Balochistan, Justice Safder Shah of NWFP, and Justice Mohammed Halim of Sindh as they could not find any direct evidence for the conspiracy to murder. While Justice Anwarul Haq in his eight-hundred pages decision dismissed all the errors and illegalities in the Lahore High Court's trial as totally irrelevant to the verdict and confirmed the death sentence. He himself wrote the judgment, dismissing the Bhutto's appeal and upholding the conviction and death sentence. J Malik Akram, J Karam Elahi Chohan and J Nasim Hassan Shah agreed with the CJP. Ironically all the four judges who upheld the death sentence belonged to the Punjab.

[*Justice Ghulam Safdar Shah expressed his sorrow over the tragedy of Bhutto's death and somewhere gave the impression that he would have accepted the argument of ZAB's defence team. This caused panic and uneasiness for Gen Ziaul Haq's team, therefore, he ordered the Federal Investigations Agency (FIA) to chase Justice Shah. He was dragged into explanations and, as per government version, was found indulged in 'wrong' practices by the FIA. With notable discrepancies the then government approached the chief justice for action against the judge. A case was referred to the Supreme Judicial Council (SJC) and J Safdar Shah was forced to resign. He left the country immediately after.*]

Justice Aslam Riaz Hussain was the only left out judge from the Supreme Court bench constituted to hear Bhutto's appeal. Reason was that once in Governor House Lahore, Gen Ziaul Haq had asked him that:

'How you people make judges. I replied that a judge should be a gentleman. Secondly he should be a gentleman. Thirdly he should be again a gentleman. Gen Ziaul Haq kept my reply in mind. Gen Ziaul Haq might have discussed my mind with the CJP at some convenient time. Later, when the bench was constituted in Bhutto's appeal, Chief Justice Anwarul Haq made sure that I was not included in it.'

Justice Malik Qayyum, in an interview published in daily **the 'Jang' dated 5th February 2006**, however, had pointed out that:

'Mr Bhutto had filed a review petition [against the final verdict of his death sentence] before the Supreme Court. My father, J Malik Akram, had written the disposal order of that review petition saying that it could better be dealt with by executive. Mr Bhutto's counsels should have urged before the court at some initial stage that the punishment be reduced as per facts available on file.

Mr Bhutto's defence lawyers had done another blunder by making a strong demand that the case should be heard by 'all available judges of the Supreme Court' including the ad-hoc judges. Had that demand not made, the bench would have been comprised of only five permanent judges. Bhutto could have avoided major punishment

If it would be so then Mr Bhutto could get a definite relief because CJP Anwarul Haq and J Malik Akram were against Bhutto but three judges named J Dorab Patel, J M Haleem and J Safdar Shah were in favour of Mr Bhutto. J Karam Elahi Chohan and J Nasim Hasan Shah were ad-hoc judges but they were included in the bench only after making demand from Mr Bhutto's defence lawyers team.

Secondly, Mr Bhutto had himself approved the bench and had categorically said before the apex court that he had full confidence on that bench of the Supreme Court.'

Moreover, Justice Malik Qayyum categorically told that:

- He'll not speak on Bhutto's case because his father Justice Malik Akram was one of the judges who had given verdict against him. He had not even read the whole judgment of the Bhutto's case.

- His father J Malik Akram had no relations or friendship with Gen Ziaul Haq. Before July 1977 he was a judge. Once Gen Ziaul Haq made Justice Afzal Cheema as Chief Justice while superseding his father, the later had tendered resignation which was not accepted and Justice Malik Akram was urged to continue.

- CJP Molvi Mushtaq Hussain should not have heard Bhutto's case because the defence lawyers had moved a no confidence on the basis of alleged bias against CJP Molvi Mushtaq in writing.

Justice Nasim Hasan Shah later became the Chief Justice of Pakistan in April 1994. After his retirement, <u>Dr Nasim Hasan Shah had once conceded that *'Bhutto could have escaped the gallows and his death sentence reduced easily'*</u>.

The former Chief Justice volunteered these contentions in a startling press interview to the ***daily Jang dated 23rd August 1996.*** He also dared to comment on the constitution of trial bench of the Lahore High Court, and said that *'Maulvi Mushtaq Hussain should have avoided naming himself as a member of the trial bench to maintain the dignity of the court in the principled tradition of justice. The grudge being that he (Z A Bhutto as Prime Minister) had superseded him (the judge) by a junior one while appointing Chief Justice of the Lahore HC.'*

The former Chief Justice had no hesitation in averring that '.......*it was in this context that during the trial, Justice Maulvi Mushtaq Hussain had made uncalled for personal remarks provoking Mr Bhutto to boycott the court proceedings.'*

J Nasim Hasan Shah when confronted by the interviewer admitted that never before in the judicial history of the country any abettor was awarded capital punishment. He further hinted that both Gen Ziaul Haq and Maulvi Mushtaq had fears that Bhutto's survival could be risky for them. So he should better be eliminated first and no chances taken.

"*I am very sorry it had to be done, had to be done*"....... a belated remorse by a participating judge who perhaps suffers pricks afterwards. Emphasis by the judge on "had to be done" speaks for itself. It was an open admission that there was immense pressure on the judges from military dictator to uphold the LHC verdict in the case.

The *'Dawn' of 4th September 2009* had opined that if any further proof was needed that Bhutto's trial was nothing but a sham to physically eliminate him, this book of J Nasim Hasan Shah was enough proof. Admitting in his book that *'he met a fellow judge, Dorab Patel, to have the three acquittals changed to guilty as a quid pro quo, is a clear indictment Nasim Hasan Shah has written against himself with his own guilty hands dripping with Bhutto's blood.'*

That was why the world jurists from former US attorney-general Ramsay Clark to a former Sri Lankan Chief Justice had declared it as '**the Murder of the Trial**' in legal interpretations.

Bhutto's judicial murder, unless honourably revoked, will forever remain the greatest slur on the face of the Supreme Court and in the annals of PLD. As popularly demanded by certain politicians Gen Ziaul Haq's symbol be hanged and retired Chief Justice Nasim Hasan Shah should be called in the dock being the only surviving judge of Bhutto's (judicial) murder and one who has provided new evidence not known or admitted at the time of the trial in the Lahore High Court then.

In nut shell, it was a pity that the superior trial and appellate courts, which should have been above mistrust and suspicion, had to earn this accusation from neutral observers and jurists of world repute because the judges succumbed to unseemly pressure from the military dictator, Gen Ziaul Haq. In ordinary circumstances, such a trial would have been vitiated and could have caused disqualification of the judges who were there on the two benches.

It was indecent haste (the statutory period of 30 days for filing an appeal was reduced to seven days) which caused circumvention of judicial norms, and the entire proceedings, both at the trial and appellate stages, left serious doubts lurking in dispassionate minds and thus its retrial by the Supreme Court under Presidential Reference no: 1/2011 contained merits because after the confessional statement of Justice Nasim Hasan Shah, the order of the LHC and SC lost their effect.

1st April 1979: Gen Ziaul Haq rejected the mercy petition of Z A Bhutto (and just 3 days after, on **4th April 1979, Mr Bhutto was hanged** to death in Rawalpindi jail). Mercilessly and despicably, he was hanged at the hands of one Tara Masih. The jurists and opinion makers all over the world termed it a **'Judicial Murder'**. That is the reason that this case has never been quoted as a reference in any court since it was decided and the judgment published. A painful chapter closed.

Justice S A Nusrat, a former Federal Law Secretary, in his interview published in print media on 25th July 1999, had contended that in Bhutto's case more fault goes to a 'defense lawyer' of Mr Bhutto (may be Yahya Bakhtiar) than judges partisanship. He told that:

'In the beginning Mr Bhutto himself committed blunders; sometimes by trying to get the trial delayed and sometimes by getting the judges influenced through "foreign appeals". Then his defence lawyer's one gross mistake decided the whole case.

Before the LHC bench, the prosecution had placed an office file of IB/FSF, originally belonging to the custody of Masood Mahmood, which was concerning Ahmed Raza Kasuri. On one page Mr Bhutto had written in his own hand 'eliminate him' referring to Kasuri. The prosecution had decided within them that no body would ask any question to anyone to get explanation of phrase "eliminate him".

All of a sudden, the defence lawyer questioned Masood Mahmood: 'what you understood from the phrase [eliminate him]'; Masood Mahmood promptly said: 'very simple, he should be killed'. The CJ Maulvi Mushtaq himself got nervous on that unexpected question. A pin drop silence prevailed in the court room and Maulvi Mushtaq's pen suddenly dropped from his hand. The cunning Justice Maulvi Mushtaq Hussain had smilingly uttered that 'today the defence lawyer has accomplished the job of prosecution.'

In an interview of July 1998, the then Governor Punjab Justice Aslam Riaz Hussain told that Gen Ziaul Haq was determined to kill Mr Bhutto by all means and at all costs because he knew that either he would survive or Bhutto at last. Justice Aslam categorically said that even if Mr Bhutto had survived through Nawab Kasuri's murder trial, he would have entangled in another sedition case with 'charges of separation of

East Pakistan' for which files were ready in GHQ. Every judge had an idea that there was no point in going against the wind.

The history points towards another odd situation that was likely to develop in Pakistan at that time. Gen Ziaul Haq had ready files, since 1977, with certain names of army Generals and Brigadiers who were to be posted as judges in superior courts if and when needed. It was only in Gen Ziaul Haq's mind that, whether or not, with the appointments of senior army officers he was going to install parallel military courts.

In a way the judges did right to stand in the game at least otherwise, irrespective of the worldly criticism, the whole system of judicial norms and traditions would have been spoiled. In that situation, they went wrong in only one case that was about Bhutto's trial, for the rest, the judiciary continued functioning as normal.

Justice Dr Javed Iqbal, in his interview published in print media dated 9th November 1991, had also mentioned the same fact. In his opinion, Gen Ziaul Haq could have finished Mr Bhutto's story within a week through a military court trial but he purposefully sent it to the High Court just to spoil civil judiciary through his cronies like Maulvi Mushtaq. Justice Javed Iqbal categorically told that:

'Gen Ziaul Haq had a plan in his mind to hang Bhutto. Had the Lahore High Court given him relief or set him free, the military court was already on papers to give the desired decision as the General [Ziaul Haq] wanted then.'

Justice Javed Iqbal had also told that Mr Bhutto had sent him a special message to join the Lahore HC bench to hear his case. Subsequently the CJ Molvi Mushtaq had also asked him to sit on that bench but he refused simply on a reason that:

'In the previous general elections I was a candidate of National Assembly's seat in my home constituency against Zulfikar Ali Bhutto, and I had been defeated by him so I cannot sit in a bench hearing case against his person; no way.'

Very few people know that a book titled '*Afwah aur Haqeeqat*', a collection of late Z A Bhutto's writings and translated in Urdu by Altaf Hassan Qureshi was got published in 1993 by Benazir Bhutto after 14 years of his father's death. Benazir Bhutto wanted to convey that her father and the PPP were not against the army and judiciary as institutions. They were against Gen Ziaul Haq only and his near associates in high judiciary.

In that book, while explaining the reasons for amendments in the 1973's constitution, late Mr Bhutto had categorically mentioned about Maulvi Mushtaq Hussain, who *being a butcher from Jallandher (India)* was purposefully obstructed to become the Chief Justice of Lahore High Court because he was known for 'raping justice'. Mr Bhutto had given details of strained relations between him and Justice Maulvi Mushtaq Hussain by quoting that:

> '*In 1966, when he was the Foreign Minister in Gen Ayub's cabinet and Maulvi Mushtaq was the Law Secretary, there prevailed a cold war between them on some petty issues. Later Gen Ayub made Maulvi Mushtaq a judge and sent him to Lahore. In 1968 Mr Bhutto was arrested in Lahore but was got ridiculed by making him appeared before the same Justice Maulvi Mushtaq Hussain.*
>
> *In December 1971, when Mr Bhutto became the Chief Executive of the country Maulvi Mushtaq met him and extended his offer that if he is made Chief Justice he would help the government even in odd matters. Mr Bhutto had declined his offer which desire was afterwards fulfilled by Gen Ziaul Haq*'.

In the same book, two letters of late Z A Bhutto, written from Rawalpindi Jail to the then Chief Justice of Pakistan Anwarul Haq, are also included in which Mr Bhutto had asked him not to sit in the Bench to hear appeal against Maulvi Mushtaq's orders because 'he (CJP) in person would not be able to deliver justice just to please his Jallandhry friend Ziaul Haq'.

This book provides enough material to believe that late Mr Bhutto was helpless at the hands of judiciary and some army Generals. He had brought amendments in the constitution to make some of the judges toothless who were inducted in the judiciary by Gen Ayub and Gen Yahya in row but ultimately the same judges had taken him to the gallows causing a judicial murder.

It had been also surfaced that had Mr Bhutto not compromised with some grave mistakes of the then Generals, he would not have faced the misery of July 1977 coup with secret patting of Gen Ziaul Haq by the Americans who were bent upon taking revenge from him [PM Zulfikar Ali Bhutto] for his nuclear programs & objectives of leading the Islamic countries at par with western powers.

Leaving all the conspiracy theories aside, putting all the explanations forwarded by the legal stalwarts at back, brushing all enlighten quotes of intelligentsia under the carpet one would like to ponder at least that Mr Bhutto might have paid the price of those murders or murderous crimes which he could not recall till his last breathing moment. He might know about them. He might not be at fault in Kasuri's case but he had paid compensation of those cries and sighs which he or his cronies had not heard when passing over some unknown dying human beings.

Referring to a veteran lawyer Akram Sheikh's interview published in daily *the 'Jang' dated 12th November 1997*:

> *'Bhutto was not wrongly punished. It is God Almighty's divine law that a man continues with his wrong doings and goes unharmed. Suddenly the divine law takes turn and that man is caught, apparently innocent, to compensate for those hidden sins & crimes which he had done earlier. No person on earth could extend him harm what to speak of judges or courts. Suddenly, he was picked up by the God Almighty to pay for his proud, hatred, double standards, cheating the humanity in the name of Roti-Kapra-Makan but from inside up keeping Jagirdari values. However, the decision was controversial and would remain so in Pakistan's judicial history for all times to come.'*

In 2004, perhaps only once in Pakistan's' Judicial History, a petition against a Former Chief Justice of Supreme Court of Pakistan was filed, seeking registration of a case against him on charges of abetting in the 'murder' of a former Prime Minister Mr Bhutto. A division bench comprising Justices Sheikh Abdur Rashid and Bilal Khan held that the petition hardly qualified for processing because the judge of a bench could not be proceeded against in a case which had already been decided 25 years earlier by a competant court.

The petition was filed by one Hanif Tahir of *People's Lawyers Forum (PLF)*. The members of the bench felt that petitioner could hardly address legal aspects of the case and certain cogent questions. One member of the bench remarked;

> *'In a situation where the judgment of a case was effective for citation as a reference, an ambiguous statement of one of the members of a panel of judges hearing the case, could in no way prejudice the decision after two decades. If such things were allowed to happen, the whole judicial system would collapse.'*

Hanif Tahir had quoted the former Chief Justice Nasim Hasan Shah as saying in two of his press interviews that the Supreme Court judgment in the appeal of the late Bhutto against his death sentence awarded by the

Lahore High Court, was a wrong decision and it was a fit case for lesser punishment. Justice Shah was part of the 7-member bench of the Supreme Court which upheld the death penalty.

Hanif Tahir had contended that comments of the former CJ amounted to a confessional statement and that he had shown no such sentiments while agreeing with the majority opinion of apex court's bench which confirmed the execution of Mr Bhutto. Hanif Tahir was relying on the text of interview as 'public document' but was unable to define the legality of public documents. The bench of the Lahore High Court on 12th February 2004 dismissed the said petition in lamina.

18th October 1979: Gen Ziaul Haq, as the Chief Martial Law Administrator, had promulgated a Presidential Order no: 21 of 1979 under which an amendment in Constitution was made where there was no National Assembly, no session in vogue. Under this order Section 212-A was added for the *'Establishment of Military Courts & Tribunals'.*

> [*Gen Ziaul Haq then told members of the Pakistan Bar Council that he had secured total collaboration from the two Chief Justices in giving effect to the idea of inserting Article 212-A in the constitution; that they had seen the draft amendment and had approved it. The General posed a question to the Bar Council members: how could he be blamed when the highest judiciary itself had accepted the imposition of martial law and the establishment of military tribunals at its own cost?*
>
> *Article 212-A was made part of the Constitution which contemplated the setting up of military courts and tribunals precluding the superior judiciary from entertaining any applications in respect of matters to which the jurisdiction of the military courts had been extended.*]

Perhaps these were the military courts which Gen Ziaul Haq was going to launch in Pakistan within moments had any of the two superior courts done justice with Z A Bhutto to set him free. Bhutto would have been trapped in some other case then manufactured in the GHQ.

Scenario 6

WHO SUPPORTED GEN ZIA (1977-88):

When the then retiring Army Chief Gen Tikka Khan refused PM Zulfikar Ali Bhutto to avail an extension of one year in March 1976, he had sent up a list of eight Lt Generals then serving in Pakistan Army with his recommendations. Gen Tikka Khan, in an interview published in *daily 'Jang' of 28th March 1999*, told that:

> *'We had never recommended Gen Ziaul Haq's name as army chief nor were we expecting his selection. He used to wear loose dress and was known as 'peon' of the Armoured Corps instead of being called a General. He had one negative report being captain which was later cleared by one Col Babar, the uncle of Gen Nasirullah Babar, but even then Mr Bhutto selected him.'*

When Gen Ziaul Haq was selected as Army Chief, the then government Secretary Ghulam Ishaq Khan (later the President of Pakistan), by chance told Maj Gen Sawar Khan that he was going to make a media announcement of seven retiring Generals as per PM's desire. Maj Gen Sawar Khan asked him to hold on, talked to PM Bhutto who was at D I Khan that day and managed to tone down the news. Three of them, Generals Akbar, Aftab & Majeed Ch were nominated as Pakistan's ambassadors in some countries whereas Gen Jilani was sent as Secretary Defence in Pakistan Secretariat Rawalpindi.

Lt Gen Faiz Ali Chishti had been the main and known supporter of Gen Ziaul Haq during starting years.

Lt Gen Faiz Ali Chishti, a charismatic character behind the army coup of July 1977, has always been measured as top die-heart companion of Gen Zaiul Haq in the history of Pakistan. He was considered a key to success for the military rule in 1970s; known for coining strategic policies for the martial law government and their implementation & control without compromises. He remained with Gen Ziaul Haq till his retirement in 1980, kept silent till 1982 under the rules in vogue [In Pakistan no officer can jump in politics until two years after his retirement] and then released some stunning facts about the perceptions then prevailing amongst the people.

Referring to an interview Lt Gen Faiz Ali Chishti conducted by *Sohail Warroich*, published in *daily 'Jang' of 20th June 1999* and later included in his book titled as 'Jarnailon Ki Syasat in Urdu (2005) some glimpses would be enough to reflect the then prevailing politics in power corridors of the military regime.

It was generally known that Lt Gen Chishti was the real strength behind Gen Ziaul Haq while the later used to say *'Murshid'* (spiritual leader) for him. The fact was that *'Murshid'* was a word Gen Ziaul Haq used to say for every colleague in an informal way and not specifically for Gen Chishti. Very few people know that previously they were simply known to each other as routine acquaintance being in army. Both the Generals were not even at good terms between March 1976 and July 1977 due to a little event in background:

> *'In GHQ Lt Gen Chishti was posted as Military Secretary (MS) and was once asked by then Lt Gen Ziaul Haq for transfer of an officer which he had refused. When in the March 1976, Gen Ziaul Haq became the Army Chief; Lt Gen Chishti at the first available chance explained that why 'that peculiar transfer was not done'. Gen Ziaul Haq had agreed with the reason apparently smilingly.*

> *Being MS on duty Lt Gen Chishti used to brief Gen Ziaul Haq that he should not shake hand with others using both hands; he should wear a proper General's cap with uniform; he should not give money to saints & clergymen and he should not bow down his body when meeting others. It was his duty to convey the Army Chief that the officers and men of his force did not like such humble and docile gestures in their army chief or commander.'*

Interestingly, it was generally known that whole of the army was with Gen Ziaul Haq for taking Mr Bhutto to the gallows. It was not the fact. Even Gen Ziaul Haq's most trusted companion Lt Gen Faiz Ali Chishti was not standing by him for that heinous act. It was purposefully made public that Lt Gen Chishti was the person to take that decision of hanging Mr Bhutto; he (Lt Gen Chishti) had gone to Rawalpindi Jail to see the 'death cells' for some reasons etc. Lt Gen Faiz Ali Chishti had denied the charges altogether by saying that:

- *'All lies. I've never visited the Rawalpindi Jail till today.*

- *Gen Ziaul Haq had never called anyone to share his plans about Zulfikar Ali Bhutto or his PPP including me. I was rather against Mr Bhutto's hanging and I used to differ with him openly in meetings. I had also argued that the mercy petition regarding Mr Bhutto's death penalty be left for the coming government.*

- *My contention remained that 'let us have elections and go'.*

- *In Mr Bhutto's death case, punishment was announced by the higher courts. No one could do anything. The real thing was the mercy petition of Mr Bhutto. An undue haste was done in processing it. When it was received by Governor Punjab Gen Sawar Khan, he sent it to Gen Ziaul Haq within 24 hours. The PM's position was of an international standing, much thinking should have been infused in that issue.*

- *This disinformation was purposefully sent to media that Mr Bhutto was subjected to torture by me. I was Corps Commander of 10 Corps Rawalpindi. I had no connection with martial law administration nor had I concern with jails. Mr Bhutto might have been beaten by Col Rafiuddin, then incharge jail from the Martial Law Admin, who was later awarded by sending to Myanmar as Pakistan's Commercial Attaché,. He was under one Brig Rahat Latif who was later promoted to Maj General.*

- *The above disinformation was sent to media on Gen Ziaul Haq's specific instructions. I had known it the same day. I was upset on the day of Bhutto's hanging. I had met Gen Ziaul Haq that day and asked harshly that 'you are calling Islam here; then, as per Islamic injunctions, why Bhutto's dead body was not handed over to his wife and daughter. Shame on you, General, Shame on you.'*

- *Mr Bhutto was actually to be hanged a day earlier. Gen Ziaul Haq had already released that disinformation to media [that Bhutto had actually died of torture done by Gen Chishti in jail] but I was not in the town that day; witness the record of GHQ.*

- *Gen Ziaul Haq rang me, called me in town but as I had known about wrong media news, therefore, I avoided obeying his orders that day. Gen Ziaul Haq postponed the execution till next day.*

- *When I refused to go as Governor Punjab, why Gen Sawar Khan agreed immediately then because he could send Mr Bhutto's mercy appeal to Gen Zia within 24 hours, I was not of that type.*

- *Afterwards Benazir Bhutto came as prime minister twice; had there been any truth in stories wrongly attributed to me, she would have taken me through a hard mill during her government.*

- *Amongst the Corps Commander's meetings at GHQ Rawalpindi, Lt Gen Jehanzeb Arbab always stood by me in making demands of elections; he was the only officer to do so.*

- *I've never met Benazir Bhutto, then or after, till today.*

In army there are two kinds of people; firstly, the yes-Sir *Laftains* to obey which are also used to extend the chief's tenures and secondly, the 'good captains'; always needed to strike and fight. Pakistan's bad luck that we have seen more yes-Sir chiefs like Ayub Khan, Yahya Khan, Gul Hassan, Tikka Khan, Ziaul Haq, Mirza Aslam Beg, Abdul Waheed Kakar and Jehangir Karamat etc. Good captain was Gen Asif Nawaz so was sent very high very soon but by whome; remains a mystry.

The elections to be held in October 1977, as originally announced by Gen Ziaul Haq in his telecasts, were postponed on the instance of Gen Ziaul Haq who always quoted that the politicians were pressing him for announcing 'no elections'. *Jama'at e Islami* (JI) and the other politico-religious parties were in Gen Ziaul Haq's pockets under the false and politicized promises of Islamization of the country but with one exception of *Maulana* Shah Ahmed Noorani of *Jamiat Ulema e Pakistan* (JUP). Throughout that 11 year's military rule *Maulana* Noorani continuously hated the General, never met him except once. When Gen Ziaul Haq announced that there would be no elections till the Islamization process would get completed, the JUP was the only party which retaliated and went furious. He never attended any meeting of Gen Ziaul Haq.

Once Maulana Abdul Sattar Niazi and Gen (Rtd) K M Azhar, both of JUP, forced *Maulana* Noorani to see Gen Ziaul Haq because the General wanted to see him desperately; he agreed. However, during meeting *Maulana* Noorani got so enraged on Gen Ziaul Haq's betrayal with the nation on election issue (recalling that famous promise of 90 days) that he abused Gen Ziaul Haq while shouting at his face. In that meeting Shah Noorani was accompanied by Maulana Niazi and Shah Fareedul Haq whereas Ghulam Isahq Khan and Gen K M Arif were there to help Gen Ziaul Haq. The meeting could not be continued further; obviously.

Gen Ziaul Haq once told Lt Gen Chishti that '*Lt Gen Rahimuddin is a paper tiger only; put him as IG Training in GHQ.*' In 1971 War, his Commander Iftikhar Janjua had recommended Court Martial for him (Gen Rahimuddin) because he had absconded from the War. He had never seen a travelling bullet throughout his army career; but later the same Rahimuddin was made a four star General brushing aside the rules

& requirements, astonishing it was; because he was (or going to be) the father in law of Ijazul Haq, Gen Ziaul Haq's eldest son.

Lt Gen Faiz Ali Chishti used to speak bluntly and loudly in Commanders Meetings at GHQ. Gen Ziaul Haq did not like him by heart but continued to tolerate him till his last day in service. After 1982, he was the first General to raise voice against Gen Ziaul Haq who was still in power then. Gen Chishti was never arrested for speaking against Gen Ziaul Haq but all politicians and media-men, whoever came to see him, were invariably arrested and taken through the usual interrogation process by the ISI then under Gen Akhtar Abdul Rehman; just to create harassment nothing else.

[Gen Ziaul Haq once had to travel in a plane which was to be driven by Gen Chishti's son. Due to security reasons and untold risk, his son was removed from the flying list. Gen Chishti, when told about it, asked his son to resign immediately. Later he joined Emirates Airlines.]

Lt Gen Chishti once told that though he was critical but Gen Ziaul Haq used to tolerate him and love him because he never expected anything more than he deserved. No complaint of corruption whatsoever but there were some Generals like Gen Akhtar Abdul Rehman, Gen Sawar Khan, Gen KM Arif and Gen Iqbal who used to twist Gen Zia's ears against him.

President Daaud of Afghanistan once came on Pakistan's tour and, due to unknown reasons, suddenly agreed to accept *Durand Line* as an international border. Lt Gen Chishtie suggested Gen Ziaul Haq to make an announcement immediately. Gen Ziaul Haq hesitated; saying that he would do it in Kabul when he would be there on tour. Later when he went on Afghan tour, Lt Gen Chishti was not asked to accompany him. He was the eye-witness to President Daaud's offer first to the Prime Minister Bhutto and then to Gen Ziaul Haq.

[*The **Durand Line** refers to the porous international border between Pakistan & Afghanistan, which is poorly marked and approximately 2,640 kilometres (1,610 miles) long. It was established after the 1893 **Durand Line Agreement** between a representative of Colonial British-Raj India and Afghan Amir Abdul Rehman for fixing the limit of their respective spheres of influence. The single-page agreement contains seven short articles and is still in vogue.*]

Lt Gen Chishti was made Chairman Election Cell and of Accountability Cell too. He remained associated with the negotiations, from March to

June 1977, used to be held between the IJI leadership and the PM Bhutto. Gen Chishti had told Mr Bhutto many times openly to go for new elections as the situation was going out of control day by day. Martial Law of July 1977 was finally decided by Gen Ziaul Haq as Army Chief, previously to be imposed on 3rd July 1977, but then held amidst the news that compromise between IJI & PM Bhutto would be signed on 4th July. Gen Zia asked PM Bhutto about it who had replied that IJI people were not coming to terms; that moment the army coup was finally decided for the next day.

The immediate cause was that PM Bhutto had called army to control the law & order situation in Lahore. An army contingent, deployed in *Anarkali Bazaar* had to fire at the crowd but a controversy had broken out within army which was taken seriously. Army was ordered to fire; 30 bullets were fired; there were only three found dead; why not 30 deaths as army was not trained to fire in the air; it was contended. Three army Brigadiers had resigned. A Channel of Command was considered broken; of course, an alarming signal for army discipline.

It was a general perception that Gen Ziaul Haq was a weak General while using shoulders of hard nuts like Lt Gen Chishti. In July 1977 and after, the two names were synonymous for that military coup but ultimately Gen Ziaul Haq survived. Gen Chishti believed in army discipline till his last breath. He believed that Martial Law was 'correctly imposed' but was not being implemented or carried through correctly. He knew that Gen Ziaul Haq was pushing the country towards devastation and wreckage but he behaved like a disciplined subordinate officer and walked away from the playground on the eve of his retirement; however, leaving the people disappointed.

Referring to an interview published in *daily 'Jang' of 4th October 1998*, Gen F S Lodhi had once commented that: *'Gen Ziaul Haq was a nationalist person and it was his ultimate wish to impose Martial Law* [that he did in July 1977']. Gen Ziaul Haq's option to fight the Afghan War was correct because the Russians were knocking at our door. Pakistan had not fought a proxy war because America joined us later.

It was rightly contended that instead of blaming Americans we should blame ourselves. In August 1988, Pakistan had debts of $7 billions; in 1998 it was $42 billion. In ten years what our politicians had done with Pakistan. One third of foreign loans went in the pockets of rulers (as per World Bank Report then published) so our politicians had eaten up $12 billions personally. Some of our key figures still take their 'pocket money' from India & America.

However, there were no two opinions that Gen Ziaul Haq had used the Islamization to extend his political rule and not for Islam. When he was made the Army Chief in March 1976, liquor was banned in army messes and the restriction was laid down by Gen Tikka Khan in Mr Bhutto's regime. The same Mr Bhutto when first time visited the army mess in Gen Ziaul Haq's period, the later had waived that constraint just to please Mr Bhutto; where was his Islam then.

Invariably in all GHQ meetings, the officers used to hold discussions over possibility of elections. Lt Gen Chishti always openly asked for elections whereas Gen Fazal e Haq (later Governor of NWFP and was shot dead in open) always opposed him saying: *'Don't follow him Sir. He wants to swing over gallows and wants us to accompany him too'*. Every officer believed that if elections were held, the PPP would definitely sweep; Gen Ziaul Haq and religious parties did not want so; the military rule continued amidst discussions.

Gen Ziaul Haq always heard the arguments about elections in detail but never commented. From inside he was sizzling. Once at last, during a meeting where all Generals were sitting, he smashed the agenda file on the floor and shouted at Lt Gen Chishti in rage: *'Ok! Come and hold the Chief's chair, you always keep on giving dictations to me'*. Chishti's contention was that the army had been hero in 1965 like wars but due to Martial Law of 1977, it was earning bad name due to Gen Ziaul Haq's false statements regarding elections and false promises of Islamization.

[**Gen K M Arif**, *in his interview published in daily 'Jang' of 30th May 1999 had, however, said that he could not recall any such event as Lt Gen Chishti had claimed.*]

Soon after Gen Ziaul Haq called a meeting (cum dinner) of politicians in which all Generals and the then Chief Justice Anwarul Haq were also present. The CJP Anwarul Haq had given six month's time to Gen Ziaul Haq to hold elections in Nusrat Bhutto case. Those six months were over. Lt Gen Chishti loudly said to the CJ:

'Sir, six months period is over. Gen Ziaul Haq is guilty of contempt of court. Call him in the apex court tomorrow, send him to jail and we Generals would announce for the general elections and place the results before your honour.'

There were murmuring and sarcastic smiles on many faces; Gen Ziaul Haq was one of them.

At the time when Gen Ziaul Haq had planned a self extension in his tenure as the Army Chief, Lt Gen Chishti had suggested to him that he should not do so. He should make any of the 40 Generals his Army Chief and go for Chairman Joint Chiefs of Staff Committee instead. Gen Ziaul Haq had flatly refused because he did not want to be a CMLA on the mercy of another COAS.

When news about differences between Gen Ziaul Haq and Lt Gen Chishti started catching leading spaces in media, the later went to see his Army Chief in his office with a written and signed resignation and placed it before him. Gen Chishti told his Chief that:

> '*To remove you from the scene and from the government is two minute's job for me (because he was the real strength; Corps Commander of the Rawalpindi Corps 10 which performs all coup operations in Pakistan) but I'll not do it because it would harm Pakistan. I've also got a list of senior army officers and politicians with me who had been advising me since months that I should send you away, but I'll not do it because it would harm Pakistan. Enough is enough General! Let me go home.*'

Gen Ziaul Haq stood up from the chair; worriedly & smilingly; torn out the resignation in pieces; embraced Lt Gen Chishti saying: '**Murshad! Nothing doing like that, cool down**'.

The stories of differences between the two Generals even continued after Lt Gen Chishti's retirement. Ch Zahoor Elahi, father of Ch Shuja'at Hussain, had been trying to bring the two Generals together. Ch Zahoor used to convince Lt Gen Chishti to tone down and to stand by Gen Ziaul Haq but the former did not agree declaring openly that Gen Ziaul Haq was a '*Munafiq*' (a hypocrite) so they would not go along. Once Ch Zahoor made a quick halt at Lt Gen Chishti's residence while going home (then in the Westridge Rawalpindi) and told:

> '*I was with Gen Ziaul Haq just now and told him that he was not going straight. I've told him that if he would not come straight then something else would be done. Mr Chishti! You were right; always right; Gen Ziaul Haq is not a trust worthy person.*'

Next day, Ch Zahoor Elahi was murdered; Gen Ziaul Haq had ordered for his elimination.

Ch Shuja'at Hussain and Ch Pervez Elahi knew this fact for long. Contrary to a general perception that Ch Zahoor Elahi was killed by Al-

Zulfikar was wrong. Later the Chaudhrys and Gen Zia's eldest son Ijazul Haq remained together in so many cabinets as ministers but went compromised with that hard fact despite tall claims of being from 'Nat' tribe, a caste of warrior *jaats*.

Lt Gen Hamid Gul had been the main supporter of Gen Ziaul Haq during his ending years.

Referring to daily *'The Nation' of 15th December 2008,* the President of Pakistan Mr Zardari had once described former ISI Chief Lt Gen Hamid Gul as 'more of a political ideologue of terror rather than a physical supporter' while giving interview to the *'Newsweek'* magazine in New York. He had further clarified that:

> *'Hamid Gul is an actor who is definitely not in our good books. Hamid Gul is somebody who was never appreciated by our government. He has not been accused in the Mumbai incident but he is more of a political ideologue of terror rather than a physical supporter. Pakistan's intelligence agencies are no longer backing outlawed groups like the Lashkar-e-Taiba. The links between the ISI and the LeT were developed in the old days when dictators used to run the country.*
>
> *The government led by his PPP had always maintained a certain position that the intelligence agencies (should) have nothing to do with politics. Since the PPP in government, we held a stated position that ISI has no political role anymore.'*

Lt Gen Hamid Gul had called Gen Asif Janjua as his senior and friend but they were not at good relations with each other for at least two reasons. Firstly; Gen Asif Janjua once said in Punjabi language that *'now we should roll back our nuclear program, we'll see it later,'* to which Gen Hamid Gul had instantly refuted by saying that *'what the hell are you talking about.'* The tone might have pinched more than words.

Secondly; the two Generals were having different views on the status of Northern Areas of Pakistan. Gen Asif Nawaz wanted to motivate politicians to take some decision on the status of the Northern Areas whereas Lt Gen Hamid Gul held the opinion that *'any such decision may extend loss to our stand on Kashmir Cause.'*

Referring to the *'Daily Times' dated 1st February 2008,* Gen (Rtd) Faiz Ali Chishti, who was heading the Pakistan Ex-Servicemen Society, which issued a blunt open letter signed by about 100 senior officers in early

2008, calling on Gen Musharraf to quit, should have apologised himself first for being a willing and core partner in the military coup of Gen Ziaul Haq in July 1977. Gen Chishti once came on TV to explain why the army did not educate the nation. His answer was: *'if the roof is leaking why put good furniture in the room.'*

[*Gen (Rtd) A Majid Malik [who was a major in 1956 when he drafted a resignation by which Gen Ayub Khan forced President Iskandar Mirza to resign] should apologise for siding with Gen Musharraf when he took over the government in October 1999 and split the PML betraying Nawaz Sharif. He should be followed by Gen (Rtd) Mirza Aslam Beg for his role in the famous Mehran Bank scandal and misuse of the ISI funds for electoral & political manipulation. Gen Beg should have apologised for bringing the Supreme Court in contempt when he admitted that he had influenced the chief justice. When confronted with challenging a general, the Supreme Court under Justice Zullah forgivably got cold feet and let Gen Beg walk away free.*

The biggest crime to which many retired Generals like Lt Gen Hamid Gul must confess, and then apologize for, is the policy of seeking 'strategic depth' in Afghanistan because the end results of this policy are now threatening the existence of Pakistan's unity on many counts.']

Scenario 7

JUDICIARY IN 1979-80:

Militarized Islamic Laws & Shariat Court:

On **1st January 1980**, interest-free counters were opened at all the 7,000 branches of the nationalized commercial banks in Pakistan. Within the framework of _Islamization of economy_, the National Investment Trust (NIT) and the Investment Corporation of Pakistan (ICP) were asked by the military regime to operate on equity basis instead of decades old routine interest as of 1st July. However, interest-bearing National Savings Schemes were allowed to operate in parallel.

The **Zakat and Ushr Ordinance** was promulgated on 20th June 1980 to empower the government to deduct 2.5 per cent Zakat annually from mainly interest-bearing savings and shares held in the National Investment Trust, the Investment Corporation of Pakistan and other companies of which the majority of shares were owned by the Muslims. Foreign Exchange Bearer Certificate scheme that offered fixed interest was exempted from the compulsory Zakat deduction. This ordinance drew sharp criticism from the Shia sect which was later exempted from the compulsory deduction of Zakat. Even Sunnis were critical of the compulsory deduction and the way Zakat was distributed. Still the Zakat Secretariat is considered the most lucrative in the provincial and federal governments.

On **9th February 1979**, Gen Ziaul Haq, through a presidential order, promulgated 'The Offence of Zina (Enforcement of _Hudood_) Ordinance 1979' which introduced concepts of fornication (voluntary sexual intercourse between two unmarried persons) and adultery into criminal law. The Pakistani Penal Code had not afforded any recognition to fornication as a crime, and adultery was only defined as an offence under section 497 if a man had intercourse with the wife of another man without his permission; the woman involved bore no criminal liability. The _Zina_ Ordinance provided for severe penalties for committing adultery or fornication, and reiterated the classical distinction between married and unmarried parties in determining punishments.

Thus, the _hadd_ punishment for a married person convicted of _zina_ is _rajm_, stoning to death, a penalty that has not been carried out by the state till today, and the _hadd_ for an unmarried person found guilty of *zina* is one hundred lashes in a public place. The Ordinance also makes a distinction between *ta'zir* and *hadd* punishments for *zina*.

It is widely believed that Gen Ziaul Haq had made a fool of the nation by introducing his half baked set of *Hudood* Laws through above mentioned ordinance of 1979. Introduction of Islamic laws was good but he *did not purposefully implement* even the basic principles of Islamic judiciary; Law of Evidence, infrastructure of *Qazi* Courts to execute the Islamic *Hudood* Laws and other administrative atmosphere in which the whole lay down of Islamic jurisprudence could be put into operation and practice for the welfare of the people of Pakistan.

As noted by one researcher **Rahat Imran** in *'Legal Injustices'* (2005) available at the internet that:

> *'While no Muslim disputes the authenticity or authority of the Qur'an, there is little doubt that the Qur'anic text can lend itself to variant interpretations that may reflect cultural biases, societal norms and social attitudes. Differences in the connotative and denotative usages of the language also opened the door to several interpretations and may at times result in "stripping the text of its meaningful connotations" as Najah Khadim, a British scholar of Islam suggests'.*

It is therefore difficult to understand the Qur'an's true spirit unless one is familiar with the historical circumstances surrounding a particular injunction. The linguistic intricacies of Qur'anic Arabic must be thoroughly understood before laws are formulated or viewpoints established. Gen Ziaul Haq had deliberately ignored these principles.

According to The Human Rights Commission of Pakistan (HRCP), every two hours a woman was raped in Pakistan and every eight hours a woman were subjected to gang rape in 2002. Gen Musharraf's government had to formulate a Commission to reconsider the *Hudood* Laws promulgated by his brother General & dictator in 1979.

The HRCP also held that the frequency of actual rapes was in reality much higher. The combination of social taboos, discriminatory laws and victimization at the hands of the police were (and still are) key reasons for why many rapes remained unreported.

Ayesha Jalal in her book titled *'The State of martial Rule'* at Page 323 had rightly concluded that 'Zia's attempt to make the legal system of Pakistan more Islamic was based largely on political motives.' Thus the first National Commission on the Status of Women was set up in 1999

61

to advise on eradicating laws discriminatory to women, which had submitted a detailed report and recommendations on *Hudood* laws in 2003. The Commission observed that the said Ordinance along with other four similar laws were hurriedly drafted and equally hurriedly enforced. In fact, a number of sections from the Pakistan Penal Code (PPC) lifted from and incorporated in the *Hudood* Ordinances with certain additional provisions, which were otherwise supposed to be in accordance with the injunctions of the *Quran & Sunnah*.

The introduction of these Ordinances was meant to give an Islamic appearance to the State and not to provide actual justice on the basis of Islamic commands. However, after the introduction of these Ordinances it was found that instead of remedying social ills, these Ordinances led to an increase in injustice against women and, in fact, became an instrument of oppression against women.

There were hundreds of incidents where a woman subjected to rape, or even gang rape, was eventually accused of Zina and thereby subjected to wrong and unjust harassment and great suffering.

More and more women were subjected to agony and torture because of these laws and the incidents of rape increased as time went by and the jails had gone filled with women on trial under the *Zina* Ordinance.

Qazf Ordinance which was meant to eliminate incidents of false accusation against women could not bring even a single conviction in 32 years. Apart from Zina and Qazf Ordinances, the Ordinance regarding property too, was of no avail in curbing incidents of theft and robbery and failed to control the spread of narcotics and illegal spirits in the country.

If we go further back; since 1983, a number of Commissions and Review Committees had examined and critiqued Gen Ziaul Haq's legacy of these laws. **Commission of Inquiry on Women, headed by Justice Nasir Aslam Zahid**, had recommended the repeal of the *Hudood* Ordinances in 1997 but PML(N)'s Nawaz Sharif, being a coward and weak administrator from inside, could not find courage to face and convince *Ulemas*. No action was taken on any recommendation.

The Commission of Inquiry, headed by the above named serving Justice of Pakistan's Supreme Court, had noted that:

'The argument that every law can be misused may be correct to some extent. But, thus stated, it addresses the wrong question. The relevant test is not whether a piece of legislation can ever be misused but rather

whether it is worth enacting at all given the potential for its abuse and the results which its enforcement would produce. This Commission is strongly of the opinion that the Zina Ordinance fails this test. Abundant data testifies that the result of this law has been the victimization rather than the protection of people, and that the law has had a particularly adverse effect on the least privileged members of society.' (**Commission Of Inquiry Report 1997 p 70**)

Furthermore, the said **Commission of Inquiry on Women 1997** was convinced that:

Firstly, all the *Hudood* laws were conceived and drafted in haste. They were not in conformity with the injunctions of Islam.

Secondly, these laws were in direct conflict both with the Constitution (such as of Article 25) and its international commitments (as made at the 4th World Conference on Women at Beijing under UN Convention on Elimination of All Forms of Discrimination Against Women).

Thirdly, in practical terms too, these laws had demonstrably failed to serve their purpose. They had not been any deterrent against crimes rather only led to proliferation of complaints in the courts, which had mostly been false or unjustified and caused undue hardship.

Thus it was recommended that:

• The Hudood laws should be immediately repealed.

• The repealed provisions of the Pakistan Penal Code 1860 should be re-enacted with an amendment to make rape a penal offence and to impose a severer punishment for rape on a minor wife.

• If the Parliament considered it necessary to make any further laws in this area, it should be done after serious debate and by reaching a consensus that the proposed laws should be in accordance with the teachings of the Holy Qura'an, Sunnah and other injunctions of Islam.

As the PML(N) government had not taken any action on the various recommendations of the Commission of Inquiry Report of 1997, the women organizations were constantly out on roads to check rising number of injustices done on the pretext of *Hudood* Laws.

Another **National Commission on the Status of Women** was constituted in 2002, to re-examine these laws with a view to determine whether or not these Ordinances ought to be repealed or whether these Ordinances could be improved through amendments. The Commission and a select Committee made by it started its job with its first meeting held in Karachi on 27th May 2002.

During the year long proceedings, it was felt that considerable confusion arose because of certain sections of PPC being lifted and included as part of the Ordinances. After receiving written comments from the Committee members, a final meeting was held in Karachi on 16th August 2003, where the members authorized Justice (R) Majida Razvi and Justice (R) M. Shaiq Usmani to draft the Report and the Recommendations of the Committee.

Justice (rtd) Majida Razvi placed her opinion on record that:

> *'Hudood Laws are full of lacunae and are badly drafted. These do not reflect the correct principles of Islamic criminal law and are not in accordance with the teachings of the Holy Qura'an & Sunnah and other Islamic injunctions. These have caused great misery to women and ought to be repealed and the original laws be restored.'*

Justice (rtd) M. Shaiq Usmani said that:

> *'Due to numerous defects and lacunae in the Hudood Ordinances promulgated by Gen Ziaul Haq in 1979, a number of anomalies have been created which have led to injustice, particularly to women, in the implementation of Zina and Qazf Ordinances.*

> *The defects in the Ordinances are so basic that amending these would serve no useful purpose and may bring about more injustice. The experience of the last 24 years (till 2003) has shown that these Ordinances have been counter-productive and have added to the misery of the people in general and women in particular. Thus he was of the view that the Hudood Ordinances ought to be repealed.'*

A veteran lawyer Syed Afzal Haider said that:

> *'After the enforcement of these Hudood Ordinances, the incidents of gang rape have increased; there are many defects as loopholes in the Hudood Ordiances and that the Ordinances ought to be repealed and the original laws be reinstated.'*

Dr Faqir Hussain said that:

> *'The Special Committee may assist the Government and Parliament by stating in the Report the reasons for its repeal and the principles of*

alternative legislation. The said Ordinance is not in accordance with the injunctions of Islam and as such should be repealed. Instead, on the pattern of Qisas and Diyat law, the offence of Zina (adultery and fornication) may be added to the Pakistan Penal Code. Most of the offences in the said Ordinance, having been borrowed from the PPC, may be reverted back to the said Code.'

Justice (rtd) Nasir Aslam Zahid gave his opinion that:

'The Hudood Ordinances of 1979, in particular the Zina Ordinance, have been (mis)used as an instrument of injustice mostly against women and helpless poor persons in the country. Consequently, these Ordinances ought to be repealed at first available chance..'

In the light of the above discussion, the Special Committee had categorically recommended that all the four Hudood Ordinances of 1979 should be repealed and the original laws with regard to the offences be restored in PPC (Pakistan Penal Code).

However it took three more years to reach the Parliament floor. The **Protection of Women** (Criminal Laws Amendment) **Bill 2006**, also informally called the Women's Protection Bill, was passed by the National Assembly on 15th November 2006 and by the Senate on 23rd November 2006. Gen Musharraf, as President granted assent to the Bill on 1st December 2006. This Bill made significant amendments to the *Hudood* laws and other criminal statutes, the most important that, the revisions or appeals in *Hudood & Zina* cases ceased to be referred to the Federal Shariat Court of Pakistan.

Federal Shariat Court: What Use?

A controversial provision in the Constitution has been the transfer of a judge from one High Court to another without his consent or after consultation with the Chief Justice of Pakistan or Chief Justices of the concerned High Courts. The original 1973 Constitution made such a transfer subject to such consent as well as consultation. A proviso added by the Constitution (Fifth Amendment) Act 1976 empowered the President to order such transfer for a period not exceeding one year, and the President Order No. 14 of 1985, issued by Gen Ziaul Haq extended that period from one to two years.

Gen Ziaul Haq, to prolong his dictatorial rule, had put the guns of his vicious wishes on the shoulders of Ulema, especially of the Jama'at e

Islami (JI) by keeping the religious cum political parties and religious scholars at his right hand side.

In 1979, Hudood Ordinance was promulgated to introduce Islamic system of punishments and to deal with the appeals against the verdicts on those ordinances from lower courts, the government brought Federal Shariat Court (FSC) in being making its principal seat, registry and the only campus at Islamabad under the Constitution (Amendment) Order 1980, which started functioning on 27th May 1980. However, it was not a new development in Pakistani jurisprudence, see the details.

[*The Presidential Order 1980 was based on provisions already available in the Constitution of Pakistan 1973 Chapter 3-A titled as Federal Shariat Court. This court was successor to the Shariat Benches of Superior Courts Order of 1978 which was created by an administrative command of Gen Ziaul Haq through President's Order no: 22 of 1978 dated 4th December 1978. This Order was originally consisting of twelve Articles.*

Article 4 mandated that there would be constituted a Shariat Bench in each High Court. Each Shariat Bench was to consist of three Muslim Judges of the High Court to be appointed by the President of Pakistan on the recommendation of the Chief Justice of that High Court. Article 5 created Shariat Appellate Bench in the Supreme Court of Pakistan while Article 6 stipulated Powers, Jurisdiction and Functions of Shariat Bench and Shariat Appellate Bench. The Shariat Benches were provincial as they were constituted in every provincial High Court.

At that time the Ulema around the military ruler had suggested him that the nature of the work assigned to the Shariat Benches demanded one Shariat Court at Federal level and not many Shariat Benches at provincial level. As a result thereof President's Order 22 of 1978 was substituted by President's Order No.3 of 1979 i.e, Constitution (Amendment) Order of 1979 dated 7th February 1979 whereby a new Chapter 3A entitled Federal Shariat Court was incorporated in Part VII of the Constitution.]

Article 203-C (4) of the Constitution, added by the Presidential Order of 1980 also provided that a judge of a High Court could be transferred to act, for up to two years, as a judge of the Federal Shariat Court, and in the event of refusal, would be deemed to have retired from the service under provisions of Article 203-C (5) of the Constitution. Ever since this amendment, the transfer provisions had been a subject of intense criticism: rightly so as the provisions were seldom used in public interest.

FSC's Justice Sh Aftab Hussain, in an interview published in the *daily 'Jang' of 25th July 1992*, told an interesting fact that:

> '*Gen Ziaul Haq had raised the FSC within one night to drag me out of Lahore High Court. I was member of that bench which was hearing petition of Air Marshal (Rtd) Asghar Khan against martial law and the bench was headed by CJ LHC Maulvi Mushtaq Hussain with Justice Zakiuddin Pal as another member. Someone told Gen Ziaul Haq that the LHC bench was going to give verdict against his martial law. The General then planned to avoid the announcement of that judgment by breaking the bench. Chief Justice Maulvi Mushtaq Hussain was sent to the Supreme Court as an ad-hoc judge and I was sent to head the said Federal Shariat Court.*
>
> *Astonishingly, I was removed in the same like sudden event. I was sent to Sudan to attend a Shariah Conference. In my absence, when I was on Umrah on my way back, I was told that I've been removed from the FSC and made an advisor to the President. It was a political slot which I had refused to join and preferred to go home.*
>
> *Both the events, of my sending to and of removing from the FSC were accomplished through promulgation of Ordinances making Constitutional Amendments; I feel proud.*'

The provisions had often been misused or abused for pressurizing the judges by the civil and military rulers so as to obtain from them favourable opinions or judgments or punish them for their upright behaviour. The Supreme Court in the case of **Al-Jehad Trust v Federation (PLD 1996 SC 324)** had examined this provision in the context of independence of judiciary and concluded that no judge would be transferred to the Federal Shariat Court against his own wish. Salute to the then Chief Justice of Pakistan Sajjad Ali Shah, the ill intentioned practice stands discontinued since then.

The Court consists of 8 Muslim Judges including the Chief Justice, appointed by the President from amongst the serving or retired Judges of the Supreme Court or a High Court or from amongst persons possessing the qualifications of a Judge of the High Court. Of the 8 Judges, 3 are required to be Ulema who are well versed in Islamic law. The Judges hold office for a period of 3 years and the President may further extend such period. Till the last day of 2008, there was a pendency of 1365 criminal appeals against convictions & acquittals and 207 cases or appeals were pending for revision.

The Court, on its own motion or through petition by a citizen or a government (Federal or provincial), may examine and determine as to whether or not a certain provision of law is repugnant to the Injunctions of Islam (Article 203-D). Appeal against its decision lies to the Shariat Appellate Bench of the Supreme Court, consisting of 3 Muslim Judges of the Supreme Court and not more than 2 Ulema, appointed by the President (Article 203-F).

The Court also exercises appellate revisional jurisdiction over the criminal courts, deciding Hudood cases (Article 203-D). The decisions of the Court are binding on the High Courts as well as subordinate judiciary (Article 203-G). The Court appoints its own staff and frames its own rules of business and court procedures.

Astonishing to note here that consistent injustice resulting from the *Zina* sections of the *Hudood* Ordinances (1979) once led the Federal Shariat Court to reach a conclusion that:

> *"We are constrained to make observations that such reckless allegations are being brought so frequently that something should be done to stop this unhealthy practice. The prosecution agencies before putting people on trail for offences of zina on flimsy allegations should be mindful of injunctions of the Holy Qur'an and the message conveyed through the decisions from the early period of pious Caliphs."* **[1991 PCr. LJ 568 FSC]**

Referring to **The Muslim, Islamabad, 9th March 1993**, the reckless misuse of this law was evident from the fact that superior courts acquitted 95% of all women accused in *Hudood* cases, said Justice Mohammad Afzal Zullah. The judge further told that:

> *'The law is a tool of exploitation in the hands of law enforcing agencies and 'family members' of women who are perceived to defy 'norms' of society by exercising their legal rights.'*

Based upon his personal experience as a sitting judge, he had observed that most FIRs were filed either:

• by mostly the under educated parents because their daughter had married someone of her own choice or

- by former husbands on the remarriage of their previous wives.

The Commission of Inquiry's review of 60 cases reported in the Pakistan Annual Law Digest of that year had found that:

- 15 pertained to the class of people who had married against the wishes of their families [mostly fathers or brothers] or guardians.

- A woman was accused of *Zina* despite possessing and producing records of the Family Court and High Court proving she was legally divorced before she remarried.

- Police officials collude with families and those seeking to abuse women through law to the extent that they had registered cases and started investigations on the basis of allegations of *Zina* received by post.

[On 18th March 1987 the Federal Shariat Court acquitted a man and a woman arrested by the police from their home on 3rd May 1980, registering a case of 'attempted *zina*' which is no crime even under the *Hudood* laws. Yet, after the couple spent seven years in prison, the Additional Session Judge South Karachi sentenced both to 5 years rigorous imprisonment and 10 lashes in January 1987. (*Pakistan Criminal Law Journal 2321*)]

When the Constitution guarantees life and liberty for all citizens (save in accordance with law), and that every citizen has the right to a good reputation, who is to be held accountable for the seven years of imprisonment, indignities and humiliation suffered by this couple?

Referring to a write up of **Dr Faqir Hussain, Registrar Supreme Court** of Pakistan, available at www.Paklegal.org the fact remains that ever since its establishment in 1980, the Federal Shariat Court had been the subject of criticism and controversy in the society. Created as an Islamisation measure by the Military Regime and subsequently protected under the controversial 8th Amendment, its opponents question the very rationale and utility of this institution. In fact this Court merely duplicates the functions of the existing superior courts.

The composition of the Court, particularly the mode of appointment of its judges and the insecurity of their tenure, is another negative point. It is alleged, that this Court does not fully meet the criterion prescribed for the independence of the judiciary, hence, is not immune to pressures and influences from the Executive.

Asia Report N°160, on 'REFORMING THE JUDICIARY IN PAKISTAN' published on 16th October 2008 categorically stated:

> *'Laws that discriminate on the basis of misusing religion and gender and mis-interpreting the Holy Qura'an & Sunnah, including the Hudood Ordinances and Qisas (retribution) and Diyat (blood money) law, are part of the legacy of military rule (widely misused and mis-applied by the then military dictator Gen Ziaul Haq)'.*

> *Given constitutional cover by military rulers and legal sanction by superior courts unwilling to uphold fundamental freedoms, these laws had undermined the rule of law, encouraged vigilantism and emboldened religious extremists. These extremists used them to advance a radical ideology of exclusion, curtail freedom of expression and discriminate against women, religious and sectarian minorities.'*

To what extent the above statements are true, intelligentsia and researchers should guide us, but the history tells us that before 1996, the Federal Shariat Court was mostly used as a dumping ground for the 'unwanted' judges of the higher judiciary and validation of the controversial *Hudood* Laws; especially the *Rajam* (stoning to death) was criticized because no male was punished.

With the adoption of **Protection of Women (Criminal Laws Amendment) Act 2006** the jurisdiction of the Court was considerably curtailed inasmuch as, appeals or applications for revision arising out of trial of offences taken out from the Offence of *Zina* (Enforcement of *Hudood*) Ordinance, 1979 are no longer filed before the Court. Since then they are filed before the High Court. Dr Faqir Hussain, Registrar SC had rightly opined then that *'there is a need for a serious discussion on the independence, utility and functions of this Court.'*

On **13th December 1980**, to the surprise of Gen Ziaul Haq, the F S Court declared the land reforms of 1972 and 1977 as eminently in consonance with Islamic injunctions. Then the so-called 'friends' *Ulema* were brought in who traditionally supported the landlord class. Thousands of tenants were forcibly evicted from the land in various districts. The martial law regime made it clear that it was not committed to redistributive agrarian policies and described the land reforms as ordinary politics to reward supporters and punish enemies.

Gen Ziaul Haq was basically focussing on all those steps which were considered 'pro PPP' by general perception. Though Z A Bhutto had not seriously implemented the 'land reforms', himself being a big landlord of Sindh, but people were hopeful of getting lands distributed some day. Military ruler did not want to take a chance even.

Three *Ulema* were inducted into the Federal Shariat Court and two into the Shariah Appellate Bench of the Supreme Court which reversed the FSC's able judgment later in 1990.

Justice Dr Javed Iqbal, in an interview published in *daily 'Jang' dated 1st July 1992*, had opined that *'there is no use of Federal Shariah Courts in Pakistan; the other superior courts can do the same job in a better way'.* The main reason he quoted firstly, was that for appointment of judges in all normal superior courts there are certain conditions, some under the constitution and some by rules, which have to be fulfilled before enrolment of a person for these superior courts BUT for judges of the FSC there exist no set rules or provisions; thus the element of 'likes & dislikes by rulers' make them un-acceptable.

Secondly; the judges of normal superior courts are appointed by the President but they can only be removed through Supreme Judicial Council under a process of Art 209 given in the constitution whereas the judges of FSC are appointed by the President and can be removed by the President at there whims and wishes.

In a way the FSC becomes a 'President's Court' though its name is Shariat Court because its judges are always found at the mercy of secretariats of the PM or the President, whatever the form of government it exists in. In Gen Ziaul Haq's times, two Chief Justices of the FSC were sent home with one stroke of pen because they were not inclined to write *'that decision which the General wanted to listen and see'.*

Main objective of the FSC was that it should see if all the prevailing laws were in accordance with the Islamic teachings. This job had already been completed during the tenure of CJ of FSC Aftab Hussain so the FSC is just an eye-wash court now causing extra burden on government exchequer nothing more.

Another side effect of this FSC is that it sometimes poses a threat to sovereignty of the Parliament which is a supreme institution of the country by Constitution. In the past [known and glaring example came up in Nawaz Sharif's second term 1997-1999] the FSC had sometimes given such decisions at their own that it posed threats to Pakistan's international business and debt commitments and the nation had to get embarrassed.

The Parliament was given six month's time to formulate new legislation to bring all the financial institutions in an ambit of 'interest-free banking system', which was not practically possible. As a result the Nawaz Sharif government had to twist the 'Islamic connotations' through re-defining the terms and review petitions etc.

Justice S A Nusrat, in his interview of 25th July 1999 published in media, had also said that:

> *'In Pakistan's Constitution of 1973 all necessities of Islamic system of governance are available; there is no need of new amendments in the name of Islam in it. No new enactments in the name of Shariah Bill are required. Shariat Court was not needed at all; it was Gen Ziaul Haq's trick to befool the people. If a case has to come in the Supreme Court at last, then why not depend upon them whole heartedly.'*

In nut shell, enough is enough, for how long we'll be betrayed in the name of Islamic Courts and Islam. Either our rulers should come up with courage to bring true Islamic way of governance or true democracy but being truthful by all means.

A historical saying: *'you can make some people fool for ever; you can make all the people fool for some time; you cannot make all the people fool for all the times.'*

Scenario 8

ARMY & JUDICIARY IN 1981-83:

PCO of 1981:

Provisional Constitutional Order (PCO) of 1981 was the first extra-constitutional order promulgated on **24th March 1981,** by the military dictator Gen Ziaul Haq, which suspended the Constitution of Pakistan. It was the earliest Provisional Constitutional Order in the history of Pakistan. Judges of the Superior Courts were asked to take oath of the office under the PCO.

Referring to an essay by **Justice (rtd) Sajjad Ali Shah** appeared in daily the*'Dawn'* of 7th January 2008.

> *'Judges of the superior courts are required to take oath as prescribed in the third schedule to the Constitution, and calls on them to preserve, defend, uphold and act according to the law and constitution itself. If the Constitution stands suspended, the oath of a judge remains intact because he acts according to law which includes a suspended Constitution. Pakistan's constitutions were abrogated in 1958 & 1969 and martial laws imposed, but the judiciary continued as it was, without any removal of judges.'*

After 1969's martial law, many government officers were dismissed or retired on grounds of misconduct, without a mandatory inquiry but some were retired in consultation with the Chief Justices of the respective high courts of Pakistan.

During Gen Ziaul Haq martial law of 1977 the Supreme Judicial Council was approached to investigate whether any judges in the high courts were selected for political reasons. After inquiry and the right of personal hearing, several were retired as political appointees. As if this was not enough, the 1981 PCO was promulgated. PCOs are normally promulgated to get rid of certain upright or unwanted judges to whom the military governments declare 'non-cooperative'.

Gen Ziaul Haq's martial law was validated on 10th November 1977 by a unanimous decision of the Supreme Court bench comprising of 9-member court headed by Chief Justice Anwarul Haq, under the doctrine of necessity, while dismissing Nusrat Bhutto's petition challenging detention of former Prime Minister Z A Bhutto and 10 others. Strange enough that the PCO of 1981 was announced after four years delay and as a result, many judges were retired from the Supreme Court and the high courts without having their say.

Question arises that why after four years then. Answer lies that in those days whatever petition was filed in Balochistan High Court (BHC), the CJ BHC Justice Murri used to announce judgment against the military government invariably in all petitions. Gen Ziaul Haq was continuously feeling disturbed for that. A chance happened that on similar petitions the Sindh High Court (SHC) gave different verdicts, nearly favouring the military government and much different than those of BHC. It was much confusing for the legal community as well as for the government.

The then Federal Secretary Law, Justice S A Nusrat, approached the then CJP Anwarul Haq and requested him on behalf of the military government to consider the issue of two judgments on the similar petitions from two different subordinate high courts and bring forward one verdict. For unknown reasons the CJP declined to consider government's request saying that *'the Supreme Court has other more important cases to deal with'*.

That was the beginning of thinking about PCOship in military minds of Pakistan. Had CJP Anwarul Haq taken those opposing verdicts from two high courts seriously to reach a just conclusion or judgment, there was no possibility of PCO in 1981. It remains a fact that the said PCO was neither coined in the Federal Ministry of Law nor any of its officers including Justice Nusrat were asked to join them. It was all a military exercise with the aid of private legal experts.

That is why that when PCO was promulgated, CJP Anwarul Haq and the former CJ LHC Molvi Mushtaq Hussain (then a judge of the Supreme Court) were not called to take oath. The CJP contended that he was called for oath but he had himself refused to take it. Both the CJs were very close to each other and were no more in good books of Gen Ziaul Haq after Bhutto's judicial murder in April 1979.

In 1981, the Chief Justice Sindh High Court, like other high courts, was instructed by the Federal Law Secretary from Islamabad to ask all the judges of the court to reach Governor House for fresh oath except the two judges named Abdul Hafeez Memon and G M Shah. Some judges had argued that if all judges boycotted the oath-taking, other 'pliant ones' would replace them and therefore it was far wiser to fight from within. Later it transpired that many judges were not called and some judges who had declined to take the oath became heroes and were appreciated by members of the bar and the general populace.

Chief Justice Maulvi Mushtaq Hussain of the Lahore High Court, who headed the bench of five judges and sentenced PM Z A Bhutto to death was though elevated to the Supreme Court but was not invited to take oath by Gen Ziaul Haq. Chief Justice of Pakistan Anwar ul Haq, when told about the PCO, called an urgent meeting and asked his fellow judges for their opinion in that regard.

Justice Fakhruddin G. Ebrahim said that although he was not party to the judgment in Nusrat Bhutto's case but he would not take oath. Justice Dorab Patel also refrained but all other judges agreed and lastly the CJP declared that since he was the author of the judgments, both Nusrat Bhutto's case and Z A Bhutto's appeal, he too would not take oath. On Federal Law Ministry's record, a letter no: 786-81/CJP dated 25th March 1981 addressed to the President Gen Ziaul Haq is available showing that Justice Anwarul Haq himself had declined to take oath at PCO declaring the act as 'against his conscience'.

Justice Dorab Patel was the honourable judge of the Supreme Court who had refused to take oath on PCO of 1981 knowingly that he was going to be the Chief Justice after refusal of Justice Anwarul Haq and was going to stay in the post for another seven years at least.

It is worth a mention here that Justices Dorab Patel, Mohammad Haleem and G. Safdar Shah had acquitted Mr Bhutto. Even then if judges like Dorab Patel were being invited for oath it meant that Gen Ziaul Haq wanted to avail the right of pick and choose judges favoured by the government under that PCO. For Justice Dorab Patel the PCO had not only negated the spirit of independence of the judiciary but also prolonged martial law by nullifying the effect of a judgement giving military regime limited recognition. As a signatory to the judgement, Patel could not have taken the new oath, given his strict conscience.

It is also said that during that PCO of 1981, Justice Samdani of LHC, a known upright judge, was also not called to take oath. The facts were otherwise in this case. Justice Samdani was called to take oath but when he reached at Governor House Lahore to take oath, the then Chief Justice Lahore High Court Shamim Hussain Qadri met him at gate and told lie to him that his name was not included in the list of would be judges. He went back from there and then.

Prior to his posting as the judge of LHC, Justice Samdani was the Federal Secretary Law. During a high level meeting once Gen Ziaul Haq had said that *'some judges should be hanged'*. Mr Samdani was also there in the meeting who loudly said that *'some Generals should also be hanged'*. Gen Ziaul Haq got angry with Mr Samdani. There prevailed an impression that due to above given remarks Gen Ziaul Haq had not asked him to take oath, whereas it was not true. Gen Ziaul Haq did call him for oath because Samdani was widely respected for his uprightness and the General had liked that quality in Justice Samdani. J Samdani was sincere in taking oath but his CJ S H Qadri did not want him in his team.

The then Federal Law Secretary Justice S A Nusrat came to know at 10 AM that day that Justice Samdani was not asked to take oath. He rang up Governor Jilani immediately who told that *'we had called him but not turned up'*. The subsequent enquiry made clear that he had come but sent back from gate of the Governor House. Sharifuddin Pirzada was upset on the issue; he immediately told the whole story to Gen Ziaul Haq. Gen Zia promptly asked Gen Jilani to call Justice Samdani and take oath from him. Justice Samdani was called again, asked to take oath but he refused then saying that *'I've been disgraced too much'*.

At the same time, the intelligentsia and old democratic figures had felt that, motivated by self-preservation and self-interest, Pakistan's superior judiciary had failed to uphold the basic spirit of the constitution. While superior courts have been validating military coups, military regimes have manipulated judicial appointments, promotions and removals, steadily purging higher court benches of independent-minded judges. This has pushed the judiciary further towards incredibility. Judicial independence used to be hampered not only by the state but also by religious groups patronized by some military Generals.

Balochistan in Gen Ziaul Haq's Era:

After the debacle of fall of Dacca in 1971, the National Awami Party (NAP) led by Baluch nationalists Ghaus Bux Bizenjo, Sardar Ataullah Mengal, Gul Khan Nasir, Khair Bux Marri and Nawab Akbar Khan Bugti dominated Balochistan. At that time, even the Jamiat Ulema e Islam (JUI) of Maulana Mufti Mahmood (father of Maulana Fazlur Rehman) thought it fit to join hands with the ethnic nationalists to become big leaders.

Emboldened by the stand taken by Sh Mujib ur Rehman of Bangladesh, these ethnic nationalists started demanding their 'provincial rights' from

Zulfikar Ali Bhutto in exchange for a consensual approval of the 1973 constitution. But while Mr Bhutto admitted the NAP-JUI coalition, he refused to negotiate with the provincial government of Balochistan led by Chief Minister Ataullah Mengal in Quetta; thus tensions erupted. Within six months, PM Bhutto dissolved the Balochistan government, arrested the CM and the Governor along with many Baluch MNAs and MPAs, obtained an order from the Supreme Court banning the NAP and charged everyone with high treason to be tried by a specially constituted Hyderabad Tribunal of handpicked judges. In time, an ethnic nationalist insurgency erupted and Army had to launch an action.

The 1970s conflict with the separatists had manifested itself in the form of an armed struggle against the Pakistani army in Balochistan. Mir Hazar Khan Marri headed the separatist movement under the Baluch People's Liberation Front (BPLF). Marri and the BPLF fled to Afghanistan, along with thousands of his supporters. [Baluch separatists often fight today under related nicknames such as BLA, BLM, BLO etc.] The irony was that Nawab Akbar Khan Bugti served the federal government as Governor of Balochistan throughout the time of the insurgency; during this time, Bugti spoke not a word in favour of provincial autonomy.

The greater irony was that the insurgency came to an end following the army coup of Gen Ziaul Haq against Mr Bhutto's civilian government. Soon thereafter, Gen Ziaul Haq called the Baluch leadership into mainstream while providing jobs and funds from the federal government to the alienated, insecure tribal middle classes. More significantly, Gen Zia created maximum political space for the religious parties so that they could be galvanized in the jihad against the USSR in neighbouring Afghanistan. Soon the ideological jetty for the Greater Balochistan movement melted into memory over the next two decades.

The uprising itself had suffered from a lack of direction. Some Baluch wanted independence, most only greater autonomy within Pakistan. Among their grievances against Islamabad were: neglect of the economic development of the area; discrimination against the Baluchis in respect of recruitment to the civilian government services and the armed forces; the policy of resettlement of large numbers of Punjabi and Pashtun ex-servicemen in Balochistan, which was viewed by them as an attempt to reduce the Baluchis to a minority in their homeland; and non-payment of royalties to the Baluchi tribal for the utilization of their natural resources for the benefit of the rest of Pakistan.

In that backdrop the attacks were organised by individual Baluch separatist chiefs, rather than an organised type of attack. During the NAP days, the Baluch separatists hoped to get the support of the Soviets, which never happened. Also, the large Pashto and Brahvi minorities in Balochistan did not take part and were hostile to the idea of a separate Balochistan. In the meantime, Gen Zia sent Lt Gen Rahimuddin as Governor there who, being a Pashtun himself, was against the idea of greater Balochistan.

Gen Rahimuddin's unprecedented long rule (1978–84) crushed almost all armed uprisings within the province with an iron fist. His policy of isolating Baluch Sardars from provincial affairs earned increasing controversy. Previous rulers had tried to appease the feudal lords; Rahimuddin went out of his way to isolate them from any position of provincial power and addressed the common masses of the province by promoting economic growth. This policy, in retrospect, led to the most stable period Balochistan has ever witnessed after the British left. Economic expansion was also impressive during Gen Rahimuddin's reign.

In Gen Ziaul Haq's times in 1980s, when the American CIA, through Pakistan's ISI, trained and armed the Afghan mujahideen and other Islamic fundamentalist elements and used them to bleed the Soviet troops in Afghanistan, the Marris and the Mengals kept away from the anti-Soviet jihad and helped the KGB, the Soviet intelligence agency; and the Khad, the Afghan intelligence agency, in the collection of intelligence regarding the activities of the CIA and the ISI on the Pakistani side of the border.

The Jamalis collaborated with the CIA and the ISI in countering the activities of the Marris and the Mengals and their influence in Balochistan. [*During the course of this collaboration, Mir Zafarullah Khan Jamali came in touch with Nancy Powell, the US ambassador in Pakistan those days. Jamali and Nancy Powell developed a close personal friendship, which was carefully nurtured by Washington. According to some sections of the Pakistani media, it was she who suggested to Gen Musharraf later, Jamali's name for appointment as the prime minister after the elections of October 2002.*]

Dr Allah Nizar Baluch (www.sachaan.webs.com) gives a recent conversation (2011: for Daily Ibart of Sindh) with Khair Bux Marri, 82 year old, known as rebel but had been a member of Pakistan parliament, then self-exiled to Afghanistan, who believes that solution of Balochistan lies in 'resist movement'. Now establishment should realize that bitter experience was not only felt by Baluch Sardars but now it also comes in common Baluch. Matter is that: would establishment and power makers ever see this bitterness? *'I can't sit to say that Baluchs are brave nation, who never surrender in front of injustice.'*

On a question that 'how do you see nature of politics in Subcontinent;' (slightly smiling) *'this question is long; I restrict myself to Pakistan; mostly slaves like Punjabis, always do fraudulent tact (while sharing one incident), there are some proverbs for them like Punjabis & Pashtuns; give them money, Sindhis; keep them under pressure, and Baluchis; make them foolish through respectable talks (while smiling), really it happens'.*

If you give respect to Baluch, he can do any sort of work for you. Punjabis just want a box of money and Pakhtoons never be able to accept challenge, for time being they fight, suddenly they would surrender. On question that Do you see any difference between Mr Jinnah and Gandhi jee? (Loudly laughed) answer is simple that Gandhi was a man of human and Jinnah was a man of British. [It was a long interview but more reservations there]

The Soviet invasion of Afghanistan in 1979 came as a blessing in disguise for Gen Ziaul Haq. The General exploited the opportunity to bankroll numerous religious schools in Balochistan and finance its religious parties in order to save the Islamic Republic of Pakistan from the Soviets influence. According to one Ahmed Rashid, the author of *Taliban: The Story of Afghan Warlords*, there were only 900 *madrassas* in Pakistan in 1971, but by the end of Gen Zia's era in 1988 there were 8000 *madrassas* and 25,000 unregistered religious schools, with half a million students. It was alleged that these schools were kept closed for months to allow students to participate in *'jihad'*.

During the general elections of 2002, the Pakistani politico-religious alliance, the Muthida Majlis e Amal (MMA) emerged victorious with 16 seats in the Balochistan Assembly, enabling it to form a coalition government along with the PML(Q). The MMA went on to support the PML(Q)'s recommendations to the federal government to launch a military operation against the Baluch people who were demanding provincial autonomy but the allegation was not proved by figures or through independent sources.

Pashtun vs Baluch gulf among populations continued widening with the time. In the midst of this tug-of-war between the Baluch nationalists and

Pashtuns [called radical Islamists also] always posed the question whether the Baluch democratic movement could prevail. Relentless efforts by the state machinery for the past 30 years have not succeeded in radicalizing Baluch society. Gen Zia however went successful.

For example, when US forces invaded Afghanistan in 2001, the Baluch populated areas hardly witnessed any protest rally in support of the Taliban regime. On the other hand, massive demonstrations took place in the Pashtun-dominated districts of Balochistan.

Office of Ombudsman (1983):

The institution of the Ombudsman in Pakistan was established in August 1983 under the Establishment of the Office of Wafaqi Mohtasib Order 1983. The Office was equipped with the power to redress certain public complaints against administrative excesses. It was an Article 276 of the Interim Constitution of 1972 that provided for the appointment of the Federal Ombudsman as well as Provincial Ombudsmen for the first time. Subsequently, the subject was included in 1973 constitution.

The main functions entrusted to the Wafaqi Mohtasib were to diagnose, investigate, redress and to rectify any injustice done to public through mal-administration of an agency of the Federal Government. This Order provided a speedy and inexpensive mode of addressing public grievances against the state. The Mohtasib was vested with wide jurisdiction to inquire into the affairs of all the offices of the Federal Government, except the Supreme Court, the Supreme Judicial Council, the Federal Shariat Court and the High Courts. WM office could investigate any complaint, except in respect of matters which are subjudice or which relate to the Armed Forces and military personnel.

Soon after, provincial Mohtasibs were appointed in Azad Jammu & Kashmir (AJK), Sindh, Punjab and Balochistan, while a separate Federal Tax Ombudsman was appointed in 2000 to address citizen's complaints against tax functionaries. A Banking Ombudsman was also appointed on 29th April 2005, based in Karachi and with regional offices in the provincial capitals of Lahore, Peshawar and Quetta to handle complaints in the banking sector, a task earlier dealt by the State Bank of Pakistan or the Banking Circle of the Federal Investigation Agency.

By analysis, 66% applications moved before WM related to the federal agencies, while the remaining 34 % go to respective provinces. Of the complaints against federal agencies, about half are normally admitted for thorough investigation, while the remaining are rejected for reasons being subjudice, service matters or premature. An average of roughly 40,000 complaints has been received annually by the WM over past two decades.

The general populace still have no faith in this institution because their findings or recommendations are not binding on any department. It is merely considered wastage of funds and resources in practical terms. On the other hand the orders and determinations of WM are appealable before the President of Pakistan where these appeals gather dust and are subsequently disposed of without any judicial appreciation.

Flogging in Public:

During Gen Ziaul Haq's regime, year 1983 would also be remembered for giving punishments to the criminals by **flogging** & **hanging in Public**. During this period several high-profile public canings and floggings were carried out, often in stadiums with **thousands of spectators**. The offenders dealt with in this way, all were men under 50, were often serious criminals such as rapists.

The punishment was administered with a very long and thick but whippy cane across the prisoner's buttocks. Often his pants were pulled down, but the target area was then covered with one layer of thin cloth, perhaps out of Islamic modesty. The prisoner was usually tied, upright and with feet apart, to a colonial-era A-frame but in some cases was held bending over a chair schoolboy-style. Microphones were often placed close to the prisoner's head so that his moans and screams could be broadcast to the crowd. Apart from the public exhibitions, many other offenders were caned and flogged privately inside prison. Media reports told that a mass flogging of 84 people in Karachi prison only was done during 1983.

[*In the same year 1983, Barrister Akram Sheikh, a veteran lawyer, won international acclaim when he contested a human right case of Safia Bibi; still alive in history as 'blind girl' case.*]

Save Pakistan Movement (1983):

On 14th August 1983, a historical movement for restoration of Democracy was launched in Sindh against the cruel regime of Military dictator Gen Ziaul Haq. The movement was named as **'Save Pakistan Movement'** in which city areas of Khairpur Nathan Shah, Dadu, Moro, Halla, Sakrand, and Liyari of Karachi were the flag bearers.

On 29th September 1983, about 500 villagers from around gathered and blocked the National Highway near Sakrand town. Some of them started reciting the Holy Qura'an whereas the rest of the mob hurled slogans against the army and Gen Ziaul Haq's rule in general. Some army trucks appeared suddenly from a side track and opened machine gun fire on the demonstrators. The firing continued for about three hours leaving 16 dead and 54 injured on the highway.

Ishaque Soomro in his essay dated 12th April 2011; titled as '*Martyrs of MRD 1983*' available at LUBP gives an elaboration saying:

'*When I reached the spot with my colleagues for reporting there was death like silence all around and red blood was still fresh and could be seen oozing out of the dead as well as injured human bodies. The bodies were also blackened because heavy trucks were made to run over these bodies presumably to demonstrate the callousness and barbarism against protesting common people of Sindh at the hands of those who were responsible for that uncalled for operation. The belongings of the demonstrators like shoes, towels, caps, empty bullets were scattered and even leafs of Holy Quran pierced with bullets were also found scattered.*'

Fifty-four injured persons were arrested and dead bodies were taken to the army camp Nawabshah. They had paid enough prices for democracy and more than enough for Pakistan. The press termed it as the biggest incident of whole MRD movement of 1983. People were looking angry but no mourning. Ghulam Qadir Chandio, a sitting MPA & ex-senator, told the press that his old father Punhal Khan Chandio and elder brother Ghulam Abbas were also arrested along with 54 others.

Ishaque Soomro seemed to be more concerned murmuring that '*now quarter of a century has passed; but people of this country are still fighting for real democracy and for the bright future of this country. People of Indus valley have sacrificed a lot; but they still believe in democracy and prosperous Pakistan.*'

Scenario 9

ARMY & JUDICIARY IN 1984-85:

Qanoon e Shahadat:

On **28th October 1984**, the *Qanun-e-Shahadat* (law of evidence) Order 1984 replaced the Evidence Act 1872, though it essentially restated the original legislation, but as it was intended to bring the law of evidence closer to Islamic injunctions, there were changes which specifically impacted upon women. This Order of 1984 introduced changes to the law as it related to the presumption of legitimacy. The original Evidence Act did not provide for a minimum period of gestation, and the maximum was 280 days. Through the new enactment, the minimum gestation period was set at six months and the maximum at two years, placing the provision in accordance with the majority position in classical Hanafi *fiqh*.

Article 151(4): *'When a man is prosecuted for rape or an attempt to ravish, it may be shown that the prosecutrix was generally of immoral character.'* This provision was enough to spread anarchy and lawlessness in the society because if someone rapes a woman and subsequently proves that she was of bad character so the criminal would walk away free. The influential groups of Pakistan, especially the landlords and employers used this provision mostly that is why none of them has ever been punished since 1984 till at least 11th February 2009 when a full bench of the Federal Shariat Court held it against the teachings of the holy *Qura'an & Sunnah*. It should have been addressed much earlier.

The bench, consisting of Chief Justice Haziqul Khairi, Justice Dr Fida Khan, Justice Salahuddin Mirza and Justice Zafar Yasin, held that Article 151(4) was repugnant to the holy *Qura'an & Sunnah* and directed the president of Pakistan to take appropriate steps for repealing the provision within six months, after which the provision would cease to be effective, even if it is not repealed. The court held that the provision was discriminatory on the basis of gender and was in violation of the constitution, adding that it negated the concept of gender equality as enshrined in the holy Qura'an.

The bench observed that it had failed to comprehend *'what tide of wisdom had prevailed upon lawmakers to add Sub-article 4 [of Article 151] as it served no useful purpose.'* It said even if assumed that the victim was of a **'generally immoral character'**, it would not exonerate the man accused of raping or attempting to rape her. The act would still be a crime, it was held.

At different occasions, so may times the human activists, NGOs, Bar Councils and the media had raised their demands to re-write this Qanoon e Shahadat (1984) because it was only promulgated in the name of Islam but actually so many basic teachings of Islam were ignored or twisted when made in haste under military umbrella. During the first week of March 2010, the Chief Justice Iftikhar M Chaudhry was approached by a political figure of PML(N) to take *suo-moto* notice of it but the promise was not fulfilled yet.

The intervention of apex court was considered necessary because thousands of innocent citizens, especially women were suffering at the hands of blackmailers, therefore, redressing this issue would be vital to ensure the sanctity of law & justice in the country. The controversial laws like mentioned above should be repealed or amended in way that all lacunas could be removed, as they were crafted by various dictatorial regimes aiming at narrow political goals. Such laws were blemish on the original 1973 Constitution of Pakistan as well; hence, they needed to get purged for the revival of original 1973 constitution.

It was observed that the lacunas of the controversial Qanun-e-Shahadat were resulting in denial of justice and being used by blackmailers against the innocent and law-abiding people of Pakistan, especially the weaker segments of the society including women.

This order except with few exceptions, and the repealed Evidence Act, 1872 are subjectively the same but objectively they are poles apart. It is an admitted position that all Articles or the Order 1984 are substantially and subjectively mere reproduction of all sections of the repealed Act with exceptions of Article 3, Article 4 to 6(with reference to Hudood), addition of Article 44 and addition of a proviso to Article 42 if compared with corresponding sections of the repealed Act. The term 'Qanun-e-Shahadat' is an Urdu or Arabic translation of English term 'Law of Evidence'.

The significant change made in the Qanun-e-Shahadat is that 'Court Martial' covered under the Army Acts besides a tribunal or other authority exercising judicial or quasi judicial powers or jurisdiction have been included. The repealed Evidence Act, 1872 was applicable to 'affidavits' but in the Qanun-e-Shahadat Order 1984, affidavits are not immune from its application. Only the proceedings saved are the proceedings before an Arbitrator, the reason thereof is obvious that award, if any, announced by the Arbitrator is subject to strict scrutiny under the Arbitration Act, 1940.

The Object of Qanun-e-Shahadat Order 1984 is evident from its preamble which has never been the object of the repealed Evidence Act. With reference to the preamble, Intention of object of introduction this Order, as stated therein, is to bring all the laws of evidence in conformity with the injunctions of Islam as laid down in the Holy *Qura'an & Sunnah*.

An interpretation of all articles of Qanun-e-Shahadat must be done in conformity with the injunctions of Islam as laid down in the Holy *Qura'an & Sunnah* instead of adopting old interpretation of the repealed Evidence Act 1872. However, principles of Islamic Law of evidence so long as they are not codified or adopted by Qanun-e-Shahadat, 1984 are not per se applicable Order apply to all judicial and quasi judicial proceedings. All technicalities have to be avoided and calls for doing substantial justice between parties are to be heeded.

Gen Ziaul Haq's Referendum:

19th December 1984: Gen Ziaul Haq had held a referendum in Pakistan by virtue of which he 'declared' himself as President. On 17th April 1984, an act to amend the Referendum Acts 1942 to 1983 was passed and called as Ninth Amendment of the Constitution Bill, 1984. On this basis the said referendum was held on 19th December 1984 in all the four provinces under the control of Election Commission of Pakistan.

Gen Ziaul Haq wanted to establish a pseudo-democracy in Pakistan, to continue as President under a civilian setup. Gen Ziaul Haq took a number of steps in this direction; the first was the establishment of the *Majlis-i-Shoora* to take the place of National Assembly but without any legislative powers. Gen Zia's second step was to ask the public to endorse his rule. This appeal was in the form of a referendum, which was so worded that a "Yes" meant that Gen Ziaul Haq himself would be further endorsed, even though the referendum did not refer to this directly. The Referendum had put forward a complex question to the citizens, in fact, seeking endorsement of the process of *'Islamization'* initiated by him.

The referendum was manoeuvred in a way that the people had no choice except to mark 'yes' on the ballot paper. The question given was that:

> *"Whether the people of Pakistan endorse the process initiated by General **Muhammad** Zia-ul-**Haq**, the President of Pakistan, for*

bringing the laws of Pakistan in conformity with the injunctions of Islam as laid down in the Holy Qura'an & Sunnah of the Holy Prophet (PBUH) and for the preservation of the Islamic ideology of Pakistan, for the continuation and consolidation of that process, and for the smooth and orderly transfer of power to the elected representatives of the people."

In the ballot paper, the part of the paper having the above question and the place to mark 'yes' was printed in green and 'No' was in white part. When the MRD gave a call to the general populace to boycott the referendum, it was declared 'a criminal offence' to make such appeal. In the words of **A S Ghazali**:

'In fact, the opposition leaders were detained throughout the country a week before the referendum. Troops patrolled the streets in Karachi. 'Unauthorised persons' near polling stations were banned, making an independent check of the turnout virtually impossible.'

The stage of referendum was set but on 19th December, the polling day' most of the polling stations were deserted. Even then the announcement made in the evening told that in total 62.15% turn over of voters had been registered out of which 93% had said 'yes'.

The Chief Election Commissioner Incharge of that Referendum, Justice S A Nusrat had subsequently told in an interview published in media on 25th July 1999 that:

'The said Referendum Order was prepared by Sharifuddin Pirzada and not by the Law Ministry nor by Election Commission. The golden idea behind was to bring Gen Ziaul Haq towards democracy gradually. National ID card's condition was also waived and the ballot boxes were even placed in mosques so how there could be a check on fake votes.'

The state propaganda was made in media and PTV, the only channel then available, that:

'The overwhelming mandate in the Referendum was convincing demonstration of the people's confidence in Gen Ziaul Haq's leadership: his achievements during the last seven & half years and his dynamic policies and plans for the future. Under his most dynamic leadership, the Nation has witnessed the implementation of the cannons of Islam in every walk of life-social, political, economic, judicial and cultural.

*Also Promulgation of Zakaat and Ushr, rejuvenation of the Council of
Islamic Ideology and Ministry of Religious Affairs, establishment of the
Federal Shariat Courts, Qazi Courts, Federal Law Commission, the
Islamic Research Council and the institution of Wafaqi Mohtasib;
implementation of interest free banking, complete prohibition of
alcoholic drinks, Laws relating to Qisas and deyat, Hudood Ordinance
and giving true and meaningful rights to the minorities of Pakistan - are
glimpses of the great many constructive steps taken by the President.'*

The world media was there to laugh at us and our courts remained mum.

Economist.com/1100672: In 1984, another military usurper, General
Ziaul Haq, also used a referendum to win a semblance of legitimacy as
president. He did it by proclaiming that he wanted to establish an Islamic
system of government and asking them whether they were for or against
Islam. Since Pakistanis, who are almost all Muslims, could hardly say
they were not for Islam, most stayed home rather than vote against him.
In the event he claimed a 95% "yes" vote, even though independent
observers said the turnout was barely 10%.

It is interesting to note the post-1984 referendum events. Gen Ziaul
Haq had presumed that the people would vote 'yes' because of the
linkage between his extension and issues such as the injunctions
of the Holy *Qura'an & Sunnah* of the Holy Prophet, future of the
ideology of Pakistan and a promise to transfer power to the elected
representatives. The idea was to seek extension in the garb of value laden
issues. The bluff was called. The people of Pakistan gave blatant thumbs
down by virtually boycotting the referendum and refusing to come out
to vote.

The 20th December 1984 issue of daily *The Muslim* reported merely 10%
turnout for voting. A displeased military contingent banned the issue's
public circulation and lifted all of its copies from the market and
newspaper's office in Islamabad.

The question was, by all standards, a very complicated and complex one,
particularly for the un-educated rural class. It was a loaded question that
simply asked: **'Do you wish Pakistan to be an Islamic state?'** An
affirmative vote in the referendum was to result in a five-year term for
Gen Ziaul Haq as President of Pakistan. After the referendum, Gen Ziaul
Haq announced that the elections for the National and Provincial
Assemblies would be held in February 1985, on a non-party basis.

Militarized Elections of 1985:

In January 1985, Gen Ziaul Haq announced a plan to hold elections on non-party basis. The move was clearly aimed at not allowing the Pakistan Peoples Party (PPP) to participate in the elections. Till then he had not defined the role and powers of the Majlis e Shoora (MeS) for which the PPP had already announced that none of its candidates would be able to contest the election under the flag of the PPP. No party tickets were at all issued to anyone.

The elections were held on 25ᵗʰ February 1985 for the National Assembly (MeS) and polling for the provincial assemblies took place on 28ᵗʰ March 1985. **A S Ghazali** writes in his e-book in Chapter VIII:

> 'More than eight hundred prominent politicians were arrested in a pre-election crackdown; campaigning was forbidden by a ban on political parties, processions, rallies and even loudspeakers. However, the voters took both the government and banned political parties by surprise. They ignored the call of the MRD to boycott the polls. The verdict was a rebuff for the government, for the opposition and for the religious parties which cooperated with the martial law regime.
>
> Apart from six cabinet ministers, a presidential adviser, two provincial ministers and three city mayors were defeated. Over half of the members of the nominated majlis-i-shura were not returned to the new house. Virtually the entire leadership of the Jamaat-i-Islami was wiped out. The party won only eight of the 63 national seats contested. Karachi, the traditional stronghold of the party, turned it down.'

The historians observed that it was a deliberate effort of Gen Ziaul Haq to bring the landlords & Jageerdars of Punjab and Sindh, religious *gaddi nasheens*, Gen Jilani's newly wealthy friends (Sharifs), sardars of FATA and Balochistan and retired army officers to occupy seats in the Assemblies. The purpose was obvious. The only change was that the younger generation of landlords had taken over from their elders.

The social background of the new members of MeS could be judged from the fact that this National Assembly had 117 landlords, 17 tribal leaders, six religious leaders, eight urban professionals, seven former army officers, two student leaders and 42 businessmen in its fold. Most of these tycoons had opted to enter into politics in vengeance against Pakistan Peoples Party (PPP)'s anti-business policies.

Even earlier, Gen Ziaul Haq had hand-picked MeS (parliament) on 24th December 1981 under Presidential Order (PO 15 of 1981) and its 284 members were nominated by none other than the General himself, therefore, they had to raise their hands whenever they were pointed to do so, especially while making cogent amendments in the Constitution of 1973.

They were allowed to take rest at home or to sleep in the assemblies because all the legislation and control were to be administered from the Army House. Most of these families were snubbed and sent home during elections of 1970 and 1977 in which PPP earned the sweeping victory.

THE 8TH CONSTITUTIONAL AMENDMENT:

During the third week of March 1985, Gen Ziaul Haq pronounced certain changes in the Constitution to keep ultimate powers with him in the name of president when the members of MeS were waiting to be called for their first session and oath taking. By virtue of these self-assigned powers he got authority to 'select' the prime minister, governors and chiefs of the armed forces in the capacity of president.

In addition, he had absolute power to decide his powers under the constitution and indemnity clauses ensured that he would not be questioned. He had also assumed powers to dissolve parliament at his discretion. Any laws inconsistent with fundamental rights were to be taken as void but excusing president's orders. The whole set of that power snatching scheme was called 'The Revival of the Constitution of 1973 Order 1985'.

In fact Gen Ziaul Haq had re-introduced and revived the 'presidential form of government' so that the chosen prime minister would not be able to mess about while in chair. After ensuring his safeguards, he called the first session of the new MeS after three days and nominated one Mohammad Khan Junejo as his Prime Minister on the recommendation of Pir Pagaro of Sindh.

Thus the constitution which he had suspended altogether in 1981 was re-instated after installing himself as president via referendum in 1984, and through Presidential order no: 14 later ratified as 8th Amendment in the Constitution of 1973 by his handpicked parliament on 17th October 1985. The Junejo government had persuaded the National Assembly (then Majlas e Shoora) vigorously to pass it through.

It was a general perception then that the MeS had ratified the said 8th Amendment under hidden threats of continuing martial law because it was lifted on 31st December 1985 only after approval and consents given by the two houses. Criticizing the 8th constitutional amendment, the International Commission of Jurists had said:

> 'Its foremost purpose is to uphold the rule of the present President, Ziaul Haq. The constitution contains nothing to prevent the President from reintroducing martial law.'

The **Financial Times London** had commented that: *'The constitution has been personalized by Zia.'*

As discussed before, Gen Ziaul Haq took it upon himself to 'Islamise' the society, and thereby effected more than one hundred amendments to the constitution on sectarian lines. *'This meddling with the constitution was so ruthless and crude that its democratic spirit was mutilated and it amounted to a completely new constitution brought in through a blanket constitutional amendment in 1985. This amendment introduced, apartheid style, separate electorates on sectarian lines and a parallel judicial system, the Federal Shariat Court, empowered to undo any law passed by the legislature deemed as 'un-Islamic'.'* An advocate named **Naeem Shakir** of LHC observed in his essay **dated 8th August 2004.**

The most notorious clause of this 8th amendment in the Constitution was Article 58(2)(b) which was:

(2) Notwithstanding anything contained in clause (2) of Article 48, the President may also dissolve the National Assembly in his discretion where, in his opinion,

> **(a)** a vote of no-confidence having been passed against the Prime Minister, no other member of the National Assembly is likely to command the confidence of the majority of the member's of the National Assembly in accordance with the provisions of the Constitution, as ascertained in a session of the National Assembly summoned for the purpose; or

> **(b)** a situation has arisen in which the Government of the Federation cannot be carried on in accordance with the provisions of the Constitution and an appeal to the electorate is necessary.

In the political history of Pakistan, the 8th Amendment is normally taken synonymous with Article 58 2(b), a provision that gives power to the sitting president to dissolve the National Assembly. However, the 8th Amendment was in fact a compromise between the Parliament elected in the non-party elections of 1985 and then President Gen Ziaul Haq.

During 6 years rule before the 1985 election, Gen Ziaul Haq had already made numerous amendments to the Constitution of 1973 through various Constitutional Amendment Orders, the most significant being the Revival of Constitution of 1973 Order (President's Order No. 14 of 1985) mentioned above. The clause of Art 58(2)(b) was included in it with similar wording. By virtue of that *'the test of the constitutional functioning of the government was not required for the President to dissolve the National Assembly.'* The first session of the 1985 National Assembly was held on 20th March 1985 and Article 58(2)(b) had received a vote of confidence on 24th March 1985.

The more significant aspect of the 8th Amendment was that the elected Parliament endorsed all Orders made by Gen Ziaul Haq by substituting the Article 270A introduced by the said President's Order No. 14 of 1985 by a slightly modified version, preserving the text declaring the validity of all of Gen Zia's actions, including his takeover of 5th July 1977 and subsequent constitutional amendments done during the previous six years.

Tariq Butt placed certain facts on *www.saudigazette.com.sa* that many sitting legislators, including Prime Minister Syed Yousaf Raza Gilani, had not only supported Gen Ziaul Haq's referendum of December 1984, but were also part of the parliament that had approved the 8th Constitutional Amendment in November 1985, which gave him discretionary powers to dissolve the National Assembly under Article 58(2)(b).

The 1985 parliament had earlier endorsed a Constitutional Order on 2nd March 1985 through which a large number of amendments were made to the Constitution. More interestingly these Pakistani politicians, hailing from all political parties, once again successfully deceived the people of Pakistan when they 'unanimously voted to erase the name of Pakistan's longest - serving military ruler, Gen Ziaul Haq, from the Constitution for his unconstitutional acts during his tenure (1977-1988).'

In fact they did so to keep away themselves, to delete their names, from the dark pages of Pakistan's history so that the future generations should not be able to see their blackened faces in the mirrors of military dictatorships. But according to Gen Zia's son and former federal minister, Ijazul Haq: *'They cannot delete Gen Ziaul Haq's name from history till Articles 62 & 63 of the Constitution are there.'*

25 years old history archives reveal that the military dictator was also supported whole heartedly then by the PML's Chief Nawaz Sharif, the Chaudhrys of Gujrat (Chaudhry Shujaat Hussain and Chaudhry Pervez Elahi) and the Chief of Jamiat e Ulema Pakistan (JUI) Maulana Fazl-ur-Rehman, Jamaat-e-Islami, Makhdoom Sajjad Hussain Qureshi, father of PPP's former Foreign Minister Shah Mehmood Qureshi, Gilanis of Multan, Nawabs of Bahawalpur and several others.

The present stalwart of the PPP, PM Mr Gilani had organized a huge political meeting in support of the 1984 referendum at Qasim Bagh Stadium Multan; Nawaz Sharif had become Punjab's Chief Minister after the 1985's non-party elections, courtesy Gen Ziaul Haq and the then military Governor of Punjab Gen Ghulam Jillani Khan.

Similarly, some robust politicians of Khyber PK (then NWFP)'s Saifullah family, former NWFP Chief Minister Pir Sabir Shah, late Khawaja Safdar (father of the fiery PML(N) leader Khawaja Asif), Chaudhry Nisar Ali Khan, late Khaqan Abbasi (father of PML(N)'s Shahid Khaqan), Sardar Assef Ahmed Ali, sitting PML(N)'s MsNA Rana Nazir Ahmed, Javed Hashmi, & Senator Zafar Ali Shah were all members of the 1985 National Assembly which had made laws under the military umbrella to facilitate Gen Ziaul Haq.

For record, the salient features of this 8th Amendment of the Constitution (1985) are summarized below:

> Article 41 (3) of the Constitution was substituted whereby Provincial Assemblies became part of the Electoral College for election to the office of the President.

> Article 58(2)(b) under which the President was empowered to dissolve the National Assembly in his discretion where, in his opinion, a situation had arisen in which the Government of the Federation cannot be carried on in accordance with provisions of the Constitution and an appeal to the electorate was necessary.

> Article 270 A was inserted into the Constitution by means of President's Order 14 of 1985 to facilitate transition of power from military to the civilian authorities. It reads:

> "270 A (1): The Proclamation of the fifth day of July 1977, all President's Orders, Ordinances, Martial Law Regulations, Martial Law Orders, including the Referendum Order, 1984 (P.O. No.11 of 1984), under which, in consequence of the result of the referendum

held on the nineteenth day of December 1984, General Mohammad Zia-ul-Haq became the President of Pakistan on the day of the first meeting of the Majlis-e-Shoora (Parliament) in joint sitting for the term specified in clause (7) of Article 41, the Revival of the Constitution of 1973 Order 1985 (P.O.No.14 of 1985), the Constitution (Second Amendment) Order 1985 (P.O. No.20 of 1985), the Constitution (Third Amendment) Order 1985 (P.O. No.24 of 1985), and all other laws made between the fifth day of July 1977, and the date on which this Article comes into force are hereby affirmed, adopted and declared, notwithstanding any judgment of any court, to have been validly made by competent authority and, notwithstanding any thing contained in the Constitution, shall not be called in question in any court on any ground whatsoever.

270 A (2): All orders made, proceedings taken and acts done by authority or by any person, which were made, taken or done, or purported to have been made, taken or done, between the fifth day of 1977, and the date on which this Article comes into force, in exercise of the powers derived from any Proclamation, President's Orders, Ordinances, Martial Law Regulations, Martial Law Orders, enactments, notifications, rules, orders or bye-laws, or in execution of or in compliance with any order made or sentence passed by any authority in the exercise or purported exercise of powers as aforesaid, shall, notwithstanding any judgment of any court, be deemed to be and always to have been validly made, taken or done and shall not be called in question in any court on any ground whatsoever.

Ms Benazir Bhutto had filed a petition under Article 184(3) of the Constitution in the Supreme Court challenging the *vires* of the amendments made in the Political parties Act, 1962 as violative of Articles 17 and 25 of the Constitution, the *vires* of the Freedom of Association Order, 1978 and the constitutionality of Article 270A in so far as it curtailed the power to judicially review its content or restricted the jurisdiction of the Superior Courts to protect Fundamental Rights of the citizens including the right to form or be a member of a political party under the Constitution as it existed before the 5th July 1977.

The Supreme Court in the judgment reported as ***Benazir Bhutto* v. *Federation of Pakistan* (PLD 1988 SC 416)** held that the Constitution of Pakistan envisaged parliamentary democracy with a cabinet system based on party system as essentially it is composed of the representatives of a party, which is in majority and therefore the future election would be held on party basis.

Scenario 10

DEMOLISHING THE CIVIL SERVICES STRUCTURE:

In 1950, when the Civil Service of Pakistan (CSP) was re-established as it was in the India before partition, the cabinet secretariat had decided that 10 per cent of its strength would be raised from the armed forces but the decision was never implemented. After Gen Ayub Khan seized power in 1958, he desired to revive the 1950's decision and made a list of perspective army officers to be sent to civil services. It was agreed that the said induction would be done through the Federal Public Service Commission (FPSC) from among the list sent by the GHQ.

Zulfiqar Ali Bhutto's administrative reforms of 1973 introduced the concepts of lateral entry and horizontal mobility into the civil service. Bypassing the FPSC, selections were largely made on the basis of nepotism and political affiliations. In his tenure (1972-1977) the PM Bhutto appointed 83 army officers to the secretariat, foreign affairs, tribal areas and district management groups whereas between 1960 and 1963, only 14 officers were appointed by Gen Ayub, then the scheme was discontinued.

In July 1977, Bhutto was ousted in a military coup by army chief Gen Ziaul Haq and executed in 1979. The military regime, which lasted until his crash in 1988, forcibly suppressed political opposition and launched a far-reaching *Islamisation* drive to achieve domestic legitimacy with support from the religious right. A traditionally secular civil bureaucracy was then compelled to reframe 'the ideological orientation of the civil servant' through measures such as a uniform dress code and enforced prayer breaks during office hours. There was a 'minimal emphasis on professional work' as long as officials were deemed 'good' Muslims.

Gen Ziaul Haq had made a commission on civil service reforms, which proposed a number of radical departures from Bhutto's system such as abolishing all occupational groups; creating several technical services to accommodate specialists in fields such as agriculture, education, engineering and medicine; revamping district administration; and creating numerous in-service training institutions. However, Gen Ziaul Haq largely retained the old system.

Referring to the daily *Dawn of 4th September 2011* ['Military in Civil Service' by Aminullah Chaudhry], Gen Faiz Ali Chishti, Gen Zia's right-hand man, said that Mr Bhutto had destroyed the institution of the civil service by recruiting his own party men and Gen Zia did more. If the PPP was Mr Bhutto's party, then the armed forces were Gen Ziaul Haq's party.

During both Gen Ayub and PM Bhutto's regimes, induction of few retired or released military officers into the civil serces was made, but the practice was never institutionalized. Gen Ziaul Haq not only recruited many more officers and placed them in higher ranks of the bureaucracy, but also institutionalized the practice by making sure of 10% military quota at lucrative posts in the civilian bureaucracy for serving and retired military officers.

The practice, however, remained confined to the induction [of the commissioned officers from Army, PAF & Navy] into the District Management Group (DMG), Foreign Service of Pakistan (FSP), and Police Service of Pakistan (PSP). Usually officers of captain rank were short listed by MS Branch of GHQ and selected against this quota after the permission and direct approval of the Chief of Army Staff before an eye-wash interview process. The interviews were though conducted by a committee headed by the Chairman FPSC, apparantly same as in the case of regular candidates but the wish of the COAS mostly prevailed.

When the barriers lifted by Gen Zia the ADCs of the serving Generals, staff officers of corps commanders, sons and brothers of senior army officers and even doctors availed the blessings. The successive political governments did nothing to reverse the trend. Chief Minister Punjab Nawaz Sharif had 'relaxed' the relevant rules and appointed two principal staff officers (a colonel and a major) his chief pilot and two majors to the provincial services. During Gen Musharraf's rule the large-scale influx of army officers into the civil service was masterminded by Lt Gen Tanwir Naqvi of the National Reconstruction Bureau (NRB).

In an interview with Ayesha Siddiqa in 2002, Maj Gen Rashid Qureshi had said that *'the average military officer is better qualified and more intelligent than the average civil bureaucrat'*. Till 2011, out of roughly 650 DMG officers, around 100 are from the army, air force and navy.

Alleged that Bhutto's 1973 Constitution and his Civil Service Ordinance carrying 'Lateral Entry' & 'Horizental Mobility' had destroyed the whole structure of the civil service. The main challenge was that the politicians and military officers who wanted to bring about this change preferred to have a weak and subservient civil service rather than a strong and independent one. PM Bhutto removed the civil services protection by taking it out of the 1973 Constitution to make sure the bureaucracy became completely docile and malleable.

In the late 70s and early 80s Gen Ziaul Haq initially wanted to restore some of the guarantees to the civil bureaucracy but then went silent. Certain politicians had suggested to Gen Musharraf to restore constitutional protection to the civil service but he had avoided too. Contrarily he himself wanted the powers to remove civil servants without any reasons given.

Asia Report No; 185 dated 16th February 2010 compiled by International Crisis Group mentions that Gen Ziaul Haq had institutionalised military induction into the civil service, a practice that had been conducted on an ad hoc basis by earlier regimes, permanently entrenching the military's presence in the bureaucracy. In 1962, Ayub Khan had once thought a 50 per cent reservation for ex-servicemen in bureaucracy but only appointed eight army captains to the elite CSP. Bhutto's lateral entry scheme had resulted in as many as 83 military officers appointed to senior public service positions.

While Gen Ziaul Haq initially re-employed only retired military officers on a contract basis, in 1980, he decreed that 10 per cent of vacancies in the federal bureaucracy at Basic Pay Scale (BPS) 17 & 18 would be reserved for retired or released military officers. These officers were not selected by the FPSC but by a High Powered Selection Committee headed by Gen Ziaul Haq himself being the *Ameerul Momineen or Khalifa e Waqt*.

The committee was also tasked to fill 10 per cent of senior vacancies (BPS 19-22) in the Secretariat Group, Foreign Affairs Group, Accounts Group and Information Group. Former military officers were mostly employed on three to five year contracts. Many officers of the rank of brigadier and above were thus inducted as federal and provincial secretaries. In 1982, eighteen out of 42 ambassadors were retired military officers. In 1985, a serving major general was chosen to head the Intelligence Bureau, the country's main civilian intelligence agency, for the first time in Pakistan's history.

By 1985, 98 former military officers were permanently inducted in BPS 17 & 18 posts, while 111 held senior appointments on contract. The civil bureaucracy was thus *'reduced to a wholly subordinate role by the regime's policy of grafting military officers to key jobs in the central and provincial administrations, public sector industries as well as other semi-government and autonomous organisations'.*

Like the previous army ruler Gen Ayub Khan, Gen Ziaul Haq also used local bodies to cover a highly centralised, authoritarian system of government under the garb of decentralisation, through non-party elections in 1979, 1983 and 1987. Civil bureaucrats, commissioners and deputy commissioners, were reduced to ex-officio, non-voting members of the City & District Councils. It is alleged that Gen Ziaul Haq had further eroded the neutrality of civil officers through large-scale postings and transfers, both at the district and policy-making levels in the federal and provincial secretariats, with calculated intervals.

The fact remains that during 1990s, the Pakistan Peoples Party (PPP) and Nawaz Sharif's PML(N) both had their own 'teams' of civil servants who were patronised and promoted not on merit but on their perceived loyalty to their respective political masters. Appointing senior civil officers known for their political affiliations rather than their professionalism, Benazir Bhutto and the two Sharifs created *"an atmosphere where the corrupt could get away with their schemes – be they politicians, tax-evading businessmen, or self-serving civil servants"*. Names of numerous Saeed Mehdis and Salman Farooquis would be remembered in the history for spoiling the Pakistan's political structure, inviting army to take over and nullify their 'precious advices' to their political masters.

The military exploited this perception of rampant corruption advised by some known civil bureaucrats to justify its political interventions, masking the actual goal, to retain control over foreign and domestic policies. On the basis of ill intentioned suggestions of these corps of political bureaucrats the post Zia governments gradually dissolved local bodies in the NWFP in 1991, in Sindh in 1992, and in Punjab in 1993. The primary motivations were political, rather than the desire to improve governance and curb corruption.

Getting scared of the electoral influence of local officials, who had served as willing clients of the military regime, the PPP and the PML(N) opted to appoint administrators to run local councils sending the actually competent civil bureaucracy on *'Khudday Line postings'* in secretariats while keeping their numbered loyalists in the cabinet corridors to make out pseudo-national policies for respective political parties.

In fact Gen Musharraf's military regime, like Gen Zia's, took the practice of appointing serving and retired military officers into the civilian caders to 'unprecedented' levels. During much of his rule, all the major civil service institutions were headed by retired military officers. The Federal Public Service Commission responsible for overseeing recruitment, main civil service training institutions like NIPA and Admisistrative Staff College, National & Provincial Accountability Bureaux and even the Civil Service Reform Unit, all were placed under the militarized control.

Quite naturally this practice, especially in the Foreign Service, was seen as a cause of growing disgruntlement amongst civil servants who saw their promotion prospects blocked by military appointees. In earlier years, the civil service had viewed the military as their natural allies and politicians as the major threat to their influence but the large-scale inductions of military officers into senior positions of the civil services gradually reversed that perception. Facts told by an ex-bureaucrat are that:

> *'Twenty years ago the Army was a state within a state. Today the Army is the state—everything else is appendages. The Army controls all state institutions—civil service, foreign policy, economic policy, intelligence agencies, judiciary and the legislature. They've monopolized policymaking. At the same time; the civilian bureaucracy is suffering from institutional decay and moving in the opposite direction. This has changed the power balance from the colonial era and the first two decades after independence when the civilian bureaucracy was the strongest institution'.*

Pakistan's political scenario brings frustration no doubt; democratic traditions have been ruined collectively through 18th Amendment introducing a culture of civil dictatorship, but the military cannot ignore the general civil society altogether. It had to accommodate the growing domestic and international pressures to govern the populace. This was vividly demonstrated by the lawyers' movement of 2007 and 2008, which helped force Gen Musharraf to hold general elections in February 2008 and to resign as president six months later.

The *Arab News of 24th February 2010* opined that the majority of Pakistanis view the country's 2.4 million civil servants as inefficient, unresponsive and corrupt. *'Military rule has left behind a demoralized and inefficient bureaucracy that was used to ensure regime's survival. Low salaries, insecure tenure, obsolete accountability mechanisms and political interference have spawned widespread corruption and impunity. Thus rising public resentment could be used by the military to justify another spell of authoritarian rule.'*

Scenario 11

OJHRI CAMP EPISODE (1988):

In *'the News London' of 6th May 2011*, a column written by Haroon Rashid titled [*LAIKEN*] has given a brief description of 'Ojhri Camp Episode'. In the column the theme concerning that tragedy was described as translated under:

> *'..... the only fact was that **it (Ojhri Ammunition Depot) was set to fire by the Americans themselves** because they (US authorities) did not want that the said ammunition should be passed on to the Afghan Mujahideen fighting with Soviets. The reason behind was that the America had secretly negotiated with the Soviets for their safe exit back. The tussle between Gen Ziaul Haq and America had taken start because Gen Zia wanted to establish a 'national government' in Afghanistan before Soviet's exit.*
>
> *Gen Ziaul Haq wanted so because he did not want 'civil war' in Afghanistan. In Pakistan, all political parties were with **PM Junejo** who was then acting under **US Influence** (?). Geneva Accord was signed and a 'true Pakistan Loving' Gen Ziaul Haq was killed by Americans afterwards.'*

History available on record tells that the basic facts were otherwise. The episode is still alive in the newspapers and various research archives of libraries. The inquiry reports might be lying in the Cabinet Secretariat and a copy thereof in the defence ministry.

The history witnessed that who was the American stooge; Gen Ziaul Haq or PM M K Junejo. Who can imagine that in military regimes, a nominated prime minister could have control over Ammunition, Afghan *Mujahideen* (religious fighters), policy on Afghanistan, strategy of armed fighting with Soviets, decisions regarding ISI's relationships with Afghan fighting factions and above all with the Americans direct. The reality might be altogether different but the written (and secret) material at hand does not lead us to above paragraph of fiction.

On **10th April 1988** the military ammunition depot at Ojhri Camp Rawlapindi, blew up and unleashed an inferno that sent all sorts of rockets all over Rawalpindi and into neighbouring Islamabad. Lying there was about 10,000 tons ammunition, about 30,000 numbers of

107mm rockets, millions of bullets of various sizes, thousands of anti-tank mines, mortar bombs and hundreds of Stinger missiles which were bound to reach the fighting factions of *Mujahideen* contingents inside the Afghanistan territory.

After finalizing the Geneva Accord, America did not want that this ammunition should go to Afghan *Mujahideen* because they could pose two serious threats to firstly; for fleeing Soviet platoons from Afghanistan and secondly; the *Mujahideen* could abolish Najeebullah government in Afghanistan to establish Taliban's own rule. Both situations were not acceptable to America. *(Ref: Irfan Siddiqui in Daily 'Jang' dated 18th August 2011)*

It also let to a sequence of events that led to the ouster of the then Prime Minister Mohammed Khan Junejo and, depending on which conspiracy experts believe, to the death of the then President Gen Ziaul Haq. The US officials had blamed sabotage for the explosion. Others held that the said explosion was done by Pakistan army agents to cover up a pilferage of the weapons stocks, including Stinger missiles. The true cause of the explosion still remains a mystery.

In Pakistan, it was another dark period of the military rule and of militant *jihadism* acceptable to the Americans against a back drop of Soviet Russia's attack on Afghanistan on 25th December 1979. Gen Ziaul Haq was pleasing the West particularly America and its allies were supporting the *Mujahideen* groups. Then Osama Bin Laden was America's most favourite freedom fighter who was leading the Western inspired Jihad against the Soviets on the Afghanistan soil. Billions of dollars were pouring in for Pakistani military to manage this Jihad in Afghanistan whereas millions of dollars were also spent on providing weapons and logistical support for the *Mujahid* (religious fighter) groups through Gen Ziaul Haq's team.

Most of this American and British weaponry were dumped at Ojhri, a camp near the centre of Rawalpindi city which was directly controlled by the ISI. The ISI's cell which used to control the Afghan War under direct command of one Gen Akhtar Abdul Rehman, was not even answerable to the GHQ's routine channels of command nor its officers but directly to one Gen Ziaul Haq only.

One **Tariq Mehmood,** a former journalist of 'The Frontier Post' had recalled this episode in this way:

'The people of Rawalpindi and Islamabad did not know the reason of missiles attack. American stinger missiles which had been given for fighting in Afghanistan had found their way into the hands of the Iranians. They were stored in Ojhri dump, and it was pretty obvious that those looking after the dump had sold them on to the Iranians, pocketing the money. A team of American navel investigators was in mid-flight, on its way to Ojhri to investigate. They entered Pakistani airspace, when the dump was blown up.

Two days after the explosions at Ojhri, Gen Ziaul Haq had compared what happened to the disasters at Russia's Chrenobyl and India's Bhopal. He refused to admit that Ojhri was a transit dump where weapons were destined for Afghanistan. The deed was blamed on foreign agents refuting that it was an insider's job.'

Allegations of foreign hand could not hold ground because *'stinger missiles do not just go off, they had to be primed. Army ammunition dumps, are built in such a manner that an explosion should not affect the other. But here were truckloads of the stuff over ground, and much more underground, all going off.'* By the time the Americans arrived, 1000 people were dead as per available reports of local Red Cross office. Officially announced figure of the death toll was 30 and prominent among those killed was a sitting Federal Minister Khaqan Abbasi whose car was hit by a flying missile while he was on his way to Murree, his hometown.

The *'New York Times'* of 17th April 1988 had told that: *' .... the explosion killed at least 93 people and wounded about 1100 people.'* Credibility could not be assigned to any agency in respect of figures.

The people of Pakistan, media and the foreign correspondents were never told that what kind of ammunition was dumped there in Ojhri and in what quantity. It remained a secret between Gen Ziaul Haq and Gen Akhtar Abdul Rehman, the then in-charge of Afghan War against the Soviets but *'The Dawn' of 11th April 2008* had revealed that:

'Ojhri Camp had about 30,000 rockets, millions of rounds of ammunition, vast number of mines, anti-aircraft Stinger missiles, anti-tank missiles, multiple-barrel rocket launchers and mortars worth $100 million in store at the time of blasts that destroyed all records and most of the weapons thus making it anyone to check the stocks.'

The fact remains that there were so many unexploded bombs and missiles left behind and the army had no idea how to defuse them. Trial and error method was applied but each error cost the life of an army officer. About 1000 more died in this process alone and there remained much confusion around. On 17th February 2007 two workers died in Rawalpindi from unexploded ammunitions from Ojhri dump. In Tariq Mehmood's words: '... *reminding about callousness of the rulers who stored so much weapons in side a major city like Rawalpindi, and then those who colluded to blow it up.'*

One of the fallouts of Ojhri episode was that Gen Ziaul Haq had lost all his credibility in Pakistan and in America. That is why the later planned to eliminate him and at last succeeded on 17th August the same year when the two above mentioned Generals, Ziaul Haq & Akhtar Abdul Rehman, along with other 17 had lost their lives in a plane crash. Ojhri event was a crime against humanity.

Mohammad Khan Junejo, the then Prime Minister of Pakistan, had displayed his concern with the then President and Army ruler Gen Ziaul Haq over the issue and demanded punishment for the army officers and Generals who were deemed responsible for the catastrophe while Gen Ziaul Haq (who kept portfolio of the Army Chief even after lifting of the martial law by extending his own term of office) could not afford to see an interference in his domain.

PM Mohammad Khan Junejo had openly blamed Gen Akhtar Abdur Rahman, because he was sure of the fact that the camp had been blown up deliberately just before the arrival of a US Defence Audit team, to cover up the fact that some Stinger missiles had been sold off to other countries, most probably to Iran.

In the last, PM Junejo had also managed to get nominated Gen Aslam Beg as Army Chief as per seniority whereas Gen Ziaul Haq wanted to post his second in command as the next Army Chief.

The final showdown took place on 29th May 1988. Three days earlier the PM had asked his Principal Secretary to take the 'fact finding report' regarding Ojhri blasts with him on his foreign tour to Seoul and Manila. This report was compiled by a committee of senior members of the Parliament who were allocated this job by the PM Secretariat. The report was shocking. On his way back from Manila PM Junejo had approved the given recommendations and signed by virtue of which the top army Generals had to face the consequences including court martial. The Military Secretary accompanying the Prime Minister, somehow, had managed to communicate the report's final outcome to Gen Ziaul Haq through pilot's wireless system from the cockpit.

Gen Ziaul Haq immediately planned to get rid of his PM, Mr Junejo and had called a press conference in the Army House Rawalpindi. The number one team of correspondents was present at the Islamabad Airport to receive the PM and were hoping de-briefing by the PM after his foreign tour. But on an urgent call from the Press Secretary of Army House, the number two team of correspondents had to attend Gen Ziaul Haq's press conference in which he, under article 58(2)(B) of the amended constitution, dismissed PM Junejo's government and dissolved the national and provincial assemblies. In sacking Prime Minister M K Junejo, Gen Ziaul Haq had made the following allegations against the Junejo government:

- The law and order in the country had broken down to an alarming extent resulting in tragic loss of human lives.
- The life, property, honour, safety and security of the citizens of Pakistan were rendered totally unsafe.
- The integrity and ideology of Pakistan have been seriously endangered and doubts generated in this regard.
- The president's conscience always pricked that he had not fulfilled his promises regarding the enforcement of Islam made to the people in the referendum of 1984.
- The public morality had deteriorated to an unprecedented level.
- A situation had arisen in which the government of the federation cannot be carried on in accordance with provisions of the constitution necessitating an appeal to the election.

So when PM Junejo came out of his plane, he was no more Prime Minister. No cabinet minister, none of the three force's Chiefs, no government officer or no media correspondent was there to welcome him. He had to leave the Airport in a private car to his home.

An essay appeared in *'The News' on 14th April 1998* titled *'Ojhri disaster saw end of Junejo govt:'* written by **Kamal Siddiqi** desribed that:

> *'The government of prime minister Muhammad Khan Junejo, installed by General Ziaul Haq, was dismissed shortly after the Ojhri camp blasts and the newspaper says that an inquiry report by Junejo's government was the reason for the dismissal.'*

The *'Indian Express'* of the same day had given details as:

> [Two committees were formed by the government to look into the affair. The first was the military committee headed by a serving

General. This committee's findings and recommendations were ignored since it called for the removal of Gen Zia's right hand man, Gen Akhtar Abdul Rehman, along with other senior military officials. Its report, presented within one week of the incident, was rejected.

Another more interesting committee was the one set up by Prime Minister Muhammad Khan Junejo. This was a political committee headed by a Cabinet minister and comprising four federal ministers. Controversy surrounded the findings of this committee. The members could not reach a consensus on who was responsible for the Ojhri tragedy. In his remarks, the head of the committee, Aslam Khattak (probably the Minister for Interior then) had concluded, 'No one was responsible. It was an act of Allah.'

However, the minister of state for defence, Rana Naeem Mehmood, a hawk in the Junejo cabinet and a die hard proponent of democracy, prepared a non paper which was signed by three of the five members of the political inquiry committee. The paper recommended the court martial of senior Generals and laid the blame on Gen Akhtar Abdul Rehman. 'Many believe that this paper cost Junejo his government.'

The newspaper report also gives another interesting angle: an interview with General Hamid Gul, a senior member of the Army Command at the time. Gul says: Before the blast, the first draft of the accord said both the Soviets and the Americans would stop arms supplies to Afghanistan. But after Ojhri, the Americans accepted negative symmetry, agreeing that both sides would continue with their supplies.']

BBC of 10th April 2008 had narrated *(www.bbc.co.uk)* that there had been fire and periodical blasts in the half burnt ammunition heaps at Ojhri. In the above report of 'The Indian Express', the first Military Committee was headed by a serving General named Lt Gen Imranullah Khan. The report with recommendations of Court Martial against the then In-charge Afghan Operations (Gen Akhtar Abdul Rehman) was sent to the President's Secretariat where it was shelved like so many other important files wanting attention.

During Gen Musharraf's rule some opposition members called for making these reports public but the then PML(Q) government took the position that it would not be *'in the larger national interest'*. Gen Musharraf did not want to tarnish the image of their Army colleagues. Irony of the fate was that after 1988, the PPP and the PML(N) got power and mandate to rule for two terms each consecutively but none of them opted to declare these two reports open.

Although there exists some pointers in the Charter of Democracy, signed in 2006 at London by the PPP and PML(N), which could be pursued to make such reports public, but neither the President Zardari nor the Opposition Leader Nawaz Sharif dared to take such a bold step. Interestingly, both the major political parties had made demands while being in the opposition but none of them bothered to do anything about it when they came to power.

Contrarily, **Michael R Gordon** of the *'New York Times'* got published an official version of the State Defence Department **on 17th April 1988** by giving a categorical version that:

> *'One week after a major explosion at a Pakistani ammunition dump, Defence Department officials say that it was sabotage but Pakistani leaders have made contradictory comments about the blast. At first, Gen Ziaul Haq called the explosion "an extraordinary accident," then on Friday, Gen Ziaul Haq said the blast was the result of sabotage.*
>
> *Defence Department officials say they believe that the blast was the result of sabotage because of the circumstances surrounding the explosion. The explosion appeared to be part of a pattern of attacks last weekend, including an attempted rocket attack on an oil storage installation in Peshawar that didn't work; a fire at an ordnance factory in Lahore and a bomb that was discovered and defused in Islamabad.*
>
> *But the State Department officials insist on understanding that the significance of the explosion is exaggerated.'*

It may be the case that the then American government did not want to make Gen Ziaul Haq angry in the backdrop of on going Afghan War against Soviet infiltration but the then ISI Chief Gen Hamid Gul is alive to give testimony in this respect.

Imran Ali Teepu gives some details of explanations given by Gen Hamid Gul, the then ISI Chief's explicit interview in 'The *Dawn' of 10th April 2010* by saying:

> *'Even Gen Hamid Gul, who was then heading the Inter-Services Intelligence (ISI), is amazed that the facility run by the agency for funnelling US-supplied arms to the Mujahideen fighting the Soviet army in Afghanistan, was located in a densely populated area of Rawalpindi but then it was a 'strategic compulsion' to hide its weapons stockpiles from Russia's spy satellites.*

Gen Hamid Gul categorically stated that: 'It is wrong to say that the tragedy occurred because the Americans were due to inspect the ammunition depot. The Americans always conducted inspections. We had nothing to hide from them. The archives room of the facility was not damaged, claiming that it provided ample proof of the military establishment's innocence.'

From the above narrations it becomes crystal clear that our political and military dictatorship never wanted to share cogent facts of our history with the people they govern. It amounts to distrust in the people and reflects lack of confidence in our successive rulers from whichever background they belonged.

Let us pray that our coming leaders should come up with devotion and truthfulness for the sake of their nationalism at least.

Scenario 12

JUNEJO GONE & GEN ZIA CRASHED (1988):

In the history of Pakistan, 1988 can be seen as one of the most volatile and proactive years. During the last week of May 1988, Gen Ziaul Haq had used the sword of Art 58(2)(b) first time to cut the throat of his PM M K Junejo and with the orders of dissolution of the then National Assembly. In the third week of August 1988, Gen Ziaul Haq was sent upstairs in the sky through a sabotage activity while his C-130 met an air crash at Bahawalpur. 19 other senior military brass of Pakistan, one from US army and a serving US Ambassador were also accompanying him to meet their fate. During November 1988, general elections were held and Benazir Bhutto started her first innings of the PPP government.

The above three main events of 1988 are remembered by all books and columns. The fourth equally most important development was a tint of 'judicial activism' which actually took start in 1988, if the writers of judicial history peep into the related events and their repercussions. Let us travel a few years back.

When in 2005, Chief Justice Iftikhar M Chaudhry held reins of the Supreme Court of Pakistan; he immediately started exercising the court's *suo moto* judicial review powers. *Suo moto*, meaning 'on its own motion,' apparently beginning with the case of **Darshan Masih v The State** (1990), where the Supreme Court had converted a telegram sent by bonded labourers into a writ petition, the apex Court rapidly fashioned for itself the power to take up cases of its own accord, based on letters or media reports. The court also relaxed other procedural requirements and public interest cases had increasingly come to acquire an inquisitorial or administrative inquiry mode rather than the strict adversarial model of adjudication that a common law system used to imagine.

Better to refer to Articles 184(3) & 199 of the Constitution of Pakistan, which place judicial review powers in the Supreme Court and the High Courts respectively. The majority of these powers are based upon the prerogative writs of *certiorari*, *mandamus*, prohibition and habeas corpus. Under Article 199 of the Constitution of Pakistan, the High Court's powers include issuing orders:
(i) directing any person performing "functions in connection with the affairs of the Federation, a Province or a local authority, to refrain

from doing anything he is not permitted by law to do, or to do anything he is required by law to do;

(ii) declaring that any act or proceeding ... has been done or taken without lawful authority and is of no legal effect;

(iii) directing that a person in custody be brought before it so that the Court may satisfy itself that he is not being held in custody without lawful authority or in an unlawful manner; and

(iv) Requiring a person ... holding or purporting to hold a public office to show under what authority of law he claims to hold that office."

In addition, Pakistani courts may, subject to certain restrictions, make an order giving "such directions to any person or authority ... as may be appropriate for the enforcement of any of the Fundamental Rights" conferred by the Constitution.

Referring to *'Pakistan: US AID Report on Rule of Law published in November 2008'*, although the above quoted powers were conferred on the courts in 1973, it was only in 1988 when the Supreme Court decided **Benazir Bhutto v Federation of Pakistan (PLD 1988 SC 416),** that these broad constitutional powers were 'discovered' and the seeds of public interest or social action litigation were sown. A subsequent judgement of 2002 of the apex court said:

> *'It is true that as held in Benazir Bhutto's case (PLD 1988 SC 416) and Asad Ali's case (PLD 1998 SC 161) the person desiring to invoke the jurisdiction of this Court under Article 184(3) of the Constitution need not necessarily be an aggrieved person, nevertheless the person approaching this Court under the aforesaid provision has to demonstrate that the question raised concerns the public at large.'*

PM M K Junejo Sent Home (1988):

In 1988, there prevailed a tension between Gen Ziaul Haq and the then Prime Minister M K Junejo who was chosen three years back for his weak political personality. The major bone of contention was the civil interference in top military appointments and the Afghan situation. Gen Ziaul Haq was angry with PM Junejo for holding Geneva talks against his wishes thus he had refused to sign the Geneva Accord. Junejo got organized a round table conference of opposition leaders to get his way. Secondly, Junejo challenged the appointment of two Generals amidst the main demand that Gen Ziaul Haq should also announce retirement from the post of the Army Chief, long overdue then.

On Afghan issue: the Russians were going back from Afghanistan. For America their purpose was over as that had taken revenge of US defeat in Vietnam but for Gen Ziaul Haq it was the start of a new era in the region. In Gen Ziaul Haq's view America and PM M K Junejo both should have wait till the new but some stable government in Afghanistan was made. With Geneva Accord a new phase of uneasiness started in Afghanistan in the form of a civil war amongst various factions. Thus for Pakistan the tension prevailed as such.

The Mujahideen had assembled again and toppled Najeebullah's government in Afghanistan which the Soviets had left while leaving the region after defeat. These Mujahideen were being controlled by all the three Gulbadin Hikmetyar, Ahmed Shah Masood and Burhanuddin Rabbani and all the three reached Kabul simultaneously to make an interim set up.

It was pretended in a calculated move that Junejo's government was not providing funds to relocate Ojhri ammunition depot away from Rawalpindi. It was a lame excuse because army otherwise keep major part of the budget cake and such operations were neither told to the civil government nor funds were ever provided by the civil authorities. Gen Akhtar played this tune on behalf of the president Gen Ziaul Haq. To subvert the blame, the PM Junejo demanded punishment for the army Generals who were held responsible for the catastrophe according to an inquiry report prepared by the Cabinet Committee.

The Prime Minister M Khan Junejo also blamed Gen Akhtar Abdur Rahman, and rumours were spread that the depot had been blown up knowingly and deliberately just before the arrival of a six-members US defence audit team, to find facts about reports that some Stinger missiles had been sold off to private parties.

On 29th May 1988: In the backdrop of above mentioned circumstances, Gen Ziaul Haq used powers of his world famous 8th Amendment [Sec: 58(2)(b)] of the Constitution of Pakistan and dismissed Prime Minister Junejo's government. Assemblies, both National & provincial, were also suspended with immediate effect.

The dissolution of the National Assembly was challenged in the Lahore High Court under its constitutional jurisdiction and through the judgment reported as *Kh Muhammad Sharif vs Federation of Pakistan* **(PLD 1988 Lahore 725)**, the dissolution of the Assembly was declared illegal and the matter then came to the Supreme Court in appeal.

On 17th August 1988, Gen Ziaul Haq died in an air crash and Ghulam Ishaq Khan, the then Chairman of the Senate assumed the office of the President of Pakistan. In an appeal to that effect, the Supreme Court vide judgment reported as *Federation of Pakistan vs Haji Saifullah Khan* (**PLD 1989 SC 166**), which was delivered on 5th October 1988 had upheld the judgment of the Lahore High Court but declined to grant relief of restoration of the Assembly on the ground that the whole nation had been geared up for election scheduled for 16-19th November 1988.

In reply to a question regarding Haji Saifullah's case, Gen Aslam Beg, the former COAS, had told the journalists in Lahore on 4th February 1993:

> *"I did try to convey to the Honourable Supreme Court that, we had given a solemn undertaking to the nation that elections to the National Assembly would be held according to the schedule already announced and that, therefore, it would be in the best interest of the nation that we stick to our promise and the said elections were allowed to be held accordingly."* (**Ref: The Dawn daily of 5th April 1993**)

Coming back, when the President dissolved the National Assembly in June 1988 in the exercise of his discretionary power both the Lahore High Court and the Supreme Court in *'Haji Saifullah Khan vs Federation of Pakistan'* did not shy away by observing that the questions involved were political and held the dissolution to be invalid on the ground that it was not premised upon objective considerations.

At the same time, however, considering that the assembly was elected on a non-party basis and as the fundamental right to form a political party stood suspended by the Martial Law regime and the whole nation was geared up for a proper party based elections to be held in November 1988, the Court declined to restore the dissolved assembly by refusing to exercise discretionary jurisdiction.

Eventually, an amendment was brought about in the constitution requiring that whenever such order was passed the matter would be instantly referred to the Supreme Court for a final verdict.

Gen Ziaul Haq's Crash (1988):

On **17th August 1988**, Gen Ziaul Haq, along with his nineteen (19) top brass military Generals, was blown in the air just after seven minutes of their flight from Bahawalpur airbase. They all had gone to Hasilpur, a town at the brink of deserts, about 55 km away from Bahawalpur to see inaugural functioning of a new American Tank. The then US Ambassador in Pakistan was also one of the dead, considered to be on 'marketing tour' to convince and persuade the high command of Pakistan Army for a green signal to buy those tanks against a hefty budget. Gen Zia's 2nd in command Gen Mirza Aslam Beg had seen them off in an army aircraft C-130, considered one of the most securely built military air carrier. Gen Beg, being the only left over and the senior most had succeeded Gen Zia as a new army chief.

Theories started coming up immediately that it was a sabotage activity or a technical fault with the plane's engine or allied security systems. The record available with FIA carries a detailed probe (probably in association with the IB team) that if the Al Zulfiqar, the underground terrorist organization set up by Z A Bhutto's son, Mir Murtaza Bhutto, had played a role to avenge his father's hanging.

One theory referred towards elements within the Pakistan Army, mostly advocated by Gen Ziaul Haq's son, Ijazul Haq, who alleged that Gen Aslam Beg was behind the crash because he had abstained to accompany the others. The fact remains that Gen Aslam Beg had travelled out from Bahawalpur alone in another similar army plane that day. Moreover, the army was not allowed to cooperate with Justice Shafi ur Rehman Commission which was set up to look into the issue.

Another theory was also given attention during probe if the Iranian or Shia factor could be held responsible for that tragedy because of Gen Ziaul Haq's 'Hanfi' way of Islamization or his close relationship with Saudi rulers. Yet another theory saw the American hand in the incident on the grounds that Gen Ziaul Haq had successfully crossed over the Americans by putting Pakistan's nuclear program on fast track with the help of US aid manoeuvred to manage under disguised military arsenal. No document is available on record to show if the inquiry people had succeeded in getting any positive clue in that direction.

Apparently convincing and in those days widely believed reason behind the clash was linked with Ojhri Camp of Rawalpindi episode of 10th April 1988. On that day the military ammunition depot, blew up and unleashed an inferno that sent all sorts of rockets all over Rawalpindi and into neighbouring Islamabad. Tens of citizens were killed and injured. An inquiry committee was formed consisting of the then cabinet members which was ordered by the then Prime Minister Muhammad Khan Junejo without the formal consent of Gen Ziaul Haq which was considered an alarming step to degrade the army establishment. The committee had finalised its recommendations but the report never surfaced in public.

On 29th May 1988, when PM Junejo was returning from Seoul & Manila tour after a state visit, the PM's staff officer had placed that inquiry report for final approval and signature. The ADC, an army officer accompanying the PM, succeeded in conveying the event direct to the Army House Rawalpindi from the cockpit of the plane. Result was the immediate response. When the plane landed at Islamabad airport, there was no media person to question about the official tour; no protocol of cabinet ministers and the PM's car was there without flag. PM Junejo was fired, while his plane was still in air, by Gen Ziaul Haq using his powers under Article 58(2)(b) of the 8th Constitutional Amendment. The conspiracy experts believed that military dictator's that action had led to his death in crash.

It remained a mystery even till today, mostly for the American themselves because they had lost their top diplomat, Arnold Raphael and an American General, too. In Pakistan there was no such expertise available then either with army or the civilians to conduct a serious inquiry into an air crash incident except that an FIR was initiated in the local police station and the enquiry was subsequently handled by an FIA team in routine.

The things go more blurred when one considers that after Geneva Accord, the American authorities believed that they had taken revenge of their humiliation of Viet Nam War from the Russians by forcing them out of Afghanistan. Taking this philosophy on, it could be believed that America wanted to take away all the 'war players' away from the battlefields especially the two top heads; Gen Ziaul Haq and Gen Akhtar Abdul Rehman. The US was not at all interested that in Kabul, the Najibullah's government be overturned to bring the Taliban in. The US did not want Islamic government in Kabul because then all the Islamic countries in a row could form a block and could create problems for America & Europe in future.

That may be one reason that the American themselves had never bothered to launch a solemn, conclusive, or even comprehensive inquiry into the crash. After the crash the FBI was told to 'keep out of Pakistan' by Secretary of State George Schultz, though the US had the authority to investigate suspicious plane crashes involving US citizens.

The special team to look for forensic evidence was not deployed. The US experts assigned to the official board of inquiry appointed by Pakistan

Inam R Sehri

included six air force accident investigators but no criminal, counter-terrorist, or sabotage experts. The US team was expected to reach at the spot immediately to examine the scene of occurrence and to collect, or help the Pakistani teams to collect, the first hand information, pieces of forensic evidence and other related material.

In an interview published in *'Jang' dated 19th November 2001*, Lt Gen Hamid Gul, the most concerned person being Chief of the ISI then, had categorically stated that:

> *'The Americans were responsible for Gen Ziaul Haq's air crash. The American team told us that the plane crashed due to a technical fault because one of its (air) pumps was blocked. Later the team found that pump from the residue and sent it to the manufacturer company named 'Lockheads'. They reported back that the pump was working right – no fault seen in it; perfectly working it was.*
>
> *Robert B Oakley, the then American Ambassador in Islamabad came to me and urged to give back the earlier inquiry report. I asked PAF Chief Mr Hakimullah of the Inquiry Commission NOT to return the report in any case.'*

Media record tells us that *'New York Times'* had tried to unearth certain facts in independent capacity but could not claim a break through because of certain barriers concerning national security affecting both the US and Pakistan. Its bureau chief in South Asia, Barbara, had sent a report suggesting that *'the infamous Israeli secret agency 'Mossad' (whose motto is 'with clandestine terrorism we will conduct war') most probably killed Gen Ziaul Haq.'* The Israelis wanted to stop Pakistan from developing nuclear technology. They had attacked Iraq's nuclear facilities at Osirak in 1981 and believed that Gen Ziaul Haq was very near to then commonly known as 'the Islamic Bomb' and feared that formal atom-bomb testing could take place any time then.

The suspicion was also endorsed by **John Gunther Dean,** who was the American ambassador to India in 1988 and had named his written article & opinion as **'Smoking Guns'** but his reasons were shelved even by the US declaring Mr Dean a 'psychiatric case.' However, the record was available to prove that:

> *'During Mr Dean's stay in India as an ambassador, various pro-Israel Congressmen and other US policymakers constantly asked him why he wasn't cooperating with the Israelis to thwart Pakistan's nuclear program and demonize Pakistan.'*

Mr Dean was forcibly sent on retirement in 1988, as was noted down by
Irshad Saleem at www.DesPardes.com

World Policy Journal had claimed that *'still another theory accused the
Ahmadiya community of masterminding General Ziaul Haq's end. At
the time, and until now, there was no mention of the Israelis.'* The
available documentation did not support any of the versions relating
with Israel's Mossad or *Ahmadiya* group because no piece of evidence
was available showing their presence or leading to their connection up to
that airbase or into the plane.

The **Press Trust of India,** through a write up of **7th September 2009,**
assured that US and 'internal powers' were behind the 1988 plane crash
that killed Gen Ziaul Haq, while referring to Brig (r) Imtiaz Ahmed,
former chief of Pakistan's Intelligence Bureau. IB Ex-Chief had then told
a news channel that *'former army chief Gen Mirza Aslam Beg also said
that Zia's plane crash was not an accident, but sabotage,* as Gen Ziaul
Haq had come to power after overthrowing the PPP's Prime Minister
Zulfikar Ali Bhutto in July 1977.'

But the fact remains that Edward Jay Epstein's report published by
Vanity Fair had ruled out Bhutto family and their Al-Zulfikar from the
crash scene altogether. It is on record that Gen Ziaul Haq and Gen
Akhtar Abdul Rehman were *'immensely persuaded from within army'* to
go to Bahawalpur suggesting that a *'faction in the Pakistan army was
bent on an invisible coup d'état.'*

Referring to an interview of Lt Gen Asad Durrani, published in the daily
'Jang' dated 7th March 1999:

> *'Many people be astonished to know that Gen Ziaul Haq's coup of
> July 1977 was not at all approved by the army at large. His orders
> were obeyed because he was the army chief but his decision was not
> hailed. Many army officers were especially upset when PM Bhutto
> was arrested. When Gen Zia's rule entered 9th or 10th year, the army
> people had built up their opinion to get rid of him.*
>
> *Gen Ziaul Haq's Afghan policy was right rather appreciable but we
> army people did not approve his policy of Islamization of Pakistan
> because we all knew that the name of Islam was being misused to
> prolong the military rule. Further, Mr Bhutto was wrongly hanged that
> was why the people compensated the PPP by calling Benazir Bhutto in
> power after nine years.'*

Justice Dr Javed Iqbal, in an interview published in *February 1993 in the Daily 'Jang'* held that:

> 'Since the day Gen Ziaul Haq had given us the "gift" of Islamic Hudood Ordinance, the crime rate soared up. In the history of Pakistan the crimes against women were never as high as now after that Ordinance. The reported rape cases had never been as high as now after that Ordinance. In my opinion Gen Ziaul Haq had met with a severe kind of humiliating death due to cries and sighs of those women who had been victims of sexual maltreatment due to his Ordinance in which he had ridiculed Islam to get his own peculiar motives.'

Referring to *Khalid Hasan's* essay published on *18th June 2004* in media: In Epstein's opinion Soviet Union might have hand in the said crash because immediately before they had accused Gen Ziaul Haq for violating Geneva Accord. Earlier, in August 1988, the Soviet Union had temporarily suspended troop withdrawals from Afghanistan in protest. Gen Ziaul Haq had also counter attacked Soviets with same like allegations. The Soviets had summoned the US ambassador Jack Matlock and told him about Soviet Union's intentions to teach Gen Ziaul Haq a lesson. Epstein shunned the possibility of Soviet's involvement due to American envoy's presence on plane in the back drop of possible strained relations with Washington.

May be noted, however, that neither the American envoy Raphael nor Gen Wassom, head of the US military mission, was supposed to fly back with Gen Ziaul Haq, so Soviet involvement could not be ruled out.

On the other hand, Rajiv Gandhi had also warned Pakistan two days earlier that it should regret its behaviour on arming Sikh separatists. The United States too was unhappy with Gen Ziaul Haq for diverting a good deal of aid and weapons to Gulbuddin Hekmatyar whom it considered an anti-American extremist. They were also worried much about Gen Ziaul Haq's nuclear programme being continued even after knowing about Mr Bhutto's tragedy at its back-drop.

The details of the enquiry were told by the head of the US team, Col DE Sowada, later that no evidence of a mechanical failure had been found. The official Pakistani report had said the same thing. The US findings, contained in a 365 page report, established that the plane had not exploded in midair but hit the ground intact. It had not been hit by a missile either, nor had there been an on-board fire. No autopsies were done, except one on the US General who was sitting with Gen Ziaul Haq in plane.

The Pakistani report categorically said that *'no engine failure; fuel not contaminated; electric power found working normal and no pilot's error'*. The report did mention of traces of explosive particles and related chemicals, or it could be poison gas in cockpit. Thus the findings pointed towards sabotage. The report recommended a criminal investigation in detail. Gen Hamid Gul, then head of ISI, had told Epstein that *'at the request of the government, the agency had called off its inquiry and transferred it to a "broader-based" authority headed by F K Bandial, a senior civil servant.'* The report was never made public.

At the time of crash, three other planes were flying in the area. Their crew members were interviewed. The last words heard by the control tower were "Stand by" and then a faint voice saying "Mash'hood, Mash'hood", the name of the captain. The voice was that of Gen Zia's MS, Brig Najib; a long silence between "Stand by" said by Mash'hood and Mr Najib calling the pilot's name. Eyewitnesses saw the plane pitching up and down; Lockheed told that this pattern was characteristic of a pilot-less plane, which meant that the pilots were either dead or unconscious.

Possibility was that a gas bomb placed in the air vent of the plane which went off when pressurised air was fed into the cockpit. Epstein's inquiry concluded that any military or civilian mechanic could install such gas bomb in vent within two hours.

Such a gas was widely used in Afghanistan by the Soviets. VX, a US-made gas, could cause paralysis and loss of speech within 30 seconds. If used, it left behind phosphorus and traces of phosphorus were found in the remains of crashed plane. Autopsies could have determined the cause but not done, though the bodies were not returned to the families until two days later. A PAF doctor told that autopsies were routinely performed on pilots after crashes. The remains of human bodies were brought to CMH Bahawalpur but before US or Pakistani pathologists could arrive on next day, they were laid in coffins, sealed and despatched.

One last theory had surfaced, too that the crash was revenge against the then killing of a Shi'a cleric in Peshawar and the pilots of both Gen Ziaul Haq's crashed plane and the standby C-130 were Shi'a. One Mash'ood died in crash, the standby plane's Flt-Lt Sajid was interrogated and even tortured; the PAF had to launch a strong protest for that. It was held by Epstein that:

> *'The Shiite red herring theory was only one of several efforts to limit the investigation into the air crash of Gen Ziaul Haq and divert attention from the issue of sabotage.'*

Another theory published in the *'International Herald Tribune'* of *16th June 1999*, coined much later by Selig Harrison, a well-known American analyst, divulged that:

'Gen Ziaul Haq picked up Gen Musharraf (then a Brigadier) in 1987 to command a newly-raised Special Services Group (SSG) base at Khapalu in the Siachen area. Gen Musharraf had earlier spent seven years in two tenures with the SSG and remained proud of an SSG commando till his last moment in power.

In May 1988, the majority of Shias in Gilgit revolted against the Sunni administration. An SSG group commanded by Gen Musharraf was sent there to suppress that uprising. Gen Musharraf transported a large number of Wahabi Pakhtoon tribesmen from the NWFP to Gilgit to teach the Shias a lesson.'

In concluding paragraphs Mr Harrison opined that Gen Ziaul Haq was said to become the first victim of the crusade of Gen Musharraf on the Shias of Gilgit. Though there is no definite report on record from any committee, which enquired into the crash of Gen Zia's plane on 17th August 1988, it was widely believed in Pakistan that a Shia airman from Gilgit named Mash'ood, opted to take revenge for the May 1988's massacre, was responsible for the crash.

In support of his theory Selig Harrison also referred to Monthly *'Herald'* *Karachi of May 1990* saying that:

'In May 1988, low-intensity political rivalry and sectarian tension ignited into full-scale carnage as thousands of armed tribesmen from outside Gilgit district invaded Gilgit along the Karakoram Highway. Nobody stopped them. They destroyed crops and houses, lynched and burnt people to death in the villages around Gilgit town. The number of dead and injured was in hundreds.'

More so, Gen Musharraf had started a policy of bringing in Punjabis and Pakhtoons from outside and settling them down in Gilgit and Baltistan in order to reduce the Kashmiri Shias to a minority in their traditional land and this is continuing till today.

The *'Friday Times'* of *October 15-21, 1992*, quoted one Muhammad Yahya Shah, a local Shia leader, as saying:

'We were ruled by the Whites during the British days. We are now being ruled by the Browns from the plains. The rapid settling-in of

Punjabis and Pakhtoons from outside, particularly the trading class has created a sense of acute insecurity among the local Shias in and all around Gilgit.'

But still there is no concrete evidence surfaced to put this theory in belief.

The records of calls made to Gen Ziaul Haq and Gen Akhtar A Rehman prior to the crash were destroyed. Military personnel posted in Bahawalpur at the time of the crash were soon transferred. All leads pointed towards 'insider's job' proposition with a well-organised cover-up.

Ijazul-Haq, being a federal minister twice, could gain access to classified information, could do a lot being a son, a citizen of Pakistan and as an elected parliamentarian, to determine facts, but he preferred not to dig the files so deep.

One uncounted casualty in 17th August 1988's crash was the truth; let us agree with Epstein.

(Part of this essay was published at *www.Pakspectator.com* on 17th August 1988)

Scenario 13

ARMY & JUDICIARY IN 1989-90:

In August 1988, after the death of Gen Ziaul Haq, Ghulam Ishaq Khan (GIK), Chairman of the Senate, took over as acting President.

It remains a blackened page of Pakistan's history that an army institution ISI went so deep in political manoeuvring that it openly fabricated a political alliance named IJI (Islami Jamhoori Ittihad) to block the way of Pakistan Peoples Party (PPP). A former Chief of the ISI, Lt Gen Hamid Gul, once told that he was the only person to formulate and run the IJI. It was a concerted effort of many high ups and he was the front-man only. He flatly told that:

> 'All the stalwarts politicians, mostly belonging to Islamic religious parties of those days, used to approach and contact the army virtually begging that elections should not be announced. They have been enjoying at peak in Gen Ziaul Haq's days and they wanted to continue with the same bonanza.

> It was written on wall that the PPP was going to win the elections but even then army and the Presidency were determined to hold general elections because the army wanted rest. IJI was only formed as 'balancing factor' that was why the PPP was given the government despite the fact that they were having only 92 seats in the Assembly.'

However, the above proposition cannot be taken as simple. The facts were that after Gen Ziaul Haq's crash, the US government had suddenly increased their pressure to hold elections in the country. The American agenda was also notified. To oppose that agenda or to neutralize their pressure the IJI was tabled. The America's ambition was comprised of three items:

- Firstly; change in Afghan policy. Taliban were not acceptable to them.

- Secondly; Roll back of the nuclear program at the earliest.

- Thirdly; change in Kashmir's hardliner policy to keep India satisfied generally.

The army circles still maintain that had there been no factor like IJI, there was no possibility of any general elections in 1988. After sending the PM

Junejo home in May 1988, the Sindhis wanted compensation so Ghulam Mustafa Jatoi was made president of the IJI. Nawaz Sharif had no calibre of being a leader; he was just a mediocre business man but Benazir Bhutto's undue opposition made him leader; should have been ignored.

When there is a talk about IJI, one cannot ignore Lt Gen Hamid Gul, the real figure behind it but what happened in the power corridors, see the following paragraphs.

About eight months before retirement, Lt Gen Hamid Gul was transferred to Heavy Rebuild Factory (HRF) in mid 1991 which was an out of army cadre posting being a project of Defence Production Division. He talked his Army Chief (and a senior friend) Gen Asif Janjua and told that if he was not to be retained as Corp Commander, he could be transferred to any non-attractive posting at GHQ. Two written requests were also made. When not hailed to he had decided to proceed on retirement. He was asked to wait because the then PM Nawaz Sharif and the COAS Gen Asif Janjua both were on tour abroad.

When Nawaz Sharif came back, he sent Gen Hamid Gul a message that he should not resign but next day he had signed his retirement orders without assigning any reasons. He was the same PM for which Lt Gen Hamid Gul as DG ISI had made IJI after Gen Ziaul Haq's crash and one Army Chief Gen Mirza Aslam Beg had distributed Rs 140 million amongst those IJI candidates in general elections of 1990 to go against the PPP and bring Nawaz Sharif up. On this account a stigma on the army history of Pakistan would prevail for ever.

Lt Gen Hamid Gul must apologise first to the PPP for having done the sordid deed; after that, he must apologise for lack of wits because the IJI could not maintain its two-thirds majority for long.

At another moment, Lt Gen Hamid Gul demanded (referring to his interview appeared in daily *'Jang' of 19th November 2001*) that:

> *'If you are serious in Ehtesab then start it from high leaders. Had it been so the process was of only three months. They should have started from Nawaz Sharif asking him to explain that from where the Raiwind Palace & Estate come from. How he had gained 32 manufacturing units and factories with three years Chief and two years Prime Ministerial slots. If could not get convincing reply, confiscate every thing. They should have asked me the same questions about my living.'*

Coming back to the original topic: general elections for the National and Provincial Assemblies were held on 16th & 19th November 1988 respectively. During elections the PPP had surfaced as the winner party. The President GIK appointed Benazir Bhutto as Prime Minister of Pakistan on the condition that she would offer full support to him in the forthcoming presidential elections. According to deal between the President and Benazir Bhutto, the PPP Parliamentarians voted for GIK who was also the candidate of Islami Jamuhri Ittehad (IJI) then being headed by Nawaz Sharif in Punjab.

Constitutional Amendments made by the PCO and the 8th Amendment, that had given the President massive powers, inevitably led the President and the Prime Minister into conflict in two major areas; appointments of the Military Chiefs and the Supreme Court Judges.

The PPP though earned most of the seats in elections but could not have simple majority in the house. Ms. Bhutto entered into discussions with smaller parties to form a coalition government. Ultimately, the Mohajir Quami Movement (MQM) added its 13 seats to the PPP's. There were 237 seats in the National Assembly, of which 205 were contested and 30 seats were reserved for women and minorities. The PPP won 92 seats, and the IJI led by Nawaz Sharif won 55 seats. The results of the provincial elections gave PPP a majority in Sindh and NWFP only.

The IJI's control of Punjab was seen as a serious challenge to Bhutto's government. The Pakistan Muslim League (PML) was the dominant political party in Pakistan from 1986 until 29th May 1988 when Prime Minister M K Junejo was sent home. Soon after the death of Gen Ziaul Haq, the Pakistan Muslim League (PML) had broken into two factions; one led by Fida Muhammad Khan, the former governor of NWFP and Nawaz Sharif, the Chief Minister of Punjab.

After Benazir Bhutto's take over as prime minister, several early actions appeared to strengthen her ability to deal with rising problems. In choosing her cabinet, for example, Benazir kept the portfolios of finance and defence for herself but appointed a seasoned bureaucrat, Wasim Jafari, as her top adviser on finance and economic affairs. Her retention of Gen Ziaul Haq's foreign minister, Sahibzada Yaqub Khan, signalled continuity in pursuit of the country's policy on Afghanistan.

As stated above, MQM had agreed to support the PPP government at both federal and provincial levels. However, Benazir Bhutto was described as autocratic because she was inexorably tied to her father's political legacy, which included harsh repression of political opposition. Further, appointment of her mother, Nusrat Bhutto, as a senior minister without portfolio, followed by the selection of her father-in-law Hakim Ali Zardari as Chairman of the Public Accounts Committee, was viewed as ill-advised nepotism by Benazir Bhutto.

Benazir's government had also set up the controversial Placement Bureau, which made political appointments to the civil bureaucracy, although the bureau was later abolished. Benazir let the political legacy of her family intrude, for example, when the able public servants, who had earlier harboured disagreements with her father PM Zulfikar Ali Bhutto, were dismissed for reasons other than job performance or for personal score balancing games.

Benazir Bhutto narrowly survived a no-confidence motion in the National Assembly in October 1989. Her government did not compile a record of accomplishment that might have helped to offset her other difficulties. No new legislation was passed, except some minor amendments to existing legislation. Benazir Bhutto raised much hue & cry complaining that legislation was thwarted because the Senate was dominated by her opposition.

Benazir's problems were further accentuated in February 1990 when an MQM-directed strike in Karachi escalated into rioting that virtually paralyzed the city. The strike had been called to protest the alleged abduction of MQM supporters by the PPP. The resulting loss of life and property forced Benazir to call in the army to restore order. In addition to the violence in Sindh and elsewhere, she had to cope with increasing charges of corruption levelled not only at her associates, but at her husband Asif Ali Zardari and father-in-law Hakim Ali Zardari.

On the international front, Pakistan faced heightened tensions with India over Kashmir and problems associated with the unresolved Afghan war. All these miseries added in Benazir Bhutto's account continued building a rift between the two, president and the PM.

On **6th August 1990**, the President Ghulam Ishaq Khan levelled various charges including corruption and mal-administration, violations of the Constitution etc, dissolved the National Assembly, dismissed only 19 months old government of Benazir Bhutto under Article 58(2)(b) of the Constitution and ordered fresh elections. The conflict between the President and the Prime Minister had its drop scene. GIK said:

'His actions were justified because of corruption, incompetence, and inaction; the release of convicted criminals under the guise of freeing political prisoners; a failure to maintain law and order in Sindh; and the use of official government machinery to promote partisan interests.'

A nationwide state of emergency was declared, citing both "external aggression and internal disturbance." Benazir called her dismissal "illegal, unconstitutional, and arbitrary" and that the military was responsible.

The order of dissolution of Assemblies and Benazir Bhutto's government was challenged before all the four High Courts. However, the cases from Balochistan and Sindh were consolidated and heard by the High Court of Sindh at Karachi.

Likewise, the cases from NWFP and Lahore were consolidated and heard by the Lahore High Court. Both the High Courts in their separate judgments, distinguished *Haji Saifullah Khan's case* and upheld the order of dissolution of assemblies and observed that the President was justified in forming the opinion that the government of the Federation was not being carried on in accordance with the Constitution.

The matter came to the Supreme Court in appeal in the case reported as *Kh. Ahmed Tariq Rahim* v. *Federation of Pakistan* (**PLD 1992 SC 646**) but the Court refused to grant leave to appeal against the judgments of the High Courts and consequently the dissolution order was maintained.

Fresh elections were scheduled on 24th October 1990 and one Ghulam Mustafa Jatoi was appointed as the caretaker Prime Minister.

[*Benazir Bhutto immediately announced that her government was sacked by the army and the President GIK was the front man only. It was true; Gen Mirza Aslam Beg had played the main role from behind and it was true.*]

Relying upon *www.defencejournal.com* wherein an opinion is available under scripts of *July 1998:*

During Benazir Bhutto's first premiership from December 1988 till August 1990; despite the military's mistrust of the PPP, she was welcome in power after the PPP's visible victory in the general elections of November 1988. The PPP gained 92 seats (government & ISI sponsored IJI had got only 56 seats) so the prerogative to make government was allocated to Ms Bhutto. The 'Emergency Council', under the chair of Admiral Iftikhar Sarohi, Chief of Joint Staff Committee, formulated a charter of governance for her. The top conditions contained the following allowances for the military:

- To continue with President G Ishaq Khan for another term of 5 years, Gen Zia's loyalist who enjoyed the military's support;

- To keep Lt Gen Yaqub Ali Khan (Gen Zia's Foreign Minister) in her cabinet to ensure continuity in Afghan policy; and

- Not to touch the issue of defence expenditure whatsoever.

She agreed to admire military's role in restoring democracy and vowed to strengthen the armed forces by all means. The military budget continued to rise during her term, Afghan policy continued and nuclear program was kept on priority.

Benazir Bhutto's relations with the military soured, allegedly because of her unprofessional economic conduct and bitter confrontation with her political opponents that brought her administration to stand still. Senior army commanders got disturbed at growing civilian interference in the military's internal affairs especially relating with appointments and transfers, which are summarized below:

- The first dispute arose in May 1989, when Benazir Bhutto changed the DG ISI to reduce ISI's involvement in domestic politics. Army Chief Gen Mirza Aslam Beg reluctantly agreed, but was annoyed by her decision to appoint retired Maj Gen Shamas ur Rehman Kallue, an old friend of her late father Zulfikar Ali Bhutto.

- Gen Beg had also resented Benazir government's efforts to persuade Army for concessions to the officers who had been once removed from service for indiscipline after her father's execution in April 1979.

- A more serious row developed when the government unsuccessfully attempted to retire Admiral Iftikhar A Sirohi, Chairman of the Joint Chiefs of Staff Committee, in 1989 amidst interference with extension of some senior officers in mid 1990.

- Benazir Bhutto's wish to cultivate India's PM Rajiv Gandhi during his visits to Pakistan in December 1988 and July 1989 was seriously suspected. Army intelligence reports on dialogue between the two leaders had spoiled the whole image of Benazir Bhutto in military record posing her unreliable on security matters.

During 1989-90, serious law and order situation developed in Sindh on ethnic issues. Army troops were assisting Sindh's civilian authorities but refused to go beyond a certain point to settle scores against PPP's political opponents. Army had also once refused to take dictations from the Sindh and Federal governments. Army had demanded permission to set up the military courts and to restrict the superior judiciary's powers to enforce fundamental rights in areas under army control. As prime Minister Benazir Bhutto had refused.

A more serious blow to already strained civil-military relations had been seen because the Army Chief started releasing public statements on the Sindh situation in bitter tones. The political opponents of PPP brewed benefits out of this situation and moved nearer to the Army command by supporting their demands.

On the Judiciary's front: During 1990-91, Justice Mehboob Ahmed was the Chief Justice (CJ) Lahore High Court (LHC). Once in a meeting at Governor House Lahore, where Altaf Hussain Chaudhry, Governor Punjab, and Benazir Bhutto as Prime Minister were heading the meeting on issue of appointment of judges. Some vacancies of judges were lying vacant in LHC. CJ LHC briefed the meeting that:

> 'He (Chief Justice LHC Mehboob Ahmed) had sent some names to the previous Chief Minister Punjab Nawaz Sharif but no appointments were made. Now there are more vacancies because of two more retirements thus I'll send some fresh names.'

Benazir Bhutto told that there were some recommendations with her too.

CJ LHC Mehboob Ahmed immediately refused to take dictation without knowing about the names Ms Bhutto was going to forward. He told Ms Bhutto that only capable people would be taken whether they belong to the PPP or Muslim League. Ms Bhutto then asked the CJ to take some lady judges on list. The CJ LHC opined immediately that in Lahore Bar he was not able to find even a single woman to be a judge.

Ms Bhutto told about her political restraints but CJ Mehboob Ahmed had no such compulsion. The CJ categorically told Benazir Bhutto that he would not accommodate even a single name in the list already sent nor the President or the Prime Minister should compel him.

The meeting lasted for 90 minutes but CJ could not agree. Meeting ended and after some days CJ's services were transferred to the Federal Shariat Court as judge as per rules then prevailing since Gen Ziaul Haq's time. CJ Mehboob Ahmed had refused to go to the Federal Shariat Court but was sent home after three months. *(Ref: 'Adlia kay Urooj o Zawal ki Kahani' by Sohail Warraich 2007 P 186-87)*

A confrontation between Benazir Bhutto and Punjab Chief Minister Nawaz Sharif played a pivotal role in tarnishing civil-military relations. Both leaders were trying to let down each other in every administrative step taken by either side; thus mystification and doubt prevailed to high pitch; big leaders but having small minds.

During this tug of war Nawaz Sharif maneuvered to win the president GIK playing him against Benazir Bhutto. President, being the Supreme Commander of the army, criticized her political and economic managerial skills. The Troika broke down. President and the Army Chief joined hands and after taking the top brass in confidence through a Corps Commander's meeting in late July 1990, the President GIK sacked Benazir Bhutto on 6th August.

[*Earlier on 3rd June 1990, the President GIK rang up Adml Iftikhar Sarohi, the Chairman Joint Chiefs of Staff Committee, to visit him at his HQ. All the Chiefs of three wings were already there in connection with their own meeting so the President rushed in. Soon he started talking about Pakka Qila Operation of Hyderabad, escalating corruptions and some other political issues. As per military tradition, the Air Chief Hakeemullah floated his opinion first and concluded that* **'the PPP government is not going good'.** *The same types of briefings were given by the Naval Chief and Army Chief.*]

Since that day the President had started his home work to send Benazir Bhutto home.

Scenario 14

PAKISTAN: ISI RIGGED ELECTIONS:

Now a day much proclaimed news in the media from Prime Minister of Pakistan, Yusaf Raza Gilani that **'we are with our ISI; their functions and operations have government backing'** (Ref: media news of 28th April 2011). Till the recent past it was not the case. PPP had series of grievances with the ISI (Pakistan's Inter Services Intelligence, a military organ) though it could not be ascertained whether it was the ISI's role which caused complaints or PPP's own wrong choice of team selected at nepotism and not on the basis of their professional skills and competency. Let us go through some facts of our past history.

An American broadcaster Mark Corcoran presented his report in late 2001 describing that:

> *'Pakistan's feared Inter Services Intelligence Agency (ISI) is a maker and breaker of governments. As the Americans and their allies venture further into the quagmire of Afghanistan, they are dependant on the ISI to be their "eyes and ears" on the ground. The only problem is the ISI was until September 11, the Taliban's closest ally - in fact the agency was instrumental in bringing the Taliban to power.*
>
> *While General Musharraf has signed up on the side of the US, the ISI has other ideas. Already Musharraf has sacked his ISI boss (Lt Gen Mahmood Ahmed) for encouraging the Taliban to resist the US. (Former PM Benazir Bhutto tells Mr Mark that) the ISI is "a state within a state", and blames it for her own political demise. According to experts, the ISI has a track record of political assassination, state-sponsored terrorism, and drug running.'*

Starting from fifty years back; it has been generally perceived that the PM Z A Bhutto dragged the ISI in the politics. It is widely spread that it was Bhutto who had first time assigned political tasks to the ISI in Pakistan. It is not the whole truth. Actually it was the Field Marshal Ayub Khan who had used ISI to seek political motives during his presidential rule in the backdrop of his growing distrust in the Intelligence Bureau due to the presence of Bengali officers. When war broke out in Kashmir in mid 1965, Ayub Khan had started feeling a collapse of the operations of all the intelligence agencies including ISI because the agencies were concentrating on the surveillance of possible domestic political activities against him.

In the words of Wajid Shamsul Hassan:

> 'The covert infiltration plan in the Indian-occupied Kashmir, codenamed Operation Gibraltar – a brainchild of GHQ and ISI turned out to be an intelligence fiasco. According to analysts ISI had overestimated so-called "local support" to Pakistani commandos in Kashmir and underestimated the Indian response to the plan. The ISI's colossal failure got exposed when Operation Gibraltar met reverses and the Indians, in order to teach Gen Ayub Khan a lesson, broadened the theatre of war beyond Kashmir into Pakistani territory.
>
> What added insult to Gen Ayub Khan's injury was the failure of ISI to locate the Indian armoured division that had sneaked into a position when Lahore could have fallen to the Indian Army without much upheaval; as per authentic secret reports.'

In a top brass meeting, Gen Ayub Khan pulled up the then ISI chief Brig Riaz making him responsible for ISI's utter failure to locate a whole Indian armoured division that caused loss of hundreds of army commandos in the *Operation Gibraltar*. Brig Riaz flatly told that *'it was busy keeping surveillance on his political opponents'*.

Wajid Shamsul Hassan adds that:

> 'This was a slap on Gen Ayub Khan's face and he appointed a committee headed by Gen Yahya Khan to examine the working of the ISI and other intelligence agencies. The Committee found that ISI had been deeply involved in domestic politics and, had been devoting its time and energy in monitoring the activities of Gen Ayub Khan's political opponents'.

Since its first day of independence, the army intelligence units including ISI used to report to the Commander-in-Chief of the Army (C-in-C) as it was natural. After 1958's Martial Law all the intelligence agencies including Intelligence Bureau were made answerable to the President and Chief Martial Law Administrator. The intelligence agencies then started competing to demonstrate their loyalty to Gen Ayub Khan. All the agencies tried to over take each other in giving Ayub Khan a rosy picture of the country. They kept him in the dark about the freedom movement in former East Pakistan which ultimately disembarked.

ISI's role during Gen Ziaul Haq's rule is quite evident in Benazir Bhutto's autobiography *'Daughter of the East"* on how the martial law regime sought to suppress the PPP. The ISI not only kept tabs on the Bhutto family when they were in the country but also during their stay abroad. In one instance a Pakistani surveillance team attempted to keep track of Benazir Bhutto even while she was in political exile in London. She then telephoned Scotland Yard and complained about some men waiting outside her house. On their interception the intimidation ceased.

Benazir Bhutto had, however, known that the ISI had once lost its political importance when her father Z A Bhutto assumed power in 1972. He was very critical of its role during the 1970-71 general elections, which triggered off the events leading to the break up of Pakistan and creation of Bangladesh. [*Of course, she had also kept the knowledge that it was his father Z A Bhutto who had injected new blood in the ISI in 1975 and made it flag bearer secret organization for all future politico-armed moves taking place in Pakistan.*]

In early seventies ISI's Chief Gen Jilani gained confidence of the then PM Z A Bhutto by secretly telling him about the alleged conspiracy by Gen Gul Hassan to overthrow his government. This information, true or false, brought Gen Jilani nearer to Z A Bhutto and he had ensured that his confidante Gen Ziaul Haq succeeds Tikka Khan as Army Chief. Gen Ziaul Haq was given rapid and unprecedented promotions by Mr Bhutto thus had himself signed his death warrants.

[*Gen Ziaul Haq instead of remaining loyal to his benefactor decided to bite the hand that had fed him fat. He used his ISI to conjure an alliance of different political parties; got PNA formed and ignited a fake movement that looked real to topple the Prime Minister Z A Bhutto's government.*]

The same Gen Ghulam Jillani, being Governor Punjab later, had expressed apprehensions about being under surveillance by his own ISI, during Gen Ziaul Haq's regime. Gen Jilani had asked Brig Syed Ali Tirmazi, who was then serving as the Director in ISI Directorate, whether he was under surveillance. Gen Jillani was a father figure credited with nurturing the ISI rise from a peripheral to a powerful organisation in Pakistan. He had served as DG ISI in three regimes beginning with Gen Yahya Khan, PM Z A Bhutto and Gen Ziaul Haq. Like his predecessors, Gen Ziaul Haq too did not hesitate to use ISI for his political interests and provided a guide for future military dictators.

Gen Ziaul Haq became all powerful following his coup against Bhutto in July 1977. He expanded its role and made this organization responsible for collection of intelligence about the PPP, with a special focus on organizing ethnic and religious groups in order to divide Sindh's political power. A golden opportunity then cropped up for both Gen Ziaul Haq and ISI to become the sole arbiter of power in the region following the Soviet invasion of Afghanistan. He had Washington and London on their toes to help him to carry out their jihad.

However, with the withdrawal of the Soviet Union from Afghanistan his utility was over but leaving behind a new class of 'wealthy politicians' like Humayun Akhter and Ejaz ul Haq whose fathers had minted billions of dollars from American ammunition received for operations against the Russians in Afghanistan. Ojhri Camp episode is a case study in that respect which also has lessons for many.

Another father figure of the ISI, Lt Gen (Rtd) Hameed Gul, according to his confession, formed IJI to deny Benazir Bhutto an absolute majority in elections after air crashed death of Gen Ziaul Haq, to avert what he called 'democratic dictatorship'. Two sons of a pseudo industrialist Mian Sharif were selected to rule over Punjab. His accomplice, of course, was his boss Gen Aslam Beg who had conceded later before the Supreme Court of Pakistan on 16th June 1997 that he had distributed 140 million Rupees, secretly amongst the Bhutto's opponents to help PPP's defeat and ensuring IJI's victory in elections.

Air Marshall (Rtd) Asghar Khan was not the only voice challenging the role of ISI in the Supreme Court of Pakistan on the pretext of those Rs: 140 million scam. Benazir Bhutto had also made a committee to ascertain and review the role of Intelligent Agencies under the chair of AM (Rtd) Zulfiqar Ali Khan. When recommendations of the said Committee surfaced, Ms Bhutto was no more in her office of the PM. Later, when Lt Gen Hamid Gul, the then ISI Chief, was questioned about his involvement, he said that:

'If I had not formed the IJI, there would have been no general elections in the country because the smaller parties have been fearful of taking on the PPP individually.'

On 4th January 2010, Hamid Gul the former DG ISI, while speaking on a live TV program admitted that:

'He played a role in forming the Islami Jamhoori Ittehad (IJI) and any accountability of the issue should be started from him. The former

Prime Minister Nawaz Sharif was against self accountability; the Saifur Rehman Accountability Cell was one sided. The people had hoped that the then president Farooq Laghari would do justice through accountability, but he gave protection to journalists, Generals and judges. When he would be probed about the IJI formation, he would reveal the names of those politicians who requested the military leadership not to hold elections.'

To move further, lat us first have some glimpses of Lt Gen (Rtd) Hameed Gul through scripts available in media at occasions.

Lt Gen Hamid Gul used to call Gen Asif Janjua [who was the Army Chief next to Gen Aslam Beg] as his senior and friend but they were not at good relations with each other for at least two reasons. Firstly; Gen Asif Janjua once, during a Corps Commander's Meeting at the GHQ, said in Punjabi language that *'now we should roll back our nuclear program, we'll see it later,'* to which Gen Hamid Gul had instantly refuted by saying that *'what the hell are you talking about.'* The tone might have pinched more than words especially in a hall full meeting.

Secondly; the two Generals were having different views on the status of Northern Areas of Pakistan. Gen Asif Nawaz wanted to motivate politicians to take some decision on the status of the Northern Areas whereas Lt Gen Hamid Gul held the opinion that *'any such decision may extend loss to our stand on Kashmir Cause.'*

Referring to *'The Nation' of 15th December 2008,* the President Zardari had once described former ISI Chief Lt Gen Hamid Gul as 'more of a political ideologue of terror rather than a physical supporter' while giving an interview to the Newsweek in New York. He clarified that:

'Hamid Gul is an actor who is definitely not in our good books. Hamid Gul is somebody who was never appreciated by our government. He has not been accused in the Mumbai incident but he is more of a political ideologue of terror rather than a physical supporter. Pakistan's intelligence agencies are no longer backing outlawed groups like the Lashkar-e-Taiba. The links between the ISI and the LeT were developed in the old days when dictators used to run the country.

The government led by his PPP had always maintained a certain position that the intelligence agencies (should) have nothing to do with politics. Since the PPP in government, we held a stated position that ISI has no political role anymore.'

Referring to the *'Daily Times' dated 1st February 2008*, Gen (Rtd) Faiz Ali Chishti, who was heading the Pakistan Ex-Servicemen Society, which issued a blunt open letter signed by about 100 senior officers in early 2008, calling on Gen Musharraf to quit, should be taken in accounts first for being a willing and core partner in the military coup of Gen Ziaul Haq in July 1977. Gen Chishti once came on TV to explain why the army did not educate the nation. His answer was: *'if the roof is leaking why put good furniture in the room.'*

[*Gen (Rtd) A Majid Malik [who was a major in 1956 when he drafted a resignation by which Gen Ayub Khan forced President Iskandar Mirza to resign] should apologise for siding with Gen Musharraf when he took over the government in October 1999 and split the PML betraying Nawaz Sharif. He should be followed by Gen (Rtd) Mirza Aslam Beg for his role in the famous Mehran Bank scandal and misuse of ISI's huge and secret funds for electoral & political manipulation.*

Gen Beg should have apologised for bringing the Supreme Court in contempt when he admitted that he had influenced the chief justice. When confronted with challenging an army General, the Supreme Court under Justice Zullah got cold feet and let Gen Mirza Aslam Beg walk away free proudly and smilingly.

The biggest crime to which many retired Generals like Lt Gen Hamid Gul must confess, and then apologise for, is the policy of seeking 'strategic depth' in Afghanistan because the end results of this policy are now threatening the existence of Pakistan's unity on many counts.']

Nevertheless AM Zulfikar's findings were based on public admissions and statements by Generals Mirza Aslam Beg, Asad Durrani and Hamid Gul which were available to the people through media but no government considered them worth implementation.

Former President Ghulam Ishaq Khan (GIK)'s dismissal of the then PM Benazir Bhutto using his powers under Art 58(2)(B) on 6th August 1990 was a significant development highlighting the role of an intelligence agency in national politics. The reasons officially stated were charges of corruption, failure to work with the provinces and attempts to question the powers of the armed forces. Ms Bhutto contained that the ISI was involved against her government. The ISI as the 'eyes' and 'ears' of the military had influenced the President, the Supreme Commander of Armed Forces to take a decision against Benazir Bhutto.

The game had started from Benazir Bhutto's first day on political arena in September 1988, when the ISI then headed by Lt Gen Hamid Gul had paved together the opposition parties in Pakistan and formed the IJI in order to defeat PPP from coming to power. The then Chairman Senate and caretaker President GIK and the COAS Gen Beg were not keen on Benazir Bhutto's success in elections and they used all the available sources like ISI, the MI, the IB and the police special branches to keep her away from gaining political power. She was young and inexperienced thus was compelled to stick to certain conditions of the military leadership before taking oath as PM. Those conditions included:

- To continue the late Gen Ziaul Haq's Afghan policy, by keeping former Foreign Minister Yaqoob Ali Khan intact in the cabinet.
- Allow Gen Mirza Aslam Beg and Lt Gen Hamid Gul to continue in their appointments as Chief of Army Staff and Director General ISI respectively.
- Not to cut or depress the defence budget.
- Not to initiate any accountability proceedings against army personnel, serving or retired.

Benazir Bhutto, after taking over office of the PM, started feeling psychological problems carrying on the ISI and the IB with her because till a day earlier they were working against her person and party. Due to them her father was taken to the gallows against the people's wish. In tune with this mindset one of her first moves was to sack Brig Imtiaz from the ISI and close down its political division in early 1989. Lt Gen **Asad Durrani, a former Chief of ISI, held** a specific view on this act:

> 'In Operation 'Midnight Jackals' there was no role of ISI as such as an organisation. When Brig Imtiaz had performed that operation, the ISI had not allocated this task to him. Brig Imtiaz was in the ISI but he had performed that act in an independent capacity. In those days Benazir Bhutto was in power and Gen (Rtd) Kallue was the DG ISI.
>
> Brig Imtiaz had done a wrong job by betraying his organisation in which he was serving. He was sent back to his parent army unit from where he was punished later and was prematurely retired.'

Secondly, she appointed Major (Rtd) Masood Sharif, a close friend of her husband Asif Zardari as the Director IB, who was otherwise an incompetent and inexperienced later proved to be total failure to hold such an important and responsible assignment.

Benazir Bhutto soon developed serious differences with the ISI over its Afghan policy in early 1989 resulting a rift between the PM and the ISI leadership. The DG ISI Lt Gen Hamid Gul was relieved from office and a retired Lt Gen Shamsur Rehman Kallue, happened to be a close associate with Z A Bhutto, was appointed as new DG ISI. The COAS Gen Mirza Aslam Beg had transferred all the dossiers on political leaders and other records related to political intelligence from the ISI HQ to the MI. This move neutralised the appointment of Lt Gen Kallue as DG ISI and also taken away the effectiveness of ISI in political field.

[*This exercise was once again repeated in the Pakistan's history in 1999 when Nawaz Sharif appointed Gen Ziauddin, an officer from Engineering Corps, to take over ISI as the DG. The then Army Chief Gen Musharraf had taken out all functions and record concerning the 'political surveillance' & the Afghanistan related Operations from the ISI for onward placement at the disposal of MI Directorate in GHQ.*]

Benazir Bhutto then focussed on strengthening the role of the Intelligence Bureau (IB) for intelligence gathering within the country in order to marginalise the participation of the ISI but miserably failed. IB's budget was increased to four times the previous figure, 20 senior positions at the joint director level were created and subordinate level staff was increased thrice to strengthen the management structure but all resources went in vain because the Director IB, Masood Sharif, a young retired major, was lacking all the management and professional skills who misused the huge budget on re-employing young retired captains and colonels with zero experience of intelligence work.

IB under the command and control of Maj (Rtd) Masood Sharif became another organisation of army but of retired and redundant young lads. Naturally, they were not in a position to see eye-in-eye towards their seniors who had once sent them home when they were not found fit for promotions beyond the ranks of captains or majors.

IB under Masood Sharif's charge had gone so lethargic that on 17th July 1989 an army intelligence wing under COAS had clandestinely recorded the conversation between Prime Minister Benazir Bhutto and the Indian PM Rajiv Gandhi while the latter was on a state visit to Pakistan. The room was bugged by the army intelligence agency. The transcriptions later disclosed that the two leaders in the course of their private meeting at Islamabad had discussed, among other issues, the possibility of mutual troop reduction in India & Pakistan.

Benazir Bhutto had agreed in principle to the proposal of reducing the respective army ranks. Soon after the Chief of Army Staff Gen Aslam Beg and President GIK met each other on 24th July 1989 and decided to topple the Benazir Bhutto's government. In order to convince the Opposition and obtain their backing for the need to destabilise the government the recorded tapes were played to them. The IJI, after hearing tapes, opted to plant a no-confidence move in the Parliament against Benazir Bhutto.

Masood Sharif's IB kept sleeping and they could not get even the air of the whole episode. When the news of no-confidence motion caught air in media, Masood Sharif's IB planned another disgusting 'operation' to keep Benazir Bhutto on their positive side.

In this backdrop, Masood Sharif's IB had planned their **'Operation Midnight Jackals'**, a much trumpeted affair in the history of IB. The said operation had started with one Arif Awan a PPP activist and MNA from Shiekupura district, who pretended to offer him for sale in order to penetrate into the group of decision makers of the IJI. MNA Arif Awan became a PPP 'plant' aimed at neutralising the hostile strategy of the IJI. The IJI pushed their team comprising of Malik Naeem, Senator Gulsher Khan, Brigadier (retd) Imtiaz, Major Aamer and Arif Awan's nephew in FIA Malik Mumtaz into the game who initially contacted PPP's Arif Awan.

Soon MNA Arif Awan started attending IJI's meetings. Mr Awan also got initial success in recording conversations between members of the group from 28th September – 6th October 1989 at his nephew Malik Mumtaz's residence. The plan of action was for Arif Awan along with three other PPP MNAs to offer to become *'lotas'* and a deal was clinched against Rs 5 million. On their part the PPP MNAs promised to vote along with the Combined Opposition Parties MNAs in forthcoming no-confidence motion. The deal also assured that one of the *'lotas'* would be made a Federal Minister if the IJI proved successful in its venture.

In the proposed no-confidence move of 1st November 1989, the attempt failed but both the teams decided to remain intact for next years move. Benazir Bhutto accused the ISI and unknowingly attributed the blame to them for this move of no-confidence. She might not know the actual number game being manipulated by her own IB team. In the meantime, the details of the said 'Operation Midnight Jackals' were picked up by the media, possibly through a Peshawar based correspondent, thus causing another blow to PPP's cause.

Amidst all these rifts and misunderstandings, ultimately, President GIK had opted to send Benazir Bhutto home on the flimsy charges of corruption and mal-administration which were never proved. There were well documented stories in news media that the President GIK had taken that decision on the advice of the GHQ since coming in pipeline from the days they had caught conversation of Benazir Bhutto with Rajiv Gandhi as detailed earlier. Lt Gen Asad Durrani, the former ISI Chief, in his interview published in daily *'Jang' dated 7th March 1999* had dispelled that impression saying that:

> *'Benazir Bhutto's first government was dismissed by the President himself and army had no contribution in it. Even the army could only get air of it about 10 days earlier through secret means. When he came to know about it being incharge MI, he had immediately rushed to the Army Chief Gen Beg and told him about the source report. Gen Beg had said: it was in his knowledge that the President was not happy with BB but astonishing that GIK would go so hard against her.'*

ISI's play in general elections of Pakistan was not ended with Benazir Bhutto's political demise in 1990, it continued thereafter too.

Referring to an interview published **on 24th February 2008 in The News,** a daily English newspaper of Pakistan, Maj Gen Ehtesham Zamir, the head of the ISI's political cell in 2002, admitted manipulating the elections of 2002 *'at the behest of President Musharraf and termed the defeat of the King's party, the PML(Q), this time a reaction of the unnatural dispensation (installed in 2002).'* He categorically emphasized that the ISI together with the NAB was instrumental in pressing the lawmakers to join Gen Musharraf to form the government and to help the military dictator stay in power.

Looking down back into the memory lane and recalling his blunders which, Maj Gen Ehtesham admittedly pushed the country back instead of taking it forward, later felt ashamed of his role and conduct. He was massively embarrassed because he was the one who negotiated, coerced and did all the dirty work for PML(Q) on orders of Gen Musharraf.

Another reference pointing towards (mis)deeds of ISI was published on 24th February 2008, in SUN of India, under the title *'Major General who rigged Pakistan 2002 polls, spills the beans'* written by Sahil Nagpal, in which Gen Zamir was quoted confirming that corruption cases were used as pressure tactics to change the loyalties of the lawmakers but:

"This tool was used not only by the ISI. The NAB was also involved in this exercise [of arm-twisting the politicians]."

[*General elections held on 10th October 2002 were stolen and rigged in favour of PML(Q) on the orders of Gen Musharraf. The history would remember that Gen Musharraf's Principal Secretary Tariq Aziz was given the assignment to deliver a pro-Musharraf parliament. To fulfil this assignment, Tariq Aziz made blanket use of Inter-Services Intelligence (ISI) and the rogue National Accountability Bureau (NAB). Gen Musharraf's aides, as well as PML(Q) leaders, termed the opposition leaders' statements as baseless and a lame excuse not to admit their defeat in those black dotted general elections.*

Despite the 'riggings' in the 2002 elections, PML(Q) could bag only 69 out of 272 general seats. Therefore, Gen Musharraf had suspended for three days the constitutional clause pertaining to floor-crossing with the result that PML(Q) was able to form the government in the centre with Mir Zafrullah Jamali, a gentle politician from Balochistan, as Prime Minister of Pakistan.]

The fact remains that the intensity of anti-Musharraf vote did not give the government machinery and the Chaudhrys of Gujrat [Ch Shuja'at Hussain & Ch Pervez Elahi] enough space to carry out massive rigging, however, the ISI managed to do it selectively and a bit more discretely to give some respectability to PML(Q), the friends of Gen Musharraf.

Later, Lt Gen Jamshed Gulzar Kiyani had also disclosed that majority of the corps commanders, in several meetings, had opposed Musharraf's decision of patronising the Chaudhrys. Gen Musharraf was repeatedly told that the PML(Q) leaders were the worst politicians who were thoroughly involved in co-operative scandals and writing off loans but he never heard their advice. One of Gen Musharraf's colleagues, who were Chief of the NAB at that time, had even sought permission to put dog collar around the necks of Chaudhrys but he was always refused permission to proceed against them despite his insistence.

The disclosures made by Generals Gulzar Kiyani and Ehtesham Zamir should serve as eye openers for the nation and future planners of the Army rule in Pakistan. Though the elections of 2008 were described as fairer than 2002, Gen Zamir could not rule out the possibility of 2008 polls being rigged. According to a generally held view, COAS General Ashfaq Kiyani had ensured army's non-interference in polls that is why there was comparatively less institutional interference of intelligence agencies in 2008 as compared to the last time in 2002.

The tragedy remained that the PPP was found repeating the same mistake by going on nepotism, favouritism, bias, partiality and discrimination ignoring merit and more.

On 2nd May 2011 evening, PPP ultimately joined hands with PML(Q) and offered them 18 slots in executive allocating them different assignments, mostly carrying ministerial perks. The young generation knows them little from days of Gen Musharraf when they remained in shared power with a military ruler but more after assassination of Ms Benazir Bhutto who had nominated them as her 'killers'. However, PML(Q) has its own history; who brought them in power and how were they favoured, is altogether a different scenario. What has been the role of ISI in that political manoeuvring can be understood from various archived essays.

(Part of this essay stands Published at www.Criticalppp.com (LUBP) on 01st May 2011)

Scenario 15

ISI RULED POLITICS OF 1990S:

[**Note:** *Some lines of this essay belong to SAT since died in Nov 2005. After correcting certain facts, it is being placed here to keep the history in tact and sequence.*]

In early 2011, the relationship between PPP and MQM were once more established (though only lasted for few months again) despite the bitter accusations on each other many times and on many counts throughout our political history. The general perception prevails that MQM was given birth and nurtured by Gen Ziaul Haq through Karachi Wing of the ISI in early 1980s just to counter or suppress the nationalist voices then raised by G M Syed, his associates and other similars. Whether it is true or not MQM people can better guide us.

The fact remains that in all the previous governments, civil or military, ISI had always been labelled with charges of playing important role in Pakistan's politics. However, ISI contributed much less in 2010-11 being least interested in breaking or repairing PPP-MQM relationships.

Testifying before the Supreme Court on 16th June 1997, in a petition filed by Air Marshal (retd) Asghar Khan, former chief of the Pakistan Air Force, had challenged the legality of Pakistan's Inter Services Intelligence (ISI)'s Political Division accepting a donation of Rs.140 million from Mehran Bank for use against PPP candidates during elections. Gen (retd) Mirza Aslam Beg, former Chief of the Army Staff (COAS), had affirmed that the ISI was (and is) manned mainly by serving army officers. It was a part of the Ministry of Defence then and it used to report to the Prime Minister and not to the COAS.

Contrarily, many Pakistani analysts correctly understand that the ISI, though *de jure* remained under the Prime Ministers during the political regimes but had always been controlled *de facto* by the COAS and that its internal Political Division had been in existence at least since the days of Gen Ayub Khan. Formally floated in 1948, ISI was purely a military organisation by objectives. It was Pakistan's first military ruler Gen Ayub Khan, who in late 1950s expanded its role to keep an eye on politicians but their reports were never made known to media or even to discuss in high level army meetings. It was for the personal knowledge of the Army Chief perhaps.

It may not be out of place to mention that the first martial law in the country was actually manoeuvred by the ISI in 1958. The nuisance of Military take over was started by the ISI while forcing Gen Ayub Khan to topple the government of Iskandar Mirza and thus paving way for Gen Ziaul Haq and then Gen Musharraf to launch their respective takeovers in succeeding years of 1977 and 1999.

Immediately after 7th October 1958, the day Iskandar Mirza had taken over the government with the help of Field Marshall Ayub Khan, the then Commander in Chief of Pakistan Armed Forces, a plan was chalked out to upset the original take over plan. Col K M Azhar (later became General & Governor NWFP) the Acting Director ISI had caught air of that upset plan. One Brig Qayyum of 51 Brigade had called Col Azhar of ISI that he had received a telephone call from 'high ups' to cancel the original plan of 7th October and act as per new plan. Col Azhar asked him to come to ISI HQ in person. Brig Qayyum reached there and told that he had received instructions from Gen Musa Khan to act at new plan.

Acting Director of ISI Col Azhar soon picked the conclusion that it was a fake call as Gen Musa was based at Rawalpindi those days. When the ISI secretly investigated the 'source of orders' it revealed that there existed no replacement plan; the call was actually fake. The matter was immediately brought in the notice of C-in-C Gen Ayub Khan.

Without taking formal approval from the CinC, ISI conveyed CinC's implied consent and the investigation was extended to senior army officers like Gen Hamid, Gen Yahya Khan, Gen Musa and Iskandar Mirza because these four were perspective beneficiaries of the new game plan. All were subjected through flip-flop interrogation; ISI eliminated the first three officers and Iskandar Mirza was declared as the only and prime suspect.

During the same days, one Air Commodore Abdul Rab received another similar phone call that 'the high ups want that you go and arrest so & so three senior army officers and report back'. AC Abdul Rab told Col Azhar of ISI about the suspicious call because how an Air Force officer could arrest the senior army officers. When Gen Ayub Khan came back from East Pakistan's tour, he was told about that later development also.

Conclusion: Gen Ayub Khan was suggested that Iskandar Mirza was using him as a tool and as a yes-sir man, breaking up the cabinet; changing the PM at its own and wanted to push out key Generals to go sovereign powerful person. Gen Ayub Khan was not agreeing to take any action and had discarded ISI's briefings. Col Azhar of the ISI then went to senior army officers and pumped them against Iskandar Mirza. Ultimately Gen Azam, Gen Yahya, Gen Hamid and Gen Burky went to Gen Ayub Khan, asked him to take over the government from Mr Mirza while announcing Chief Martial Law Administrator himself.

Field Marshall Ayub Khan had refused to accommodate his four senior Generals but ultimately surrendered because all the four had threatened to resign collectively. Then these four Generals went to Iskandar Mirza and asked him to step down voluntarily if he wanted pension and other benefits. Later it surfaced that those two phone calls were manipulated by Col Azhar of ISI himself and also pumped the senior Generals to take share of the booty.

ISI had played his first game successfully in which Col Azhar used all the above mentioned fabricated and concocted reports by putting guns on the shoulders of one Brig Qayyum and AC Abdul Rab. He was perhaps having some personal grudge against Iskandar Mirza for which he had also spread some fake stories of Naheed Mirza's corruption in the army circles using ISI network.

Gen Ayub Khan had issued the first notification for its changing role after his successful military coup of October 1958 thereby providing that the organisation would be directly answerable to the President of Pakistan. As per constitutional provisions then available it was unfair and illegal but no body raised voice for this unlawful government directive; neither in any court or otherwise. Later, the role of internal Political Division of ISI was redefined making it more assertive set up within the organisation by Prime Minister Z A Bhutto in 1975. Since then the ISI has been performing that role assertively as one can see now.

One can recall an interview of Maj Gen (Rtd) Ghulam Umar published in *daily 'Jang' dated 20th September 1998*, who had told that:

> "Yes! ISI and MI have been playing [role in Pakistani politics]. In Z A Bhutto's days, the political wing was reinforced. During previous eras the ISI had been doing political jobs but not in a way that 'this particular desk would only do political job, not at all'. Such orders affect the organizational ability of ISI. In our days, the ISI was such that if a Division Commander of Deccan in India was ordered to move out to Kashmir, the news reached us before the notification was received by that Div Commander who had been ordered to move."

It was pity that A M Asghar Khan's petition went almost undecided through unwarranted and undue delay. Still it is pending with the SC for want of decision. Two former Air Chiefs' condemnations of ISI are available on the court's record. The charge of maneuvering of three general elections in which the people of Pakistan were deceived and cheated thrice had been so momentous that delaying action on it should have been taken as criminal negligence on the part of judges sitting on the helm of affairs.

More instances to be recalled; the conspiracy to divide MQM was initiated during Benazir Bhutto's first regime but took concrete shape later. At that time Lt Gen Asif Nawaz Janjua was Corps Commander Karachi and was keen on eliminating the anti-state elements including MQM. The MQM leader Altaf Hussain got smell of the army's plans to split his party in February 1991. Thereafter, on 2nd March 1991 he had expelled 19 members from his party because they were holding contacts with ISI and MI. [*The same group later developed itself as the MQM-Haqiqui and started its political activity independently*]

Altaf Hussain, the MQM Chief, had complained to the then President that the ISI was conspiring to divide the MQM. During May 1991 a couple of prominent MQM leaders were killed in Karachi by masked gunmen. The foreign electronic media, though having no evidence, had speculations that those MQM leaders were shot by some intelligence personnel alleging the ISI.

On 21st August 1991, the split in MQM formally took place during a convention of the MQM (Haqiqui) wherein Amir and Afaq, two activists of MQM and close buddies of Altaf Hussain, had expelled their own leader and founder from the party. This split was defined as between Mohajirs of Uttar Pradesh origin (in Altaf Hussain's MQM) and those of Bihar origin in the splinter anti-Altaf Hussain group called MQM (Haquiqi). In Altaf Hussain's MQM itself, the ISI did try to create a gulf between the Sunni and Shia migrants from Uttar Pradesh but remained unsuccessful, it was generally perceived.

Altaf Hussain of MQM, once known as a product of 'secret agencies', had accused ISI of this split and for massive violations of human rights in Karachi. The whole anti-MQM operation by the Army on 19th June 1992 and onwards had helped destroy Karachi's economy. Politics was tarnished, stained and got a bad image. The media propaganda against MQM (that the party harbours criminals and is not patriotic) was true or false but were the 'agencies' a right antidote of such accusations.

When the MQM of Altaf Hussain lead a revolt in late 1980s in Karachi Division, Hyderabad and Sukkur (three main cities of Sindh province), the ISI allegedly provided equipment and arms to certain sections of the Sindhi nationalist elements to kill *Mohajirs* to leave a lesson for many. No proof in that context anyway.

After assuming office of the prime minister on 19th November 1990, Nawaz Sharif promoted the DG ISI Maj Gen M Asad Durrani and hunted to reverse the Benazir Bhutto regime's move to downsize the ISI. The next logical step was to reduce the importance of the IB which Benazir Bhutto had strengthened against ISI to deal with the internal and political intelligence. Nawaz Sharif was heading the IJI-led government in which MQM was also included.

Soon an issue cropped up when the PM opted to spy on their alliance partners especially the MQM which they came to know in December 1990. The IB had installed bugging devices in the rooms of all MNAs of MQM including their parliamentary leader named Aminul Haq. This brought a major embarrassment for the ruling IJI because MQM was an important ally at that time. Nawaz Sharif, however, handled the issue, offered apologies admitting mistake amidst explanations of misunderstanding but the distances set to widen.

Once, during Benazir Bhutto's second tenure of 1993-96, Opposition leader Nawaz Sharif had released secretly recorded tapes of a conversation to gain political advantage against her. These tapes contained a conversation between NWFP Chief Minister, Aftab Sherpao and top officials of Mehran Bank as 'conclusive evidence of horse-trading' in order to challenge the PML government of CM Sabir Shah on 1st December 1994.

This time again, the game was played between two political rivals and ISI had no hand in it.

In the Pakistan's history, there have been three instances when Directors ISI were at daggers drawn with their own boss Army Chiefs. The first instance was during the first tenure of Ms Benazir Bhutto as Prime Minister (1988 to 1990). To reduce the powers of the ISI, to re-organise the intelligence community and to enhance the powers of the police officers in the IB, she discontinued the practice of appointing a serving General as DG ISI. Instead she appointed Maj Gen (retd) Shamsur Rahman Kallue, a retired officer close to her father, as the DG in replacement of Lt Gen Hamid Gul in 1989 and entrusted him with the task of winding up political wing of the ISI.

The role of collection of internal intelligence was then entrusted to IB providing them more powers and funds. But the IB was proved a total failure under the command of one retired major Masood Sharif, a classmate and friend of her husband Asif Ali Zardari; the details are available in all leading articles of those times. Writing in *'the Nation' of 31st July 1997, Brig A R Siddiqui*, who had served as the Press Relations Officer in GHQ said that:

> *'This action of hers marked the beginning of her trouble with Gen Mirza Aslam Beg, the COAS, which ultimately led to her dismissal in August 1990. Gen Beg made Maj Gen Kallue persona non grata (PNG) and stopped inviting him to the Corps Commanders conferences. Not only confined to the dismissal of the government, Gen Beg made sure that PPP should not earn enough seats in the Parliament in the forthcoming elections.'*

Gen Beg had distributed Rs: 140 million amongst the IJI and PML candidates on which the above referred A M Asghar Khan's petition cropped up in the SC.

> [*Gen Mirza Aslam Beg had given a press statement in early 1994 that Younus Habib of Mehran Bank had collected Rs: 140 million from the Business Community of Karachi for general elections of 1990. That money was handed over to the ISI which was distributed by them further. Lt Gen Asad Durrani, then DG ISI, was asked in 1995 to submit a statement in that respect before a judicial tribunal. Lt Gen Asad Durrani sent the details available on record to the judicial tribunal with a copy to the then PM Benazir Bhutto. In 1996, Benazir Bhutto presented that letter in the Parliament; it was her prerogative.*]

It was then generally presumed that Lt Gen Durrani was an 'inner associate' of Benazir Bhutto. The PML and Nawaz Sharif had openly said that he had helped the PPP through 'engineered elections of 1993'. It was a wrong allegation. Lt Gen Durrani was retired from service on 3rd May 1993 whereas the general elections of 1993 were held in October. How much an ordinary citizen could affect the general elections of a country to be labelled as 'engineered'. However, Gen Durrani's association with PPP was a fact because soon after Benazir Bhutto's take over, he was sent to Germany as an ambassador, a well deserved slot after retirement.

Coming back; the second instance was during the first tenure of Nawaz Sharif (1990-93), who appointed Lt Gen Javed Nasir as DG ISI, a fundamentalist Kashmiri officer, against the recommendations of the then COAS for the post. Gen Asif Nawaz Janjua, the then COAS, also made Lt Gen Nasir a PNG like Gen Kallu in the previous regime, banned his entry in GHQ and extended the same harsh treatment to him.

During her second tenure (1993-96), Benazir Bhutto avoided any conflict with Gen Abdul Waheed Kakkar and Gen Jehangir Karamat, the Chiefs of the Army Staff in succession, on appointment of the DG ISI. Her action in transferring part of responsibility for operations in Afghanistan including handling of the Taliban, from the ISI to the Federal Interior Ministry headed by Major Gen (retd) Nasirullah Babar, who used to lever Afghan operations in the ISI during the tenure of her father, did not create any friction with the army since she had ordered that Lt Gen Musharraf, the then DG Military Operations, should be closely associated by Major Gen Babar in the Afghan operations.

However, certain dissident and hired trained men of the ISI, said to be close to Farooq Leghari, the then President of Pakistan, were allegedly involved in the assassination of Murtaza Bhutto, the surviving brother of Benazir Bhutto, outside his house in Karachi on 20th September 1996, with the complicity of few local police officers and started a disinformation campaign in the media blaming her husband Asif Zardari for that murder. This campaign was proved to be lethal for her dismissal by President Farooq Leghari in November 1996.

The third instance was during the second tenure of Nawaz Sharif (1997-99) when his action of appointing Lt Gen Ziauddin as the DG ISI, over-riding the objections of Gen Musharraf, led to the first friction between the two. Lt Gen Ziauddin was an engineer by profession and had zero experience in intelligence gathering. He was given this slot only having one merit that he was a Kashmiri clan brother of Nawaz Sharif. Gen Musharraf transferred Lt Gen Aziz, the then Deputy DG ISI, to the GHQ as the CGS and transferred the entire political surveillance wing to him as per previous exercise of Benazir Bhutto's days.

Gen Musharraf, as COAS, made Lt Gen Ziauddin PNG as per previous practice and stopped inviting him to the vital Corps Commanders conferences. Lt Gen Ziauddin also proved himself unfit because he could not even smell the planning and implementation of the Kargil operations for his boss Nawaz Sharif though it was spread over eight months.

But otherwise, during his second tenure Prime Minister Nawaz Sharif had used the ISI in an ill-effective manner to investigate financial dealings abroad by various politicians and bureaucrats particularly those of Benazir Bhutto and her husband. Those investigations included major contracts signed with foreign companies like Cotecna & CSG and the kick-backs deposited in Swiss Bank accounts. This exercise was carried out in rogue association with one Hasan Waseem Afzal, then Director Ehtesab Bureau, spending millions of dollars from secret funds of ISI for which no accounts were ever submitted.

The critics maintain that to that extent, the ISI was misused under Lt Gen Ziauddin because the said task was of Ehtesab Bureau or more precisely belonged to FIA's jurisdiction alone and not of an intelligence agency. Nawaz Sharif had realised this anomaly later and that is why he was planning to open a new intelligence wing in the FIA in that connection but his government collapsed after wasting millions of dollars by that pseudo-bureaucrat who was purely performing the political job on behalf of PML.

During the last months of Nawaz Sharif's regime, various intelligence agencies were working against each other. The DG ISI used to send reports to the PM (but was under the COAS for organisational control) whereas the DG MI reported to the COAS. In the process the political and military leaderships were at loggerheads with each other and competition between their respective intelligence agencies only proved to be purely extension of clash of interests.

Daily *'the Nation' of 28th June 1997* had once commented on the ISI involvement in the Mehran Bank scandal that:

> 'The case has amply attracted public attention on what is widely perceived to be a government within a government. They (ISI's) are virtually autonomous while playing role in the political affairs of the country. The baneful influence of the intelligence agencies of Pakistan has spread its malign shadow over the political destiny of the country.'

Reportedly, a 105 pages report on the lack of utility of Pakistan's strong intelligence community, was also prepared by old and experienced intelligence officers and submitted to the then DG ISI in October 1998 but its contents were never made public.

The above narrations are sufficient to reflect that whenever an elected leadership was in power in Pakistan, whether of PPP or of PML, the then serving Chiefs Of Army Staff had formulated their own operational policies. The elected Prime Ministers did not have effective control over the ISI and that the ISI, as an organization, was cornered or marginalised every time if its head appeared to show any loyalty to that elected Prime Minister of whatever political party.

(Published at www.Pakspectator.com on 13th August 2011 as 'ISI Foot-balled in Politics')

Scenario 16

JUDICIARY: NAWAZ SHARIF RESTORED (1993)

From the first day of Pakistan, the judges have been trying to match their constitutional ideas and legal language to the exigencies of on going politics. This has been the most favourite line of action. Judiciary has largely remained a tool in the hands of the rulers. As a matter of fact, various judgments of the higher judiciary pertaining specially to the validity of martial laws have made us a laughing stock in the world. The imposition of martial laws, abrogation and suspension of constitutions were acts of treason but who bothers in poor countries.

Roedad Khan, a former bureaucrat in his book *'Pakistan-A Dream Gone Sour'* has highlighted this important issue which has been hunting the nation for the last fifty years. He questioned:

'Where does the sovereignty reside in Pakistan? The higher judiciary in Pakistan created history' by validating the imposition of martial law by Ziaul Haq and granted him the right to amend the constitution. All the nine judges were a party to this. (Then giving more details of various feats performed by the higher judiciary, he continues to say worriedly) ...... where revolution is successful, it satisfies the test of efficacy and becomes a basic law creating fact was the observation on Gen Ayub's martial law.

This ruling legitimized not only Ayub's usurpation of power but opened the flood gates for others. Yahya's usurpation of power was declared illegal when he was no longer there. The Provisional Constitutional Order of 1982 was the climax to humiliate the higher judiciary which largely accepted it. Again in Junejo's case, the judgment came after the usurper was gone. Nawaz Sharif's restoration is another example. 'Gen. Waheed distanced himself from the president, his benefactor, and joined the crowd in running him down'.

Roedad Khan described it 'improper' that the military brass summoning Ghulam Ishaq Khan, the then Chairman Senate, to the Army GHQ after the crash of Gen Ziaul Haq on 17th August 1988. The proper course was that the top military hierarchy should have gone to him.

One excuse that judges speak for their weakness is that in Pakistan, the executive exercises control over the courts by using the system of judicial appointments, promotions and removals to ensure its allies fill key posts. But it is true for most of the third world countries.

As per *Robertson and Nicol:* (Ref: **Robertson & Nicol, Media Law, 3rd Edition, [1992] p 298**).

> *"..............in certain commonwealth countries there does exist an unhealthy relationship between the judges and the Government that appoints them..."*

Pakistan is also among the list of same third world countries and considers itself as member of commonwealth, so there should be no surprise if the above statements are applicable here too.

In the immediate aftermath of the October 1999 coup, the judiciary was purged of judges who might have opposed the military's unconstitutional assumption of power. The purge was accomplished by requiring judges to take an oath to Gen Musharraf's Provisional Constitutional Order — an oath that required judges to violate oaths they had all previously taken to uphold the 1973 Constitution. An element of fear that another oath would be used to remove more judges, had limited the bench's freedom. In addition, new judges were mostly found scared because the executive could follow a generally prevailing practice of removing them after a year or two by declining to 'confirm' their appointments.

An episode from the recent judicial history of Pakistan: During the hearing of Haji Saifullah's writ petition against the then president of Pakistan on the issue of dissolution of National Assembly in August 1990, Gen Mirza Aslam Beg, on 4th February 1993, briefed the national press and electronic media that:

> '*I did try to convey to the Honorable Supreme Court that, we had given a solemn undertaking to the nation that elections to the National Assembly would be held according to the schedule already announced and that, therefore, it would be in the best interest of the nation and the country that we stick to our promise and the said general elections were allowed to be held accordingly.*'

Tragedy is that it lies on record of the Supreme Court of Pakistan in the form of a statement given by Gen Mirza Aslam Beg himself in person that (when the former COAS was asked whether his above narrated action did not constitute contempt of court)':

'I definitely did not think so as the information sought to be conveyed in good faith and in national interest.'

On 20th February 1993, during preliminary proceedings, the Supreme Court censured Gen Beg for giving an 'irresponsible and careless' answer to the question asked by the press on 4th February, and remarked: 'we are very sorry to hand over the defence of the country to a person if he was so careless.' On 21st February 1993, the Supreme Court formally charged Gen Aslam Beg with contempt of court. When the trial started, Gen Beg met with the then COAS, General Waheed Kakar and through him assured President and the army leadership that he would not damage their image. *(Ref; 'The Govt of Agencies' [in Urdu] by Azhar Sohail Page 106)*

The CJ Nasim H Shah, in later moments, had also observed that:

"I do not change my opinion, even if Allah the Almighty directed me to do so."

Yet again, on 22nd February 1993, the Chief Justice addressed the reporters and respondent in anger that:

"If you fail to produce the tapes, I shall blacken many faces; I shall ensure that I send some of you to your graves and hell." (Quoted verbatim from the *'daily Dawn' of 2nd March 1993*)

Referring to A S Ghazali's book on internet: On 1st March, Gen Beg stated before the Court that the then Chairman Senate Waseem Sajjad had carried his message to the Supreme Court to block restoration of Junejo's assembly. Mr Waseem Sajjad had denied Gen Beg's statement.

Despite all the lengthy hearing in detail, stunning remarks of the Chief Justice and making the former army chief face bullshits, what happened in the end, Gen Mirza Aslam Beg was let off by 'a weary but thoroughly indignant' Supreme Court with a conviction without a sentence. On appeal, even that conviction was overturned by the same Supreme Court.

In another judgment the Court decided on 9th January 1994, to drop even that punishment against Gen Mirza Aslam Beg.

Commenting on the judgment, *The Friday Times Lahore of 11th April 1996* had thrown its candid opinion that:

'....... the (Supreme) Court was humiliated during the contempt of court hearing against Gen Mirza Aslam Beg because it knew that it

couldn't punish an army general. People made fun of Chief Justice Zullah's eccentric obiter dicta, and a witness called him corrupt inside the court.' [What a tribute to the judiciary it was]

Referring to 'Building Judicial Independence in *Pakistan: Asia Report No: 86'* published by US State Department (on Human Rights practices in Pakistan) on 9th November 2004, it is on record that:

' ..... *The superior judiciary (in Pakistan) is unable to address creeping financial corruption within its own ranks. Dysfunction in the superior judiciary also impedes reform in Pakistan's subordinate judiciary, which comprises the trial courts in which the mass of ordinary judicial business is transacted. Appalling under-resourcing and endemic corruption in the subordinate judiciary lead to agonizing delays in the simplest cases and diminish public confidence in the judiciary and the rule of law'.*

In some subject-areas and in some territories, the government simply bypasses the ordinary courts by establishing parallel judiciaries. Since as early as August 1947, the Federally Administered Tribal Areas (FATA) and the Northern Areas have had *sui generis* legal systems, more or less independent of Pakistan's ordinary judiciary. Little justification exists, as even the government seems to recognize, for the essentially colonial regimes preserved in these enclaves.

In 1997 and 1999 respectively, the respective governments established separate anti-terrorism and accountability courts and tribunals. Those tribunals contained procedural shortcuts that made them too attractive to zealous police and prosecutors. It had never been realized that in the absence of state commitment to reform constitutional ground rules and statutory laws, judges would continue to lack security of tenure and necessarily would do and announce decisions with an eye to the government's agenda.

The same sentiments can be felt in an article captioned as 'Pakistan Corruption's Trap' written by A Masroor, published in The *Pakistan Observer of 4th March 2005.* It says that:

'President Musharraf, in order to keep the genuine politicians out of the 2002 Parliament, had manipulated the electoral laws in such a way that it was not difficult for the unscrupulous to find the electoral loopholes. And during his rule President Musharraf has inducted so many retired and serving armed forces personnel into the civilian set-

up that the performance of the elected governments of the 1990s in doling out Government jobs to their party workers pales into insignificance.

The judiciary is completely at the mercy of the executive. The Pakistan Bar Council has already expressed its no confidence in the superior judiciary refusing to seek its help against the high-handedness of the executives or attempts by the military ruler to redraft the constitution to suit his agenda. Parliament is so weak that it has gone to the extent of passing facilitating a non-elected, in-service Army General to become the President of the country'.

There was a time when Judges in the Judiciary were very fond of taking *Suo-Moto* Notices particularly on those matters which indirectly or directly related with the Power. Now there are subjects like Extra Judicial Killings, Custodial Deaths, Fake Encounters, Mysterious Death or Assassinations, Illegal Confinement of Prisoners and Women and Child Abuse Reports by Human Right Watch but courts are not moved. There is no *suo-moto* notice. Above all there was no hearing on Mehran Bank Scandal of ISI which can [if these hearings are held impartially] end political bribery by ISI in body politics once and for all.

Some people opine that Judges in Pakistan were worse than Dacoits and Terrorists. How?

Famous Columnist of Daily Dawn **Mr. Ardeshir Cowasjee,** known for his judicious views, had once said on PTV:

"Today Judiciary has no respect. The judiciary has killed itself. The Judiciary is corrupt. The Government made it corrupt. The Government has got a book on all the Judges. The people looked down on the Judges. The higher the Judge, the lower he is looked down upon.....Judiciary can never demand respect. I mean these guys can threaten us that we will take you to court and charge you with contempt case.

But it's all nonsense. They should command respect and that will take a long time to come, every thing is corrupt. These remarks, the Court urges," scandalized the Superior Courts of this country and the judges comprising such courts and tended to bring them into hatred, ridicule and contempt".

The *American State Department's report on Human Rights and Democracy* around the world, released on **28th March 2005** titled 'Supporting Human Rights and Democracy' notes that:

'...constitutional amendments passed by Musharraf government have strengthened the powers of the president at the expense of the National Assembly. Parts of the report are blunt'. It stated that the military remains heavily engaged in politics, the Government's human rights record remained poor, political parties are generally weak, undemocratic institutions centred on personalities instead of policies. But it commented on Pakistani judiciary in a stinking tone that the 'judiciary is corrupt, inefficient, and malleable to political pressure.'

On **18th April 1993** the same President Ghulam Ishaq Khan dissolved the National Assembly again and dismissed the government of Nawaz Sharif under Article 58(2)(b) of the Constitution. The Prime MinisterNawaz Sharif immediately approached the Supreme Court and challenged his un-called for dismissal.

A brief background: Chief Justice Nasim H. Shah's favourable tilt towards Nawaz Sharif's Muslim League and his hostility towards PPP were well known. He had exchanged harsh words with the then Chief Justice M Afzal Zullah when the later had received Benazir at a function being an opposition leader.

He had been humiliated earlier during PPP's government when Benazir Bhutto as prime Minister had refused to sit on the same table with him. The reason was that Nasim H. Shah was one of the justices who had upheld the death sentence of Benazir's father Mr Bhutto in 1979 (Justice Shah was one of the four judges out of seven to sign a verdict for rejecting Bhutto's appeal of death sentence).

In early 1993, relations between PM Nawaz Sharif and President Ghulam Ishaque Khan (GIK) deteriorated quite rapidly and GIK was planning to ouster PML's chief and the PM. Statements attributed to the Chief justice M Afzal Zullah indicated that judiciary might act to counter president's move. President waited till 18th April 1993; the day of retirement of Chief Justice of Pakistan Afzal Zullah. In a very curious development, Chief Justice on the very day of his retirement was on a plane heading out of country.

Justice Nasim Hasan Shah was sworn in as Acting Chief Justice; another inquisitive move as he should have been appointed permanent Chief Justice of Pakistan. President dropped his guillotine on the same day sending Nawaz Sharif, his cabinet and the Assembly packing home.

PML moved their petition in the Supreme Court against allegedly undue use of presidential powers by GIK and Acting CJ Nasim H Shah was there to handle it. After short arguments, the bench resorted to restore Nawaz Sharif's government but justice Sajjad A Shah gave the lone dissenting opinion when Supreme Court announced the decision by majority. Two judges; M Rafiq Tarar and Saeeduzzaman Siddiqi had asked Chief Justice Nasim H Shah to take disciplinary action against Justice Sajjad Ali Shah for the language he had used in his dissenting note. The Chief justice did not take any action against the said Mr Justice but it caused a lasting rift amongst the two.

26th May 1993: A full bench of the Supreme Court including Justice Rafiq Tarar, Justice Afzal Lone and others, under the chair of CJP Nasim Hasan Shah, in an almost unanimous verdict, declared that President Ghulam Ishaq Khan had acted unlawfully in dissolving the National Assembly and dismissing the Nawaz Sharif's government. The Supreme Court of Pakistan had announced:

> 'On merits by majority (of 10 to 1) we hold that the order of the 18th April, 1993, passed by the President of Pakistan is not within the ambit of the powers conferred on the President under Article 58(2)(b) of the constitution and other enabling powers available to him in that behalf and has, therefore, been passed without lawful authority and is of no legal effect.'

Chief Justice Nasim Hasan Shah took the view that the president and not the prime minister had been instrumental in subverting the spirit of the constitutional provisions because:

> 'The president had ceased to be a neutral figure and started to align himself with his opponents and was encouraging them in their efforts to destabilize his government.'

An interesting fact about this judgment was that each of the eleven judges on bench had written his own, individual and separate decision and each judge had written different grounds to reinstate Sharif's government but reaching the same one conclusion except one Justice Sajjad Ali Shah who later paid a big price for that.

However, Justice Sajjad Ali Shah, the only judge of the Supreme Court from rural Sindh, in his dissident verdict pointed out that:

> 'Seemingly it so appears that two Prime Ministers from Sindh were sacrificed at the altar of Article 58(2)(b) of the constitution but when turn of Prime Minister from Punjab came the tables were turned. Indisputably right at the very outset of the proceedings indications

were given that the decision of the court would be such which would
please the nation...In my humble opinion decision of the Court should
be strictly in accordance with law and not to please the nation.'

It was a wrong set of reasons on the part of Justice Sajjad Ali Shah. The
PM was from Punjab but the bench did not comprise of all Punjabi
judges as five of them were from Urdu speaking community of Karachi,
one from rural Sindh. It was against the judicial norms & prevailing
traditions and a reference should have been filed before the Supreme
Judicial Council for his written remarks.

Throughout the proceedings, the Chief Justice gave such remarks that led
to the belief that the judges had already made up their minds. Even
before start of proceedings, CJP Nasim H Shah once said loudly that
'I would not be Justice Munir' and all the ten judges on bench had
launched a strong protest in that regard. After retirement, once he made
a statement before media that:

'The President (GIK) was right; we should not have given that
judgment in favour of the Prime Minister (Nawaz Sharif)'.

It has been pity that our Chief Justices were so careless, sentimental,
irresponsible and sloppy.

The case stands reported as *Nawaz Sharif v. President of Pakistan* (**PLD**
1993 SC 473) in which the apex court had held that the order of
dissolution did not fall within the ambit of the powers conferred on the
President under Article 58(2)(b) of the Constitution and other enabling
powers available to him in that behalf and in consequence the National
Assembly, Prime Minister and the Cabinet were restored.

However, Nawaz Sharif later advised the then President to liquefy the
assemblies on 18th July 1993. Nawaz Sharif could not survive more than
two months as Prime Minister after getting decision in his favour from
the Chief Justice Nasim Hasan Shah.

The Supreme Court apparently gave its verdict against President Ghulam
Ishaq Khan because it knew that the president has lost support of the
power arbiter, the Army. The subsequent developments confirmed this
belief as *the Chief of Army Staff, Gen Abdul Waheed Kakar forced*
Ghulam Ishaq Khan and Nawaz Sharif both to resign simultaneously.

Scenario 17

POLITICIZING JUDGES IN PAKISTAN:

A few lines from an essay of **Ardisher Cowasjee** appearing in the daily *'Dawn' dated 15th February 2009* describe the 'recruitment' of a Chief Justice as;

> *'Early in 1994, former chief justice of the Sindh High Court, Sajjad Ali Shah who had been elevated to the Supreme Court of Pakistan was sitting on the Lahore Bench. One day he received a message that the prime minister's house had telephoned asking for a convenient time for prime ministerial husband Asif Ali Zardari to call on him. A time was fixed and Asif Ali Zardari duly turned up, with Aitzaz Ahsan.*
>
> *Sajjad was told that the prime minister was considering appointing him the chief justice of Pakistan. What was his reaction? Sajjad told his visitors that he would not care to leapfrog over three senior judges, but that he would be agreeable to go back to Sindh as its chief justice. This did not fit in with the then government plan.*
>
> *Contacts between Zardari and Sajjad continued and they met thrice at Zardari's house in Islamabad when the offer of appointment as chief justice was raised again. On one occasion, Zardari, accompanied by Agha Rafiq Ahmad, "finally came out openly with the proposal that the prime minister was prepared to appoint me as the chief justice of Pakistan on the condition that I give my written resignation in advance, which would be used if I failed to oblige her. Obviously the letter was to be undated."* (***Law Courts in a Glass House** by Chief Justice (Retd) Sajjad Ali Shah - 2001*).

In 1994, there was seen a visible division amongst the judges of the Supreme Court. Then according to the seniority list Justice Saad Saood Jan was at number one; Justice Abdul Qadeer Chaudhry at number two; Justice Ajmal Mian was at number three and Justice Sajjad Ali Shah was at number four.

Justice Saad Saood Jan was simply ignored by the PM Benazir Bhutto because he had not agreed with a list of 20 names which was prepared by the PPP on the basis of their political affiliations. When Justice Jan was being considered for elevation to CJ's slot, the list was indirectly passed to him which he straightaway declined being political.

Justice Abdul Qadeer Ch was offered the slot but he had refused it saying that Justice Saad Saood Jan was senior thus it was his right. J Ajmal Mian was not touched at all and the negotiations mentioned in above paragraphs started taking place. When Justice Shah was given the position of Chief Justice, he had promptly accepted all those judges without raising any objection.

When Justice Sajjad Ali Shah was sworn in as the Chief Justice, a case was immediately filed against him by an advocate Akram Sheikh. Instead of dealing that case on merits, Mr Sheikh was proceeded against under Contempt of Court charges. Then another advocate Wahabul Khairi moved a similar petition against the CJ, he was also charged with Contempt of Court.

Then another advocate named Abdul Basit took the court on horns on the same issue but again the contempt of court proceedings were initiated against him also. That was enough protest against an injustice within the apex judiciary itself. Shameful days those were in the history of Pakistan.

Astonishing fact of the history is that the same CJP Sajjad Ali Shah had taken 180 angle view two years later. See the next paragraphs.

On 20th March 1996, under his dominion the Supreme Court announced judgment in the 'Judges Case' which was considered as a milestone in the judicial history of Pakistan. This judgment was announced by a larger bench. With that decision, the Supreme Court of Pakistan tried to stabilize country's constitutional framework on firm foundations that paved the way for future of democracy and supremacy of law. It was a full bench unanimous decision of the Supreme Court. The basis of the decision was:

> '.....dictatorship, army or civil, is another name of centralization and monopoly of authority, whereas democracy stands on the basis of supremacy of constitution and rule of law. Therefore it is necessary in a modern state to achieve this end through proper checks and balances.'

The observation was hailed by all sections of the society. Prof Khurshid Ahmed of *Jama'at Islami* (JI), in one of his releases on internet then, had rightly pointed out that:

> '........limiting and encircling the powers of judiciary, appointment of favourites in judiciary by ignoring the principles of merit, wholesale appointment of favoured judges in the High Courts and in the Supreme

Court, dismissal of trusted and experienced judges, transfer of not only senior judges but the Chief Justices of High Courts without due consultation and dumping them into Shariat Court ultimately forced the Supreme Court to announce its verdict to save the judicial system of the country - the verdict of 20th March.' (**Translation of Isharaat from 'Tarjuman Al Quran' for 1st December, 1997**)

The said decision of 20th March 1996 enumerated:

'......Article 270 determines Qura'an and Sunnah as the basis for legislation and for the oath that is taken by the President, the Prime Minister, the Chief Justice, the Ministers, the judges and the members of the Parliament before they assume office.

In Pakistan the parliamentary democratic system should ensure distribution of powers to the three institutions with absolute balance. Parliament enjoys powers of legislation, running of the state is the responsibility of administration that consists of Prime Minister, his Cabinet and subordinate bureaucrats, and the judiciary has the authority to monitor the enforcement and implementation of law.

The judiciary should be completely independent and segregated from the administration and its system of appointments, demotions and transfers should be based on transparent principles to ensure merit and must be free from the intervention of political elements and self seekers.

It was resolved through this decision that two main fundamental rights of an ordinary person had been recognized; firstly that even if one is not directly an aggrieved party but on the basis of fundamental rights, one could knock at the door of law and secondly if in the lower courts, a case is lingering on (as was then the case of 'Jehad Trust' which had been unnecessarily kept pending for 3 years and hearing was not fixed), the apex Court could be approached provided it involved fundamental rights.

With the announcement of this decision, interpretation of the Constitution and law became the sole prerogative of the judiciary. In other words the judicial review was declared the constitutional right and responsibility of the higher courts'.

With the announcement of this ruling it was for the first time in the history of Pakistan that *judiciary* had fortified itself in a way it could function as an independent and powerful institution and the fortification

157

is the *sine quo non* for the protection of fundamental rights, supremacy of law and attainment of justice. But, unfortunately the then political leadership was not prepared to accept the essentiality of this ruling, which was not a good omen for democracy.

Nawaz Sharif, who was the leader of Opposition then, had branded the resistance of Benazir Bhutto's government as treason against the constitution and had paid tributes to the Courts. But he turned around when he himself assumed power in February 1997. His party men challenged the right of the apex court to interpret the Constitution.

PML brought out an ordinance to reduce the number of judges of the Supreme Court (which had to be withdrawn later under enormous pressure from all corners). Appointment of judges was delayed till last hour. When the Chief Justice had advised President to take action under Article 190 and when the President and the Chief of Staff refused to support and ratify the unconstitutional attitude of the then government, they made appointments as per advice of Chief Justice in 'public interest'.

Prof Khurshid Ahmed had then rightly quoted a reference of three living legends of judicial history while commenting on the respective government's behaviour in this respect.

Leonard Jason L, in his book *"The Constitution" (published: London, François 1996 pp 42)* writes about the British parliamentary system:

> *'Though in our constitutional system parliament is the supreme institution for legislation; Courts, which are formed by judges, have the power to see that laws are properly implemented. It is courts who decide on the vires of laws and their legitimacy. Since parliament's legislation can neither address every human error and nor can it cover all unlawful deeds, it is, therefore, for courts to interpret a law or even give direction for necessary legislation where there is either no law or exists an ambiguity about its meaning in the given circumstances.'*

Thus, judges themselves perform the task of legislation. The British 'common law' is simply based on judge's legislation made on issues not found in Parliamentary Acts. Moreover, the exercise of Judicial Review is an important means with the help of which the British Courts keep government (and even legislation, to an extent) in control. It is the field of judicial review which is now making fast progress in the UK.

> *[Lord Diplock has described that there are three basics of judicial review i.e. to decide about a law whether there exists some element of*

illegality in it, whether there was irrationality in it, or there is procedural impropriety.]

Secondly; in America, Chief Justice Marshal had settled this principle in a case known as *'Marbury vs. Madison'*. It was recognized as an absolute principle of constitutional law despite certain reservations of the justice prone governments of that time.

When the US President Roosevelt had tried to take revengeful action against the Supreme Court for declaring certain laws of his renowned *'new ideal'* as void and planned to increase the number of judges so as to appoint some of his liking, the Congress had refused to accept it. Thus collective support was attained for the supremacy of constitution, freedom of judiciary and its judicial review.

Thirdly; an important instance is India where the Supreme Court in a famous case *Kesavananda vs. Kerala* (**AIR 1973 SC 1461**); commonly known as fundamental rights case, settled this principle that:

' .... *Parliament is not empowered to make any constitutional amendment that runs counter to the basic structure of the constitution. It is because the parliament is not constitution-making body. It can, however, exercise authority to amend the constitution formed by the constitution-making body. Therefore any amendment that distorts the constitution itself is not an amendment rather it is constitution-making, for which the legislature enjoys no authority.'*

It was further explained by the Supreme Court of India, in a case *Indra Gandhi vs. Raj Narain* (**AIR 1973 SC 2294**) and clearly decreed that:

'..... *it can never be the purpose of constitution-makers that the Prime Minister should be made an oriental despot through a constitutional amendment. Parliament's authority for amending the constitution (Article 368) despite its overt phraseological expanse confers only limited authority - not absolute authority.'*

In order to counter it, when Indra Gandhi added two amendments (clauses 4 and 5) to Article 368 through constitutional amendments, and thus ended the authority of the courts to declare any constitutional amendment being counter to constitution, the Supreme Court in 1980 in *Mai Nirwamal* case (**AIR 1980 SC 1989**) cancelled this amendment (42nd amendment) and through it not only frustrated the claim of the parliament that it enjoyed unlimited authority to amend the constitution but also refused to recognize its right that parliament can restrict the powers of judiciary. This is the position of judiciary in a democratic parliamentary system.

Contrarily, the attitude adopted in Pakistan once by Prime Minister Nawaz Sharif and his aides, through delay in appointment of five judges, amounted to disregarding the advice of the Chief Justice of Pakistan. They had deliberately avoided respecting verdict of *the 'Judges Case'*, which was basically the settlement of certain principles and regulations with regard to the appointment of judges and the freedom of judiciary. It was unanimously ruled that:

- ...... the appointment of judges should be on merit and transparent by way of 'mutual consultation' amongst the government and the higher courts. This consultation was declared as mandatory between President, Chief Justice, and Governor of the respective province as the case may be.
- ...... this consultation should be meaningful and purposeful leading to consensus to eliminate any shade of irregularity, political considerations, influence or individual discretion. Mere linkage with a political party in the past should not necessarily be a disqualification but it should not be a political bribery in any way.
- .... the administrative head, President or Governor, could render advice about the background and moral character of an individual but the person's legal capability and acumen would be verified by only those who possess legal experience and excellence. Therefore, the advice of the Chief Justice High Court and Chief Justice of Pakistan would be final.

[In other words the final authority to appoint remained with the President but he would neither go against nor without the advice of the Chief Justice to suggest any other name. If the President would like to differ with the advice of the Chief Justice, he should record reasons for doing so and the Chief Justice would have a right to discuss dissenting reasons concerning legal capability, aptitude, capacity, standing and repute of the perspective candidate.]

- ... after appointment, promotion should be on the basis of seniority and the same principle would be held for Chief Justices of all the four High Courts of Pakistan.
- ......the judges working as Additional judges would be given the first right for confirmed appointment unless there was something against them on their service record.

- ...... the appointment as Acting Chief Justice should be purely temporary - in ordinary circumstances 30 days and in extraordinary circumstances (e.g. death) at the most 90 days. The Acting Chief Justice should dispose off day to day routine matters but his advice in regard to appointment of judges would not take effect.
- .... the existing vacancies of judges should be filled up within one month. The question of filling posts that were likely to fall vacant must be considered ahead of time so that appointments are made within 30 days.
- ..... by no way such posts in the superior judiciary should remain vacant for more than 30 days, at the most 90 days.
- .... the appointments of Supreme Court judges as Acting Chief Justices of High Courts or shifting Supreme Court judges or Chief Justices High Courts to Shariat Court disregarding their wishes would be taken against the Constitution and freedom of judiciary. There should be no transfer against their will by way of penalty as per Article 209 of the Constitution.
- ...... the appointment of adhoc judges in the vacancies of permanent judges would be treated as incorrect.

A very interesting fact from our judicial history: when the judge's decision was announced on 20th March 1996, CJP Sajjad Ali shah was very happy and feeling proud. In the tea room the fellow judges congratulated him and at the same time two judges loudly said that:

> 'Mr Chief Justice you should follow your own judgment of today and by principle of seniority you should also set an example by stepping down voluntarily in favour of Justice Saad Saood Jan who still have five months till his retirement. If you'll do justice with your fellow judges also by keeping adhered to your own verdict, Pakistan's judiciary could be seen at sky and your name would become legendary, worth writing in gold for ever.'

CJP Sajjad Ali Shah had gone angry on that suggestion; justice in Pakistan is what suits to the power player in whichever place he is, whether PM or the CJP or Army Chief.

Now an excerpt from a paper, presented by **Mr Khalid Anwar** - a close aide of the then Prime Minister Nawaz Sharif and the Law Minister - at a seminar held in the Institute of Policy Studies, Islamabad in Nawaz Sharif's era, is reproduced here:

"Judicial power is a fundamental aspect of secular as well as religious constitutions..... It operates to restrain parliament from transgressing their constitutional limits. There is nothing unusual in this exercise of judicial power and, instead of considering it as usurpation of the powers of the parliament; it is indeed the exact opposite. It is an attempt to prevent the parliamentary organs from usurping a power which does not vest in it".

But when a moment for practical implementation came up, Mr Khalid Anwar stood with his PM Nawaz Sharif pushing back his own words. It is the routine ever prevailed in Pakistan; we are Muslims.

This judge's case was **revisited later in 2002** when the Supreme Court's judgment in Constitutional Petition No 1 (Supreme Court Bar Association through its President *Hamid Khan vs Federation of Pakistan*) and Constitutional Petitions No 6 - 10 and 12 of 2002 dated 10th April 2002 surfaced on the arena of Pakistan's judicial history. In these petitions, the appointment to the Supreme Court of three LHC judges, namely Justice Khalilur Rehman Ramday, Justice Mohammad Nawaz Abbasi and Justice Faqir Mohammad Khokhar, who were at number 3, 4 and 13 on the seniority list respectively, was challenged.

A five-member SC bench headed by the then Chief Justice Sheikh Riaz Ahmad examined the Judge's Case (till then commonly known as **Al Jihad Trust Case** also) of 1996 and Malik Asad Ali case of 1998, setting guidelines for the elevation of a High Court judge to the Supreme Court. In para no: 23 of the verdict, the Supreme Court said:

(i) The Chief Justice of Pakistan being the *pater familia* of the judiciary of the country is the best judge to ascertain and gauge the fitness and suitability of the judges working in the high courts for appointment as judge of the Supreme Court; and

(ii) Neither the principle of seniority is applicable as a mandatory rule for appointment of judges in the Supreme Court nor has the said rule attained the status of convention.

Paras no: 24 - 28 further elaborated the role of the CJP and the status of his recommendation declaring that:

'If seniority is to be considered the sole criterion, the role of Chief Justice of Pakistan stands undermined and the process of elevation of the most senior judge of the High Court to the Supreme Court would become a mechanical process.'

It was also held that *'if a lawyer or a retired judge is to be appointed judge of the Supreme Court, as our Constitution does permit this* (and lately it was practised by CJP Abdul Hameed Dogar under the PCO while recommending some retired judges of the Sindh High Court and Lahore High Court to the Supreme Court soon after 3rd November 2007 emergency), *then the principle of seniority stands vitiated, and only the recommendation of the Chief Justice of Pakistan regarding fitness of the candidate will hold field'*. Therefore, the CJP's recommendations are almost imperative and binding on head of the executive of Pakistan. (**Ref: www.supremecourt.gov.pk**).

In Pakistan, the practical way of appointment of judges remained different and above the provisions given in the framework of 1996's decision or of 2002's re-interpretation. Most of the times the heads of political parties like Pakistan Peoples Party and Pakistan Muslim Leagues, whenever they come in Power, tried to bring their own party workers belonging to the lawyer community as judges of higher courts.

On one side they bribe, pay back or compensate their party workers while they jeopardize and compromise with the demands of justice by showing their sympathies with the political parties they belong secretly and sometimes quite openly.

As a practice in Pakistan, when a political government comes in power, the Governors of the provinces make out a list of perspective judges and hand over to their respective Chief Justices for on ward pass on to the President. The Chief Justices have little say in those names. What happens we all get a corps of political judges? When a military dictator takes over, he does not need any list from their governors even.

The ISI and MI make lists for them and the only qualification comes up as 'loyalty to the army' and the presence of germs of *'PCO-ship'* in the candidates. In Pakistan, it is because after taking oath, those judges have to complete uphill tasks of issuing green slips to crooked presidents, dishonest prime ministers, corrupt ministers and their deceiptful associates in cases presenting before them.

After reinstatement of CJ Iftikhar Chaudyry and his colleague judges in March 2009, the situation has suddenly changed. The first instance came up in May 2009, when a constitutional petition was moved by Sindh High Court Bar Association (SHCBA) against the appointment of judges on permanent basis and extension of their tenures. The said order of appointments was issued without consulting the Chief Justice of Sindh High Court.

The notification was issued for converting appointment of Justice Bin Yameen to permanent basis on his post as Justice of Sindh High Court, and the extension of the tenures of Justice Arshad Noor Khan and Justice Peer Ali Shah for further six months. The decision was given on the basis that in respect of three alleged justices there was no disagreement of opinion from the constitution. The said petition was dismissed by a full bench comprised of Justice Khilji Arif Hussain, Justice Maqbool Baqar, Justice Gulzar Ahmed and Justice Fasial Arab.

A misconception normally prevailed that there existed a controversy between the parliament and the judiciary and that judiciary was aiming at grabbing the powers of the Parliament. In democratic states each of them is independent in its respective sphere but none is supreme over the other. The real problem in Pakistan is that every government wished to establish its supremacy over the *Parliament and the judiciary both* and to make them totally subservient to the one ruling person and thus the state had always suffered.

In the past the judiciary herself, as the history witnessed, preferred to lie down in the lap of successive political and military masters, therefore, this misconception might be the natural outcome. That is why, it has become a popular voice of today that **'Ehtesab' is equally necessary in the judiciary and Army** so that it could put the nation to Ehtesab candidly and carries it out in the most transparent manner (in Constitution Article 209 deals with the judiciary only).

Judiciary is the institution which the nation is prepared to accept on all times to come but as above board and blotless, despite the deteriorations whatsoever. It is their longing and their desire. It is essential for the survival of democracy as well. Therefore, judiciary should also take care of it within the prevailing system whatsoever.

Scenario 18

IS HAMAM MEIN SAB NANGEY:

On **25th April 1994, daily Dawn**, a leading English newspaper of Pakistan, had published an editorial titled **'Our secret godfathers'**, which opened up with:

> *'Two basic points emerged from General Aslam Beg's admission that in 1990 he took Rs 140 million from the banker Younus Habib [and business community of Karachi] and that part of this money was spent by the ISI during the elections that year . . '.*

And closed by saying that: *'it is time now for some sort of check on the rogue political activities of our intelligence agencies'.*

It was another alarming tragedy that this amount of Rs: 140 million was collected by the President Mehran Bank, Younus Habib, from the business community of Karachi, out of bank regulations, on the instance of secret agencies through clandestine instructions. Otherwise Pakistan's history is stuffed with many breath-taking financial scandals like Cooperatives scam, in which poor and middle class people lost billions of rupees in the hope of getting some fixed incomes for their livelihoods. The fake financial corporations deprived off the economy with huge unpaid bank loans owed to the politicians and top level businessmen.

The **'Mehran Bank'** scandal was a story of massive corruption of that age in Pakistan. The arrest of the Bank's chief executive, Yunus Habib, on 7th April 1994, had lifted curtain from one of the biggest financial fiasco of the country in which he had siphoned off an amount of five billion rupees and doled out millions to certain politicians and serving Generals of army in order to cover up his crime. His arrest was made by the Federal Investigation Agency (FIA) on a complaint lodged by the State Bank of Pakistan for committing misappropriation in the sale proceeds of 'Dollar Bearer Certificates' to the tune of $36.7 million.

> [*Younus Habib was actually arrested on 24th March 1994 for siphoning off money from both Habib Bank and Mehran Bank he was kept under 'informal custody' by the FIA or the ISI for interrogation off the record. He was forced to 'deliberately forget & omit' certain important names and 'some' transactions and to save skins of many*

*big guns that were once part of the deal. He was put on formal arrest
later after two weeks when media cried.*]

The national media had also felt the vague and ambiguous attitude
of the government and Superior Courts towards the facts (of open state
sponsored financial and political corruption) on record.

The general populace of Pakistan then wanted (and expected) from the
Supreme Court to put some guiding principles, ways & means and
procedures to keep the army organisations away from political
interferences in future. The people wanted an able ruling of the apex
court for justified use of public funds on national development cause and
not sending it to the big politicians or Army Generals as bribes and
looted shares. Their expectations were based on the proceedings which
were going on in the Supreme Court for about one year.

This black & hard fact of Pakistan's history was further confirmed when
in 1994 a stunning revelation about that scam was made in a session
of the National Assembly of Pakistan. Exposing the manipulation of
Pakistan's political affairs by the anti-democratic forces of the country,
the then Federal Interior Minister, Major Gen (Rtd) Naseerullah Babar
had disclosed to the nation about army establishment's undercover
financing of certain politicians of IJI to oppose Pakistan Peoples Party
(PPP) in the 1990's general elections.

Opposition leader Nawaz Sharif added fuel to the fire on 31st May 1994
and announced that President Farooq Leghari was involved in the
scandal and had used Mehran Bank to inflate prices in his own land deal
involving a Rs: 15 million transaction. The President confirmed that
Younus Habib had facilitated the deal but denied charges about any
illegalities. The government then appointed two judicial commissions to
investigate the MBL scandal and the President filed libel charges against
Nawaz Sharif and his political companions.

Why Gen Beg did so to down the PPP power? Reason may be that
Benazir Bhutto, being the Prime Minister of Pakistan, had appointed
former Air Chief Zulfikar Ali Khan to head an Enquiry Commission in
1989 to look into the working of various intelligence agencies including
ISI, IB, ASF, and Special Branch of Police and also to recommend
measures to improve their performance and keep them away from the
political arena. In fact, similar exercises had been done before as well;
Gen Yahya Khan did it for Gen Ayub Khan, Rafi Reza for Z A Bhutto,
and Sahibzada Yakub Khan did it for Gen Ziaul Haq; but not a single

page is available on record showing implementation of recommendations of these commissions.

To support his statement, Gen Babar had presented a letter from another retired Army General, Asad Durrani, addressed to the then Prime Minister Benazir Bhutto, confessing the distribution of those secret funds worth 140 million rupees in the capacity of DG ISI. Gen Durrani was later designated as Pakistan's Ambassador to Germany during Benazir Bhutto's government in 1994.

Here is the verbatim copy of that letter dated 7th June 1994:

"My dear Prime Minister,

A few points I could not include in my 'confessional statement' handed over to the Director FIA. These could be embarrassing or sensitive. (a) The recipients included Khar 2 million, Hafeez Pirzada 3 million, Sarwar Cheema 0.5 million and Mairaj Khalid 0.2 million. The last . . . . [illegible] someone's soft corner that benefited them. (b) The remaining amount of 80 million were either deposited in the ISI's 'K' fund (60 m) or given to director external intelligence for special operations (perhaps the saving grace of this disgraceful exercise. But it is delicate information.)......... .

[Noted in the margin of this paragraph by Gen Babar or Benazir Bhutto: "This is false. The amount was pocketed by Gen Mirza Aslam Beg (of Friends)"]

The operation not only had the 'blessings' of the President (GIK) and the wholehearted participation of the caretaker PM (Ghulam Mustafa Jatoi), but was also in the knowledge of the army high command. The last mentioned will be the defence of many of us, including Gen Beg (who took his colleagues into 'confidence' but that is the name that we have to save & protect).

The point that I have 'war-gamed' in my mind very often is: what is the object of this exercise?

(a) If it is to target the opposition, it might be their legitimate right to take donations, especially if they come through 'secret channels'. Some embarrassment is possible, but a few millions are peanuts nowadays.

(b) If the idea is to put Gen Aslam Beg on the mat: he was merely providing 'logistic support' to donations made by a community 'under

instructions' from the government and with the 'consent' of the military high command. In any case; I understand he is implicated in some other deals in the same case.

(c) GIK [President Ghulam Ishaq Khan] will pretend ignorance, as indeed he never involved himself directly.

(d) Of course, one has to meet the genuine ends of law. In that case let us take care of the sensitivities like special operations and possibly that of the army [of Pakistan].

It was for these reasons that I desperately wanted to see you (the PM) before leaving. I also wanted to talk about my farewell meeting with the COAS (General Waheed Kakar). In the meantime you must have met often enough and worked out what is in the best interest of the country [the Pakistan].

I keep praying that all these natural and man-made calamities are only to strengthen us in our resolve and not in any way reflective of our collective sins [as Pakistanis].

With best regards and respects

Yours sincerely, *Asad*

Filed also in the court was a note, attached to Gen Durrani's letter written in his own hand, reading:

"YH TT Peshawar A/C Sherpao For Election 5,00,000; Anwar Saifullah for MBL deposit 15,00,000; Farooq Leghari PO Issued 1,50,00,000. Another 1,50,00,000 paid through Bank. There are a host of other political figures who received funds like Liaquat Jatoi [later Chief Minister Sindh], Imtiaz Sheikh etc."

Gen Durrani's above revealing had claimed that in September 1990, he had received instructions from the then Chief of Army Staff (COAS) Gen Mirza Aslam Beg to provide logistic support to the disbursement of *'donations made by some businessmen of Karachi'* to the election campaign of *Islami Jamhoori Ittehad* (IJI). Astonishingly no body could find any clue for this presumption that how these donations were collected, who collected and who were the businessmen to make these donations. The fact remains that it was the money 'donated' by Mehran Bank nothing else.

These disclosures by the then Interior Minister had provoked former air force chief and leader of an almost defunct political party, *Tehreek-e-Istaqlal*, Air Marshal (Rtd) Asghar Khan, to urge the Supreme Court of Pakistan to take a *suo moto* notice of the issue. In his 'Human Rights Petition no: HRC 16/96' addressed to the Chief Justice Sajjad Ali Shah on 16th June 1996, Asghar Khan contended that:

> '......*the action of Gen (Rtd) Mirza Aslam Beg and Gen (Rtd) Asad Durrani amounts to gross misconduct and I am writing to ask that you may be pleased to initiate legal proceedings against both these persons who have brought the Armed Forces of Pakistan into disrepute and have been guilty of undermining the discipline of the Armed Forces.'*

Proceedings of the case during next one year had amply proved, beyond reasonable doubt, that politics in Pakistan was plagued by capital investments by the under-cover intelligence agencies. Even Gen (Rtd) Aslam Beg who denied his personal involvement in the transaction of Rs 140 million, secretly deposited and withdrawn from various branches of Habib Bank to finance leading politicians of the country, had admitted it in the Supreme Court earlier.

Explaining his role as the COAS in the ISI's funding for IJI, Gen Aslam Beg maintained before the Supreme Court that:

> '*In 1990 when the money was donated by Younas Habib, ISI was acting under the directions of higher authorities. As COAS at that time, when I was informed of the matter, my only concern was that the money received by the ISI was utilized properly and an account was maintained and beyond that, I had no concern with that money.'*

Ironically, the former COAS had not hesitated to accept his contribution to the evil of corrupting the political culture, as he probably saw the situation as one of the Establishment's routine covert activities undertaken 'in the best interest of the country'.

The times when this scandal had hit the print-media headlines, most political analysts had focused on the issue as a classic instance of undue manipulation of political actors and events by our intelligence agencies. A number of editorials, columns and news-reports published during the course of the revelations questioned the *'ability of intelligence agencies such as ISI to secretly use public funds for purposes which amount to the strangulation of our infant democracy and are also beyond the scope of their legitimate activities'*.

It is also a fact that questions were also raised in the past regarding the justification for maintaining the so-called Political Cell in the ISI since 1975, an initiative which goes to the discredit of former Prime Minister Zulfikar Ali Bhutto.

More pathetic situation is that despite all these confessions on record the Supreme Court remained silent and did nothing for the poor nation, passed no stricture, no judgement, no reprimand and no line of action for such future lootings because the respondents were Generals, the ruling elite for whom the country was in fact made.

The matter did not end for all. Still there were hopes when a replica of Gen Naseerullah Babar's words, spoken on National Assembly's floor in 1994, was highlighted in the national press later. People were of the view that in the light of their own decision on 'Corruption & Corrupt practices', the Supreme Court would take cognizance of the facts already on record.

Reference is being made to the daily *'Dawn' of 4th August 2002* in which *Ardsher Cowasjee* had shouted that:

> '....... Naseerullah Babar also filed in court a copy of a bank account sheet headed "G/L Account. **Activity Report: Account 12110101 G. Baig** (sic.) The column heads read "Transaction, Date, Particulars, Debit and Credit." The numbered transactions took place between October 23, 1991, and December 12, 1993. The first transaction listed was "Cash-P.O. Karachi Bar Association A/C Gen. Baig (sic.), debit, 5,05,680" (advocate Mirza Adil Beg, Aslam Beg's nephew, the then president of the KBA, confirms that the KBA received the money). In January 1992 USD 20,000 was sold @ 26.50 and 5,30,000 was credited to the account. Thereafter all debits: "Arshi c/o Gen. Baig (sic.) 2,90,000; Cash paid to Gen. Sahib 2,40,000; Cash Friends 1,00,000 [Aslam Beg's organization, FRIENDS, Foundation for Research on National Development and Security]; Cash TT to Yamin to pay Gen. Shah 3,00,000; Cash TT to Yamin Habib 12,00,000; Cash Friends 1,00,000; Cash Friends 1,00,000; Cash paid through YH 10,00,000; Cash Friends TT to Salim Khan 2,00,000; Cash 1,00,000; Cash Towards Friends 5,00,000; Cash Asif Shah for Benglow 35,000; Cash Friends 1,00,000; Cash Friends 1,00,000; Cash TT through Yamin for Friends 1,00,000; Cash paid to Fakhruddin G. Ebrahim 2,00,000 [he confirms having received the money from General Beg as fees and expenses for defending him in the contempt of court charge brought against him - PLD 1993 SC310]; Cash paid through TT to Yamin for Friends; Cash paid to Fakhruddin G Ebrahim 1,28,640 [he

confirms receipt for fees/expenses for contempt case]; Cash Guards at 11-A 10,500; Cash TT for USD 240,000 Fav. Riaz Malik to City Bank (sic.) New York 68,76,000; Cash Friends 1,00,000; Cash Guards at 11-A 10,500; Cash Mjr. Kiyani 10,000; Cash mobile phone for Col. Mashadi 28,911; Cash TT fav. Qazi Iqbal and M Guddul 3,00,000; Cash Mjr. Kiyani 10,000; Cash TT to Peshawar 3,00,000; Cash deposited at Karachi A/C EC [Election Commission] 3,00,000; Cash Guards 24,000; Cash TT to Quetta 7,00,000; Cash mobile bill of Col. Mashadi 3,237; Cash TT to Peshawar Br. 4,00,000; Cash deposited at Karachi Br. 4,00,000; Cash Guards 11,520; Cash TT to Peshawar for EC 2,00,000; Cash TT to Quetta for EC 2,00,000; Cash Guards 5,760; Cash Mjr. Kiyani 5,000; Cash A/C Guards 8,640; Cash to YH 2,00,000; Cash A/C Guards 5,760; Cash TT to (an apparently unknown person named) Salim Khan 1,00,000."

The *"host of other political figures who received funds" from an ISI account were revealed in the Supreme Court when Asghar Khan's petition was being heard. Interalia, Nawaz Sharif received (in rupees) 3.5 million, Lt General Rafaqat [GIK's Election Cell] 5.6 million, Mir Afzal 10 million, Ghulam Mustafa Jatoi 5 million, Jam Sadiq Ali 5 million, Mohammed Khan Junejo 2.5 million, Pir Pagaro 2 million, Abdul Hafeez Pirzada 3 million, Yusuf Haroon 5 million [he confirms having received this for Altaf Hussain of the MQM], Muzaffar Hussain Shah 0.3 million, Abida Hussain 1 million, Humayun Marri 5.4 million.* (**Source: File Records of the Supreme Court of Pakistan**)

Citing one A S Ghazali's analysis in his e-Book, one can also add other testimonials, already available on Supreme Court's record, in which there was a mention of payments made by Yunus Habib of Mehran Bank directly to Generals, politicians and political parties from his bank. The main beneficiary of this national booty was former Army Chief Gen Mirza Aslam Beg who had received the main amount. Besides Rs. 140 million, other names & amounts in the documents included:

'Jam Sadiq Ali (Rs. 70 million from Habib Bank and Rs: 150 million from Mehran Bank); MQM's Altaf Hussein (Rs. 20 million); Yusuf Memon for Ejaz-ul-Haq and one more (Rs. 50 million); Nawaz Sharif (Rs. 6 million); Chief Minister of Sindh Muzaffar Hussain Shah through his secretary (Rs.13 million); MQM Haqiqi (Rs. 5 million); former Sports Minister Ajmal Khan (Rs.1.4 million); Jam Mashooq Ali (Rs. 3.5 million); Liaquat Jatoi (Rs:1 million); Dost Mohammad Faizi (Rs. 1 million) and Jam Haider (Rs. 2 million) to mention some of them; all respectable politicians of today.'

On 16th June 1997 Gen (Rtd) Mirza Aslam Beg said before the court that Lt Gen Asad Durrani had received the money and spent Rs 60 million for funding certain candidates as per above details and 'some' to more names while the remainder on 'other' operations. He added that Gen Durrani had kept him informed about the developments.

Kamran Khan of News had also confirmed to the press that the amount of Rs: 140 million, given to Gen Beg was deposited in the 'Survey Section 202' account of Military Intelligence (then headed by Maj Gen Javed Ashraf Kazi). From there Rs 6 crore was paid to President Ghulam Ishaq Khan's Election Cellmates (General Rafaqat, Roedad Khan, Ijlal Hyder Zaidi, etc.), and Rs: 8 crore transferred to the ISI account. *(Referred to Daily Dawn of 21st July 2002)*

These documents and many others, filed in the Supreme Court, are a matter of public record. In this regard, reference should be made to paragraph 111, 'Corruption', of the judgment of the Supreme Court of Pakistan on the Proclamation of Emergency dated 14th October 1999 (approved for reporting), delivered by Chief Justice Irshad Hassan Khan and his eleven Brother judges, sanctifying Gen Musharraf's takeover. It was a document presented by Attorney-General Aziz Munshi, dating back to 1990, with the lists of ISI's payments, Gen Naseerullah Babar's and Gen Asad Durrani's affidavits being amongst them.

The innocent people of Pakistan have a right to question that why not all these corrupt, bribed political people who shamelessly accepted the people's money for their own political ends, and who have never denied having received such payoffs, were not disqualified for life?

A question was once asked from the Chief of *Jama'at Islami* (JI), Qazi Hussain Ahmed, on the issue of involvement of agencies in toppling the governments in Pakistan.

> **Question:** '*The Supreme Court took up a case filed by Air Marshal (R) Asghar Khan. During the proceedings the ex-Army Chief, Gen Aslam Beg and some other people alleged that the official agencies and ISI etc have been spending huge sums in favour of one party or to topple the other. How the Jama'at would react to it. Further, does it not prove that many a past elections held in Pakistan were dubious and unjust?*'

> **Answer:** '*..... We offer no specific and detailed comment on it, because the matter is before the court, which alone can decide whether the allegations were right or wrong. What any body can see however, is*

that Gen Aslam Beg first stated that so much was paid to such and such (party or person). When Asghar Khan filed the case, the Gen denied what he stated earlier. ....Further comments will only be possible when the court makes its final judgment [which has not surfaced till today].'

Leading politician Ch Shujaat Hussain had openly confirmed that he and Ch Pervez Elahi were offered millions of rupees by the then Army Chief Gen Aslam Beg in 1991 for political purposes from Mehran Bank accounts. Referring to his interview appeared in daily *The News of 23rd April 2003*, he was courageous enough to reopen the controversy over Army's role in politics by admitting that Mehran Bank scandal had cost Rs 9.92 billion to the national exchequer. He told that the two brothers, he and Pervez Elahi were called in the Army House Rawalpindi in 1991 to strike the deal but they refused to involve themselves in that sort of state bribery to politicians.

In this interview, Ch Shujaat Hussain had also confirmed the names of certain recipients of public funds distributed through the ISI to change the election shades. He, interalia, narrated that:

'Gen Beg is accused of distributing Rs 140 million among different politicians like Nawaz Sharif the former Prime Minister, Farooq Leghari the former president, Jam Sadiq the former Sindh Chief Minister, Altaf Hussain the MQM Chief, Yousaf Memon advocate for disbursement to MNA Javed Hashmi and others, Liaquat Jatoi the former Chief Minister Sindh, Afaq Ahmad of MQM, Imtiaz Sheikh, Muzaffar Shah the former Chief Minister of Sindh, Ajmal Khan the ex-Federal Minister, Jam Mashooq, Dost Mohammad Faizi, and Mr Adnan son of Sartaj Aziz the then Finance Minister.'

Air Marshal Asghar Khan is still waiting to have an announced verdict from the Supreme Court of Pakistan since about a decade, heard by the CJP Saeeduzzaman Siddiqui. Many of the witnesses like Gen Naseerullah Babar have already expired.

It should remain in mind that the Mehran Bank had been doing badly since its very inception, and banking experts unhesitatingly attributed this poor performance to Yunus Habib's affinity and weakness for 'extra-curricular banking activities.' In fact, the only reason why the bank had managed to stay afloat was the protection and patronage enjoyed by Yunus Habib, whereby hefty institutional and government accounts were brought to Mehran Bank.

Mehran Bank was in imminent danger of being declared near insolvent. Gen Aslam Beg, the then Army Chief, and the ISI Chief Gen Javed Nasir came to its rescue and, in the process, unwittingly sealed its fate. Gen Javed Nasir deposited his organization's foreign exchange reserves near about 39 million dollars with Mehran Bank, which was in clear violation of government rules that such banking must be conducted through state-owned financial institutions.

Yunus Habib started dipping into this huge deposit to finance his customary dealings on the other side. After Gen Javed Nasir, Lt Gen Javed Ashraf Qazi took over as the new DG ISI in January 1993 and decided to transfer this money to a safer bank. When it tried to withdraw such a huge amount, Yunus Habib's bank was in no position to cough up. And it was precisely for this reason that Yunus Habib was picked up first time by a law enforcement agency (FIA) in 1993. A deal was reportedly struck, with Yunus Habib promising to return the money.

Yunus Habib was formally arrested by the Federal Investigation Agency (FIA) on 7th April 1994, on a complaint of State Bank of Pakistan for misappropriation in the sale proceeds of the Dollar Bearer Certificates (DBCs). He subsequently admitted that out of the 36.7 million dollars generated through the sale of DBCs (a federal government bond that the State Bank sells through commercial banks) he had used 20 million dollars to pay back a portion of the amount owed to the ISI and used the rest of the money to meet some other pressing obligations.

According to the State Bank of Pakistan rules, proceeds from the DBC's (Mehran Bank was given 40 million dollar worth) had to be deposited within 72 hours of the sale. Yunus Habib did not meet this deadline — in fact, never deposited the money at all — and as the State Bank governor alleged, misappropriated the funds.

Gen Aslam Beg denied any personal gains in the above quoted scandal. His organization FRIENDS claimed that the money was 'donated' by Yunus Habib and that the amount was deposited directly into the account of 'a government agency.' Accounts in the name of an intelligence agency were opened in four separate banks; Allied Bank, National Bank of Pakistan, Muslim Commercial Bank and United Bank Limited and an amount of 140 million rupees was deposited in these accounts between 16th September and 26th October 1990.

The said money was taken out almost soon after it was deposited, and is said to have gone towards running the 1990 election campaigns of certain politicians of IJI then being headed by Nawaz Sharif. This was not done out of generosity, but allegedly only to further the career designs of Gen Aslam Beg, who wanted an extension in his tenure as Army Chief from the President GIK but was refused.

Pakistan's intelligence agencies, especially in military regimes, had gone much deep into politics and still it is so. It is because of this sinister nexus that in Pakistan politics, events taking place behind the scenes have often been more important than anything taking place on the surface. Indeed, some senior ISI officials like Lt Gen Hameed Gul, recall with a sense of pride, their role in this regard and claim it as their prerogative in open and live TV programs.

Referring to an internet site *www.Freedomfiles.org*, the Mehran Bank proved to be a club for spies and politicians to collaborate illegally against each other. The intelligence agencies prevailed upon politicians from different parties to trade their loyalties for a price. The objective of the intelligence agencies was to destabilise an allegedly hostile government [of PPP] and then put in place a 'friendly' [IJI & Nawaz Sharif's] regime. The scandal comprises the entire gamut of financial crimes like fake loans, kickbacks, illegal transactions and bribes unprecedented in our history.

At the same time it also speaks about our inept and lethargic judiciary which had dealt with a case in which all the needed evidence was on record along with the confessional statements of the accused. Because of the fact that the persons charged were the high ranking Army Generals, the Supreme Court did not felt courage to pass any cogent judgement in this connection. Nor the judiciary could initiate any proceedings against the high profile political figures that were named among the beneficiaries of the Mehran Bank because the judges had not dealt with the Generals in a rightful way. The compromising attitude of the judiciary was not less damaging; the following illustration is there to prove it.

In July 1994 a commission, comprising five judges, was formed to investigate the Mehran Bank scandal. It took eight months to complete its inquiry in February 1995 but its report was never published. However, parts of the reports were released on 8th December 1996, according to which the commission had exonerated President Leghari from any wrong doing in his *benami* deal. But the commission did not mention to whom the land was sold by the President for Rs. 15 million and from which account the money was debited to make the payment.

The said Commission had also cleared the former Chief Minister of the NWFP, Aftab Sherpao and one Senator Anwar Saifullah, who were accused of being the main beneficiaries of the Mehran Bank, of all the allegations. Details are available in daily *'The DAWN' of 9th December 1996*. On 13th May 1997, the then Commerce Minister, Ishaq Dar informed the Senate that the report was missing from the Law Ministry. According to Mr Dar, the Mehran Bank scandal cost a total of Rs. 9.92 billion to the national exchequer.

[No *analysis can be offered that why the report could not be released open in 1995 and what happened behind the curtain. The Commission's report, as it was reported in the inner circles, had declared involvement of notable politicians in corruption. It was not made public perhaps because some of those politicians were members of the ruling PPP and Benazir Bhutto had not opted to drag them in the mud.*

In November 1996, Benazir Bhutto's government was dissolved by Mr Leghari using Article 58(2)(b) of the Constitution. After that the report was (unofficially) called in the President House, re-considered or may be got amended to suit certain people, partly released as per requirement and the file was not returned to the Ministry of Law till the moment of statement given at the Senate floor by FM Ishaq Dar at least.]

Shortly thereafter Chief Justice Sajjad Ali Shah received a letter from Air Marshal (Rtd) Asghar Khan, copied to the then COAS Gen Jehangir Karamat, drawing his attention to the matter. On the basis of this letter, attached press clippings and an affidavit signed by Asad Durrani listing the politicians to whom money had been paid, the Supreme Court had decided to initiate action under Article 184(3) of the constitution.

Hearings commenced in February 1997 and continued through the year. On 6th November 1997, the statements of Gen Babar and Gen Durrani were to be recorded. The Court, under Chief Justice Sajjad Ali Shah, was faced with the awkward question as to the law under which the ISI and its political cell had been set up. Gen Beg's counsel, Akram Shaikh, after fulsome praise of the agency and its great achievements – greater than those of RAW, the KGB or MI 5 – explained how the political cell had been established in 1975 under the orders of Mr Bhutto.

The Court asked the Attorney-General to provide the relevant documentation as to the scope of the activities of the political cell and to clarify whether, under the law, part of its duties was to distribute funds for the purpose of rigging elections.

The Attorney General, of course, wriggled out of that one by stating that the matter was of such a 'sensitive' and 'delicate' nature that it could not be heard in open court. Air Marshal Asghar's lawyer, Habib Wahab ul Khairi, countered by saying that as the entire matter had been aired in the press, with all the names involved fully listed, there was little left to warrant in-camera proceedings, and besides, the people had every right to know how their money had been used and whether the use in question was permitted by law.

The court, however, allowed the recording of Gen Naseerullah Babar's and Gen Asad Durrani's statements and their cross examination to be held in camera on 19-20ᵗʰ November.

Seven days later, on 27ᵗʰ November 1997, the Supreme Court was stormed by Nawaz Sharif's goons and shortly thereafter Chief Justice Sajjad Ali Shah was sent home. The people heard no more about this petition, filed truly in the national interest, until *The Herald, a monthly magazine*, in its issue of *April 2000* published a report by Mubashir Zaidi ('Forging democracy') which made mention of it :

> *"The case has since been heard and on 11th October 1999, just a day before the military overthrew the 'heavily mandated' Nawaz Sharif government, the sitting Chief Justice, Saiduzzaman Siddiqui, announced that he had reserved judgment on ISI case."*

Almost three years later, after a deafening silence from the Court, on 10ᵗʰ August 2002, Asghar Khan addressed a letter to the then Chief Justice of Pakistan, Sh Riaz Ahmed; its subject being 'HRC No.19/96, Air Marshal (R) Asghar Khan versus Gen (R) Mirza Aslam Beg.' It read as:

> *"I should like to draw you attention to my letter MAK/12/5 addressed to your predecessor on 8 April 2000, requesting that the above case may please be reopened. I have received no reply to this letter and elections are due on 10 October, 2002.*
>
> *Many of the people [Pakistani politicians] who are guilty of misconduct will, if the case is not heard, be taking part in the elections and the purpose of those elections will thus be defeated. I would request an early hearing and decision in this case."*

> *(Ref: We never learn from history by* **Ardeshir Cowasjee** *published in* **'DAWN' dated 5th August 2007**)

Again, nothing happened.

In the election year of 2007, ISI and its sister agencies once more got into the act, the reinstated Chief Justice of Pakistan, Iftikhar Chaudhry, could not take up the Asghar Khan's petition which was of vital importance to the future political scenario as it should have eliminated and disqualify many aspiring public representative hoping to lord the nation again.

The stalwarts of the Supreme Court Bar Association did not help the retired Air Marshal – when he needed legal representation.

Mehran gate is just a tip of the iceberg. There are hundreds of banking and financial scams involving politicians and Generals that have yet to surface. It seems that all politicians, whether they belong to the ruling coalition or the opposition, are part of this corrupt political culture. The charges and counter-charges made by both seem to have only one aim: *Lutto tay Phutto.*

Who cares for the coward, clumsy and hopeless judiciary in Pakistan?

Scenario 19

RISE OF PAN-ISLAMISM IN PAKISTAN:

During the Pakistan movement, the role of religious leaders, normally called as *'Ulema'*, remained dormant. Some historians are of the view that they had opposed the ideology of Pakistan on certain occasions. Maulana Hussain Ahmed Madni of *Jamiat Ulema E Hind* had openly criticized Mr Jinnah and remained in opposition till the Independence Day (14th August 1947). Thus the emergence of Pakistan on the world map left these religious leaders wounded and crying. While leaving their followers in the lurch in post-independence India, the self-styled preachers of the 'Law of Islam' fled to 'Islamize' Pakistan.

Soon after independence, when the administration of the new state was coping with huge problems arising out of partition of the subcontinent, the *Ulema* began moving religious passions of the people to get the "Islamic Constitution" passed by the Constituent Assembly. The cry of 'Islam in danger' remained a powerful weapon in all times. Every contemporary politician was aware of the risk that any adventurous policy would be greeted with the words like 'Islam betrayed' and it happened so many times in the history of Pakistan.

Incidentally, it was Zulfikar Ali Bhutto who fell as first prey in the hands of *Ulema*. He went too far in pleasing them during 1977 uproar against so called 'manoeuvred' national elections. It is a hard fact that to reach a compromise he had to be a torch bearer of the *Islamization* process in the country. This was the time when he declared *Ahmadis* as non-Muslims in a constitutional mend.

To Islamize the society, he declared Friday as holiday instead of Sunday, and introduced the subjects of *Islamiyat* as compulsory subject for the students at all levels. He invited the Imam of *Ka'ba* to Pakistan to lead the prayers at certain places. Drinking of wine or alcoholic drink and selling of liquor by Muslims was declared banned in Pakistan in early 1977 by the then PM Z A Bhutto and punishments of imprisonment and fines were provided in that law.

However, these initiatives could not save him from the ultimate disaster and he became the victim of fate when almost all the religious parties joined hands in launching a campaign of slogans like 'Hang Bhutto' and ultimately he was hanged.

When Z A Bhutto was waiting his death appeal in the Supreme Court of Pakistan, Gen Ziaul Haq on 2nd December 1978 delivered a nationwide address on the first day of Islamic Hijra calendar vowing to enforce *Nizam-e-Mustafa* (Islamic System) for Pakistan accusing most politicians of exploiting the name of Islam. Afterwards, the history witnessed that he himself was the champion of such exploiters.

Very few people know that when Gen Ziaul Haq promulgated his martial law on 5th July 1977, soon after he called the top *Ulema* especially *Maulana Tufail* of *Jama'at e Islami* (JI) and told them that he wanted to bring Islamic way of governance. *'I'm here for three months or so; bring the outline of Islamic system under which we shoud rule Pakistan.'* Gen Ziaul Haq had urged rather pressed the scholars but any of them did not have ready home work nor had they concrete suggestions in that regard.

That was a mix lot of politicians who had raised roaring voices against Z A Bhutto just a month back and resorted to create a law & order situation in the whole country, by offering group arrests in all cities on daily basis, as per instruction of their joint command of Pakistan National Alliance (PNA).

Their aimed politics started against Bhutto when they demanded ban on *Ahmedia* sect. Forgetting Qaid e Azam's manifesto that all the religions and sects, irrespective of their way of worship, origin or language, Pakistan belongs to all as equal citizens; Bhutto accepted PNA's demand and got them declared 'non Muslims' under a Parliamentary act.

Then the PNA leaders demanded ban on manufacturing, import, selling and consuming alcohol. Declaring manufacturing of spirits and many organic chemicals in distilleries of sugar industry illegal for export though caused a great recurring loss to the Pakistan's economy but PM Bhutto accepted their demands and termed alcohol a banned trade.

What happened at last? The PNA pushed the *Ulemas* ahead to make calls for Islamic way of governance; but later developments told that the PNA was using them to oust Mr Bhutto not anything less.

This exercise had earlier been carried out in 1963, when the Governor West Pakistan (now the whole Pakistan) Nawab Amir Mohammad Khan had once asked his Advocate General Khalid Ishaque, a veteran lawyer from JI, to bring the Islamic System Code so that it could be implemented in West Pakistan at least. Khalid Ishaque went to Karachi next day, called all the Islamic scholars and asked them to give him a manuscript at the minimum. For full one year they could not bring an Islamic Code of governance, due to their own sectarian differences perhaps, so the *Ulemas* kept on differing and fighting each other with no progress.

In 1964, Khalid Ishaque gathered the prominent known Islamic lawyers at Lahore, most of them having tilt towards & affiliations with JI, and asked them to bring an Islamic Code for government telling them that the *Ulemas* had not come up with any suggestion. Astonishingly, they discussed many things mutually but ultimately a loud announcement was made in media on behalf of JI that:

> *'At the moment we do not feel that Islamic Code is necessary. When JI would get power to rule the country then the consolidated Islamic code would also be framed for the people.'*

The matter ended with Khalid Ishaque's resignation as the Advocate General of West Pakistan.

Gen Ziaul Haq depended much on Council of Islamic Ideology (CII) for his plans regarding implementation of the Islamic laws but the Council had an inbuilt defect in it. The members of CII were to be selected from all sects of Islam so when ever they gathered to discuss an issue, every representative had forwarded their own peculiar viewpoint according to his own school of thought or *fiqah*. The result was that none of the law could be truly consented.

Gen Ziaul Haq, in ending 1977 announced that no law would go against the Qura'an & Sunnah as a broad and workable guideline and authorised the superior Courts to take care of the Islamic injunctions while taking decisions. To implement that policy in practice, certain amendments in the then existing laws were needed. Heavy homework was done in that regard but ultimately had to be shelved because some stalwarts, very close companions of Gen Ziaul Haq like Ghulam Ishaque Khan, J Afzal Cheema Chairman CII and A K Brohi advocate, had created enormous hindrances and blockades.

Gen Ziaul Haq had taken start by announcing the establishment of *Shariat* Courts remarking that:

> *'Every citizen will have the right to present any law enforced by the government before the Sharia Bench and obtain its verdict whether the law is wholly or partly Islamic or un-Islamic.'*

But at the same time he had signed an overriding clause:

'......(Any) law does not include the constitution, Muslim personal law, any law relating to the procedure of any court or tribunal or, until the expiration of three years, any fiscal law, or any law relating to the collection of taxes and fees, state levies or insurance practice and procedure [in vogue in Pakistan].'

It meant that all important laws which affect each and every individual directly remained outside the purview of the *Sharia* Benches. The whole game was to befool the people.

A referendum was held by Gen Ziaul Haq in 1984, with a reported 98.5% voting in his favour because it contained a very simple question for the people to answer: '**You like Islamic System of government in Pakistan. Answer yes or no.**'

If the answer is yes: ———— Gen Ziaul Haq will be the President of Pakistan for next five years.

Referring to Haroon Rashid's column in the daily *'Jang International' of 27th August 2011*:

"Religious fundamentalism and extreme secularism both have spoiled Pakistan and Qaid e Azam had not approved any of them. Most people of Indo Pakistan are suffering with inferiority complexes thus they love sectarianism based on decades old orthodox ideas and interpretations. Our Qaid e Azam had declared Pakistan as modern Islamic state; neither mullaism is required here nor the secularism.

Simple Islam based on Qura'an and Sunnah; not on rituals based on old Arab territorial history. Some 'maulvis' had labelled him [Qaid e Azam M A Jinnah] as 'Kafir e Azam' in those days but the Qaid was a better Muslim in fact; truthful and straight."

At present Malaysia, Indonesia, Dubai, United Arab Emirates, Morocco, Turkey, Iran etc are Islamic but booming.

To cut short, Gen Ziaul Haq fully utilized the process of *Islamization* to achieve his political ends and sought legitimacy by dramatizing implementation of Islam as an ideology of Pakistan. Gen Ziaul Haq, with the help of state institutions, weakened the progressive forces and in February 1979 he introduced the *Hudood, Qisas & Diyat* in the legal system of the country. The Federal Shariat Court was established through an amendment (Article 203 D) in the constitution with the powers to examine and decide the question whether or not any law or provision of law is repugnant to the injunctions of Islam.

Chief Justice Sh Aftab Hussain of the Federal Shariat Court, in an interview published in the *daily 'Jang' of 25th July 1992*, commented over the scenario then prevailing in Pakistan:

> *'Qaid e Azam made Pakistan by eliminating sectarianism in Indian Muslims but Gen Ziaul Haq revived the same evils again when he came in power. Before Gen Ziaul Haq's rule there was complete harmony amongst Shias, Sunnis and other sects in Pakistan at all levels. Gen Ziaul Haq first divided the nation into Shias & Sunnis and then encouraged 'Brelvi and Deobandi sects' to expand their influences even through government institutions. He developed Mullaism in the country all around.*
>
> *In Constitutions of 1956 & 1973 it was decided that no law would be framed in the country against Qura'an & Sunnah and that was all an Islamic state needed. In Gen Zia's era negative legislation started cropping up. On Zakat issue, the Jafferia sect went apart which was opposed by making 'Sipah e Sohaba'. Melad was previously held in every home but when it was brought to mosques it officially created another sect [Ahle Hadith].*
>
> *In nut shell Gen Ziaul Haq believed in ad-hocism. He did every thing and only up to that extent which suited to keep his military rule and government intact.'*

The Council of Islamic Ideology, another constitutional body then framed, had restricted itself to a negative role; to identify what is 'repugnant' to Islam without spelling out alternative which should be 'in conformity' with Islam. *The Islamization process was used as a lethal political weapon. Wrong interpretation of Islam had resulted in the rise of fundamentalism, obscurantism and retrogression.'* A S **Ghazali** noted it with concern in his book released on internet.

Later, the interpretation of the *Shariah* Act of 1991 was challenged in the Federal Shariat Court (FSC). Sections 3(2) and 19 of the Act, which safeguarded the existing political system and the country's financial obligations (including interest payments) were declared un-Islamic by the FSC because of the *riba* (interest) involved. In its ruling of January 1992, [*the FSC ruling was actually passed in November 1991, but the 50-page document giving court's opinion was circulated to bankers and government officials in January 1992*] the Court held that rules and regulations relating to interest were repugnant to the *Qura'an* and *Sunnah* and should be brought in accordance with Islam.

This ruling was embarrassing for Nawaz Sharif, the originator's own government, while on one hand they wanted to satisfy the traditionalists; on the other hand the ruling was not in accordance with the government's international obligations. A private appeal was thus lodged with the Supreme Court against the FSC decision but with no cogent outcome.

This issue of interest-free economy continued hounding PML in their 1st term as their government had tried to avoid this sensitive issue through different means but could not fully succeed except some flip-flap changes in nomenclature like replacing 'interest' with 'profit-loss account' etc whereas the working of financial institutions and banks practically remained the same. During the second term, which began in February 1997, Nawaz Sharif's majority government was still facing continuous pressure to introduce an Islamic system in the country from powerful religious groups like the *Jamaat-e-Islami*. To satisfy them and for his own agonistic desire to become *Ameer ul Momineen*, he moved the Supreme Court in July 1997 for ruling and guidance on 'interest free' banking.

This appeal filed by the PML Government of Nawaz Sharif had again raised several fundamental questions about introduction of an interest free economy mentioning Pakistan's obligation towards other countries and international financial institutions which had given loans worth billions of dollars to the country on interest. The appeal had also argued that the change in system would question the validity of the banking system in the country and sought a time frame of at least two years to suggest and implement the needful in this regard.

Ultimately, **on 19th April 1998** the Pakistan government had to withdraw that appeal from the country's apex court against FSC's decision which had declared *'riba'* (interest) un-Islamic and directed the authorities to immediately introduce an interest-free economy.

In an arena of parallel judicial systems then prevailing in Pakistan the superior courts could not help women class which became the special victim of militarized laws and its effects. The *Zina* Ordinances, which went particularly discriminatory against women, continued to be the law despite all the demands from women's organization. In 1992, there was an interesting case in the Supreme Court where the court had declared Section 7 of the said ordinance to be against Islam.

Military Courts of 1997-99:

In 2nd term of PML's governance in 1997-99, PML was in a coalition government in Sindh with the MQM but when PML developed differences with the MQM and the MQM began looking to form a government with the help of the opposition Pakistan People's Party (PPP), the PM dismissed the government. The law and order had already broken down in Sindh province; the Prime Minister Nawaz Sharif on 30th October 1998 dismissed the elected provincial government and had placed the province under Governor Rule. Under the Pakistan Armed Forces (Acting in Aid of the Civil Powers) Ordinance 1998, promulgated on 20th November 1998, Article 245 of the Constitution of Pakistan was invoked and the army called in to assist the police in Karachi.

Earlier on 10th November 1998, the federal government had also suspended the powers of Speaker and Deputy Speaker of the Sindh assembly after they tried to get convene the session to discuss a no-confidence motion against the then suspended Sindh Chief Minister, Liaqat Jatoi of PML.

Karachi had faced its worst social and political crisis in 15 years those days, the history witnessed. Sindhi and Mahajir communities had lived peacefully together until 1983, when Gen Ziaul Haq and MQM's Altaf Hussain joined hands against the movement for democracy. The banned political parties at that time formed the Movement for Restoring Democracy (MRD). [*In 1998 alone, more than 600 people had lost their lives in ethnic clashes, terrorist attacks and fights between MQM activists and police.*]

In the back drop of that serious law and order situation, Nawaz Sharif's government formed special military courts, supposedly for speedy trials to deal with the terrorist activities in Karachi. The courts made judgments in one or two weeks and the government had already carried out two executions from its decisions. On 4th January 1999, the PM escaped an attempt on his life. [*Referring to The Guardian UK of 17th May 2002, Riaz Basra of LeJ was suspected of involvement in a plot to assassinate Nawaz Sharif, the then prime minister. A bridge near Mr Sharif's home was blown up minutes before his motorcade was due to cross.*] After the attack, the government decided to establish military courts in all four provinces of Pakistan.

The Military courts did not allow defendants to present a full defence in the restricted time available for the trial and seriously limited the right to appeal. These courts were subsequently abolished to prevent further miscarriages of justice. Two of the people sentenced to death by the military courts were executed till that moment. The executions were carried out despite the fact that petitions challenging the constitutionality of the military courts were pending in the Sindh High Court and in the Supreme Court of Pakistan.

Challenging the constitutionality of the summary military courts, lawyers in Pakistan pointed out that in 1977 a full bench of the Lahore High Court held that military courts could not be set up under Article 245 of the Constitution to try ordinary civilians. Other judgments of the higher judiciary in Pakistan had laid down that criminal trials should only be conducted by properly trained judicial officers, independent of the executive and under the judicial supervision of the higher judiciary.

The setting up of summary military tribunals was considered against the spirit of the Constitution of Pakistan which in Article 4 states that: 'To enjoy the protection of law and to be treated in accordance with law is the inalienable right of every person'. In Article 9: 'No person shall be deprived of life and liberty, save in accordance with law'. Trial by special tribunals also contravenes 5th Principle of the United Nations Basic Principles on the Independence of the Judiciary [as endorsed in 1985]. It states: 'Everyone has the right to be tried by ordinary courts or tribunals using established legal procedures. Tribunals that do not use the duly established procedures of the legal process shall not be created to displace the jurisdiction belonging to the ordinary courts or judicial tribunals.'

One Mohammad Saleem was sentenced to death on 19th December 1998 along with three adult men on charges of murdering three police officers. Their trial had lasted 12 days. He was acquitted for want of evidence and ordered to be released while the death sentence of the three other men was commuted to life imprisonment.

UN Convention on the Rights of the Child clearly forbids the death penalty for anyone who is under 18 at the time of committing the offence. 13 years old Saleem and at least 10 other people were reportedly sentenced to death on charges of murder, rape and kidnapping after summary trials by military courts in early December 1998. A report of amnesty International dated 7th January 1999 described about Saleem's acquittal, 20 days after he was sentenced to death by a military court.

Scenario 20

PAKISTAN'S JUDICIARY IN 1997- I

12th January 1997: In MAHMOOD KHAN ACHAKZAI *VS* FEDERATION OF PAKISTAN case, cited at *PLD 1997 SC 426* on a question about basic structure of the Constitution, the Chief Justice of Pakistan Sajjad Ali Shah had given the verdict that:

> *'The question cannot be answered authoritatively with a touch of finality but it can be said that the prominent characteristics of the Constitution [of Pakistan] are amply reflected in the Objectives Resolution which is now substantive part of the Constitution as Article 2A inserted by the Eighth Amendment'.*

The Objectives Resolution was preamble of the constitutions made and promulgated in Pakistan in 1956, 1962 and 1973. Its thorough perusal indicates that for scheme of governance the main features envisaged are federalism and Parliamentary form of government blended with Islamic provisions. The 8th Amendment was inserted in the Constitution in 1985, after which three elections were held on party-basis and the resultant parliaments did not touch this Amendment demonstrating its ratification in letter and spirit. The preamble categorically stated that:

> *'.........The State shall exercise its powers and authority through the chosen representatives of the people; and the principles of democracy, freedom, equality, tolerance and social justice as enunciated by Islam shall be fully observed. Wherein shall be guaranteed fundamental rights including equality of status, of opportunity before law, social, economic and political justice and freedom of thought, expression, belief, faith, worship and of the association, subject to law and public morality'.*

Even this wording of the preamble remained un-changed in all the three previous constitutions of Pakistan and was maintained in 1973 Constitution also. While commenting upon the Parliament's procedure to amend the said Constitution under the provisions of Article 239, the judgment stated that:

> *'Article 239 cannot be interpreted so liberally to say that it is open-ended provision without any limits under which any amendment under the sun of whatever nature can be made to provide for any other*

187

system of governance, for example, the monarchy of secular, which is not contemplated by the Objectives Resolution. Clause (6) of Article 239 provides for removal of doubt that there is no limitation whatsoever on the power of the Parliament to amend any provision of the Constitution [of Pakistan].

It therefore, follows that the Parliament has full freedom to make any amendment in the Constitution as long as salient features and basic characteristics of the Constitution providing for the Federalism, Parliamentary Democracy and the Islamic provisions are untouched and are allowed to remain intact as they are.'

It has been debated much that Article 58(2)(b), inserted in the Constitution through Eighth Amendment had changed the shape of the Constitution from Parliamentary to Presidential. In fact this apprehension may not be based on factual analysis. It is stated that Eighth Amendment was brought in by Parliament which was not elected on party basis then after that three elections took place on party basis in 1988, 1990 and 1993 which did not touch the said Amendment showing that they had full faith in it which amounts to ratification by implication.

Therefore, six out of seven judges on the bench were of the unanimous and considered opinion that Eighth Amendment including Article 58(2)(b) had come to stay in the Constitution as permanent feature.

However, it would remain open to the Parliament to make amendment to the Constitution of any provision of the Eighth Amendment as contemplated under Article 239 as long as basic characteristics of federalism, parliamentary democracy and Islamic provisions as envisaged in the Objectives Resolution/Preamble to the Constitution are not touched. Just for academic consumption, one should not forget a note, embodied in this judgment by Justice Saleem Akhtar, who had opined that:

'There are some characteristic features in every Constitution which are embedded in the historical, religious and social background of the people for whom it is framed. ..... It cannot be made rigid because such rigidity if confronted with the social and political needs of the time is likely to create cracks in it. (In nut shell) rigidity is one of the main features of a written Constitution. But this rigidity is often tuned to flexibility by the provisions of the Constitution itself and interpretations made by the Courts. Rigid Constitution may provoke violence.

...... The Courts enjoy power to strike down any law which is in conflict with the provisions of the Constitution; however, they do not have power to strike down any provision of the Constitution which may be in conflict with any of its provisions, even in the presence of Article 2A as a substantive part of the Constitution. In view of the legal dispensation resting on the judgments of this Court we agree and approve the observations of the CJP Ajmal Mian the impugned judgment that:

'it is not open to the Court to hold that a provision of the Constitution can be struck down on the ground of its being violative of the Objectives Resolution or of national aspirations or of higher ethical notions or of philosophical concepts of law or of the basic structure.'

The Achakzai's judgment had clearly stated that 'by employing the words "any law", the intention of the Constitution seems to be that Article 8 will apply to all laws made by the *Majlis-e-Shoora* (Parliament) be it general or any law to amend the Constitution.

[Likewise no enactments can be made in respect of the provisions of the Constitution relating to judiciary by which its independence and separation from executive is undermined or compromised. These are in-built limitations in the Constitution completely independent from political morality and force of public opinion.]

Most of the jurists agree with this viewpoint.

20th January 1997: Supreme Court of Pakistan was informed that false and fictitious documents were used by the then President of Pakistan Farooq Leghari to make out grounds for dissolution of government and the Parliament in November 1996. Resuming his arguments before a seven-member bench of the Supreme Court, Aitzaz Ahsan mentioned a particular letter submitted by President Leghari written on 13th November 1995 regarding an incident which actually occurred on 21st November. Another document had a date of 8th November on it but related to an incident which occurred on 15th November.

It was also pointed out that President Leghari had submitted another false document in which he had claimed that a company, in which Asif Zardari's brother-in-law held an interest, was illegally allotted land by the Capital Development Authority (CDA). The fact was that 'the person referred to by the supporting documentation, Mir Munawwar Ali, was not Zardari's brother-in-law (Mir Munawwar Ali Talpur) but some one else, that only the names were similar.

189

Referring to another document allegedly signed by PPP's Nahid Khan recommending employment for some one, the Court was informed that the letter on which the president had relied was a forged document and the criminals involved in forgery were being prosecuted.

Once Gen Raja Saroop Khan, the former Governor Punjab, in his interview published in daily *'Jang' dated 17th January 1999*, commented upon Farooq Leghari as:

> *'Farooq Leghari had developed a very bad habit of talking nice in presence of Benazir Bhutto and passing sarcastic remarks against her in her absence. We all knew it and Benazir Bhutto too. Most people started avoiding Mr Leghari. Mr Leghari had lacked courage to talk to Benazir Bhutto directly. For instance, to convey his point of difference on 'judges' case' Mr Leghari never talked to the PM [Benazir Bhutto] directly but always used to pass remarks before others. An objectionable person was he as the President of a Muslim country.'*

29th January 1997: The Supreme Court upheld President Farooq Leghari's orders dissolving the National Assembly and dismissing Benazir Bhutto's government.

The Supreme Court by a majority decision upheld President Leghari's proclamation dissolving the National Assembly and dismissing Benazir's government. Justice Zia Mahmood Mirza was the only dissenting judge who had said that:

> *'The presidential order was illegal, can not be sustained and the prime minister along with her cabinet should stand restored'.*

Six of the seven judges on the bench upheld all the charges leveled by the president excluding the murder of Mir Murtaza Bhutto saying this was subjudice before a tribunal. The allegation of extra-judicial killings in Karachi was the main charge in the presidential proclamation dismissing the Benazir Government. The court held that it was not necessary that all the material should be before the president to form his opinion before the dissolution of the assembly as was claimed by Aitzaz Ahsan; held that:

> ['*Partial evidence was enough for forming the opinion and there was no harm if corroborative and supportive material was produced after the dissolution of the assembly'.*]

The six judges of the bench disagreed with Benazir Bhutto's lawyer, Aitzaz Ahsan, that his client may also be given the same relief as provided to Nawaz Sharif, the restoration of the assembly and her government. Justice Zia Mehmood Mirza disagreed with the majority judgment and said loudly that requirements for using powers under Article 58(2)(b) had not been fulfilled.

Justice Mirza stated that law laid down in the previous dissolution cases (Haji Saifullah case, Khawaja Tariq Rahim case and Mian Nawaz Sharif case) of complete breaking down of the constitutional machinery was not fulfilled in this case. The Judge had further held that president, who had praised the government at numerous occasions for doing great job in Karachi, had no material before him at the time he made his mind to dissolve the National Assembly.

Justice S A Nusrat, in his interview of *25th July 1999*, published in the media, told that:

> *'I've seen Supreme Court's judgment written by CJP Nasim Hasan Shah in Nawaz Sharif's case of 1993. It was OK. In 1997, CJP Sajjad Ali Shah should have given a similar decision because the grounds of using Art 58(2)(b) were more or less the same. CJP Sajjad Ali Shah had dissented in 1993's judgment on the basis of Sindhi & Punjabi PMs which made him totally controversial in the judicial history of Pakistan] but he himself as the CJP behaved opposite when he wrote Benazir Bhutto's judgment.*
>
> *Basically, the CJP Sajjad Ali Shah had developed very intimate relations with President Farooq Leghari, quite contrary to the judicial norms, which made him controversial otherwise he was a perfect & nice judge altogether.'*

It is interesting to note that four weeks before the Supreme Court judgment, the Caretaker Prime Minister, Malik Meraj Khalid, told a seminar in Karachi, that the IMF had agreed to release the loan instalment only after his government dispelled the impression that the deposed government of Benazir was being restored. Meraj Khalid told that:

> *'When Pakistani team was negotiating with the IMF, a telephone call was made, asking them not to sign any accord because the Benazir government was being restored. The IMF officials were irked over the telephone call and the negotiations had run into snag because the international institutions were not inclined to dole out anything in this situation. With great difficulty the government convinced IMF that nothing of that sort was happening.'*

191

The conspiracies amongst the stake holder institutions have been the major cause of obstructions faced by Pakistan in its way to development. *Nawaz Sharif's interview with Sohail Warroich* in the name of his book *'Gaddar Kaun'* very interestingly describes the personality traits of the then President Farooq Leghari saying that:

> *'Farooq Leghari was the personal choice of Benazir Bhutto as her most*
> *confident aide. The PPP had nurtured and then tolerated Mr Leghari*
> *for 30 years, a long way; otherwise he could simply be a chief of his*
> *little tribe not a politician. It was the PPP which had offered him the*
> *presidency in a plate, who in 1996, turned eyes from his PPP when*
> *developed relations, better to say friendship, with CJP Sajjad Ali Shah*
> *and the Army Chief Gen Jehangir Karamat. Ultimately he stabbed his*
> *own party, his own leadership and got blackened his own face.'*

In nut shell, President Farooq Leghari had used his power of Art 58(2)(b) considering that Benazir Bhutto's government was involved in corrupt practices. He had not bothered to look into his own image in mirror that once he was also dragged into grave-sands of corruption.

A sale of 531 acre farm, situated in *Darkhawst Jamalkhan* (a village of District Dera Ghazi Khan) sold by Sardar Farooq Leghari, several times an MNA & Federal Minister in PPP governments and later President of Pakistan, was one of many episodes linked with Mehran Bank.

This land belonged to Mr Leghari and his family members. It was sold to six people from Karachi alleged to be fronting for banker Yunus Habib, which gave a new and dramatic twist to the Mehran gate scandal. The president's integrity and his image, as an honest politician, came under question when Nawaz Sharif alleged that Farooq Leghari was involved in the Mehran Bank scandal. Releasing photocopies of bank drafts worth 17 million rupees deposited in Mr Leghari's account in Mehran Bank, Nawaz Sharif charged that the money was a pay off by Yunus Habib in return for Leghari's bailing out Mehran bank.

On 4th June 1994, President Farooq Leghari conceded that the documents produced by Nawaz Sharif, the then sitting on opposition benches, were related to the sale of a farm that had been owned by him and several of his family members. However, he defended the deal, saying that there was nothing illegal about it.

President Farooq Leghari had told the *Newsline,* a monthly magazine of Karachi:

"I did ask Mr. Yunus Habib to see if he could arrange for any buyers for the land ... But I didn't know those six people (who eventually bought the land). I am not aware of whether they were fronting for Mr Yunus Habib or if the land was actually bought by Mr Yunus Habib and his family.... As a seller, my only interest was to make sure that I got the price of the land."

President Farooq Leghari, however, admitted, that he was approached by Yunus Habib in April 1993, when he was Finance Minister in the interim government (April/May 1993) to save Mehran Bank from collapsing. Mr Leghari referred Yunus Habib's request to the State Bank, but before getting any reply, the interim government was dissolved and Mr Sartaj Aziz, who became the Federal Finance Minister in the revived government of Nawaz Sharif in April 1993, had ordered the demanded relief given to the Mehran Bank.

President Farooq Leghari had categorically stated that:

"The allegation of my having helped Yunus Habib and saved Mehran Bank is false. It was done by Sartaj Aziz and Nawaz Sharif. But I have the moral courage to say that yes, I also wanted to do the same and if I had a longer stay as Finance Minister I would have done the same."

In July 1994 a commission, comprising five judges, was formed to launch investigation into the Mehran Bank scandal. It took eight months to complete its inquiry in February 1995 but its report was never published. However, some parts of the reports were released on 8th December 1996, according to which the commission had exonerated President Leghari from any wrong doing in his *benami* deal. But the commission did not mention to whom the land was sold by the President for Rs. 15 million and from which account the money was debited for the payment.

Earlier, on 14th December 1995 Younus Habib had been awarded 10 years rigorous imprisonment and fined Rs 36.7 million in a fraud case by the Special Banking Court of Sindh.

Coming back; had Farooq Leghari not done so, the history of Pakistan would have been different. He would have continued with his portfolio as president for long. In the first week of April 1997, just about forty days after the SC's decision, when he was having rest in his village home, Prime Minister Nawaz Sharif got a constitutional amendment okayed by both houses of the Parliament during the same night at 11 PM and at 3 AM a helicopter was landing in Mr Leghari's village with that amendment to be signed finally depriving him off his powers of Article 58(2)(b). After a few months he was lastly asked to pack off from the Presidency too.

24th February 1997: COAS Gen Mirza Aslam Beg told the Supreme Court that he was not answerable to it regarding the alleged funding of the *Islami Jamhoori Ittehad* (IJI) election campaign in 1990.

> [It was proved through record that ISI had distributed 140 million Rupees of army secret fund to various people of IJI to make sure defeat of PPP's candidates in general national elections in 1990. Full details are given in a separate chapter.]

2nd March 1997: Prime Minister Nawaz Sharif got Justice (Rtd) Rafiq Tarar and Justice (Rtd) Afzal Loan elected as senators.

One can re-collect that this was the reward from Nawaz Sharif for having their favours for restoration of his government in April 1993 when they were the sitting judges of the Supreme Court of Pakistan. This nexus went a long way.

Prime Minister Nawaz Sharif once paid a courtesy visit to the Chief Justice Sajjad Ali Shah in mid 1997. Majid Nizami of daily *'Nation & Nawa i Waqt'* was also accompanying him. The PM asked the CJP to refrain from accepting petitions or cases involving Sharif family in corruption and also to shun the routine judicial process against them. In those days there were numerous petitions under regular hearing with ample documentation on alleged corruptions done by the Sharifs and the prime minister was feeling embarrassed due to numerous stories appearing in row at print and electronic media.

Nawaz Sharif had then asked the CJP that what he intended to do after retirement which was due after three months. If he (CJP) extended favours to Sharifs in petitions lying before the SC, he would be able to get 'big favour' from the PML in return.

The CJP Mr Shah told Nawaz Sharif that he intended to go to *Madina Munawwara* after retirement. The PM asked him to stay here and *'he would be nominated as the president if he considers'*. The CJP thought for a while and then refused to accept that 'bargain' because he intended to deal with those petitions of corruption against Sharifs on pure merits.

In November 1997, when the relationship deteriorated between the PM and the CJP, Justice (Rtd) Rafiq Tarar played a vital role in winning the judges of Balochistan High Court which helped Nawaz Sharif's move of sending CJP home. In reward Rafiq Tarar was offered that presidential slot through Mian Sharif, PM's father, which he gladly accepted.

10th March 1997: An ordinance titled *'Registration of Printing Press and Publication Ordinance, 1997'* was got issued by PM Nawaz Sharif to curb the press and freedom of expression. Article 29 authorized magistrates and low-ranking police sub-inspectors to get in the way of the Press, hold them and to initiate executive actions including the forfeiture of newspaper copies without the process of judicial review and restraint.

Among other negative points, the ordinance obstructed the newspapers from publishing any account of the proceedings of the National Assembly or the Senate or a provincial assembly if such account contains any matter which is not part of the proceedings of such an assembly and which is prejudicial to the maintenance of public order or is opposed to morality, or amounts to contempt of the court, defamation or incitement for the commission of an offence.

The police and respective magistrates were authorized to forfeit the copies of a newspaper containing any material inciting an offence or violence or amounts to false rumours or causing hatred or contempt of the government with intent of causing defiance of the government authority.

This suppression of press freedom was taken as the first negative point for the Nawaz Sharif government which ultimately harmed him in October 1999 when all the press and media welcomed Gen Musharraf along with his army team because they were living in a frightening atmosphere for the last two years.

13th Amendment Bill:

2nd April 1997: At midnight, rules and procedures of the parliament were suspended all of a sudden and the 13th Amendment Bill was rushed through both houses, signed by the president the next day, and notified on 4th April. By this amendment, the president was disempowered and the Prime Minister further empowered. The President was left with no power to dissolve the National Assembly under the provisions of Art 58(2)(b), he could not appoint governors at his discretion but on the advice of the prime minister, the provincial governors could dissolve their assemblies.

Further, the president, though he was the supreme commander of the Armed Forces, but was not able to appoint or sack the services of the chiefs without consultation and recommendations of the prime minister.

On the issue of appointment of judges, Benazir Bhutto as prime minister and Farooq Leghari as president had filed separate references before the Supreme Court. The PPP had then levelled an allegation that the Supreme Court had accepted the reference of the president on Sunday by opening the court doors especially for him.

Justice Sajjad Ali Shah had himself refuted this allegation later by saying that the reference of Farooq Leghari was in the hearing process since much before Benazir Bhutto's dismissal. Mr Farooq Legahri's presidential reference was basically concerned with certain explanations of 'Judges Case' *vis a vis* Article 2A of the Constitution.

In the same reference Mr Leghari had particularly asked the SC to guide <u>'if the PM's consultation is mandatory before the president's orders for appointing judges are released.'</u> All law officers including Attorney General had tried to convince the court that PM's consultation should not be there because PM's office was 'political' and thus the judges would also be carrying certain political influences. Justice Sajjad Ali Shah CJP gave a categorical verdict that:

'As our constitution gives approval for parliamentary system of government, therefore, Prime Minister's consultation should be incorporated in the decision making process while appointing judges in the superior courts of Pakistan.'

The then President Farooq Leghari had gone home in Dera Ghazi Khan for a week in the last week of March 1997 and in his absence the special sessions of Senate and the National Assembly were made to sit midnight. The PML(N) had two third majority in both the houses thus it took only seconds to pass this amendment. During the same night time a special helicopter was sent to President Leghari's home 300 miles away, he was awakened and asked to sign the bill passed, a much humiliating way to tell somebody that your powers have been snatched.

4th April 1997: 13th amendment in Pakistan's Constitution got enforced by the then PM Nawaz Sharif. Under the provision of this amendment, the powers to dissolve the Assemblies or sending home the Prime Minister were taken back from the President.

Ehtesab Cell Modified:

29th May 1997: The National Assembly amended the Ehtesab Ordinance to introduce major changes in the accountability process to suit Nawaz Sharif. In that era of political victimization and tyranny all the higher courts remained mum rather shown a visible bias and partisanship. Mostly the goals were achieved through judges like Justice A Qayyum Malik whose face was blackened by his fellow judges in 2001 while his audio tapes were caught having 'glorious' instances of miscarriage of justice.

The most significant amendment was the shifting of the starting date for accountability from the original 31st December 1985 (when General Zia lifted the martial law) to 6th August 1990 (when the first government of Benazir Bhutto was dismissed). It was done so because Nawaz Sharif himself remained in saddles of the Punjab Government.

The amendment also transferred the power of investigating the corruption charges from the Chief Ehtesab Commissioner to the Ehtesab Cell set up by PM Nawaz Sharif. This amendment in Ehtesab Bill steam-rolled through the National Assembly made a mockery of accountability because Nawaz Sharif had taken out himself and his family members from accountability process for the period he remained as Finance Minister, Interim Chief Minister and Chief Minister of Punjab.

During the same abolished period of 1985-1990, he had got written off bank loans of Rs: 212 billion taken on their family projects from various banks and Financial Institutions. (Ref telecast program of *Kashif Abbasi dated 8th April 2011 on ARY News*)

During this period Nawaz Sharif, in his capacity of Chief Minister of the Punjab, was strengthening and consolidating his industrial and political base. Reports were on record that:

> *'There were 167 cases of major loan defaults which included 107 cases involving top leaders of the PML(N) who got the benefit of huge write-offs during 1985-1990 during his rule on Punjab.'*

The transfer of power of appointment of the Chief Ehtesab Commissioner from the President to the federal government reduced the office of the CEC to a mere post office. The real powers were soon transferred to the Accountability Cell in Prime Minister's secretariat. The head of the Cell, Senator Saifur Rehman Khan, was accountable only to the PM. The amendment also extended ex post facto legal sanction to the Prime Minister's Accountability Cell, which was under attack in a number of petitions and challenges in the Lahore High Court.

The original ordinance had empowered the Ehtesab Commissioner to initiate a case on a reference received from the appropriate government, on receipt of a complaint or on his own accord. Under the new amended law, if the CEC deems a reference necessary, he must refer it to the A Cell for investigation. With all the accountability functions and powers concentrated in Saif ur Rehman's Cell functioning in PM secretariat, PM Nawaz Sharif was able to keep strict check not only on the opposition and the bureaucracy but on his own party-men also.

On **4th February 1998,** Nawaz Sharif got amended the Ehtesab Act, replacing the name 'Ehtesab Cell', with 'Ehtesab Bureau', and provided powers of an SHO, (like an officer in-charge of a police station) to the Bureau Chief or any other official designated by him for the purpose of investigation. The amendments were introduced into the Ehtesab Act through a presidential ordinance, promulgated by the then President Rafiq Tarar on advice of Nawaz Sharif.

By amending Section 3 of the Ehtesab Act, the government had restored the original definition of 'corruption' meaning thereby that any favour by a government official to any person other than his/her spouse or dependents would also fall in the definition of corruption, and he would be held responsible for that. A reference made to the Ehtesab Bureau was treated as a report under Section 154 of the code with powers to examine all the material, evidence and proof. No other agency will have a power to look into the matter.

After the amendment, the Ehtesab Bureau was also empowered to ask the Chief Ehtesab Commissioner (CEC) to make a request to any court for the withdrawal of any case pending in a court. If the court grants permission, the said case will be transferred to the Ehtesab Bureau. The Chief Ehtesab Commissioner was given powers to arrest an accused at any stage of proceedings against him.

The amendment had provided a right of appeal to the CEC if the court or Ehtesab Bench acquitted any accused. Earlier this right was given only to the accused. It was also provided that on the grant of pardon from the CEC, a magistrate appointed by the CEC himself will examine an accused [what a judicious joke it was].

When the Ehtesab Bureau became an independent investigating agency with teeth of its own and therefore not dependent, as it formerly was, upon the powers of the FIA, a cold war had taken start between Saifur Rehman and Ch. Shujaat Hussain whose FIA and interior ministry were made paralyzed. The first and most striking change was to strip the original law of its neutrality and place all the powers in the Prime Minister Secretariat Islamabad.

In Pakistan, the word 'accountability' has only one meaning: to malign and persecute political opponents. Glimpses of the full story can be culled from the report of Mehran Bank Commission along with the evidence provided by Gen Asad Durrani and Hameed Asghar Qidwai, as well as the jailed chief executive of the failed bank, Yunus Habib.

Several references were filed against the former PM Ms Bhutto and her husband and 87 senior bureaucrats were suspended hastily amidst a blaze of publicity. Meanwhile, the list of bank defaulters remained as long and potent as ever with hardly anything returned to the banks or the financial institutions or state.

The annual 1997 Human Rights Report of US State Department said:

> *'The Accountability Commission, which was established by the caretaker government and headed by a retired judge, had been overshadowed by an Accountability Cell, headed by a close associate of the PM Nawaz Sharif. This cell had been accused of conducting politically motivated investigations of politicians, senior civil servants, and business figures, designed to extract evidence and, in some cases, televised confessions of alleged wrongdoers. There are numerous examples of televised confessions extracted from Salman Farooqi, Secretary of Commerce under Benazir Bhutto; Ahmed Sadiq, Benazir Bhutto's Principal Secretary; and Zafar Iqbal, Chairman of the Capital Development Authority Islamabad and many more like them.'*

16th June 1997: A writ petition was moved in the Supreme Court to close down political cell of the Inter Services Intelligence (ISI), Pakistan Army's spy directorate. The PML had backed it in fact.

14th Amendment Bill:

1st July 1997: the National Assembly had unanimously adopted the Constitution Bill, the Fourteenth Amendment. This *Anti-Defection (Floor Crossing) Bill* earlier passed by the Senate and later by the

National Assembly with a large majority, was a structural reform to end the practice of switching party loyalties and blackmailing party leadership for ministerial slots, bank loans and other concessions.

After being rushed through Parliament, the 14th Constitutional Amendment was hailed as the remedy against the scourge of floor-crossing, which had de-stabilized the democratic political system in the post-Ziaul Haq era. On the other hand, by vesting party leaders with sweeping powers to unseat legislators and denying judicial redress to the latter, it was seen as having imposed party dictatorships and political regimentation making it the 'family dynasty' in politics.

All these issues went before the Supreme Court and its 6 to 1 verdict has only partially validated the controversial Amendment. The six judges in favour had struck down the portions curbing the legislators' right to express dissent inside and outside Parliament. However, almost certainly with an eye to the bitter realities of our political culture, they maintained the compulsion for legislators to vote according to party dictates so as to "bring stability to the polity" by eliminating floor-crossing.

Even in allowing this right of verbal dissent, there was a 4-2 split among the honourable judges. Justices Saiduzzaman Siddiqui and Irshad Hassan held that even dissent outside the legislature was ultimately damaging to party discipline inside the House and, thus, for political stability generally. They believed that principled dissent required the legislator to resign the seat won under a party flag. Hence, they favoured upholding the 14th Amendment in its entirety.

However, the six judges were unanimous in diluting the vast powers given to party bosses by upholding the right of an unseated legislator to seek remedy from the superior courts. A very interesting situation had cropped up in Pakistan on that 14th Amendment issue, which ultimately 'inspired' the then ruling party of Pakistan Muslim League (PML) to launch an attack on the Supreme Court of Pakistan.

A Supreme Court judgment of 11th July 2002 describes it as under:

> ' ..... A tug of war started between the Prime Minister (Nawaz Sharif) and the Chief Justice of Pakistan (Justice Sajjad Ali Shah). The Prime Minister introduced the 14th Amendment to the Constitution as a result of which the persons elected on the ticket of a particular party were debarred from speaking against the policies of the party concerned at the floor of the house or outside.

A petition was moved challenging this amendment on the ground that it infringed the fundamental right of freedom of speech and the then Chief Justice suspended the operation of the 14th Amendment which was resented by the party in power. The justification advanced by the party in power to introduce 14th Amendment was that they were trying to bring an end to the floor crossing.

The suspension of the operation of the 14th Amendment made the Prime Minister and others to ridicule the Chief Justice and certain derogatory remarks were made against this Court, which led to initiation of Contempt of Court proceedings against the sitting Prime Minister Nawaz Sharif and his cronies.

Although the Prime Minister appeared in Court but as expected this Court desired to proceed further in the matter which again infuriated the party in power and thus through a concerted effort this Court was attacked by an unruly mob to deter the Court from hearing the contempt case as a result of which the Chief Justice of Pakistan and other Judges had to leave the Courtroom. Crocodile tears were shed by the party in power over the incident. The mob which attacked this Court included elected members. .....'

Before passing that 14th Amendment, probably during 2nd week of May 1997, the CJP J Shah had once called Barrister Akram Sheikh and handed over a draft of that proposed amendment carrying imposing of restrictions over freedom of parliamentarians, which was going to be taken through the Parliament. Next day, Akram Sheikh tried to see PM Nawaz Sharif to speak on that proposal but could not see him. Akram Sheikh, however, made out a text suggesting the PM to refrain from calling such an amendment on the floor and faxed it to the PM with copies of that text to all PML's MsNA. On 15th May when PML's parliamentary meeting was held, all the members placed that Akram Sheikh's fax before the PM and urged him to cool down.

Two days later, that fax was published in all print media. Nawaz Sharif went sentimental, had conveyed his displeasure to Barrister Akram Sheikh and announced to go with the draft proposal at all costs which ultimately became the basis of 14th Amendment.

Throughout the history of Pakistan, the 'party changing process' had contributed to a sense of immunity on the part of members of the ruling party, and to rampant corruption among leading politicians. The 14th Amendment, had however, helped some dictators and particularly contributed to the overwhelming popular support for Gen Musharraf's coup in 1999. The same Supreme Court had subsequently validated the coup on the grounds that the 13th & 14th Amendments had created a situation for which there was no constitutional remedy.

Anti Terrorist Courts 1997:

On 18th January 1997 Mehram Ali, a Shia militant member of an organization called *Tehrik Nifaz Fiqh-i-Jafaria* (TNFJ), planted a remote controlled bomb in the grounds of the district court complex in Lahore. He detonated the bomb. When the debris settled the bodies of twenty-three victims were found, including those of Maulana Zia-ur-Rehman Farooqi and Maulana Azam Tariq, Chairman of the *Sipah-i-Sahaba Pakistan* (SSP), a militant Sunni organization. The victims were brought to the Additional Sessions judge's Court from the Kot Lakhpat jail where they were serving sentences related to their earlier anti-Shia crimes. 55 others were injured in the blast.

One Mehram Ali was caught at the scene but his trial before the Sessions court dragged on. The case generated considerable press coverage and provided the context, perhaps pretext, for the introduction of the Anti Terrorism Act of 1997 which came into effect on 20th August.

The Anti-Terrorism Act of 1997 was the brainchild of the Nawaz Sharif administration, which had been returned to power in February 1997 following a landslide victory that left PML(N), with an overwhelming majority in the national assembly. During his first premiership, Nawaz Sharif had earlier introduced an anti-terrorism strategy, through 12th Amendment in the Constitution, which added Article 212-B to the document.

The said amendment allowed for the "establishment of Special Courts for the trial of heinous offences" on 28th July 1991. This device was designed as a temporary measure that would stand repealed, if not confirmed by the parliament, three years after its enactment. Thus, the 12th Amendment & Article 212-B expired on 28th July 1994, died its own death and stood nullified at its own.

On 13th August 1997, an *Anti-Terrorism Act (ATA)* was bulldozed through the parliament and was severely criticized by all including many members of PML and its coalition allies. Yet on the day of its presentation it was endorsed within three hours. It was widely felt that the ATA would turn the country into a police state violating the constitution. The law was to equip the law enforcing agencies and army with a license to kill any person on mere suspicion. It also empowered the police to search a house and arrest a person without warrant.

The ATA provided an appeal against the special court judgment before a tribunal of two High Court judges. A person accused under the ATA was not able to move any court for bail even the High Court. Thus the judiciary also opposed the ATA and many feared that the law would be grossly abused. In a mutual meeting on 20th August CM Punjab, Shahbaz Sharif, had failed to convince the then CJP Justice Sajjad Ali Shah of the need to establish special courts under the ATA. The bar associations had also condemned the law.

The then Federal Law Minister Khalid Anwer first surprised his colleagues by allowing the government to push through this piece of dubious legislation but afterwards proceeded to distance himself when it was enacted. He even went so far as to declare that he would have opposed the law, had he been in the opposition. The situation went so tense that PM Nawaz Sharif had to announce that the law would be phased out once the situation was under control.

Six special courts started working in the Punjab province on 25th August but with smooth profile. When the special courts were established in the Sindh province the fears came true because the police had started sending cases to special speedy trial courts at rocketing speed.

The Punjab Forensic Science Laboratory used to be kept under pressure from the government to issue 'positive results' about weapons used in cases being tried by the special courts set up under the ATA. For instance, the same four weapons were repeatedly sent to the Punjab Forensic Science Laboratory at Lahore to ascertain whether or not they were used in about 1000 cases by an accused during a sectarian attack for which he was being tried.

Interestingly, all the weapons tested were declared positive by forensic experts, providing sufficient evidence for the prosecution to obtain maximum punishment for the accused. On the basis of those bogus reports as many as 55 people were sentenced to death, 32 people sentenced to life imprisonment or so.

Reportedly in some cases the bullet shells collected from a crime scene years ago matched with the weapons recovered from the accused on arrest. It was ironic that some officials had insisted on matching the shells recovered from a scene of crime in 1990 with that of a weapon recovered from the accused in 1997.

It was CJP Justice Sajjad Ali Shah who had tried to block the mode of this tyrannical way of governance for which he had to pay ultimately in November same year when he was shown way to home in an un-ceremonial way. In February 1999, the Supreme Court had declared these Military Courts unconstitutional and ordered their dissolution. There was no way out except to obey the Apex Court's orders. Nawaz Sharif, taking it as a note of humiliation for his person and premiership, got formulated and issued an ATA Ordinance in April 1999 to continue his dictatorial, despotic and oppressive governance.

Under this Ordinance, those ATA Courts, previously run by the military officers and commonly called as special military courts, were later replaced with Anti-terrorist Courts. Through amendments to the ATA, the jurisdiction of Anti-terrorist Courts was extended to cover the same types of offences as had been tried before by Military Courts, and the executive completed the transition by transferring Military Court cases to the Anti-terrorist Courts. These courts again lacked essential due process and fundamental rights guarantees, including the right of appeal. As was the case with Military Courts, Anti-terrorist Courts were also established to dispense with the summary justice, conducting and concluding trials mostly within seven working days.

Coming back to the earlier cited case, after promulgation of ATA 1997, the Mehram Ali case was transferred to the newly constituted special Anti-Terrorism Court (ATC) in late August, where Ali was awarded a death sentence, convicted for twenty three counts of murder, and various other sentences related to the bombing. He filed an appeal before the newly constituted Anti-Terrorism Appellate (ATA) Tribunal, also having a seat at Lahore.

The ATA upheld his conviction. The petitioner then filed a writ petition before the Lahore High Court claiming, among other things, that the formation of the special courts violated provisions of the constitution. The Lahore High Court claimed jurisdiction to hear the appeal, but held that the conviction should still stand. Mehram Ali then filed an appeal to the Supreme Court of Pakistan.

The motives for the introduction of the Anti-Terrorism Act were, in a way, justified. Clearly, Pakistan had suffered from very significant communal and sectarian violence for the past several years, and the regular criminal justice system had not been able to curb such violence. In this context, the ATCs, with their "promise" of speedy justice, unencumbered by the procedural niceties of the regular court system, would serve as a deterrent to would-be terrorists. The Chief Justice Sajjad Ali Shah CJP had opposed this development in mid 1997 but the PM Nawaz Sharif sent him home later.

His successor Justice Ajmal Mian, the then Chief Justice of the Supreme Court, also held the opinion that the supervision and control over the subordinate judiciary (including the special courts) should go with the High Courts. Moreover, no parallel legal system could be constructed that bypassed the operation of regular court system. Despite this finding the Supreme Court had shown sympathy for the government's affirmed intent to speedy justice.

In a concurring opinion Justice Irshad Hassan Khan had stated:

> '[The] speedy resolution of civil and criminal cases is an important constitutional goal, as envisaged by principles of policy enshrined in the constitution. It is therefore, not undesirable to create Special Courts for operation with speed but expeditious disposition of cases of terrorist activities/heinous offences have to be subject to constitution & law [then in vogue in Pakistan].'

In the light of this finding, the Nawaz Sharif government had no recourse but to amend the Anti-Terrorism Act and incorporate the changes ordered by the Supreme Court. Accordingly, on 24 October 1998 the *Anti-Terrorism (Amendment) Ordinance, 1998* was issued. The new act met all of the objections raised in the *Mehram Ali* case.

Thereafter, Special Anti-Terrorism courts remained in place but the judges of such courts were granted tenure of office (two years, later extended to two and half years); the special Appellate Tribunals were disbanded, appeals against the decisions of the Anti-Terrorism courts would henceforth allowed in the respective High Courts; and restrictions were placed on the earlier act's provisions regarding trial in absentia to accord with regular legal procedures.

Scenario 21

PAKISTAN'S JUDICIARY IN 1997-II:

In summer 1997, Chief Justice of Pakistan Sajjad Ali Shah proceeded to an overseas trip. Incidentally second senior most justice Ajmal Mian was also abroad. Justice Saeeduzaman Siddiqui was in Islamabad when he was told that chief justice had left the country. He adjourned the proceedings, consulted lawyers and then called upon all Supreme Court registries to stop working. He declared that there was a constitutional crisis since no acting chief justice was appointed. He sent a letter to the federal government advising it to issue notification for appointment of acting chief justice. As he was the next senior judge, Justice Siddiqui was appointed as acting Chief Justice.

This caused a lot of bad taste between J Saeeduzaman Siddiqui and the CJP and on his return. CJP Sajjad Ali Shah conveyed his disapproval in writing and kept it on record.

In August 1997, Chief Justice Sajjad Ali Shah recommended elevation of five judges to Supreme Court without consulting with the government. Government in return issued an order duly signed by the president reducing the strength of the Supreme Court from seventeen to twelve.

It was done by the PM Nawaz Sharif without consulting his closest legal advisor Barrister Akram Sheikh, who was told on 22nd August 1997, about this 'structural reduction' of the Supreme Court by the Swiss authorities in Geneva, where he had gone to attend an International Human Rights Conference. Akram Sheikh did not believe it but when he reached his hotel room, a fax message was waiting for him, sent on behalf of the PM Nawaz Sharif, containing the news about that reduction.

Akram Sheikh immediately left that meeting in between and straightaway rushed back to Pakistan. He advised the PM to take back that executive order because no sane person would approve that. The PM said that the CJP wanted to add his favourite five judges in the Supreme Court to make his lobby strong. Akram Sheikh had urged to accept those five judges; if they would go honest, well & good; if not we'll find out a legal and better way to deal with that wrong judge under Art 209 of the Constitution.

In the meantime, the Supreme Court Bar Association passed a resolution to challenge the PM's decision. Sharifuddin Pirzada had also given the same advice to Nawaz Sharif.

Few days later the Chief Justice Sajjad Ali Shah, while presiding a three member bench, suspended the said notification and the government had to withdraw its decision.

During the same days judges of the Supreme Court started dragging each other in clashes over tiny issues like the colour of the Supreme Court flag. The chief justice arranged for the inauguration of incomplete building of the new Supreme Court because he wanted to be in the limelight before his retirement. A number of judges opposed this ridiculous idea and they were not invited for the ceremony. There were many such gimmicks which marked 1997 a laughing stock. (Ref: *Judicial Jitters in Pakistan by Hamid Hussain in Defence Journal, June 2007*)

Sitting PM called in for Contempt:

3rd November 1997: Chief Justice Sajjad Ali Shah issued notices to the Prime Minister Nawaz Sharif on a 'contempt' petition and on 19th November 1997, the Supreme Court issued charge sheets to the Prime Minister Nawaz Sharif and 11 others in the same contempt case.

Referring to the '*World News....Story page*' of CNN dated 30th November 1997 which described accusation of the then Prime Minister Nawaz Sharif against President Farooq Ahmed Leghari and Chief Justice Sajjad Ali Shah for trying to undermine his government and vowed to fight against the 'conspiracy' in the 'national interest.' Nawaz Sharif said in a 30-minute televised address to the nation:

'I have uncovered a greater, deeper conspiracy but I will fight. I will, inshallah, face every difficulty because the question is not that of my personal interest but of the national interest. I will not allow my people to become a victim to this conspiracy.'

Nawaz Sharif's accusations came as the Supreme Court was to resume his trial for contempt of court — part of a power struggle that erupted two months earlier and had led to factional fighting that threatened to escalate into a full-blown constitutional crisis. The government was scared that if the Supreme Court found Nawaz Sharif guilty of Contempt of court, he would be disqualified from office of the Prime Minister.

Nawaz Sharif's confrontation with the judiciary began when both he and the Chief Justice Sajjad Ali Shah claimed their rights to appoint judges to the Supreme Court though there might be other issues also. Allegedly Prime Minister Nawaz Sharif wanted to forward names of certain people who were either their family members or friends or their intransigent and die-hard party workers.

After weeks of refusing to back down, Nawaz Sharif had at last told the Parliament that it was up to the Chief Justice and said he was making decisions in the interests of nation and to prevent further confrontation between the two pillars of the state.

To understand the real perspective of enmity and confrontation between the two giants, one has to go back deep into the past events like:

- Justice Sajjad Ali Shah was the only dissenter in the 11-member bench whose decision restored Mr Nawaz Sharif to power in May 1993 after he had been booted out by the then President Ghulam Ishaq Khan on the charges of corruption.
- Chief Justice Sajjad Ali Shah ordered the release of some civil servants who were arrested and hand-cuffed from Faisalabad by order of the Prime Minister Nawaz Sharif.
- The main sour point was the establishment of special Courts by Nawaz Sharif, established in contravention of the Chief Justice's judicious advice. These special courts, which were established to benefit the Prime Minister's allies and supporters, eventually proved to be a humiliating blot on the face of justice in Pakistan.
- The Chief Justice wanted to fill five vacant positions of judges in the Supreme Court on merit and promotion, to be able to carry out the business of dispensing justice in a speedy manner, the Prime Minister not only refused to grant the request but went ahead and abolished those vacancies altogether through a parliamentary move.
- The PM Nawaz Sharif had to restore the judges vacancies under pressure but refused to fill them up.

The Prime Minister eventually gave in but shortly afterwards summoned to the Court to answer allegations of contempt of court, arising out of remarks he had made about a court decision. He had criticized the decision to suspend one of his early pieces of legislation, which had outlawed the practice of members of parliament switching sides, commonly known and understood by the people of Pakistan as '*Horse Trading or Lotacracy*'.

As per daily **Dawn of 30th October 1997**: *"...... while commenting on suspension of the 14th amendment; Nawaz Sharif had said that the Chief Justice's action was 'illegal and unconstitutional' and that it would revive 'horse trading or lotacracy' in the parliament. He also maintained that the Chief Justice of Pakistan had created a situation that was both unfortunate and undemocratic."*

In the 3rd week of November 1997, PM Nawaz Sharif was formally charged with contempt of court in a dispute that threatened to unseat the leader elected just nine months ago. The charges were made during Nawaz Sharif's second appearance at the Supreme Court to respond to allegations that he made at a news conference showing contempt of the top judicial institution. In Pakistan it was (and still it is so) objectionable and un-wanted to publicly criticize the judiciary. The CJP Sajjad Ali Shah should have reconciled the matter when sitting prime minister had appeared before the apex court himself. It was enough.

Nawaz Sharif had tendered his apologies on the next hearing day, which his lawyer recited on his behalf before the Supreme Court. Nonetheless his comments offended Chief Justice Sajjad Ali Shah, conveying that:

> *'It was his job to keep the people of my country informed in the light of varying opinions. I [Nawaz Sharif] have neither committed contempt of the apex court, nor do I intend to do that'.*

It was not clear whether Nawaz Sharif's apology had satisfied the court. Chief Justice Sajjad Ali Shah adjourned the hearing until next day, so he could review videotapes of the news conference.

At this stage one can recall that 'Public Confidence' in the context of contempt of court was a hot topic in the developed world and was so since the last two decades. The courts have vigorously punished offensive speech directed at the judiciary on the grounds that intemperate criticism of the court leads to erosion of public confidence in the judiciary. It is a well established principle that public confidence in the judiciary is both vital and fragile and therefore requires special protection from offending free expression.

Referring to David Pannick (*Judges*, Oxford University Press [1987] p 110) as explained that:

> *'......the grandiloquent fear that criticism of the courts may endanger civilization has, in the twentieth century, continued to lead to the*

209

punishment of persons who have insulted members of the judiciary or impugned their impartiality.'

Similarly in Australia, when Norman Gallagher, a trade union leader greeted his acquittal on a contempt of court charge with the comment that it was the demonstrations of his trade union members which changed the mind of the court trying him, he was again charged with contempt. The very court which had just acquitted Gallagher of the charge of committing contempt felt compelled to try him for scandalizing the court, albeit, of course, on a different cause of action. Gallagher was ultimately found guilty.

Gallagher lodged an appeal to the Australian High Court but it was dismissed, holding that:

> *"...what was imputed was a grave breach of duty by the Court ...and.... there can be no doubts that the offending statement amounted to a contempt of court, and if repeated was calculated to undermine public confidence in the Federal Court."* (Ref: *Gallagher v. Durrack* **[1985] LRC (Crim) 706 Aus HC**)

One can compare Gallagher's case exactly fitted in Nawaz Sharif's shoes. May be that Gallagher was not attacking the Court at all. Nor was he leveling direct criticism which could be viewed as 'willful insult'. But in the case of Nawaz Sharif, the Supreme Court might have felt the insult hidden in his expression made in the above referred statement in the name of 'Public Confidence'.

Coming back to our topic, S M Zafar (Nawaz Sharif's lawyer) said he had hoped the Chief Justice would drop the contempt charges after viewing video tapes of the news conference. Nawaz Sharif looked angry as he left the packed courtroom shortly after the Chief Justice had announced his decision.

Next day, in a move that seemed to anticipate the Supreme Court's decision, Parliament amended Pakistan's contempt law giving Nawaz Sharif a right of appeal and suspending a conviction while the appeal is being heard. This controversy had driven the country into a constitutional crisis. The bill needed the assent of President Farooq Leghari with whom Nawaz Sharif was not at good terms.

One of Nawaz Sharif's first acts when he came to power in early 1997 was to pass a constitutional amendment on 2nd April 1997 stripping President Leghari of the power to sack governments under the provisions of section 58(2)(B) of the constitution, a power that had been used at least five times since 1985.

[Afterwards the military ruler Gen Musharraf got the same power back through an amendment made under military orders and then got it regularized and converted into supreme law under the title of 17th Amendment in the Constitution of Pakistan.]

Nawaz Sharif had insisted on the right to defend himself and wanted an ordinance carrying amendment to the contempt of court law so that he could appeal, should he be found guilty. However, Farooq Leghari, the then President, had refused to sign that amendment, and that prompted Nawaz Sharif to try to impeach the president. The impeachment proceedings were halted when the army stepped in to mediate in the beginning of November 1997.

Then one black Friday of November 1997 came when the court proceedings against Nawaz Sharif were interrupted. His supporters stormed the Supreme Court and a major scuffle ensued with the judiciary. There were riots with the police on duty too. The details of incidence are given below.

Supreme Court Attacked:

28th November 1997: The building of Supreme Court at Islamabad was attacked. The workers of Pakistan Muslim League Nawaz Group [PML(N)] were brought in thousands in buses arranged by the elected members of National & Provincial Assemblies around to ransack the buildings and sanctity of the Supreme Court. Pakistan grappled with its worst-ever constitutional crisis when that unruly mob stormed into the Supreme Court, forcing Chief Justice Sajjad Ali Shah to adjourn the contempt of court case against Prime Minister Nawaz Sharif. Thousands of PML(N) supporters and members of its youth wing, the Muslim Students Front (MSF), breached the police cordon around the courthouse when defence lawyer S M Zafar was arguing PM's case.

A journalist had rushed into the courtroom and warned the bench of an impending attack. The Chief Justice got up abruptly, thanked S M Zafar and adjourned the hearing. While judicial members left the courtroom soon after, the mob entered it shouting slogans, and damaged furniture.

The unruly mob, led by ruling party member from Punjab *Sardar Naseem* and Col (Rtd) *Mushtaq Tahir Kheli*, Sharif's political secretary, chanted slogans against the Chief Justice. The mob had also beaten up

PPP's Senator Iqbal Haider. The police managed to restore normalcy after baton charging and tear gassing the mob, both inside & outside the courthouse. The court which assembled at 9:45am could continue the proceedings for about 45 minutes only.

[On 5th November 1997, as recounts Gohar Ayub Khan in his recently published book 'Glimpses into the Corridors of Power', Nawaz "asked me to accompany him to the PM's House. In the car, the PM put his hand on my knee and said, 'Gohar Sahib, show me the way to arrest the Chief Justice and keep him in jail for a night'. Naturally, Gohar Ayub was shocked, as has been a disciplined officer and advised him not even thinking about it.

But deep-thinking Nawaz thought further, and in November of that same year he had his goons physically storm the Supreme Court of Pakistan while CJP Sajjad Ali Shah was hearing a contempt case brought against him (Nawaz) and then proceeded to engineer, with the help of Sajjad's brother judges, the successful removal of their Chief Justice.] (Ref: Ardeshir Cowasjee in daily **'DAWN': 5th August 2007**)

After the incident, Justice Sajjad Ali Shah requested the then Chief of Pakistan Army, Gen Jehangir Karamat to send troops to dispel a mob attack on Pakistan's Supreme Court. Gen Jehangir Karamat refused CJP's plea straightway and pointed out that:

'There is an established chain of command and any instructions of that sort should have come from the elected prime minister and the president, who is also the supreme commander of armed forces'.

It may be an interesting fact of the history that when the Supreme Court was being attacked by the guided mob of the PML's 'danda bardar force', Lt Gen Javed Nasir was supervising the on ground situation from a helicopter in air.

Sitting Chief Justice ousted:

On **25th November 1997,** Senator Rafiq Tarar had flown to Quetta with Shahbaz Sharif and briefcases (the opponent group of judges said it as blatant lie because relations between J rafiq Tarar and J Irshad Hassan Khan were never good) on a special aircraft to meet with Justice Irshad Hasan Khan, then a senior judge of SC Bench at Baluchistan.

[Unprecedented in the history of Pakistan judiciary, a strange row of events was seen. The Quetta bench of the apex court held the appointment of CJP Sajjad Ali Shah in abeyance till further orders and restrained him from performing judicial and administrative functions. The bench had also held in abeyance the operation of the notification of 5th June 1994 in that regard.]

(When Dr. Nasim Hasan Shah retired as Chief Justice of the Supreme Court in 1994, Justice Sa'ad Saud Jan should have taken his place but Ms Benazir Bhutto by-passed three senior judges and appointed Sajjad Ali Shah as Chief Justice of Pakistan)

On 9th February 1998, the Lahore High Court accepted the constitutional petition filed by (Senator) Rafiq Tarar against his disqualification by the (former) Acting CEC and declared him qualified to contest for and hold the office of President. The acting CEC, Justice Mukhtar Junejo of the Supreme Court, had found Mr Tarar, a former Supreme Court Judge, guilty of propagating views prejudicial to the integrity and independence of the judiciary at the time of his nomination as a presidential candidate under Article 63(G) of the Constitution of Pakistan and debarred him from the December 1997 contest. [Courtesy: Excerpts from ISLAMIC PAKISTAN: ILLUSIONS & REALITY by Abdus Sattar Ghazali]

The Chief Justice Sajjad Ali Shah, declared the order of the two-member Supreme Court bench at Quetta 'without lawful authority', and directed the assistant registrar, Quetta registry, not to fix any case before the two judges till further orders. Justice Shah, whose appointment as the chief justice was held in abeyance by the two-member bench, continued working as the CJP.

In his order the chief justice observed that under Order XXV of the Supreme Court Rules 1980, a petition of Article 184(3) under the original jurisdiction of the Supreme Court was to be filed only at the principal seat and not at any other registry. He said;

'In this respect there are orders and directions that if any such petition under that provision of Article 184(3) is filed at any other registry, it is to be forwarded straight-away to the principal seat for orders to be obtained from the Chief Justice for its fixation before a proper bench.'

Chief Justice Shah observed that if any orders had been passed in that petition they should be deemed to have not taken effect for the reason that proper procedure had not been followed. He had further observed that even registration number could not be given to such petitions at the registry without the permission or express orders of the Chief Justice.

The CJP directed that the record of the above mentioned petition may be summoned immediately from Quetta Registry for placement before him for further orders in this respect and also the 'honourable' judges present at the Quetta registry had acted without lawful authority.

When these two ad hoc judges of the Supreme Court were asked by the Chief Justice not to perform their judicial functions; the Quetta bench of the Supreme Court had used the words that *'the impugned executive order of the Chief Justice is nullity and is to be ignored'*. The Quetta bench had also over-ruled the executive order of Chief Justice Syed Sajjad Ali Shah regarding not fixing the cases before it. One of the senior judges used the phrase that;

> *'it is misconduct on the part of Chief Justice as none of the Supreme Court judge can be restrained from the work on executive order and said that judicial order had already suspended the Chief Justice to perform his duties as Chief Justice of Pakistan'.*

The full bench after ignoring the orders of the Chief Justice disposed off 10 cases. These cases were fixed before the bench by Advocate General Balochistan and the counsels of different petitioners. The court had also ordered the CJP that he should not perform his judicial and administrative duties as Chief Justice till the decision of the said bench regarding the petition comes up. Notices in this regard were issued to Attorney General (AG), Deputy AG and others.

The Supreme Court's circuit bench at Peshawar had also endorsed the verdict of the Quetta bench on a petition challenging the appointment of Justice Sajjad Ali Shah as Chief Justice of Pakistan. But Justice Sajjad Ali Shah continued hearing the contempt case against the sitting Prime Minister Nawaz Sharif.

A division bench of the High Court of Sindh requested the CJP Sajjad Ali Shah to convene a full court meeting of the SC to consider the controversy surrounding his appointment. But at the same time, the Supreme Court Quetta bench maintained its interim order suspending the Chief Justice Syed Sajjad Ali Shah and barring him from performing administrative and judicial functions. The SHC bench had referred the matter to the full court at Islamabad for final decision.

As a matter of fact, the judges were harvesting the crop which was sown by Benazir Bhutto in 1994 by superseding three judges to bring Justice Shah at the top. Justice Sajjad Ali Shah was never been accepted by heart by any of judges even the junior one being power thirsty.

CJP Shah should have placed himself before the full bench excluding him; J Mian Ajmal abstained at his own being an interested party. The other judges once made this proposal and the CJP Sajjad Shah had informed the 10-member bench that he would contest the case, and engaged *Abdul Hafeez Pirzada*, a prominent lawyer, to represent him.

However, a severe blow to CJP Mr Sajjad Ali Shah came when President Farooq Leghari tendered his resignation saying he could not violate the Constitution and the law to oblige Government. Speaking at a press conference Mr Leghari said he had opted to resign because he did not want to become a party to the violation of law and the Constitution. He had received a summary from the Government asking him to de-notify the appointment of Chief Justice Sajjad Ali Shah.

[The fact available on record is that on 2nd December 1997, President Leghari was conveyed messages of 'impeachment' and thus forced to quit. PM Nawaz Sharif wanted to bring Justice (Rtd) Rafiq Tarar, then senator, as president. In Muslim League circles his image was being portrayed as a rubber stamp.]

26th November 1997: Justice Irshad Hasan Khan of SC-Quetta Bench held Sajjad Ali Shah (Chief Justice)'s appointment in abeyance.

'The background may also be kept in mind that in his self-imposed war against the Chief Justice Sajjad Ali Shah, Nawaz Sharif (the then Prime Minister) succeeded in dividing the judges into two camps. The group of judges that sided with the Prime Minister said openly that "if Justice Sajjad Ali Shah gives up trying cases of Contempt of Court against Mian Nawaz Sharif, they will accept him [Justice Sajjad Ali Shah] as the Chief Justice."

The infamous Article 58(2)(b) was restored and suspended within minutes by two separate benches of the Supreme Court of Pakistan assembled against each other.

A three member bench headed by CJP Sajjad Ali Shah suspended the operation of the 13th Amendment restoring the powers of the president to dissolve the National Assembly, a verdict which was within minutes set aside by another 10-member bench.

The 10-member bench of the SC headed by J Saeeduzzaman Siddiqui granted stay against the chief justice's order minutes after it was passed, even without receiving any formal petition or the copy of the order on the subject.

All efforts to resolve the judicial crisis failed as both the judge's groups stuck to their stance and issued separate cause lists. The dissident judges, who did not acknowledge Sajjad Ali Shah as chief justice, issued a fresh cause list for 13 member's full court session. The full court, headed by Justice Saeeduzzaman Siddiqui, took up petitions questioning the validity of CJP's appointment'.

Justice Malik Qayyum, in an interview appeared in the daily **'Jang' dated 5th February 2006** had commented that:

'The two judges then making Quetta bench were nice and upright but they should not have issued injunction against a sitting chief justice whatever was the cause. If at all they wanted to do so then instead of issuing judgment from Quetta, they could come at principal seat at Islamabad and could have held a full court bench. It was a degradation event for the office of the Chief Justice not a person. Can some one think such an activism in army or any other institution?'

23rd December 1997: A Supreme Court bench declared Justice Sajjad Ali Shah's appointment as Chief Justice illegal. Justice Shah was already barred on 3rd December to sit on CJP's chair and Justice Ajmal Mian was given the charge of acting CJP since then. On 23rd December he was elevated to take oath as the new Chief Justice of Pakistan after a judicial order passed by a 10-member bench. Critics were also there to say that role of Justice Ajmal Mian was controversial in that scenario as he effectively allowed a coup to occur within the Supreme Court of Pakistan against a sitting chief justice.

The 10 member bench had earlier directed the CJP's office not to take any further orders for constituting benches from the Chief Justice Sajjad Ali Shah (under restraint) and orders regarding day-to-day working and administration of the court should be obtained from Justice Ajmal Mian till the appointment of Acting Chief Justice.

The 10-member bench which was hearing the petitions challenging the appointment of Justice Sajjad Ali Shah as Chief Justice of Pakistan was also constituted by Justice Ajmal Mian being the senior most in routine. He was retired as the Chief Justice of Pakistan on 30th June 1999.

[Points to ponder: Justice Ajmal Mian, was the only judge in the country's recent history who did not receive any residential plot in Islamabad or anywhere else, unlike most of his colleagues including Justice Riaz A Shaikh, Justice Irshad Hasan Khan and Justice Iftikhar M Chaudhry.

PM Nawaz Sharif once wanted to oblige the CJP Sajjad Ali Shah so the same evening a Mercedes EEL320 car was purchased from open market and sent to the CJP. After Justice Shah's departure Justice Ajmal Mian got CJP's slot and thus that car got allotted to him. Next day CJP Ajmal Mian sent back that car to the pool that he was not entitled to keep that car in the given official capacity.]

29th December 1997: Justice Junejo was forced to vacate Chief Election Commissioner's seat because he had dared to reject Tarar's nomination papers on 18th December on the basis of his dismal background.

[Justice (Rtd) Rafiq Tarar, was considered accused of corruption. According to media reports he was the person who reportedly passed on 'brief cases' to certain members of Baluchistan Judiciary to influence the judges in PM vs Sajjad Ali Shah row.

When the Chief Election Commissioner rejected nomination papers of Justice Tarar as unfit to stand for election, Nawaz Sharif's pocket man Justice Qayyum, who was on leave for a death in his family, left the condolence mat to return to office and passed the order that Justice Tarar be allowed to contest elections. As a result, on 1st January 1998: Justice (Rtd) Rafiq Tarar, later Senator, became President of Pakistan]

Coming back; the judiciary's clash with the PM Nawaz Sharif prompted the chief justice to call for army protection for the court building and his home. These clashes also drew a callous and hurtful attack from President Leghari, who effectively accused Prime Minister of incompetence saying:

'There can be no greater evidence of the dismal failure of your government's administration than that provided by the unprecedented shameful events of the last two days.'

Nawaz Sharif had replied by accusing President Leghari of 'intemperate language' and rejected his call for army protection for the Supreme Court. A new crisis loomed within the judiciary on next Sunday when two separate agendas were issued for Monday's Court proceedings against Nawaz Sharif. It was unprecedented in the judicial history of Pakistan. One agenda said the Chief Justice would take up the contempt of court case against Nawaz Sharif, while another agenda said a full Court, comprising 15 judges, would take up petitions challenging appointment of the CJP.

The Chief Justice Mr Shah issued an order cancelling the full court meeting, saying it was being convened illegally to prevent him from deciding cases against the prime minister. No body heard him then. PM's brother Shahbaz Sharif and Justice (Rtd) Rafiq Tarar, a Nawaz Sharif's party Senator then, had approached the judges of Baluchistan Bench, formed a lobby with like minded judges of Northern Frontier province, and had started proceedings against the sitting Chief Justice on the pretext of his illegal appointment to the apex office.

End result....Chief Justice Sajjad Ali Shah was sent home.

But, Justice Shah deserved that treatment because once he had betrayed his *'Mohsina'*, a lady PM who had blessed her with excessive grace.

[On Dr Nasim Hasan Shah's retirement as CJP in 1994, Justice Saad Saud Jan should have taken his place. But Ms Benazir Bhutto threw tradition overboard when she appointed Sajjad Ali Shah as Chief Justice of the Supreme Court by superceding his senior judges. Later she was dismissed by President Farooq Leghari on charges of corruption and Sajjad Ali Shah along with 6 other members of the Supreme Court upheld this decision. Reading from a 12-page short order, CJP Sajjad Ali Shah had said:

'The presidential order contained enough substance and adequate material had been provided to conclude that the government could not be run in accordance with the provisions of the constitution and that an appeal to the electorate had become necessary in the given circumstances.'

Scenario 22

JUDICIARY IN 1997-III:

Shameful Judgments & Judiciary:

This hard fact of Pakistan's history made the people believe that some judges of superior courts could be puppets in the hands of wealthy politicians. On the other hand, for some judges of the superior courts, their personal differences are dearer to them in comparison to judicial values. Some judges had practically demonstrated that they had no courage to announce decisions contrary to the wish of sitting rulers. It was pity. It is Pakistan's painful judicial history.

It is a common saying that one who digs a pit for others will fall into it himself. The same thing happened here. Nawaz Sharif had promulgated the 'Contempt of Court Ordinance 1998' to find a way of appeal for himself if he would have declared guilty. The side benefit of this ordinance was to tackle his political opponents too but himself fell prey to it along with his companions during his own regime.

The political scenario changed suddenly in October 1999 and hence the mood of the courts.

In the first week of December 1999 the ousted Prime Minister Nawaz Sharif had appeared before the Supreme Court, in a hearing of re-opening of a contempt of court case against his political party. A petition was moved before the Supreme Court by a 'private person' to re-open this case. Nawaz Sharif was then also waiting for a special anti-terrorism Court to frame formal criminal charges against him for actions leading to the military takeover in October.

The former prime minister was brought before the Supreme Court amid tight security. Nawaz Sharif had also been named in this lawsuit. Although he was not charged in the case, the Supreme Court ordered Nawaz Sharif to testify. The Court then adjourned the case until 12th January 2000 to allow the parties to prepare responses.

[The fact may be kept in mind that during Gen Musharraf's regime, the judges of superior courts became particular targets of a lethal criticism from the opposition parties as well as the Supreme Court and High Court bar associations for accepting three-year extension in service through the controversial Legal Framework Order (LFO).

Gen Musharraf's military government opted to counter these voices by promulgating another ordinance on contempt of court though the Parliament sessions were running there during 2003. The apparent ruling party, Muslim League (Q), had not moved the bill on the floor but instead got the army wishes implemented through the military commander and the President in one chair.]

Mohammad Shehzad of *'One World'* had rightly pointed out in his essay titled 'Pakistan Law Muffles Opposition to Army-Judiciary Nexus' **dated 27th July 2003** that:

'................ *while widening the scope of law on the subject (of Contempt of Court), the military regime had in fact issued the draconian Contempt of Court Ordinance 2003, that made even mere criticism of a judge a punishable offence, sparking off widespread protests from the intelligentsia. The ordinance, issued in July 2003, was facing huge criticism. According to the Lawyers Action Committee, it only furthered the impression that army judiciary nexus was going full tilt to gag all opposition.'*

Qazi Hussain Ahmed, a key leader of the alliance of six religious parties, the *Muttahida Majlis-e-Amal* (MMA), condemned the manner in which the ordinance was issued as shameful, unlawful, and unconstitutional. Mr Qazi had pointed to the ordinance as 'law's back door entry', when there was perfectly legitimate route through Parliament, and said that:

'It *is another wicked attempt to suppress criticism of the crooked judiciary by politicians & lawyers and its reporting by the media.*'

Khwaja Sa'ad Rafiq of the PML(N), the party of ousted Prime Minister Nawaz Sharif, said that:

'Gen *Musharraf has shown his contempt for the country's Parliament by issuing the said ordinance.*'

This statement reflected another replica of Pakistani politician's character; a tragedy...... that Nawaz Sharif and his party had already accomplished the same illogical act in 1998 when he had promulgated an ordinance on the same subject, Contempt of Court Ordinance 1998, with the signatures of the then President Rafiq Tarar though the parliament sessions were also in the row.

On **7th February 2008,** another petition against former Prime Minister Nawaz Sharif was filed in Lahore High Court (LHC) seeking action under contempt of court act.

S Naeemul Hassan Sherazi, advocate, on behalf of Ch Siddiq Sarwar, Safia Naureen and Farzana Kausar in the petition had challenged an advertisement message which was published in daily newspapers on 8th January 2008 on behalf of or instigated by Nawaz Sharif. The petitioners said in their application:

> 'The respondent has committed contempt of court wilfully and intentionally in order to scandalise the honourable court which is grievous contempt of court. He had criticised various policies of the previous military government, particularly saying "Agar Tum Mann pasand judges Sey Mann-pasand Faisalay Laina Chahtay ho to Tumhara Yaum-e-Hisab Qareeb Hay" (if you desire to get decisions of your own choice by your beloved judges then the day of your accountability has come true or nearby at least).'

Nawaz Sharif is known for creating such occasions for committing contempt of court. History is the witness to it.

Let us move a step further. A script from column of **Ardisher Cowasjee** *dated 15th February 2009* appearing in daily the *'Dawn'* of Karachi reads as under:

> 'Come Nawaz Sharif as prime minister in 1997, with Sajjad Ali Shah as chief justice of Pakistan. A prickly person, not open to wheeling and dealing, he did not suit Nawaz Sharif or his designs to assume full and complete power, transforming himself into an amir-ul-momineen and the country into his vision of a citadel of Islam. The tussle reached its peak in November 1997.
>
> Later, on Nov 28, Sharif did the unthinkable. He arranged for a mob of his party storm troopers to physically invade the Supreme Court building at a time when its chief justice was sitting hearing a contempt of court case that had been brought against the prime minister and various others. Pakistan was disgraced in front of the world. Many of the attackers were identified, but, the judiciary being the judiciary, they got off lightly'. The PML was 'however' feeling proud.

Pseudo Trial in SC Attack Case:

During the first week of March 1999, a full bench of the Supreme Court indicted six legislators of the then ruling PML (N) by framing contempt of Court charges against two Members of Parliament and four Members of Provincial Assembly Punjab, besides head of the 'Nawaz Sharif Force' in the case of ransacks, bullying and attack on the apex Court building on 28th November 1997.

Those, who were charged with offence of the contempt of Court under the Contempt of Court laws read with Articles 3 and 4 of the Constitution, included PML (N) MNAs Tariq Aziz and Mian Muhammad Munir; PML (N) MPAs Ch. Tanvir Ahmed Khan, Akhtar Rasool, Sardar Naseem, Mehmood Akhtar and a leader of the PML (N) Youth Wing, Shebaz Goshi.

The show-cause notice served earlier on the political secretary to the then prime minister Col (Retd) Mushtaq Tahirkheli was withdrawn. Islamabad Secretariat police had registered an FIR against these leaders soon after the incident took place. No investigation into the matter could be started as Pakistan's political culture never allowed any agency to enquire into or investigate any issue if it would be related to the sitting government's favourite persons.

The bench, designated to hear this contempt case, was headed by Justice Nasir Aslam Zahid and comprising Justice Munawar Ahmed Mirza and Justice Abdul Rehman Khan. The charge-sheet, which after a prolonged hearing was served on the seven PML leaders, stated:

> "You were the part of the crowd gathered in and around the building of the Supreme Court in the morning of 28.11.97 and were involved in acts of rowdyism including raising of slogans and display of banners against the judiciary with the intention of bringing the authority of this Court into disrespect or disrepute and lower its authority and to disturb the decorum of the Court and rendered yourself liable to punishment under Article 204 of the Constitution read with Articles 3 and 4 of the **Contempt of Court Act, 1976.**"

The alleged contemnors were served with the show-cause notices on 3rd July 1998 as per procedural demands.

Leading columnist of daily The Dawn, Aredsher Cowsjee had assisted the Court in identifying the contemnors and provided the Court with two video films of the incident; one recorded by the close circuit video camera of the Supreme Court and the other shown by the BBC and CNN. Some 13 press reporters had appeared before the Court as witnesses while on the orders of the Court newsmen and newspapers provided the photos of the incident appeared in the daily newspapers.

The SC bench headed by Justice Nasir Aslam Zahid did not allow any counsel of the alleged contemnors to argue and directed them to speak on the matter themselves.

It was May 1999. Those were the days of Nawaz Sharif's rule being the prime minister so how the court, how high level it was, could dare to hear the contempt case against Prime Minister's colleagues and party leaders. The available evidence was 'declared' insufficient to prove the allegations. The critics though remembered that *video tapes of BBC, CNN and of Supreme Court's own security cameras were there on the Courts record* along with bundles of national and international newspapers having details of events and photographs of the political stalwarts involved.

Just for academic discussion, one should not forget the other scripts on the court's file. For example Justice Nasir Aslam Zahid, heading the three-member bench, during regular hearing of this contempt case, had reacted and asked the then Inspector General of Police (IGP) Islamabad, Salim Tariq Lone, whether or not they lathi-charged people gathering outside the Parliament, Presidency, Prime Minister's house or for that matter the Supreme Court?

Though the IGP Mr Lone had tendered his apology at the very outset of the proceedings on that day but the judge further said:

'When the police knew that a thousand or two three thousand people had gathered in front of the Court, why the entire Constitution Avenue was not blocked for traffic?'

The Politicians & political workers; the planners, muggers and assailants were not asked even a single question.

The Court, including Justice Munawar Ahmed Mirza and Justice Abdur Rehman Khan as its other members, had expressed dissatisfaction over the police performance that after the lapse of seven months police could not identify the miscreants whose TV footage had been run by the Court's close circuit cameras and international media. Even after viewing the footage of CCTV, press videos and press photos, the politicians and political attackers were not found guilty of any charge, police was there to be bullied. What an independent judiciary the Pakistan had.

Responding to the Court, the then IGP Salim Tariq Lone said that about 30 people were identified, 15 of whom arrested till then. The officer offered regrets, when the Supreme Court had expressed its dismay that no further action taken and the issue was still pending, as it was.

The IGP had also placed it on record that an inquiry was conducted by the Chief Commissioner of Islamabad but its report was not officially given to them yet.

He said two police officials were suspended following the incident. Why it was delayed, the Supreme Court asked. IGP Lone told the Court of his satisfaction with the security arrangements on 28th November and said some of his colleagues had advised not to use force, as they feared, the situation might get out of control. The IGP was reprimanded that as head of the department he should have immediately started investigations of the incident. The politicians and attackers were declared angels, not found guilty of any charge as if police had instigated them. What a justice it was.

Javed Akram, the Chief Commissioner, in his statement before the bench said, it was not unusual for the crowd to gather in front of the Supreme Court as it would come whenever the Prime Minister appeared before the Court. He said he did not get any intelligence report that the crowd would gatecrash into the Supreme Court building. Security arrangements in and around the SC building were adequate and satisfactory, he submitted to the Court.

It was further pointed out again to the Islamabad Police Chief, Salim Tariq Lone, that an administration official Assistant Commissioner Mr Shallwani in his statement before the Court had identified a group of people among the trespassers as members of the ruling PML Youth Wing.

The judge observed that no one from police had bothered to further probe into his statement despite the fact that the statements made in the Court room were communicated to the police chief by his subordinates who attended the proceedings. The slackness was continuing as it existed on that day (when the Supreme Court was stormed); candidly observed by Justice Mirza sitting in the bench.

'I apologise. I think it was not intentional', IGP Mr Lone replied but only to be interrupted again by Justice Zahid who had observed that the crowd had threatened the dignity of the Court. The politicians and political workers were not touched, being sacred.

The senior police official, SSP Altaf Hussain, who was in charge of police deputed for security at the apex Court on the day of incident was bullied by the court. The bench had also asked for statements of many journalists who were there on that day for reporting. BUT even then, there was no decision from the court because of pressure of the PM Nawaz Sharif who had patronized his party members involved in the said case of historical misery. How independent the judiciary was. Politicians and attackers were innocent, police guilty. *Pakistani justice Zindabad.*

The evidence comprising of press videos, BBC & CNN videos and reports, CCTV footings, bundles of newspapers and press photos, statements of media-men, was shelved declaring it 'insufficient' by the apex court and the case was filed because the members of ruling party were involved in the case and they were subordinates and company men of the same Prime Minister Nawaz Sharif, who had sent their Chief Justice home about 20 months back. Justice—Hurray.

Referring to this 'judicious trial', former CJP Sajjad Ali Shah held a candid opinion that *'some of our judges and the attacking politicians'* were a joint party against the supreme Court. The attack on the SC was launched by politicians but those 'party judges' were consulted prior to actual attack. PM Nawaz Sharif was openly saying at all forums, including media that 'we are working on [brother] judges and soon the Chief Justice of Pakistan would be isolated'.

CJP Mr Shah had once addressed PM Nawaz Sharif in presence of the President and the Army Chief that:

'I can tell you Mr Prime Minister that your son in law Captain Safdar visits which judges with brief cases and who accompanies him to the judge's residences.' Both the addressees were staring at the wall.

The PM had no answer. All those judges were residing in official accommodations in front of the Punjab House Islamabad and most of them used to assemble in the Punjab House invariably every evening. Senator Saifur Rehman used to be there also to use his dictatorial influence about NAB appeals. Their meals used to come from nearby five star Marriot Hotel of Islamabad.

Shahbaz Sharif remained busy on another front while sitting in Lahore. During those days of turmoil, once he asked Justice Fazal Elahi from Peshawar Bench to stand by Nawaz Sharif, he would be made Chief Election Commissioner of Pakistan.

In nut shell, most of the 'brother judges' were paid their price by the PM Nawaz Sharf. They themselves had assured the PM that the CJP would be out soon and that too through the court orders. CJP Mr Shah tried his level best to obstruct that exit order against him through both judicial and administrative means but could not succeed because the executive was with them all. For all this exercise, the fact prevails that; judges could not stand before 'chamak'. The PM Nawaz Sharif once himself told in a private meeting that:

'[BOX]*Justice Sajjad Ali Shah's exit has cost us too much, too high.*'

It was fact also because a special plane was used to fly between and buy the 'brother judges' in all the four provincial capitals through Justice (Rtd) Rafiq Tarar, Dr Shahryar - a cardiologist of Lahore & family friend of Sharifs and Sharifuddin Pirzada.

That was the only way out for Nawaz Sharif to finish all the corruption cases against him and his family. After exit of the CJP Mr Shah, all cases were transferred to a bench of 'brother judges'; what happened to them then, history is silent on those facts.

Akram Sheikh, Pakistan's top law specialist, in an interview published in media on **29th August 1999,** had opined:

'It was categorically mentioned in the said judgment that the planning for that attack on the Supreme Court was done at some other place and at very high level. The motive behind that planning was to keep the CJP Sajjad Ali Shah away from hearing cases [of contempt and regarding corruption both] against the PM Nawaz Sharif. It was done to teach a lesson to the CJP.

The transport was provided from the same PM House. Some PML's elected members were made incharge of the people sent in those transport buses. Under a similar planning then, that PML's local leadership was got acquitted from some judges on the pretext that there was no evidence available against the 'high level planners'.

The process got immediate approval by the followers. An Additional Session Judge was hearing a case of an 'influential person'. His colleague openly conveyed the message to 'set free his man' otherwise he would be coming with 4000 people in buses. The Judge brought that threat in the notice of his seniors. Advised; that better to proceed on leave to avoid a new trouble.'

Threats, misappropriation and corruption by influential have developed as acceptable culture in Pakistan now.

Nothing new in Pakistan; no surprise! In most of the third world countries it is just a routine matter. Quoting Tanzania as an example where the judiciary also finds itself chastened by government efforts to persuade and sometimes forcefully push it to go in line with state *dictation*. According to M.K.B. Wambali and C.M. Peter, as narrated in *'The Judiciary in Context: The case of Tanzania'* Frances: London).

> "....the government and the Party play a vital, if not a decisive role in determining who will man various positions in judiciary. This in a way has a bearing on the work of this important institution. Although the constitution also provides safeguards to the judges to maintain their independence ...... experience has shown that these safe guards are formal enactments and are not all that water-tight. Judges have been transferred from the judiciary and given other responsibilities in government service.
>
> The very fact that the executive makes appointments [in the superior judiciary] has at times tended to make members of the judiciary subservient to the executive and the Party"

When our judges are so 'courageous and God-fearing' then how a nation can prosper. These judges had sworn in with the Holy Qoran in hand considering themselves as the true followers of Islam; taking oath under the constitution of Islamic Republic of Pakistan, of an Islamic state.

Contrarily they behave like a coward clerk of a municipal office who is simply afraid of any rogue BD member. They are the Respectable judges who do not remember that an ordinary *Qazi of Muhammaden* Era used to call the *Khalifa* before him to answer the allegations levelled by ordinary persons. But who could speak against them. Contempt of court for them was enough.

Here, instead of making bold decision on the basis of evidence placed before them, the judges preferred to shout at IGP and Chief Commissioner - the harmless creatures, sidelining the main culprits and finally letting them off. What kind of judgments they have drafted and what they are leaving behind as legacy. What the future law students would take out from their judgments and what would they quote. ——— Nothing but shame, filth, burnt flesh and sarcastic smiles.

One can see if the same is true for Pakistan throughout its history.

Scenario 23

SELECTION OF ARMY CHIEFS (1998-99):

Gen Musharraf Selected as COAS 1998:

Recalling good old days of Pakistan Army, the people still remember Gen Mirza Aslam Beg who could have easily occupied the seat vacated by Gen Ziaul Haq's accidental death, because of no resistance from any quarter; but he opted to take the army's depleted image to an unimaginable height by bringing in democracy. He was the first army Chief with outstanding dual qualities of professional supremacy and field dynamics. Further, he was a student leader & a devout worker of Pakistan Movement.

As per PM Nawaz Sharif's contention, Gen Jehangir Karamat had tried to influence his civil government by suggesting and then pressing hard on formation of a 'National Security Council'. Nawaz Sharif held that:

> 'Gen Jehangir Karamat had placed this proposal before senior army officers during a high level conference at Naval War College, which was not mandated by the Constitution. When we curbed his demand and intriguing efforts with greater political force, he felt sorry for his un-healthy proposals and suddenly tendered his resignation. We accepted it.'

It may be remembered that Gen Jehangir Karamat was otherwise a thorough professional soldier. The selection of a General as an army chief has always been a prerogative of the political governments. When Gen J Karamat was selected, there were other four Generals, equally competent, in the row. The other names were of Gen Tariq, Gen Naseer Akhtar and of Gen Javed Ashraf Qazi.

The *lunger gup*, however, prevailed that Army's own intelligence agency had caught documentary proof of Gen J Karamat's corruption in buying deal of armoured tanks from Karghistan. The inside pressure was built up from within army to vacate the seat of the Army Chief.

What was the truth; no body knows with certainty.

After his sent off, Nawaz Sharif appointed Gen Musharraf as Chief of the Army Staff (COAS) on 8th October 1998 superseding three senior

Generals, Gen Ali Kuli Khan being the senior most. Nawaz Sharif appointed Gen Musharraf, allegedly to gain total control of military affairs, as Chairman of the Joint Chiefs of the Staff Committee also, against merit due to which Chief of Naval Staff Admiral Fasih Bokhari had to resign from the Navy who rightfully was the deserved officer for this assignment.

Gen Musharraf was also responsible for the Kargil episode and he was the strategic planner to send Pakistan's army inside Afghanistan to fight against the Northern Alliance. After succeeding in military coup in October 1999 he opted to become an American ally in the War on Terror; laying down his neck on the table before them.

Nawaz Sharif, himself admitted (ref: *Gaddar Kaun by Sohail Warroich* pages 136-138) that he had done a blunder while choosing Gen Musharraf as an army chief by superseding three other senior Generals. The PM has especially mentioned the name of General Ali Kuli Khan, at so many occasions and at so many times. Nawaz Sharif said that:

> '*We were in utmost haste to decide about the army chief after resignation of Gen Jehangir Karamat. My colleagues advised me wrong. They told me, about each senior General, a different story of their partisanships. Secretary Defence Iftikhar Ali Khan had spoken ill of Gen Ali Kuli Khan especially so I dropped him. Subsequently I came to know that he wanted to balance his old score with the later. [PM's 2nd in Command in PML, Ch Nisar Ali Khan was real brother of that Secretary Defence]*
>
> *The more serious blunder I did was that all the intelligence reports were against Gen Musharraf advising me that the officer was not 'fit for commanding position' but even then I posted him as an army chief; my fault. Gen Nasim Rana, the then DG ISI, had himself come to brief me that Gen Musharraf's reports were not favourable in connection with Army Chief's portfolio.*

The intelligentsia, media and the insiders were shocked to know when Nawaz Sharif had nominated Gen Musharraf as the COAS while superseding Lt Gen Ali Kuli Khan CGS and Lt Gen Khalid Nawaz the Quarter-Master General. Very few people could guess that Nawaz Sharif's choice of Gen Musharraf was attributed to the following:

- He was strongly recommended by President Rafiq Tarar and Lt Gen Javed Nasir, the 'secret' advisor of the PM on intelligence.

- He had falsely associated himself with Nawaz Sharif by keeping the latter informed of the criticism over his Government's functioning by Lt Gen Khalid Nawaz at the Corps Commander's meetings under the chair of Gen Jehangir Karamat as COAS.

- That in Nawaz Sharif's books, Gen Musharraf did not belong to any 'Marshal Race' of Punjab or NWFP, thus was considered weak by 'connections'.

- The last one that though himself a Mohajir, Gen Musharraf disliked Altaf Hussain and his Muttahida Qaumi Movement (MQM), it was briefed. The PM Nawaz Sharif, therefore, wanted to use Gen Musharraf to crush the MQM in Karachi.

Nawaz Sharif's choice was once hailed in March 1999 when, as per his original thinking, Gen Musharraf appointed special military courts in Karachi to try the MQM cadres on charges of terrorism. Several of them were sentenced to death and two executed in actual.

A serious blow, however, caused when the Supreme Court, acting on a petition, declared those special military courts unconstitutional. It was alleged that Nawaz Sharif was also planning to have Asif Zardari tried as a terrorist by the military courts and sentenced to death for allegedly killing Murtaza Bhutto in September 1996.

Going into details; Gen Ali Kuli Khan was not left over on the basis of such simple factors as described above. Nawaz Sharif was told, in those days of PML vs Judiciary crisis of 1997 that Gen Ali Kuli Khan used to talk in Corps Commander Meetings that Nawaz Sharif should be sent home. He had once seriously advised Gen Jehangir Karamat to work out a cogent coup plan in which he (Gen Ali Kuli Khan) was prepared to play a key role. Might be, Gen Khan was suggesting it in the expected capacity of next Army Chief.

Secondly; Gen Ali Kuli Khan had played a vital role in as DG MI during the days of Gen Abdul Waheed Kakar in 1992-93, which all had contributed a lot in ending Nawaz Sharif's first government. In those days the DG MI was actually performing all tasks of ISI, especially the bargains amongst members of various political parties, because the PM's nominated Gen Javed Nasir DG ISI had been declared 'persona non grata' (PNG) by the GHQ.

Gen Khalid Nawaz was superseded perhaps rightly because he had nothing mentionable at his credit except the seniority. No senior officer would be happy with him. He was known for his lethargic attitudes in general but especially for making inordinate delays in taking decisions. He used to keep files on his table for weeks wanting decisions. He himself was not mentally prepared to accept such big responsibility.

Lastly, Gen Tirmizi & Gen Musharraf were equal in all respects. Both aspiring and fighters, but Gen Musharraf was then selected on the basis of aforementioned factors, docile and yes-man as Gen Ziaul Haq used to pose before Mr Bhutto. Mr Bhutto and Nawaz Sharif, both were beaten by two 'baby faced' and apparently docile Generals who were given the top slots by ignoring their seniors hoping that they would behave as they looked like; but both deceived.

Travelling back into the history: in the *'International Herald Tribune'* *of 16th June 1999,* one Selig Harrison, a well-known American analyst, made comments that *'recent information makes clear that the COAS Gen Musharraf, has long-standing links with several Islamic fundamentalist groups',* but the writer could not bring forward any cogent proof in support of his statement. Most concerned political community had not taken notice of it.

Gen Musharraf, a *Mohajir* of Karachi origin, had subsequently settled down in Gujranwala and preferred to project himself more as a Punjabi than as a Mohajir. He was commissioned in the Pakistan Army Artillery in 1964, went normal through 1980s but then picked up by Gen Ziaul Haq who had chosen him on strong recommendations made by his advisors and guides in the *Jama'at e Islami.*

His first notable assignment was the training of *'jehadis'* recruited by various Islamic groups for fighting against the Soviet troops in Afghanistan. In those days Gen Musharaff came into contact with Osama bin Laden, then a reputed civil engineer of Saudi Arabia, who had been recruited by the America's CIA and brought to Afghanistan for constructing bunkers for the Afghan *Mujahideen* in a difficult landscape.

Osama developed his reputation in Afghanistan not as a *mujahid* or terrorist, but as a civil engineer who could construct bunkers in any terrain. He also developed the technique of constructing long tunnels to reach far off Soviet and Afghan military posts and using them as underground safe passages. The *Mujahideen* used to suddenly emerge from these tunnels, fresh and ready to attack, and surprise the Soviet and Afghan troops. The links between Osama and Gen Musharraf allegedly went strong with the passage of time.

231

During his days with the SSG in the Siachen and the Northern Areas (Gilgit and Baltistan), Gen Musharraf developed a close personal friendship with Lt Gen Javed Nasir, DG ISI during Nawaz Sharif's first tenure as the Prime Minister and later his Adviser on intelligence matters, Maj Gen Zaheerul Islam Abbasi, Lt Gen Aziz, Brigadier first & then promoted to Maj General and Deputy DG ISI but later called in GHQ as Chief of the General Staff (CGS), and Rafique Tarar, then a Judge and later the President of Pakistan. In 1989, Gen Abbasi (then as Brigadier) was also posted to the Siachen like Gen Musharraf.

Reportedly, Gen Musharraf had posed himself in Gen Ziaul Haq's times as *'Deobandi'*. The above mentioned were also devoted *Deobandis* having strong links with Islamic parties particularly with the *Harkat ul Mujahideen* (HUM), previously known as *Harkat ul Ansar*, which was once declared by the US as an international terrorist organisation in 1997. Drawing its strength from a Pakistan based organization *Lashkar e Toiba*, the HUM was alleged to be a member of Osama's International Islamic Front for Jihad against America and Israel.

The late Gen Asif Nawaz Janjua, the then COAS, called him to Rawalpindi back at last.

On 8th September 1995, the Pakistani Customs stopped a car carrying heavy arms and ammunition near Kohat and arrested its driver and Saifullah Akhtar of HUM. On interrogation, they reportedly told that the weapons were procured by one Brig Mustansar Billa of the Pakistan Army posted at Darra Adamkhel allegedly meant for Kashmiri extremist groups under his [informal] command.

The GHQ took over the investigation and arrested a group of 40 army officers and 10 civilians headed by Major Gen Abbasi. Benazir Bhutto, the then Prime Minister, was briefed that this group had conspired to kill her with some senior military officers, staging a coup and proclaiming Pakistan as an Islamic state. All officers & men taken in custody were tried by a military court and sentenced to various terms of imprisonment.

M H Askari wrote in the *'Dawn' of 18th October 1995* that:

> *'It is said that the plotters had close links with Hizbul Mujahideen and the Harkat ul Ansar, which are known for their involvement in international terrorism. It is also said that the arrested officers wanted Pakistan to become militarily involved in the Kashmir freedom struggle and should go visible all over.'*

'The Nation' of 20th October 1995 reported that: *'Major Gen Abbasi had close contacts with the Harkat ul Ansar.* The 'Khabrain', an Urdu newspaper, alleged that two of the arrested officers belonged to the ISI and that one of them had worked as the staff officer to Lt Gen Nasir, when he was DG ISI [referring to Major Gen Abbasi]. *'The Nation' of 15th November 1995* reported that:

'Almost all the arrested officers are followers of the Tablighi Jamaat based in Raiwind which place [then] also considered the Punjab's HQ of Harkat ul Mujahideen (HUM).'

Retaliating Gen Ziauddin's posting as DG ISI in 1999, and perhaps to implement his plans regarding Kargil activity, Gen Musharraf transferred Lt Gen Aziz from the ISI to the GHQ along with his assignments and control of affairs concerning with Kashmir and Afghan operations. Gen Aziz was given the post of CGS at GHQ and made responsible for implementation of all kinds of military operations through the Directorate of Military Intelligence (MI).

Lt Gen Nasir was kept in the picture about the implementation of Kargil Plans, but unprofessional Lt Gen Ziauddin, even being Chief of the ISI, could not get air of it. Officially Nawaz Sharif was not told about Kargil Operation but he could not know it un-officially even because of such ineffective & incapacitated DG ISI like Ziauddin in his team.

Media reports available on record for first quarter of 1999 had conveyed an impression that some irrational religious elements in the Pakistan army known by Gen Musharraf and his retired colleagues had encouraged adventurism in Kargil assuming that:

- The morale of the Indian army was low due to bad handling of George Fernandez, the Indian Defence Minister. Lt Gen Asad Durrani, former DG ISI, had mockingly referred to him as the *'best Indian Defence Minister that Pakistan can hope to have.'*

- The BJP was a party of paper tigers, known more for their long speeches and verbal threats than for their actions.

- Pakistan's nuclear and missile capability had ensured that India would not retaliate against Pakistan for occupying the strategic border ridges in Kargil.

- The fear of the possible use of nuclear weapons would bring in Western intervention; thus internationalising the Kashmir issue.

- Pakistan would agree to a ceasefire only if it was allowed to retain the Indian Territory it occupied; not to previous position.

- Pakistan wanted to keep the Indian army bleeding in Kashmir just as, in the past, various Afghan *Mujahideen* factions kept the Soviet troops bleeding in Afghanistan in 1980s.

- Pakistan should keep on frustrating India's ambition of emerging as a major Asian power at par with China and Japan.

In May 1999, the Indian Army started reacting vigorously to the Kargil invasion and had ordered the Indian Air Force to go into action against the invaders. It was only then that Gen Musharraf told Nawaz Sharif that he had sent in a large number of Pakistan army troops to help Kashmiri fighters at Kargil border but already there were heavy casualties till then. The pressure from US and his allies for withdrawal of the Pakistan forces for restoration of the status quo ante came as another surprise for all in the government and away.

Besides Kargil, Gen Musharraf deceived Nawaz Sharif at another count during the same days. He ordered the movement of nuclear warheads from one place to some other but without placing it in the knowledge of the President being the Supreme Commander of the army, or the PM being the executive head of the state. The PM did not know this fact.

During Nawaz Sharif's meeting with Bill Clinton, the later asked a question regarding reasons and rationale behind that movement of nuclear arsenal where the PM was blank. It was a moment of utter humiliation for a PM that he was not aware of that serious matter whereas the CIA (of course the RAW also) knew it.

In March 1999, Gen Musharraf started coming out his upper skin. After taking over WAPDA (Water & Power Development Authority), he issued orders that the army would conduct all future negotiations with the independent power producers, thereby denying any role of the politicians and civilian bureaucrats in energy matters. When Nawaz Sharif questioned that order, he declined to cancel it.

Gen Musharraf got prepared a list of all payment defaulters of the WAPDA and leaked to the press having names of PM's industrial managers, colleagues, high profile politicians and their business concerns. One Abida Hussain, a cabinet member of Nawaz Sharif, was one of the major defaulters, thereby forcing her to resign. Gen Musharraf as COAS openly hinted to the media that the business enterprises of

Sharif's family top the list of defaulters. Much humiliating it was for a sitting prime minister.

The media reports of those days also tell that Gen Musharraf's policy and handling of WAPDA affairs were appreciated by the general populace being a gesture of uprightness because the Pakistani politicians are known to be above law while eating up national levies and funds.

After military coup of 12th October 1999, Gen Musharraf ruled Pakistan from 1999 to early 2007 smoothly; was going fairly popular amidst usual criticism amongst the people at large but stumbled down while suspending his Chief Justice in March 2007 and then ordering the Lal Masjid siege in July same year. His attempt to institute emergency rule failed as calls for his impeachment escalated.

The return of Benazir Bhutto and Nawaz Sharif from exile had pushed the nation towards parliamentary democracy ending Musharraf's reigns in August 2008 at last.

In February 2011, a Pakistani court issued an arrest warrant for Gen Musharraf because of his alleged involvement in assassination of Benazir Bhutto. As of June 2011, he lives in self-exile in London. He has vowed to return to Pakistan on 23rd March 2012 which has been considered doubtful by all means.

Gen Ziauddin selected as COAS 1999:

Since the start of October 1999, the senior army Generals under Gen Musharraf's command, especially who were responsible of Kargil's disaster, had gone adamant to throw away the political leadership to avoid any possible incident of sudden announcement of an Enquiry Commission into their failures. It was too late then. The best time for ordering such an enquiry was the first week of July 1999 when Nawaz Sharif had returned from America after a humiliating meeting with President Clinton, generally known as Washington Accord.

Leaving aside the facts that Nawaz Sharif had ordered to keep Gen Musharraf's jet passenger plane in air or not; Gen Musharraf and his four intimate General's team had planned it since two weeks earlier or not; it was fact that Nawaz Sharif knew it that his government's send-off was on cards but he could not handle the things intelligently.

Since 1st October 1999, there were abnormal changes seen around the PM House then. Commander 111 Brigade was changed, the army men on security duty were given new intelligence system, the visitors to the PM House were monitored and special SSG platoons were called on Dhamial base which were all unusual signs in smoothly running set ups.

On 12ᵗʰ October 1999, when Nawaz Sharif was coming back from Multan at about 2 PM, he had called Secretary Defence Ch Iftikhar Ali and Principal Secretary Saeed Mehdi at Islamabad Airport. When the PM landed, Secretary Defence was there but not the Saeed Mehdi, may be he was not able to get message from air. The PM and Secretary Defence got into the state car while Brig Javed Malik, the Military Secretary (MS) to the PM also accompanied them. During his drive to the PM House, the PM told Secretary Defence that he had decided to change the Army Chief at last.

When they reached the PM House, Saeed Mehdi was already waiting for them there. All the four officers proceeded to the PM House's lobby where Saeed Mehdi was told about the PM's decision to retire Gen Musharraf and also to bring Gen Ziauddin, then DG ISI and the next senior most General on the list, as the new COAS.

It was about 3 PM that day when Gen Ziauddin was asked on phone to attend the PM House at 4 'O'clock. In the meantime, the Principal Secretary and Secretary Defence had got ready a notification retiring Gen Musharraf and making of Gen Ziauddin as the new Army Chief. It was the notification which the same two officers had issued exactly a year earlier on 8th October 1998; only the date and names were changed. The PM Nawaz Sharif signed it.

At 4 PM, Gen Ziauddin was there in the PM House and a one to one meeting with PM was held. The two secretaries and Brig Javed Malik were later called in. All they congratulated the new COAS. The PM decorated the badges on the new COAS, which were temporarily removed from Brig Javed Malik's shoulders to honour the occasion before the TV & media staff of the PM House. Immediately after, the PM went to the President House, got the said notification approved and countersigned by President Rafiq Tarar, came back and copies issued to media & PTV for onward news release.

Gen Ziauddin, the new COAS moved in Military Secretary's office in the PM House and in descending order made hotline telephone calls to Gen Mahmood of 10 Corps, Gen Aziz the CGS, Brig Imtiaz, Gen Tauqir Zia, Gen Akram (telling him that he would be the new CGS and called him to the PM House then), Gen Saleem Hyder (telling him that he would again take over 10 Corps replacing Gen Mahmood as he had done with him a year back), Gen Yousaf of Multan Corps and lastly with Gen Usmani of Karachi Corps. Gen Usmani was asked to receive Gen Musharraf with usual protocol of a retired army chief and to keep him in a rest house till new instructions.

Later Military Secretary Brig Javed Malik had told in an interview that no instructions to delay the flight or to keep it hanging in air were conveyed; it was a subsequent concocted story.

The new CAOS was sitting in Military Secretary's room where Gen Akram, the new CGS had also arrived. Gen Salim Hyder, the new designated Commander of 10 Corps was on his way to the PM House, when at about 5 PM, Nawaz Sharif called his MS and told him worriedly that some army personnel had taken over the PTV HQ and had interrupted the news.

PTV HQ was just at 2 minutes away from the PM House. The MS did not want to go to PTV HQ under PM's orders but the new COAS was also there to instruct him. He had to proceed. Outside there was no military vehicle so he had to go in police escort car.

A scene occurred in PTV building. When the MS Brig Javed Malik reached the news room at the 2nd floor, one major of 111 Brigade was handling the affairs there with about 12 armed *jawans*. When the MS conveyed them the message of the new COAS and the PM, the armed persons took him at aim. After some minutes the major incharge was able to understand his viewpoint. The PTV news reinstated as normal.

When the MS reached back at the PM House, it was Ok as if the change of COAS had been normalized. But soon after there were army all around and the armed soldiers were crossing over the walls of the PM House from each side. The MS went outside and talked to the officer on duty; made him understand that there is nobody from the PM House to resist. Take it as they had surrendered.

'No firing, no fighting, no beating; simply do what you have been instructed,' they were told. The game was over. Inside every body was told to stay in the rooms where they were. After two hours Gen Mahmud came to the PM House. The MS, though a serving Brigadier then, was abused and beaten even by *jawans*, it was learnt later.

The unlucky new Army Chief, Gen Ziauddin could survive for three hours only and was pushed to darkness of history forever with so many others; civilians and politicians.

The historians opined that Gen Musharraf was sacked on Kargil's debacle; it was PM's prerogative but every decision should have good intentioned rationale behind it. All Generals are not J Karamats.

Gen Ziauddin of Engineer's Corps was not acceptable to any. The force respects skills not 'the genes or *brothery*' only.

Had Nawaz Sharif negotiated with Gen Mahmud at the last moment when the later himself was there in the PM House, whether his name was born on the seniority list or not, his government would have survived or Gen Mahmood would have been the CMLA; but at least Pakistan could have been saved from 'Kargil's Hero'.

Scenario 24

PAKISTAN: FACTS ON KARGIL ISSUE:

The disputed State of Jammu and Kashmir has been a continuous cause of tension and wars between Pakistan and India. A plebiscite was promised with the Kashmiri populace to be held under UN Security Council Resolutions of 13th August 1948 and 5th January 1949 but the moment never came to make it true. An unending freedom struggle since then is going on in that part of Kashmir which is occupied by India.

The plans and physical movement gained sudden momentum in 1999 when the freedom fighters made high-altitude conquests in that troubled territory. They captured high ground of a 140 kilometres long stretch of 4,500 meters high mountain ridges, near the strategic Indian-held garrison towns of Kargil and Drass. These towns lie on the only usable road between Srinagar, capital of Indian-occupied Kashmir, and the East. The cropped up situation threatened India's main supply route to its forces deployed on the Indo - Chinese border.

There had existed a sort of 'gentleman's agreement' between India and Pakistan that the armies of either side will not occupy posts from the 15th September to 15th April of each year. This had been the case since 1972, but in 1999 when the Indian forces returned to the mountains, they were surprised to find around 600 Kashmiri freedom fighters, occupying their lands five kilometres inside Indian occupied Kashmir. India alleged that these Kashmiri fighters and militants were sponsored by the Pakistan Army who had crossed the Line of Control (LoC) in an attempt to alter the de facto border by force.

South Asia Tribune dated 30th August 2004: a former ISI Chief Lt Gen (Retd) Javed Nasir held Gen Musharraf responsible for major slips in the disastrous Kargil misadventure and demanded that an inquiry commission of senior retired army officers should have been formed to determine what mistakes were made. In a press article he mentioned that:

> *'Major slips in the application of methodology and the evolution, implementation and execution of the operational instructions were made. Regretfully, unlike the Indian side, instead of sacking, some of those responsible were promoted. Though Gen Musharraf had given some detailed briefings to Nawaz Sharif but in which month Kargil was occupied and when was the first briefing given was perhaps*

deliberately omitted; this most serious issue was not cleared by anyone; neither by army nor by PM's team.'

Some facts taken from an article published in daily **The Nation** dated **30th August 2004** places a fair scenario of our contemporary history before us: that Kargil was a part of the Azad Kashmir and under the control of Pakistani troops up to 1972. Because of 'permafrost' high altitude features mostly exceeding 17,000 feet, logistic dumping in the area was always considered difficult and pain taking.

After humiliating surrender of Pakistan Army on 17th December 1971, the Indian Prime Minister Indira Gandhi surfaced as a victorious leader and knew that whatever she would dictate at Simla would have to be accepted by Bhutto. Therefore, she included a term about Kashmir in the Simla agreement that:

'The areas captured across ceasefire line (CFL) in Kashmir would neither be vacated nor given back, instead the present line held will be termed as LoC but areas captured across the recognized international borders would be given back by both sides on the western front.'

The Indian Army Chief, therefore, moved his troops to occupy the vacant snow line features in Kargil. Pakistan's Army Chief Gen Tikka Khan, not knowing details of Simla Agreement, believed that upon ceasefire all the areas under adverse occupation across the Cease Fire Line (CFL) would be vacated by the two countries and given back to the respective governments as was done in 1965.

After the occupation of Kargil, the Indian army opened the road along Shyok River to the mouth of Siachen and Ladakh which previously was dominated and overlooked by the Kargil heights and always remained under occupation of Pakistani scouts. Beyond that point the CFL towards Siachen were left unmarked in 1973 because of inaccessibility.

The Indians neither ever claimed Siachen nor challenged Pakistan's control over it. After gaining Kargil in 1972, the Indians started experimenting adventures there in early 1980s and finally occupied the Siachen heights in April 1984 before the Pakistani troops were to move in.

Gen Mirza Aslam Beg planned to play back Siachen on the Indians in Kargil and he could do so because he had the best team at GHQ Pakistan would ever have. Gen Shamim Alam as the CGS & Gen Jahangir Karamat as the DGMO were in his team to go ahead with strategic military plans. The plans were presented to the President G Ishaq Khan and PM Benazir in 1989. The response was an utter disapproval from the both based on two factors.

- That India was an established nuclear power then.

- That the freedom struggle by *Kashmiris* was at a very preliminary stage then as had been estimated by the media.

Such an armed activism could have invited undue retaliation for which Pakistan had no resources to meet with. Gen Beg got disappointed.

Pakistan's nuclear explosions in May 1998 had proved that its nuclear technology was far superior to the Indian technology and that made Indian & Western media believe that balance of power in South Asia was visible. When Gen Musharraf was appointed as the Army Chief in October 1998, within the first hour of his take over he issued transfer orders of six Lieutenant Generals of his choice which included both the CGS and Chaklala Corps Commander. The Chief had himself, while serving as DGMO, minutely gone through the 1989 script of the Kargil Plan which was turned down by Benazir Bhutto.

After minute analysis of the Kargil Plan, Gen Musharraf gave the green signal. The responsibility beyond this point was that of his team comprising the CGS, Corps Commander, DGMO and Commander FCNA but, perhaps, correct method was not followed to get the government's approval. Operation was allowed by the Army Chief, it started but the credit was attributed to *Mujahideen* for the occupation of key positions.

The fact remained that Pakistan Army was to come in by all means to thwart Indian attempts to recapture these positions, thus prior approval of the PM was a must for total support as this operation would instantly become a global issue and might lead to a war between India & Pakistan.

Gen Javed Nasir, though a former DG ISI, had learnt about Kargil's move at the end of March 1999 in Karachi. He met PM Nawaz Sharif in the first week of April 1999 and asked about Kargil Operation who had no idea till then. In May 1999, Gen Javed Nasir had met the Pakistan's Air Chief who told that:

'He and the Naval Chief had learnt about the Kargil Operation for the first time in April 1999 when Gen Musharraf told the PM about that development just as a passing reference.'

241

It was never done earlier, of course, a thorough discussion was needed which should have been through before the start of the Operation.

The Government of Pakistan tried to convince the world media that it was only the moral, diplomatic and political support that Pakistan used to extend to Kashmiri freedom fighters for their cause of self-determination. It further clarified that the heights near Kargil were occupied by indigenous Kashmiri freedom fighters and not the Pakistan's army, but it was not the whole truth.

With India's nuclear re-tests in 1998, and in the intervening period of Pakistan's nuclear tests in May 1999, Indian leaders like L K Advani threatened to occupy Azad Kashmir by force. Accompanying the declaratory threats, there was actual movements of the Indian Army seen across the LOC, with massive targeting of villages of the AJK side. However, the threatening statements also revealed the ongoing Indian military planning to alter the LOC in such a way that the rest fell into its lap.

The PML(N)'s associate columnists always narrate in media that the Kargil episode had taken away the fruit of Indian PM Vajpayee's Lahore tour of 21-22nd February 1999 and of Lahore Declaration. An article titled 'Kargil War: the Real Facts' available on www.defencetalk.com puts forward another story that:

'The fact of the matter is that Prime Minister Vajpayee himself began undermining the process when he reneged on the agreements he had signed in Lahore, especially in relation to Kashmir, as soon as he was back in New Delhi. In fact, even before he left Lahore, he remarked, in connection with his commitment to discuss Kashmir in bilateral Pakistan-India talks:

"Only history can be discussed, not the geography of Kashmir."

Other members of his cabinet then began making statements that what had been discussed in Lahore had been Indian claims over Azad Kashmir. With this approach, bilateral talks were a non-starter despite Lahore, by the time the BJP government fell in April 1999.'

In order to put the onus on Pakistan, from October 1998 to February 1999, India accused Pakistan of launching as many as 17 attacks on their posts in the Siachen area. They claimed that they had beaten back all these attacks. Those allegations were to divert Pakistan's attention and draw its forces into the Siachen sector while Indian forces tried to take over unoccupied areas along the LOC.

Another important development at the time was the reported presence of Russian technical experts who were assisting Indian troops in their trials of a high altitude bunker-busting missile system in the Kargil area.

Kargil War took place between 8th May, when Pakistani forces and Kashmiri militants were detected atop the Kargil ridges and 14th July 1999, the day cease fire implemented. During the war 524 Indian soldiers were dead and 1,363 wounded; on Pakistan side 696 soldiers and 40 civilians were killed as per statistics released by Defense Minister George Fernandez of India on 1st December 1999. Contrarily the Pakistani media had told us of 2700 Pakistani army men and proportionate numbers of officers of all ranks declared dead.

On 26th May 1999, India resorted to air strikes to drive out the freedom fighters. During this episode, two Indian aircraft entered the territory of Pakistan, one of which was shot down. The situation across LoC became tense and several innocent civilians became the targets of indiscriminate Indian shelling. The international community got concerns about the escalation of conflict between the two new nuclear powers, India and Pakistan. Talks, however, held between the two states in summer 1999 and efforts were made to resolve the crisis.

An intervention by Bill Clinton, the US President persuaded Pakistan to use its influence on the freedom fighters to avert a full-scale war with India. They, however, vacated the captured territory by August 1999.

Interestingly, Pakistan had initially blamed the incursion on independent Kashmiri insurgents but then retreated. Attacks by the Indian army and air force eventually forced Pakistani troops to come back. Pakistan had sustained enormous losses including deaths of hundreds of army men and proportionate number of officers of all ranks as given above.

The other side of this conflict was more damaging. Differences broke out between the elected government of Nawaz Sharif and the Army Chief Gen Musharraf. Very serious questions were raised that did COAS Gen Musharraf, then serving under the PM Nawaz Sharif, inform him about his plans to send the Army to occupy the Kargil heights? If so, was the COAS formally permitted to go ahead? Was the attack plan formally placed before the then Corp Commander's meeting afresh [*or the same ten years old planning worked out by Gen Mirza Aslam Beg in 1989 was as such implemented questioning that whether the PM was taken into confidence].*

These questions assumed importance in the light of two interviews given by Lt Gen (Rtd) Jamshed Gulzar Kiani on **2nd June 2008,** to the **Geo TV** and the ***Dawn Daily*** of Karachi. J G Kiani was a Major-General in the Inter-Services Intelligence (ISI) at the time of Kargil conflict and the subsequent coup against Nawaz Sharif. The ISI was then headed by Lt Gen Ziauddin, a Kashmiri origin officer from the Engineer Corps but considered to be a buddy of PM Nawaz Sharif.

The differences between Gen Musharraf and Nawaz Sharif initially developed shortly after the appointment of Gen Musharraf by Nawaz Sharif as the COAS in October 1998. The main issue cropped up was Nawaz Sharif's ruling over Gen Musharraf's objections to the appointment of an engineer Gen Ziauddin as the Director-General of the ISI. Gen Ziauddin was a close confidante of Nawaz Sharif and used to keep him informed of all actions of Gen Musharraf.

Gen Musharraf had stopped inviting Ziauddin to the meetings of the Corps Commanders. During the same period Maj Gen Jamshed G Kiani was taken into confidence by Gen Musharraf to keep an eye on the activities of his DG (ISI) Gen Ziauddin. Most of the key operations of intelligence, which were the normal domain of the ISI, were taken out from ISI's jurisdiction and were allocated to the Military Intelligence (MI) Directorate indirectly being controlled by Gen Musharraf himself.

In the above mentioned TV program, Lt Gen (Rtd) J G Kiani had levelled various allegations against Gen Musharraf regarding the Kargil episode, Gen Musharraf's post 9/11 co-operation with the US in the war against terrorism and the commando raid into the *Lal Masjid* of Islamabad in July 2007. He stated that:

> '.......*according to his [Gen Jamshed Gulzar Layani] information, Nawaz Sharif did not know any thing about the Kargil episode. He was never thoroughly briefed on the issue. I personally support the holding of a judicial probe into the Kargil fiasco'.*

In his interview to daily the ***Dawn*** on the same day of **2nd June 2008,** Gen J G Kiani said that Nawaz Sharif, the majority of corps commanders and the ISI were kept in the dark about the Kargil operation in 1999. Although Nawaz Sharif was briefed on the Kargil issue but it was fairly late and the conflict had taken start by then. *'It was not a comprehensive briefing that the Chief Executive should have been given.'*

In nut shell, Gen J G Kiani had spoken well against Gen Musharraf but in October 1999, he was one of those hand-picked conspirators who, in association with Lt Gen Mohammad Aziz, the then Chief of the General Staff (CGS), had staged a coup against Nawaz Sharif (that too in the absence of Gen Musharraf because he was in the air then on his way back from Colombo), arrested the PM because he had dismissed Gen Musharraf and appointed Lt Gen Ziauddin as the COAS. They prevented Lt Gen Ziauddin from entering the office of the COAS and arrested him subsequently against all the norms and traditions of Pakistan Army.

For so many months a debate continued in senior circles of the Pakistani intelligentsia that whether PM Nawaz Sharif's behaviour to appoint an Army Chief from Engineering Corp, ignoring all the seniority lists and traditions, was a professional decision. Of course it was not. That is why he had suffered bitterly.

Gen Musharraf rewarded Gen J G Kiani for his unforgettable services immediately and promoted him as Lt Gen and appointed him as Corps Commander within one month of October 1999 coup. The two were very close to each other. Gen Musharraf used to appreciate his cooperation before the days of 'take-over' by keeping him informed of the activities of Lt Gen Ziauddin and his links with Nawaz Sharif beyond the normal scope of ISI's charter of duties.

Not only was that, Lt Gen J G Kiani was given the most important job of controlling Rawalpindi Corps for his services. When he reached the age of superannuation in 2003, Gen Musharraf third time rewarded his loyalty by appointing him as the Chairman of the Federal Public Services Commission, which post had a fixed tenure of five years under the law.

Serious differences developed between the two when Lt Gen J G Kiani as the Chairman of the Commission did not oblige Gen Musharraf and Mr Shaukat Aziz, the former Prime Minister, in respect of some appointments of officers. Gen Musharraf asked him to resign. He declined. Gen Musharraf managed a bill passed by the National Assembly in September 2006 reducing the tenure of Chairman FPSC from five to three years. Lt Gen Jamshed Gulzar Kiani was then sent home at the end of three years.

Talking to the media on 3rd June 2008, Nawaz Sharif demanded the trial of Gen Musharraf on treason charges for his illegal act of 3rd November 2007, imposing a State of Emergency, the *Lal Masjid* carnage and keeping the nation, military officials and the then political leadership in dark on the Kargil issue. Nawaz Sharif alleged that:

*'Gen Musharraf's description of the Kargil issue in his book, **In the Line of Fire**, is a pack of lies and that the interview of Gen Jamshed Gulzar Kayani to Geo TV has upheld his [PM's] stance that he [the PM] was not informed about the Kargil operation.'*

The critics and analysts had taken Nawaz Sharif's version as misleading, too. Gen J G Kiani had not told either Geo TV or the *Dawn* that 'Nawaz Sharif was not informed.' Gen JG Kiani had categorically stated that:

'Nawaz Sharif was informed later and that too not in a comprehensive manner as has been the practice in army.'

At the same time, Gen J G Kiani had added that *'Nawaz Sharif approved the already on-going operation provided it would be successful.'*

Research & Analysis Wing (RAW) of Indian Intelligence had noted in their files, as detailed in **OutlookIndia.com,** that in the last week of May 1999, Gen Musharraf had been to Beijing on an official tour. He was in daily telephonic contact with Lt Gen Mohammad Aziz, the then CGS, in Rawalpindi from his hotel room in Beijing. All those conversations were intercepted by the RAW. The government of Atal Behari Vajpayee, the then Prime Minister of India, later decided to release the transcripts of two tapes to the media. He did it for three reasons:

- Firstly, the tapes showed that it was the Pakistan Army which had occupied the Kargil heights violating the Line of Control (LoC) and not the Kashmiri Freedom Fighters (*Mujahideen*) as had been claimed by Gen Musharraf every now & then.

- Secondly, it was the Pakistan Army which had shot down an Indian Air Force plane and asked the Hizbul Mujahideen to claim the responsibility for it so that the media people go calm.

- Thirdly, the tapes showed that Gen Musharraf had launched his operation without the knowledge of Nawaz Sharif, many of his Corps Commanders, the ISI, the Chiefs of the Air Force and Navy and his Foreign Office.

Gen Musharraf got nervous after the Indian Air Force went into action and there were reports of the Indian naval ships moving from the East to the West coast. Worried over the possibility of the conflict spreading outside Kashmir, Gen Musharraf authorised Lt Gen Aziz from Beijing to brief others about the operation at an inter-ministerial meeting chaired by PM Nawaz Sharif on 29th May 1999. At this meeting, as reported by

Gen Aziz to Gen Musharraf, there were objections to Gen Musharraf's keeping others in the dark.

According to the account of the meeting as given by Gen Aziz to Gen Musharraf in Beijing over telephone, Nawaz Sharif had defended Gen Musharraf's plans of not informing others as due to demands of operational secrecy. Nawaz Sharif claimed that he himself and other Corps Commanders were informed only a week earlier. He made it appear that Gen Musharraf's action was understandable though the facts were otherwise; but when the Indian Army hit back and the IAF went into action, he lost his nerve and informed firstly Nawaz Sharif and then other senior officers and the Foreign Office.

In reality, instead of rebuking Gen Musharraf for launching the operation without his clearance and asking him to stop it, Nawaz Sharif went along with it hoping that the operation would succeed. When it did not, he flew to the US and sought the US assistance in bringing the fighting to a halt.

It becomes clear that neither Gen Musharraf nor Nawaz Sharif nor Gen J G Kiani was telling the whole truth. Each was telling only a part of the truth which, they thought, would serve their purpose.

There were no two opinions that the PM Nawaz Sharif was not shrewd enough to understand the intrigues of power corridors. He was not skilful enough to choose Gen Musharraf as the Army Chief by ignoring his senior Gen Ali Kuli Khan. The subsequent events had made it clear that he had taken this decision simply on hear-say of his famous five kitchen cabinet members and not by going through the official records available in GHQ.

Secondly, the PM should have understood Gen Musharraf's behaviour from a test assignment that how jubilant he was when once Nawaz Sharif had asked the army to take over WAPDA, a purely civilian function, to improve the organizational working of a corruption ridden department.

A little detail of that test case of running WAPDA to end corruption and to improve its efficiency: after taking over, Gen Musharraf had immediately issued orders that the Army would not only be responsible for the day-to-day running of WAPDA, but would also conduct all future negotiations with the independent power producers, thereby denying any role of the political leadership and civilian bureaucrats in that regard. All postings, transfers & tariff adjustments were shifted towards military officers.

PM Nawaz Sharif was shocked to know all the details but the bird was out of his hands then. Gen Musharraf's writ prevailed. PM Nawaz Sharif had got a first hand knowledge about his Army Chief's way of handling the state affairs.

On 14th June 1999, B Raman, an expert media analyst, was asked by Jaswant Singh, the then Indian Foreign Minister, some crucial explanations on the Kargil issue. B Raman then tried to reply the queries in an article titled *'Pak Army Chief Caught Yapping'*. When asked that how the Prime Minister Nawaz Sharif got aware of the Pakistan Army's proxy invasion plans.

> *"He said I (Nawaz Sharif) came to know seven days back (prior to Corp Commander's meeting of 29th May 1999), when Corps Commanders were told. The entire reason for the success of this operation was this total secrecy. Our experience was that our earlier efforts failed because of lack of secrecy. So, the top priority is to accord confidentiality, to ensure success. We should respect this; the advantage we have from this would give us a handle."*

Two interpretations were floated in that regard: Firstly that Gen Musharraf had secretly planned the operation, then started the execution of this operation and informed Nawaz Sharif thereafter. The second interpretation was that in a high profile meeting convened by PM Nawaz Sharif, the Foreign Office representative had expressed their unhappiness over the Army for not keeping them in picture since they had to handle the diplomatic fall out.

The conclusion reached by Jaswant Singh was that:

> *'Mr Sharif tried to soothe their ruffled feathers by claiming that he himself was informed only seven days earlier in the interest of operational secrecy. This does not necessarily mean that Mr Sharif was not in the picture from the beginning; especially when the DG ISI was his own chick.'*

Gen Musharraf, in his book *'In the Line of Fire (2006)'* had rejected Nawaz Sharif's claim of keeping him in dark on the Kargil issue. The book contains pictorial evidence of Nawaz Sharif's visit to Camp Kel in the south of Kargil where he was briefed by the army high command on 5th February 1999. (The Indian Premier Vajpayee had visited Pakistan on 19th February 1999 when the Lahore declaration was signed)

Nawaz Sharif, in his book *'Ghaddar Kaun (2007)'*, had given his version saying that:

'The audio tapes of Gen Musharraf's 26-29th May 1999's telephonic talks with Gen Aziz Khan are with him to prove that Gen Musharraf wanted to keep me [Nawaz Sharif] in the dark about the Kargil operation whatsoever.'

The matter does not end here. Leaving aside the question of whether PM Nawaz Sharif was told about the operation or not, the real issue surfaces that why or how the operation failed. The PM was told earlier or later matters less, but once operation starts the onus of failure comes on the shoulders of the Army Chief who had thought it, planned it, worked it out and launched. It was a total failure on the part of Army Chief and his close associates.

Nawaz Sharif could only be blamed if the operation was going successful and was interfered by political bosses in between or so. Gen Musharraf could be tried for the deaths of over 2700 officers and men of the Northern Light Infantry (NLI) who were eliminated in the ill-conceived and uncalled for war. In two collective wars of 1965 & 1971 Pakistan had not lost so many lives as we lost in that ill planned activism. It was an ill conceived way of 'internationalizing the Kashmir issue'.

Going into details; when India took the Kargil issue seriously and its Air Force started bombing Pak-army bunkers, Gen Musharraf told PM Nawaz Sharif about the operation first time. It was perhaps 26th or 29th May 1999 perhaps. During those days, the secretly recorded conversation between Gen Musharraf and Lt Gen Aziz, instituted and taped by the Indian Intelligence, while Gen Musharraf was staying in a hotel at Beijing (China), were also got delivered to Nawaz Sharif by the Indian PM Bajpai through an Indian Diplomat at Islamabad.

Gen Musharraf urged Nawaz Sharif repeatedly to visit the Kargil to boost morale of his army because Indian Army was overtaking all the strategic heights there. The General time and again asked the PM to find out solution to avoid a shameful defeat. Till then the Kargil operation was known by only four persons; Gen Musharraf himself, Lt Gen Aziz the CGS, Lt Gen Mahmood the Corp Commander Rawalpindi and Gen Javed Hasan the Div Commander of Northern Area. Even the other Corp Commanders, Air Chief and Naval Chief were ignorant.

Then a series of meetings were held, sometimes in Rawalpindi Corp Commander Office, then at GHQ, once in Corp Commander Office of Lahore and ultimately a meeting of Cabinet Defence Committee was called (on 2nd June 1999) where it was decided to contact the

US President Bill Clinton for ceasefire lest Pakistan looses all of its stakes.

President Clinton showered a heavy bull-shit, then hesitated to help but ultimately summoned the leadership to Washington. Meeting was arranged. Gen Musharraf gave last briefing to Nawaz Sharif at the Airport. During an emergency meeting with the PM, the American President Bill Clinton rang up Indian PM Bajpai and asked him to stop bombing Kargil; a ceasefire held next day.

Some people believed that Gen Musharraf and his four Generals had decided to oust Nawaz Sharif the same day because they were not able to face their humiliations rising from their own guilt. More so they were expecting an enquiry anytime into the whole Kargil affair.

In fact Nawaz Sharif should have announced so, irrespective of the fact that eleven years earlier a similar enquiry into Ojhri Episode of 10th April 1988 had brought an end of the rule for the then Prime Minister Mr Junejo; but the history should have been kept straight.

However, there was another school of thought which considered that Gen Musharraf was right. Gen Tariq, during his interview dated 3rd December 2001 (ref: *Gernailon Ki Syasat by Sohail Worroich* PP 41-42) categorically stated that:

> *'Gen Musharraf stood by the Nawaz Sharif government through every thick & thin. He had recovered millions of rupees from WAPDA defaulters; searched and investigated hundreds of 'ghost schools'; helped the civil government through critical hours of 'Moharram days' and in many other political issues like censes and local elections on the instance of political Prime Minister.*

> *Kargil Operation was initially Okayed by Nawaz Sharif himself but then he backed out. On some secret talk between the two PMs Bajpaie & Nawaz Sharif, the later started double play and suddenly reached America to sign Washington Declaration to end the war. If temporarily our jawans were loosing war then what, the things were in our command and control.*

> *In governments, a Show Cause Notice is issued to expel a peon but Gen Musharraf was his Army Chief. The PM should have wait for his come back from Colombo. Gen Musharraf could have taken over earlier if he wanted so. Nawaz Sharif was wrong.'*

Ayaz Amir, at present an MNA from Nawaz Sharif's PML(N) but a veteran writer had pointed out that:

'The real question about Kargil is not whether Sharif knew or not. It is something else. What accounts for the army's institutional capacity to dream up ventures lacking any geo-strategic or political context? Kargil was a misadventure. Sharif was supposed to have a limited attention span. Kargil throws up an intriguing question. Whose intellect span was more limited, Sharif's or that of the army command?'

Lt Gen Ali Kuli Khan, who had availed retirement after he was superseded in October 1998 by Gen Musharraf as Army Chief, had analyzed that:

'Kargil was flawed in terms of its conception, tactical planning and execution. The Kargil incursion was a far bigger tragedy for Pakistan than the civil wars which led to the creation of Bangladesh and damaged the country's Kashmir cause, contrary to Gen Musharraf's often repeated claims. The Kargil episode was an unprofessional decision by someone who had served in the Pakistan Army for 40 years.

As the architect of Kargil, Gen Musharraf must answer critical questions as to whose brainchild it was and what exactly the broad strategic aim behind the operation was. Let the government appoint a Kargil Commission as had been done in India to hold a thorough investigation and let the nation know the truth about Kargil.'

In fact, the Indian government had appointed a four-member committee to determine what caused the debacle from their point of view, especially the failure of the Indian intelligence to get wind of Pakistani plans to move into the Kargil heights. Establishing the truth on the Indian side was easy, because there was only one party that was in overall command and that was the elected civilian government; the military merely carried out the orders what they were asked to do.

The experts opined that to know what actually happened and who committed the blunder in that operation, firstly Nawaz Sharif during his tenure, then Gen Musharraf after October 1999 should have constituted an inquiry commission comprising certain retired officers like Gen Aslam Beg or Gen Shamim Alam including Gen Bukhari (FF), Gen Anwar (AK) and Gen Usmani (FF) [*all officers knowing about that area through their past postings*] so the nation could know the true facts and actual plans, strategy and capability of Pakistan Army.

The historians still feel astray that before Kargil war, Nawaz Shareef was very strong in Pakistan; he sacked President Farooq Leghari, Chief justice Sajjad Ali Shah and even Chief of army staff Jehangir Karamat without anyone daring to challenge him. He was the only prime minister ever in Pakistan that had held over two-third majority in Pakistan parliament and was thinking to become *ameer-ul-momeneen* with absolute power [before Nawaz, it was Z A Bhutto but had simple majority only]. He had full cooperation of Pakistan army with his own chosen Army Chief Pervez Musharraf, his hand picked DG ISI Gen Ziauddin and absolute control over Punjab but why he failed to know about Kargil & Gen Musharraf's person.

Scenario 25

PAKISTAN: MILITARY COUP OF 1999

The Prime Minister Nawaz Sharif once told in an interview to the ARY TV Network that:

'I was sitting in Prime Minister's House when the television went off and I heard that the military was around and I saw military entering and surrounding my office. Meanwhile my wife Kulsoom telephoned me and asked about the situation and later General Mahmood in uniform entered the Prime Minister's House with dozens of armed guards and asked me and my brother Shahbaz Sharif to go with him [Gen Mahmood].'

When the PM asked Gen Mahmood why the military had taken over Prime Minister's House, the latter replied that:

'Don't you know the military has taken over because you changed the army chief without any cogent reason.

Later the Prime Minister Nawaz Sharif and Shahbaz Sharif were taken to Rawalpindi in a vehicle with tinted glasses.

Nawaz Sharif also told at ARY that:

'I gave the Army immense support during the Kargil adventure though Musharraf had deliberately hidden some aspects of the Kargil war from me. Even then I took all the blame and saved the army. I didn't ask President Clinton to call me in Washington and resolve the Kargil dispute, it was Musharraf who pressed me to meet Clinton and resolve the Kargil issue. I didn't want to take any action against Musharraf after the Kargil episode because I wanted to move forward.'

In Pakistan, General Pervez Musharraf came into power on 12th October 1999 and an elected PM Nawaz Sharif was taken in army custody under the guard of military rifles. Comments of one Rodha Kumar, a Fellow of Council on Foreign Relations, New York appeared in *'The Hindu' of 21st October 1999* as follows:

'The coup was primarily a reaction to the (then) Prime Minister, Mr. Nawaz Sharif's attempts to subjugate every one of Pakistan's institutions to his extraordinarily flip - flop dictate.

Having looted the state and packed the executive with cronies and relatives, he (PM Nawaz Sharif) tampered with the Judiciary, altered the Constitution to consolidate his power, used the peace process with India as an opportunity for both political gain through Kargil and personal gain through sugar contracts, and finally turned to playing 'divide and rule' with the army.

.......Understanding this context should not, however, detract from the fact that the coup was precipitated by the Kargil debacle, and that many in Pakistan welcomed it on the grounds that the (then) democracy .... (was) too costly for the country.....'

Ever since Nawaz Sharif and Gen Musharraf fell out over Kargil; Nawaz wanted to get rid of Gen Musharraf and waiting for a suitable opportunity. He would have probably let Gen Musharraf finish his term and avoided confrontation but Gen Musharraf once insisted that Corp Commander Quetta Lt Gen Tariq Pervaiz (a close relation of a Federal Minister Raja Nader Pervaiz) who had allegedly acted as a spy for the Sharifs; be forcibly retired because he had met Nawaz Sharif without GHQ's permission required under the Army regulations. This odd demand brought Nawaz sharif to repent on his choice of Army Chief.

According to the PML sources, there were news pouring in that Gen Musharraf, after feeling humiliation over the Kargil episode, had started cursing Nawaz sharif in private meetings of Generals and diplomats. Nawaz sharif himself told that:

'Gen Musharraf came to me once and told me that he wanted to send Lt Gen Tariq Pervez home because the later had not behaved well with him during a mutual meeting.

The actual reason for his shunting was that Gen TP, then Corp Commander Quetta, had complained that why he (Gen Musharraf) had not told them about the Kargil Operation before its launch; and if PM Nawaz Sharif would not have bailed them out, the whole image of Pakistan Army could be spoiled. We argued over the issue for a long while but, to save army relationship, I ultimately agreed.

I was astonished next day when I was told and shown all the newspapers were mainly captioned that Gen Musharraf had sacked Lt Gen TP "on the charge of having met the PM". I immediately contacted ISPR, Secretary Defence, GHQ and Acting CAOS Saeeduzzafar (because Gen Musharraf had gone to Sri Lanka) but

*could not get a satisfactory reply nor could that news be taken back by
the ISPR [Pak Army's public relations wing].*

*It was much embarrassing for me, for a PM. That was the moment
I had thought to send the Army Chief Gen Musharraf home.'*

Nawaz Sharif, however, maintained that Gen Musharraf, before
departing for Colombo, himself had chalked out a similar 'special
programme' with the help of his four buddies Generals in place who
were also looking for a chance to 'deal with the PM' at some appropriate
moment. The PM House had felt changes in the routine duties of
'Brigade 111' (responsible for security duties at the PM House); new
Commander, new special walki-talki sets, noting about visiting people,
increased strength and much more. It meant that Gen Musharraf's team
had already started the 'take over' game.

The army circles maintained their side of story that when PM Nawaz
Sharif ordered Gen Musharraf to attend Colombo SAARC Conference
whereas, at par with Indian delegation, a Lt Gen rank officer should have
gone. The PM had full plan in his mind to shunt out the Chief that was
why Gen Musharraf was sent to Colombo whereas army had no such
plan to topple the government at that moment.

The fact remains that on 12th October, Prime Minister Nawaz Sharif had
attempted to dismiss Gen Musharraf and install ISI Chief Gen Ziauddin
in his place. Gen Musharraf, who was on official tour to Colombo in
connection with SAARC meeting, was coming back to Pakistan.

Nawaz Sharif had ordered that the Karachi airport be closed to prevent
the landing of the airliner, which then circled the skies over Karachi. In
the coup, Gen Usmani, the Corps Commander of Karachi, ousted Nawaz
Sharif's administration and took over the airport. The plane landed,
allegedly with only a few minutes of fuel to spare, and Gen Musharraf
assumed control of the government some moments after he landed.

Gen Musharraf had, through his 'sixth sense', taken precautions and
prepared his two close friends and course mates, CGS Aziz and Lt Gen
Mahmoud, Corps Commander RawalPindi, for all eventualities. The
Army Chief, however, did not expect to be sacked while still in the air.

Nawaz Sharif would have succeeded if he had chosen a fighting General
to replace Gen Musharraf. Nawaz Sharif's mistake was that he had
chosen his 'boot licker' who was from the Engineering Corps. Nawaz

Sharif did not realize that officers from the fighting branches of the Army like Infantry, Artillery and Armour hate to receive orders from the supporting branch officers especially from Sharif's home servant.

There is no point in arguing whether Nawaz ordered the PIA plane to remain in air or to go to Nawab Shah or elsewhere. Nawaz Sharif had constitutional right to sack the Army Chief, but through cogent reasons. He should have called his army chief to PM's office and asked him to resign instead of announcing his removal on TV. It was not a child play.

> [*Incidentally, it was only a week before the coup d'état took place that Nawaz Sharif himself had extended Gen Musharraf's term as Chief of Staff until 6th October 2001.*]

Gen Musharraf later, through a pre-recorded message, had accused the Prime Minister of leading the country to a political, economic and security deep hole and of attempting to splinter and politicize the military in order to satisfy his hunger for power.

Nawaz Sharif was on the 'high' after having successfully removed the Chief Justice Sajjad Ali Shah, replaced Jehangir Karamat as Army Chief and earlier replacing the President Farooq Leghari. All that needed was to get the 15th amendment passed through the Senate which would have consolidated his family rule over Pakistan for the next 20 years at least. Nawaz Sharif had liked to follow Nehru dynasty; Shahbaz Sharif or Hamza Shehbaz after Nawaz & and then his son Hussain Nawaz or son in law Capt Safdar or Maryam Nawaz in due time.

A survey of Gallop Pakistan (headed by known figure Dr Ejaz Shafi Gilani, who was offered a ministerial slot by Gen Musharraf in his cabinet but Mr Gilani declined) on legitimacy of 12th October 1999 military coup had shown that 70% of Pakistanis had approved Gen Musharraf's take over and sending Nawaz Sharif home. The reasons for success in survey and the said pole were:

• Chasing of Benazir Bhutto, Mr Zardari and their close associates by Ehtesab Bureau's Saif ur Rehman and his team of 'wolves' and simultaneously filling their own pockets by twisting through Ehtesab Cell. Justice Qayyum was also a party to it.

• Launching attack on the Supreme Court buildings in November 1997, mixing political workers & judges together and buying certain angry judges to send the Chief Justice home.

- Launching covert attacks on the media offices especially on 'the Jang' and enforcing a new Press Ordinance to curtail the press and media freedom.

- Getting Pakistan's foreign policy framed by Pentagon, falsely claiming the President Bill Clinton as his family friend and allegedly surrendering Kargil before them under pressure.

- Economic development rate coming down from 6% in 1988 to 2% in actual statistics but keeping the bank counters alive to release loans of billions for Sharifs.

- The magical development of their own family owned industrial empire at the cost of other industries in competition; getting all the loans written off through arm twisting of State Bank & courts.

PM Nawaz Sharif was detained on 12th October 1999 and the military had filed a complaint in the court accusing him of criminal conspiracy, hijacking, kidnapping and attempted murder. Nawaz Sharif was made to appear before a Special Anti-Terrorist Court in Karachi in November 1999 without formally being charged (but alleged) with hijacking & kidnapping with criminal intent, the attempted murder and plotting to wage war against the state. Charge sheet was probably served on 8th December 1999.

[It may be interesting to note that nabbing Nawaz Sharif and his family members, without issuing them a formal charge sheet, was not a new phenomenon in Pakistan. Nawaz Sharif, when he assumed the office of Prime Minister in February 1997, himself adopted the same measures for his political opponents and those members of bureaucracy who had gone against him in the past.

Nawaz Sharif had brought one of his trusted companions named Saif ur Rehman (a senator) as the Chief of Ehtesab Bureau (an organization to implement accountability in the country) and through this bureau, immediately suspended 87 top bureaucrats in April 1997 who had been investigating the cases against him and his family's corruption on mass scale when he was in power during 1991-1993.

Then Nawaz Sharif and Saif ur Rehman levelled allegations of corruption against most of his political opponents specially Asif Ali Zardari, husband of Ex-Prime Minister Ms Benazir Bhutto and pushed him behind the bars. False cases/references were registered against their *companions and high ranking officers were sent home on the basis of baseless enquiries, and their family members were tortured through special powers given to Ehtesab Bureau.*

Time is the real master of fortunes. Just after 30 months of ruthless rule, Nawaz Sharif, his family members, Saif ur Rehman and his family members were picked up by the army authorities in the same way and subjected to same kind of treatment, detention without warrants, trials without issuance of formal charge sheets under the same laws and regulations and by the same agency named Ehtesab Bureau (afterwards re-named as National Accountability Bureau by the military regime) and were tried in the same military courts which were originally designated by Nawaz Sharif himself.

That is a separate question that where were the higher courts then. What they felt and what were their feelings towards rule of law.]

But why it happened so; peep into the depth of few lines from an essay written by a veteran parliamentarian of Nawaz Sharif's own party, **Ayaz Amir,** *appeared in 'the News' of 20th April 2001*, saying that:

'.... True, Nawaz Sharif had got General Jahangir Karamat to write out his resignation, an event which gave rise to the legend that after conquering other institutions he had humbled even the army. Still, this was not the same thing as having another Justice Malik Qayyum as army chief [plying as domestic servant].

This is the significance of October 12: Nawaz Sharif in Hercules mode setting out to rectify this situation by removing Musharraf and putting a fellow Kashmiri from Lahore, Lt-Gen Ziauddin Butt, in his place. The scheme went awry because it was not thought through properly or the army command had had enough and was in no mood to be pushed around.

Remember also that the army command was smarting from Kargil, a defining moment in the longstanding love affair between GHQ and the Sharifs (the Sharifs having been discovered and groomed for great things by General Zia himself, Lt-Gen Jillani, Lt-Gen Hamid Gul and a whole line of minor geniuses in ISI).

A wounded tiger and wounded Generals: the mood between them is about the same. Nawaz Sharif did not have a measure of this feeling. He was also surrounded by a school of bumpkins, the kind who act as cheer leaders to prize fighters. "Play it on the front foot" was their constant refrain. Mian Sahib played it on the front foot once too often and did not know what hit him.'

In last week of July 2011, Nawaz Sharif himself narrated the story of his arrest on 12ᵗʰ October 1999 to some closest media friends as under:

"On 12th October 1999, I was arrested from the PM House Islamabad and taken, in a car having black tinted windows, to an army mess in Chaklala where armed guards were taking care of me. The window pans of room where I was detained were covered & pasted with old newspapers. At midnight, Gen Ehsan, Gen Mahmood and Gen Orakzai came to my room, placed a typed paper before me and asked me to sign it. It was a statement saying that:

'I hereby resign from Prime Minister's slot and advice the President to dissolve the Assemblies.' I flatly refused to sign. They asked me time and again but I did not agree. Gen Mahmood got angry; resorted to threats and started abusing me. I told them categorically that even you shoot me dead, I'll not sign it. The three Generals left the room leaving me alone with that typed paper.

[The fact remains that the Generals had rather attempted to remove Nawaz Sharif by forcing him to resign and then bring in a civilian government from amongst a host of technocrats, who would be approved by the parliament. When they failed to get Nawaz Sharif on line, they declared the dissolution of parliament and dismissed all the provincial Assemblies, thus assuming the reins of powers directly.]

Next day I was taken to face a Brigadier in uniform in his camp office. He offered me chair and started putting questions, as it was an interrogation by a 'thanedar', in low and high tones. I told the officer that I'll not answer any question; I'll only speak in the court. His temperature went high he took out a newspaper from his table drawer and forwarded to me. Main caption was; 'Making a special cell in Mianwali jail for Nawaz Sharif'. The Brigadier told me smilingly to get ready for it then. I was kept in that room for about three weeks.

During one night of second week of November 1999, I was taken to Murree where I was kept in a very small room having a bed and stand-only space, with tinted in pitch black windows and with small attached bathroom. The room was kept locked from outside and I had to knock the door and wait for guard to hear me.

Once an officer in uniform attended me and I simply requested him that if he could open a side window for me enabling me to see the sun light. He very politely declined my request.

Once I heard voice of Quraan's recitation, while in the same room of Murree, from which I could imagine that my son Hussain was also around. Once I requested that army officer if I could meet my son for a while. Again I was refused. Instead he did a favour to me that while taking me out next morning, he made out way to let me pass near my son's room. We only saw each other, wave hands and said goodbye because we were going apart.

When Gen Ziaul Haq had arrested late Z A Bhutto in 1977, the later was also brought in the same rest house of Murree. Meeting between Gen Zia and Bhutto was also held at this place." (**Ref: Daily Jang London 29th July 2011**)

Ch Nisar Ali Khan of PML(N), in his interview to *Hum* TV in 2006 had given an insight over what happened on 12th October 1999 and the events which lead to the take over. According to his assessment, Gen Musharraf was a very obedient officer and considered Nawaz Sharif as the captain of the ship.

But it was the team of three other Generals, who where behind Kargil Fiasco, created misunderstandings between the two chiefs. They threatened Gen Musharraf that the PM would make minced meat out of them over the Kargil issue and the four of them would be court martialled. At the same time another team was working on the PM to take action against the Army Chief.

Other information the PM had availed was of a mock coup exercise conducted by the army officers, in which they visited president house, parliament house, Prime Minister House, Radio station and PTV station. This info was perhaps leaked purposely to the PM. More so, Gen Musharraf had a lust for power like his predecessors which lead to the coup. It was personal vendetta and a sense of fear.

Gen Musharraf had once said in an interview, that *'Nawaz Sharif would have been prime minister till today had he not removed him'*. Nawaz Sharif was flying high after having successfully removed the Chief Justice Sajjad Ali Shah, replaced Jehangir Karamat as Army Chief and finally replacing the president Leghari.

All that needed was to get the 15th amendment passed through the Senate. This would have secured his family rule over Pakistan for the next 20 years like Nehru dynasty of India.

Much later, Nawaz Sharif was tried in the same 'Anti-Terrorist Court' at Karachi which was once established by him. He got the same treatment from his own hand-made courts which he wanted to deliver to his political opponents when he had assumed power in 1997. Time is the real master. He was sentenced for imprisonment and was kept in Attock Fort, partly converted into jail, till 10th December 2000 from where he was sent to Saudi Arabia for ten years after negotiating a deal with Gen Musharraf but brokered through Saudi rulers.

Nawaz Sharif and his brother Shahbaz Sharif had signed a memorandum of understanding that they would not take part in Pakistan politics for ten years and would stay in Saudi Arabia.

[*However, they managed to come back to Pakistan on 10th September 2007 as a result of immense combined pressure from US, Benazir Bhutto and the Royal Saudi Rulers. So many times tried to wriggle out but each time was snubbed by his Saudi masters.*]

Gen Musharraf's NAB (name of Nawaz Sharif's Ehtesab Bureau was changed by Gen Musharraf to be called as National Accountability Bureau) had hired international detectives to trace an estimated £700 million in assets of Nawaz Sharif when he was allowed to go into exile.

This surprise decision to free Nawaz Sharif from a life sentence and let him and his family flee to Saudi Arabia was perhaps taken on the advice from investigators that the only way to track down the missing fortune was to let him start spending it. While he was in prison the military government could manage to locate only $6 million [£4.1 million] in accounts which were confiscated.

The evidence gathered till then by NAB had suggested that 'Mr Sharif owns seven apartments in London, including one in Mayfair and Park Lane each, and holds bank accounts in London, Liechtenstein, Austria and Switzerland. *This is a phenomenal rise in wealth for a man who, when he started in politics in 1979, owned one re-rolling foundary at Lahore shared by Mian Sharif's brothers too.*'

Throughout this rise in graphs of wealth, the Pakistani courts kept their eyes closed, rather Sharif family's personal judge Justice Malik Qayyum of Punjab High Court always provided them shelter, relief and mostly acquittals in all cases filed by the state or banks in connection with their corruption at various times.

Considering the other responsible factors; the observers of the situation in Pakistan did not rule out a change in the authority, because the demonstrations organized by the Pakistani opposition parties had been consistent those days. The opposition, which included 19 parties, had one single agenda, that is to topple government by exploiting the spirit of resentment felt by the masses in the wake of the **Washington Declaration** of June 1999 between the American president Bill Clinton and the Prime Minister Nawaz Sharif, pertaining to the withdrawal of Kashmiri fighters from the Indian side of Kargil.

It was clear from day one that the coup was staged with the blessing of America. The American warning on 22nd September 1999 was in fact deemed as a sign that the coup was imminent. America had attempted to topple Nawaz Sharif by destroying him in the eyes of masses through forcing him to withdraw the military forces from Kargil and then inciting the masses and the political parties against him.

However, Nawaz Sharif continued to cling to power and this forced the United States to remove him by a military coup, backed by a broad popular support, see 70% poll in Gallop's survey mentioned above.

Furthermore, Nawaz Sharif failed to comply with the resolutions of the IMF, mainly amongst others was that 220 billion rupees should be recuperated from influential personalities who defaulted in their repayments and returned to the banks. From inside the America knew it that this huge amount was actually taken out as loans by Sharifs and their close associates. The America had the record of all such details. Due to his dictatorial attitude, Nawaz Sharif had squandered the state's funds in buying people's loyalty, especially in the media circles.

Christina Lamb wrote in *'The Telegraph'* of 19th June 2001 under caption *'Sharif is freed to lead Pakistan to lose £700m'* that:

> *'Saudi Arabia's Crown Prince Abdullah, who negotiated the deal, had threatened to cut diplomatic ties with Pakistan if his friend Mr Sharif was not freed. Mr Sharif has been accused of corruption, but was actually jailed for attempted hijacking. Although there has been criticism within Pakistan of the decision to free him, Mr Haqqani insisted that the deal was good for the military regime'.*

A similar deal was also offered to Ms Benazir Bhutto whereby corruption charges against her, for which she was sentenced to five years imprisonment in absentia, was to be dropped had she agreed to hand over some property & foreign cash and not to participate in politics of Pakistan. Ms Bhutto had refused, arguing that this would imply guilt.

Coming back to Army's take over, the irony of fate is that every military government used to blow their brass trumpets at full volume stating and trying to prove with 'facts & figures' that they have come to save Pakistan from flood of corruption, bankruptcy and lawlessness brought by dismissed political governments. Gen Musharraf had also started his rule with the same slogans. To keep his control over the affairs of government, Gen Musharraf adopted a two way policy but mainly depending upon the historical weak character of higher judiciary.

While doing so Gen Musharraf availed that routine opportunity of getting his rule validated by the Supreme Court of Pakistan for three years, after which the Constitution was restored (after making amendments which only suited Gen Musharraf) and elections were held.

The 17th Amendment was incorporated in the Constitution permitting the President to continue wearing the uniform of COAS up to 31st December 2004 as agreed between the government and the supporting parties in the parliament and MMA (*Mothida Majlis-e-Amal*, a coalition of Islam loving parties sitting on opposition benches in the Parliament).

Gen Musharraf announced on electronic media that he would give up the post of COAS after 31st December 2004, which he never obliged till the end of 2007.

> *[In 1977, after imposing martial law, Gen Ziaul Haq had also made a similar promise on TV with the people that he, being a simple soldier, did not have political ambitions and would hold elections within three months, but he did not keep the promise and ruled for eleven years.]*

Nawaz Sharif was blamed for destroying Pakistan's economy and bringing Pakistan to a near default. Though Pakistan was facing sanctions over nuclear tests and the international trade was affected but the historians would remember some bitter facts also from which Pakistan had suffered a lot but the Sharifs got maximum benefits out of that situation i.e:

> Firstly: A week before the nuclear tests on 28th May, all foreign currency held by Sharifs and their close associates was taken out from the banks and Saif ur Rehman personally took those bags and brief cases to Dubai.

Secondly: When the foreign currencies were nationalized, the PML within two days converted all his wealth in Pakistani rupee currency into dollars from the nation's frozen foreign currency and again despatched them to Dubai as second instalment.

Thirdly: When the US government imposed sanctions, the PM announced a donation scheme named *'Qarz Utaro Mulk Sanwaro'*. The people of Pakistan donated generously but not even a single rupee was paid as foreign debt. Till today there are no accounts available for that huge collection of money. Once the then Finance Minister Ishaque Dar, while replying a stinking question about that scheme, had told the print and electronic media that:

'The money collected was deposited in the main account 'A' of Ministry of Finance'. No evidence is available on record till today.

A *'Media Forum Analysis' dated 29th October 1999* carried out by *Hizb-ut-Tahrir,* still available at www.hizbuttahrir.org seems to be more convincing because it was written by a foreign organization and just two weeks after the military coup in Pakistan. This analysis categorically told two things: Firstly that the coup had prior approval of America and; secondly it was an off-shoot of Kargil episode in which America wanted to help the Indian Prime Minister Vajpaee.

Details available were that just before the flare-up of the military hostilities between India and Pakistan around Kargil, the Indian government of PM Atal Behari Vajpayee collapsed on 18th April 1999 by a majority of one single vote, and when the Congress Party failed to form a new government, general elections were held in India. This led to a further decline in the popularity of the Congress Party whose deputies were reduced from 141 in the parliament of 1998 to 112. On the other hand the majority of the coalition of 24 parties led by AB Vajpayee had increased.

The main reason for the success of Vajpayee over Gandhi was because his coalition was presented as a **victor in the Kargil war** and propagated as capable of vanquishing the enemy. The battle of Kargil had washed away certain negative effects caused by the feuds between the coalitions of Vajpayee during its first term of office. It is well known that Atal B Vajpayee was a pragmatic politician, who held a host of radical slogans, such as 'India for the Hindus'.

It was through him and his party that America succeeded in breaking the dominance of the Congress Party over the political life in India which lasted more than 45 years.

Therefore, Nawaz Sharif's submission to the American pressure to withdraw from Kargil had led to the victory of Vajpayee in the Indian general elections and to the crushing defeat of the Congress Party that had historically been loyal to Britain, which fact the US never approved.

But was the coup justified?

The army on 12th October 1999 came forward with a common, but ever appealing slogan of *'eradication of political corruption'* for Pakistani people. Was it appropriate for the army to prosecute corruption mafia who themselves kept a blurred history in this respect? Pakistan's army, with its record of dictatorial intervention and rule and then getting legitimacy & approval through the kangroo courts of known fame, hardly qualified as exceptional.

However, despite its prolonged and best endeavours, Pakistan's army has not been able to entirely subjugate its civil institutions and especially the judiciary as in the military regimes of Spain of the past and other countries of South American continent. Many analysts had noted that Gen Musharraf's regime had done little to quash corruption. In fact, Pakistan, which was ranked 79th in Transparency International's Corruption Perceptions Index in 2001 dropped to 142 in 2006, placing it in the bottom quarter of the list, 22 spots away from the last entry. What a qualification the Pakistan possess.

As per polls done by Dawn, News, Indian Express and CNN-IBN in individual capacity and at intervals, a majority believe that corruption during this administration had increased. An Asian Development Bank report on the state of the country during the 60th year of Independence described it as a country with *'poor governance, endemic corruption and social indicators which are among the worst in Asia'*.

Once in 2007, Gen Musharraf's team cost national exchequer millions of Rupees to hire teams of expensive lawyers to represent his government in courts. In one such case regarding the privatization of Pakistan Steel Mills Corporation, whose worth was stated to be Rupees 600 billion, and which was sold out for mere Rupees 20.6 billions, the government had spent Rupees 90 million, with Sharifuddin Pirzada alone getting away with 6.6 million rupees. The Supreme Court had taken *suo moto* notice of that dubious deal and the said case had played a background role for decision of sending the Chief Justice Iftikhar M Chaudhry home in March 2007.

Most serious side effect of Gen Musharraf's rule was that the army lost its credibility as an institution. There was an escalating civil war-like situation on our north-western frontiers where soldiers were routinely being killed or kidnapped nearly daily, military installations were being attacked, and military casualties were piling up.

Most importantly, public resentment against the military as an institution was as high as one could ever recall. Arguably, not since 1971 had the Pakistan military been under such internal strain.

In Pakistan, every dictator 'General' had always taken all due cares and precautions to keep reins of the government in his hands. Gen Musharraf adopted the same methodology to extend his rule under one pretext or the other and by keeping his guns on the shoulders of higher judiciary. Gen Ziaul Haq had also done the same.

Scenario 26

MUSHARRAF'S NAB ORDINANCE OF 1999

When Gen Musharraf announced to continue the process of 'Ehtesab' by changing name of (Nawaz Sharif's) Ehtesab Cell to 'National Accountability Bureau (NAB)' after his take over on 12th October 1999, the former Chief Justice Sajjad Ali Shah had urged that the judiciary should also be included in the accountability process. However, the then Chairman of NAB, Gen M Amjad had opposed the idea of accountability of the armed forces and judiciary.

Referring to daily *'The News' of 22nd December 1999*, the justification he forwarded was that:

> 'The powers given to the NAB's Chairman have made the NAB very powerful. We need to evolve a mechanism for keeping the NAB under check and the only institution that can check the NAB is judiciary. If we start accountability of the judiciary, who will check NAB!'

[*Kashif Aziz in his essay **dated 14th March 2008** available at **www. Chowrangi.com** has given some interesting facts about Gen M Amjad, 1st Chairman NAB appointed by Gen Musharraf in October 1999. Gen M Amjad was Corps Commander Multan when he was appointed as the first chairman of NAB being a close friend of Gen Mahmood Ahmed.*

On 4th April 2002, for the first time in the history of Pakistan Army, a serving General and Corps Commander was posted as Chairman Fauji Foundation, Pakistan Army's business concern, and he was Gen Muhammad Amjad.

In 2003, Qazi Hussain Ahmed, Amir Jamat-e-Islami (JI) alleged that Gen Amjad had been allotted an expensive piece of land (plot 2-A) measuring two kanals in Lahore Cantt at throw away price, on 31st August 2003 through allotment letter No.11-1484RD-Ihr-88 dated 31st August 2003. The plot, situated on Sarwar Shaheed Road, Lahore Cantt, was leased out to the worthy General for 99 years, against an annual lease fee of 50 rupees only. The plot was worth 90 lakhs and Gen Amjad had already sold one kanal for 45 lakhs out of that.

In early 2005 a complaint was filed in NAB against its own ex-Chairman Gen Amjad, Chairman Fauji Foundation, for corruption in sales of

Khoski Sugar Mill. The Parliamentary Secretary for Defence, Tanvir Hussain, had admitted in the Assembly that the 'sugar mills had been sold at Rs. 300 million, against the highest bid of Rs. 387 million.'

But instead of coming clean on the issue, Gen Amjad and the other top Generals of GHQ had decided to challenge the jurisdiction of the Parliament to look into the affairs of Army-run businesses. The Senate Standing Committee on Defence, on 4th June received a communication from the Ministry of Defence stating that the Committee had no jurisdiction to consider affairs of the Fauji Foundation because 'it is a private sector organization.'

On 21st March 2007, KESC appointed Gen (retd) Amjad as the new Chief Executive drawing a salary of Rs. 1.1 million besides perks amounting to Rs. 0.3 million. His appointment was 'directed to be made outside procedure' while he had no technical know-how of running such a sensitive and technical outfit. That is why the KESC is still suffering with Power Crisis.]

Going back to November 1999 when the NAB ordinance was promulgated along with creation of accountability courts to try corruption cases, the NAB was granted extensive powers of arrest, investigation & prosecution. The judicial tribunals were prohibited from granting bail. The ordinance also allowed for detention periods of up to 90 days without charge and did not allow the accused access to any counsel prior to the institution of formal charges.

Further, the burden of proof at trial continued to rest with the defendant and convictions for violations could result in 14 years' imprisonment, fines, property confiscation and the loss of right to hold public office for a period of 10 years.

[However this prohibition was later modified following a Supreme Court ruling restoring the rights of the accused.]

The validity of the said draconian NAB ordinance was challenged on various grounds in the Supreme Court of Pakistan by ANP Chief Asfand Yar Wali Khan. The SC on 25th April 2001 announced its unanimous decision signed by a full bench comprising of the Chief Justice Irshad Hasan Khan, Justice Muhammad Bashir Jehangiri, Justice Muhammad Arif and Justice Qazi Muhammad Farooq. The Chief Justice Irshad Hasan Khan had authored the said judgment.

In the petition about 22 issues were raised and the SC bench had given judgment by replying each point raised therein. It was ruled therein that the Accountability Courts were competently established by the Federal Government but the Presiding Officers should be serving District & Sessions Judges qualified to be Judges of the High Court.

The Presiding Officers shall be appointed for a period of three years in consultation with the Chief Justices of the concerned High Courts and shall not be transferred to any other place or removed from service in routine. They shall perform their functions under the supervision and disciplinary control of respective High Courts but necessary funds shall continue to be paid by the Federal Government.

In that 2001's judgment, the Supreme Court held that it was absolutely necessary to create the offence of **'wilful default'** in the back drop of great loss of public revenues due to massive corruption and through huge Bank-loans. The offence of 'wilful default' was made a continuing offence declaring it prospective in nature.

On that issue, the SC believed that 30 days notice should be served upon the defaulter to explain his innocence or cause of guilt whatsoever and then 7 days notice was made mandatory for the financial chiefs to consider the explanations submitted by the accused. Any settlement arrived at with the defaulters by the Chairman NAB or compounding of any offence shall be subject to the confirmation by the respective Accountability Court after re-considering the facts.

Regarding arrest of the accused the Supreme Court held that arrest and detention of an accused for a period of 90-days is *ultra vires* to constitutional provisions. It was held that the accused shall be produced before the Accountability Court within 15 days each time for further orders if considered necessary.

It was also ordered that if sufficient and reasonable cause appears for further remand after the expiry of first 15 days, the accused shall be brought before the Court for appropriate orders. Previously there were provisions that:

> 'No accused arrested under the Ordinance shall be released without the written orders of the Chairman NAB.'

On the question of bail, the powers of the High Courts of the respective provinces under Article 199 of the Constitution were made available as per law and practice.

[Previously under Section 9(b) of the NAB Ordinance, no court, including the superior courts, were allowed to take bail of the accused charged under NAB ordinance.]

Section 12 of the NAB Ordinance had conferred unchallengeable powers on the Chairman NAB to freeze the property of an accused which order shall not accede 30 days unless confirmed by the Accountability Court. These powers were considered unjustified being 'excessive delegation' thus the period was curtailed to 15 days. Section 12 (f) provided that:

'Order of freezing mentioned in section 12 (a) to (c) would remain operative until final disposal of case by the accountability Court or the appellate forum.'

It was held unjustified, thus declared that the respective courts would decide about the freezing or releasing of the properties involved in view of available circumstances.

An amendment was also suggested by the SC that in case of acquittal of an accused, the freezing orders shall continue for 10 days to be reckoned from the date of receipt of certified copy of the final order to enable the NAB to file an appeal. If they consider it appropriate. The SC ordered that Section 13 of the NAB Ordinance should also be amended so as to allow right of appeal to the accused against freezing of property if dismissed by the Accountability Court.

The tyranny of the state was reflected through Section 14(d) of the NAB Ordinance under which an accused person was required to bear the burden of proof that:

'He had used his authority, powers or issued any directive or SRO etc. in the public interest fairly, justly etc. In the absence of such proof, he shall be guilty of the offence.'

The SC held that the prosecution would first make out a reasonable case against the accused charged under Section 9 (a)(vi) & (vii) of the NAB Ordinance. If the prosecution succeeded in making out a reasonable case to the satisfaction of the Court, the prosecution would be deemed to have discharged the prima facie burden of proof and then the burden of proof would shift to the accused to rebut the presumption of guilt levelled against him or her.

The SC held that in case of conviction, envisaged by Section 15(a) of the NAB Ordinance disqualification to contest elections or to hold public office for a period of 21 years is too excessive and through an amendment be reduced to 10 years.

With regard to 'rule of holding of open trial', the apex court held that it would remain within the discretionary power of the Accountability Court; no hard or rigid rule can be taken in consideration on either side.

Section 17(c) had empowered the Accountability Court to dispense with any provision of CrPC and to follow such procedure as it might deem fit in the circumstances of the case. The SC held that such provision was also contained in the Ehtesab Act 1997 but was not held *ultra vires* previously *(PLD 2000 SC 26)*. However, it should not go uncontrolled thus if it deemed fit to make departure from the provisions of CrPC reasons would be recorded in writing.

Section 23 of the NAB Ordinance had imposed a total ban on transfer of property by an accused or his relatives and associates etc where an investigation got initiated into an offence. It was observed that Section 23 be suitably amended so as to provide that transfer of property by accused or his relatives would not be void if made with the prior approval of the judge of the Accountability Court in writing subject to such terms and conditions as deemed fit.

Plea bargaining, envisaged by the NAB Ordinance was approved being an established method of out of court settlement of disputes in several developed societies, but the court held that firstly; it should not be in cases opposed to public policy, secondly; it should be approved by the Accountability Court and thirdly; should not be the outcome of pressure or threats from private persons or state sponsored bodies.

Section 25A of the NAB Ordinance had given an unfettered discretion to the Chairman NAB to reject recommendations of a duly appointed Committee and refuse to recognise a settlement arrived at between a creditor and a debtor. It was held by the SC that the provisions of Section 25A (e) and (g) suffer from the excessive delegation of powers and should be amended as to provide that the recommendations made by the Governor State Bank of Pakistan would be binding on the Chairman NAB except for valid reasons to be assigned in writing subject to approval of the Accountability Court to be accorded within a period not exceeding 7 days.

NAB Ordinance's section 32(d) provided that no stay of proceedings before Accountability Court be granted by any Court on any ground nor prosecuting thereof be suspended or stayed by any Court on any ground whatsoever. It was held on the strength of case laws that constitutional jurisdiction vesting in High Courts under Article 199 of the Constitution cannot be taken away or abridged or curtailed by subordinate legislation. The provision was, therefore, declared *ultra vires* the Constitutional provisions on the subject thus the said Section was ordered to be amended accordingly.

In connection with reference of Section 31B of the NAB Ordinance, empowering the Chairman NAB to direct the Prosecutor General to withdraw from prosecution of any accused, it was held that withdrawal of cases could only be resorted to if the Accountability Court so permitted. Suitable amendment in Section 31B was ordered.

Regarding appointment of the Chairman NAB, there had been much hue & cry from all corners and still it continues. Section 6 (b)(i) of the Ordinance said that the *'Chairman NAB shall hold office during the pleasure of the President'* was held to be *ultra vires* the Constitution. Section 6 was directed to be amended in a suitable way like:

- The Chairman NAB shall be appointed by the President in consultation with the Chief Justice of Pakistan.

- The Chairman NAB shall hold office for a period of three years.

- The Chairman NAB shall not be removed from office except on the grounds of removal of a Judge of the Supreme Court.

- The Chairman NAB shall be entitled to such salary, allowances and privileges and other terms and conditions of service, as the President determines for this assignment and these terms shall not be varied during the term of or his stay in office.

- The Chairman NAB may, by writing under his own hand, resign from his office anytime before his mandatory period.

The SC also held that Section 8(a) of the NAB Ordinance, regarding the Prosecutor General Accountability, should be amended as:

- The Prosecutor General shall hold an independent office on whole time basis and shall not hold any other office concurrently.

- He shall be appointed by the President in consultation with the Chief Justice of Pakistan and Chairman, NAB on such terms and conditions as may be determined by the President. His remuneration and benefits shall in no case exceed those of the Attorney General for Pakistan; the Principal Law Officer of the country and holder of a constitutional office.

- He shall hold a tenure post of not less than two years.

- His services shall not be dispensed with except on the grounds prescribed for removal of a Judge of the Supreme Court.

- He shall not be permitted to conduct private cases and in lieu thereof he may be allowed a special allowance.

- Prosecutor General may, by writing under his own hand, resign from his office anytime before conclusion his stay.

In the interest of continuity of accountability, the then incumbent Chairman NAB and Prosecutor General were allowed to carry on with NAB with the service conditions already designated for them. With regard to the Deputy Chairman NAB it was held that he would hold office for a minimum period of two years and would not be removed except on the grounds of misconduct as defined under Section 2(4) of the Government Servants (Efficiency & Discipline) Rules, 1973.

The following directions were also issued for an independent prosecution:

- A panel of competent lawyers of experience and impeccable reputation would be prepared in consultation with the Law and Justice Division. Their services would be utilized as Prosecuting Counsel in cases of significance at reasonable fee on case to case basis. Even during the course of investigation of an offence, the advice of a lawyer chosen from the panel could be taken by the NAB.

- Every prosecution which resulted in the discharge or acquittal of the accused, must be reviewed by a lawyer on the panel and on the basis of the opinion given; responsibility should be fixed for dereliction of duty, if any, of the concerned officer. In such cases, strict action would be taken against the officer found guilty.

- Steps would be taken for the constitution of an able and impartial agency comprising persons of unimpeachable integrity to perform functions of investigation and inquiry, etc.

On the subject of **'Accountability of Armed Forces'** the SC had observed that notwithstanding the constitutional safeguards provided in Articles

8(3)(a), 63(1)(g) and 199(2)(3) members of the Armed Forces would be better dealt under the Pakistan Army Act 1952 and the Pakistan Army Rules 1954 which expressly provide for prosecution and punishment in cases involving corruption, corrupt practices and illegal gratification etc.

At that moment, the apex court had forgot that for civil bureaucracy there existed Efficiency & Discipline Rules 1973, then why they were twisted, picked up, arrested and sent behind the bars in the name of 'Accountability' under NAB.

Similarly, on the subject of Accountability of Judiciary, the SC held that Article 209 of the Constitution relating with the Supreme Judicial Council, the Code of Conduct for the Judges and the law declared in *Malik Asad Ali vs Federation of Pakistan (PLD 1998 SC 161)* were sufficient to deal with the judges. Though it was held in *Zafar Ali Shah Case* that the Judges of the Superior Courts were not immune from accountability but even then they were only referred to the Article 209 in which it is for the President only to make a reference nothing more.

The said system flawed in disaster in 2001 when the malafide and corruption charges were proved on Malik Qayyum and the then CJ LHC Rashid Aziz but simply they were sent home smilingly. Whereas when bureaucrats were handled under NAB Ordinance, their careers gone OK but rest of their lives ended in jail.

Numerous examples are available in Nawaz Sharif's days when Saif ur Rehman, the Ehtesab Lord then, had published a list of 87 officers and half of them were sent to jail because they had dealt with Income Tax of Ittefaq Group, Customs duty of Ittefaq Foundary's scrap; Loans raised on Hudaibya Sugar Mills, Hudaibya Paper Mills, Raiwind Palace, Phalia Sugar Mills, Ramzan Sugar Mills, Brother Sugar Mills Sahiwal and many fraudulent loans up to Rs:212 billion taken by Sharif's and got them washed through Judges like Malik Qayyum.

The whole nation ponders that if in our society only bureaucrats and politicians are corrupt, not the judges or army Generals. Why so that:

- The intelligent white collared criminals prefer to engage 'judges' instead of going to expensive lawyers.

- The intelligent people like to send their sons in forces instead of making them doctors or engineers because an army officer's ending years ensure billions in fortune.

Coming back; persons charged with corruption by Gen Musharraf's NAB then included former Prime Ministers Benazir Bhutto and Nawaz Sharif. In April 1999 during PML era, Benazir Bhutto and her husband, former Senator Asif Ali Zardari, were sentenced to five years imprisonment by a stooge judge of the Lahore High Court named Malik Qayyum on corruption charges to please Nawaz Sharif.

In April 2001, the Supreme Court overturned those convictions following revelations concerning the political manipulation of above named judge, the then Chief Justice of LHC named Rashid Aziz and the then Federal Law Minister Khalid Anwar.

Various tape recordings surfaced which demonstrated that the then head of Accountability Bureau, Saifur Rehman, had directed High Court Judges to impose the maximum sentence convicting Ms Bhutto and Mr Zardari. Thus the Accountability Bureau & courts were mostly determined to deny due process and fair justice.

An article written in Urdu by a celebrated columnist Irshad Haqqani, appeared in *Daily Jang of London of 4th October 2003*, captioned as: *'A Test Case for Election Commission and NAB'* gave a factual start by saying that:

'If we don't betray ourselves then should we admit that there prevail no basic values of supremacy of law in Pakistan'?

Historically speaking Pakistan is a country where the constitution remained either suspended or mutilated or subjected to emergencies floated by various rulers or implemented under the hammer of Army Rule since its independence in 1947. This situation prevailed amidst flavours of militarized [and mostly coerced] slogans of democracy for more than three decades since then and after.

Educationists understand that a nation can be labelled as cultured only if there is rule of law. Those countries where these values exist and where the notions of 'equal justice for all' prevails and where the law is bound to earn respect at all echelons and where the courts are able to deliver decisions without fears or favours can be called civilized or cultured. The remaining stuff can be taken as a group of living people in given geographical boundary but cannot be called a 'nation'.

Each time when a new ruler took over reigns of control in Pakistan, there was some person to challenge his illegal action in the apex courts. These challenges were granted acceptance and the writ petitions were heard in length each time by panels of senior judges. But it is also a history that each time the superior courts gave a decision in favour of the sitting rulers; invariably to all the army adventurers.

No body was ever punished, no ruler dethroned and no military General made angry rather they all were blessed with certificates of approval in the name of *'doctrine of necessity'*. It is a known fact that in Pakistan any powerful tycoon of political or financial status can twist any law in one's favour, at all levels and in all circumstances.

Ijaz Hussain, professor of International Relations in Qaid e Azam University Islamabad also holds the same opinion (conveyed through *South Asia Tribune of 13th September 2003*) that:

> *'The judiciary in Pakistan does not have an edifying history. Most jurists agree that its weak-kneed response to the excesses of the executive early in the country's history have gone a long way in impeding the progress of democracy in Pakistan.'*

Thus, in this context Pakistan has a shameful position because here the law and judiciary are not the strongest institutions rather these are the weakest. Ministry of Law & Parliamentary Affairs exists at the Federal level but it is considered to be the most unattractive slot in the cabinet. Secretariats of Law & legislation are there at all federal and provincial levels but no bureaucrat, officer or subordinate, wants to be posted there happily. That is why there exists no real or fair institution for 'practical accountability' who would deal the matters on merits.

On the other hand, it is also a fact that the people of Pakistan are really scared of Accountability Bureau or NAB, an organisation always remained under the direct command of the Chief Executive, whether a politician like Nawaz Sharif or a military ruler like Gen Musharraf. It always enjoyed tremendous special powers (mostly above constitution & general law) of arrest, investigate and prosecute any person on any reference pertaining to any time in the past.

No court has any jurisdiction to interfere in their activity, no procedural code is applicable to them, practically no rules of physical or judicial remands are followed by them and they do not bother for any thing. It is all because the NAB members have no agenda as their own. They only deal cases of those political and bureaucratic high profiles for which the orders are conveyed by their civil or military commanders.

A press statement issued by the PPP on 1ˢᵗ October 2003 is referred here which said that:

> '......... *we strongly condemn the continued victimisation of Pir Mukarram ul Haq, the spouse of Ms. Farzana Raja MPA in a bid to pressurise her to succumb to the regime. Pir Mukarram has been shifted to the Adiyala jail from Federal Services Hospital in Islamabad yesterday, the 30th September, where he was under treatment of his illness. Immense pressure was exerted on the hospital authorities to relieve him from the hospital.*'

Makhdoom Amin Fahim of PPP then told the media that the NAB authorities had arrested Pir Mukarram, the former Managing Director, Printing Corporation of Pakistan on 21ˢᵗ June 2003. The references against him were not filed till that moment. It should be recalled that at the time of his arrest, the protest against the LFO and the president in uniform was at its peak in the Punjab Assembly. Ms Farzana Raja MPA, being a PPP stalwart was vocal against the military regime and they wanted to strangulate her voice.

Makhdoom Amin Faheem abhorred the heavy handedness of the regime and said that:

> '....... *to use NAB as a weapon against political opponents is not only contemptible but also a grave violation of human rights.*'

Another statement published in media on 3ʳᵈ October 2003 from a spokesman of the Pakistan Peoples Party (PPP):

> "........... *welcomed the requirement of declaration of assets and liabilities by the legislators as an element of transparency, public scrutiny and good governance. The Party has accordingly directed its legislators to comply with the law and submit to the Chief Election Commissioner a statement of their assets and liabilities as on 30th June 2003.*
>
> *The Party has also noted with deep concern the media reports that at least two sitting ministers of the government namely Finance Minister Mr Shaukat Aziz (afterwards the Prime Minister of Pakistan) and Education Minister Ms Zubeda Jalal have failed to submit the required declarations by the due date.*
>
> *This is a matter of grave concern as it shows the scant respect the ministers have for the laws of the land and also that the law is intended to be another coercive instrument against opposition.*

The Party (PPP) also believes that transparency, public scrutiny as elements of good governance and accountability should not be confined to the 1170 legislators alone. For the law to have some measure of credibility and equity, it must also require the Generals and senior civil servants to make public every year their assets. If the assets of 1170 legislators can be advertised every year in the name of transparency and public scrutiny what is the justification to exempt the 400 odd generals and senior bureaucrats from the ambit of such a law?

The people of Pakistan have a right to know how many residential and commercial plots, agricultural lands, plazas and bank balance was owned by an officer upon entry into the defence service and how much was owned at the time of exit as a General and the magic of the multiplication of their wealth beyond known mathematical formulae.

The Party hopes that the Chief Election Commissioner would also make public his assets and liabilities. There may be no law requiring the CEC to make public his assets. However, the CEC's call to the legislators to declare assets will have great moral force if he were to also declare his assets and no minister of the cabinet would be able to flout the law with impunity as it seems is the case at present."

[The point to ponder remains that whether the PPP itself adhered to the above maxims of judicial advice when it assumed power in 2008 and how its members behaved during subsequent 3.5 years of rule at least.]

On 18th June 2002, Nayyer Bokhari, of the Pakistan People's Party sent a letter to the Chief Justice of Pakistan, then Sh Riaz Ahmed, on the basis of published reports in media that the Chairman of Evacuee Trust Property Board (ETPB) named Lt Gen (rtd) Javed Nasir had extended a loss of three billion rupees during his six years stay in the organization; it was not a military related assignment.

The Chief Justice of Pakistan was requested to take *suo moto* notice of the matter but the Supreme Court did not bother and no action was initiated even on PPP's written complaint to the Apex Court. The matter was also brought in the notice of NAB vide Complaint no: 9 of 2002 but no action was taken because the accused was a senior military officer.

The main allegations were that:

- Lt Gen Javed Nasir the Ex-ISI boss, following his retirement from the Army, was appointed Chairman of Evacuee Trust Property Board where the controversial 20 land deals resulting in a loss of three billion rupees was caused to the state exchequer.

- One deal involved land on main Ferozepur Road Lahore. The land was sold at Rs: 3,48,000 against the market price of Rs: 4.5 m.

- In another deal in Karachi, a plot of market value of Rs: 267m was sold at Rs: 5.6m only for no reason on record.

- In a sale to 11 persons, another estimated loss of Rs: 243 million was caused. A plot on Super Highway Karachi was disposed of at Rs: 48m against its actual price of Rs: 240m.

- A plot on main Raiwind Road Lahore, was sold at Rs: 46m against market price of about Rs: 90 million.

- Land between Lahore Airport and Defence Housing Society was sold for Rs: 8.01m against market price of Rs: 91.85m.

- Further allegations relate to the leasing out of PASSCO godown in Lahore and construction of the ETPB complex and Trust Plaza in Islamabad. It was alleged that a loss of Rs: 320m was caused in the civil works alone.

According to a leading editorial in the *Daily Times of 25th August, 2002* captioned "**Another blot on the ISI**". Gen (Retd) Javed Nasir was a born-again Muslim who converted from a playboy to a "pious" man of the reactionary variety. He nursed a flowing beard and ran the biggest *Deobandi* congregation in Pakistan, the *Tableeghi Jamaat* annual "jalsa" at Raiwind. He was placed atop the ISI on the request of another ISI officer, Imtiaz Billa, who was also later tried for build up a private empire of properties when in office. He was also the man who facilitated the aides of Osama bin Laden to build terrorist bases in Afghanistan.

After Gen Javed Nasir was removed from the ISI in 1993, it was discovered that he had pared off big sums of money by buying property for the ISI at inflated rates. It was also discovered that he had taken the entire ISI foreign exchange budget and placed it in Mehran Bank, which later collapsed. Although he was an engineer in the army, he steadily advanced in career because of his "Islamic" guise.

Another interesting scoring game played during the last week of July 2005, when one Shah Khawar Advocate on behalf of PPP had filed an application under section 5 & 18(B)(II) of the NAB Ordinance 1999, referring to a news item published in media on 14th June 2005.

It was revealed that in 1989 during the government of PPP, the ISI had given the respondent Sh Rashid Ahmed MNA of Rawalpindi, the then a Member of Opposition, hundreds of acres of prime land in the Rawalpindi areas. Totally wrong accusation it was. When the then PPP government took up this matter with the ISI, it was informed that the land was given for support to the Kashmiri groups. Later, Gen Musharraf had stopped training of Kashmiris.

The baseless question raised in the petition was that under what circumstances, huge piece of land was given to the respondent by ISI and after the change in the policy regarding Kashmiris, under which authority the respondent was retaining the said land worth billions of rupees and why the lands were not being taken back. The then ISI authorities and the respondent were termed responsible for causing financial loss to the nation but the enquiries told that the blame was unfounded.

Chairman NAB was called upon to initiate investigation in the matter but he declined; the petition brought enough shame for the originators.

A news clipping from The Dawn dated 26th May 2006, saying that despite insistence of the audit department, the Public Accounts Committee (PAC) showed reluctance to refer the *'Kamra grid station scam'*, in which an army brigadier was allegedly involved, to the NAB. The retired brigadier had allegedly paid Rs: 20.278 million extra (original contract was of Rs: 60.50 million in 1995) to a private company for the installation of grid station and in return received Rs:12 million in kickbacks.

Ruling party's MNA, Col (Rtd) Ghulam Rasool Sahi, who headed the two-member sub-committee on defence production, with PPP MNA Chaudhry Qamar uz Zaman Kaira as member, met to investigate the Aeronautical Complex Kamra Grid Station scam, did not differ with the viewpoint of the audit people but did nothing except giving sarcastic smiles; a retired army officer was in dock.

Col Sahi had also directed Maj Gen Tariq Saleem, additional secretary of the ministry of defence production to pursue Brig Shah to refund the embezzled amount as directed by the AGP and court of inquiry but who cares in Pakistan; Pak Army Zindabad.

The contractors had completed the same grid station at Heavy Mechanical Complex Taxila for just Rs: 40 million. The court of inquiry had found that two officers, Brig Zulfiqar Ali Shah and Section Officer M Younus were involved in awarding the contract to the private company, AEG International, and had received Rs: 8.950 million and Rs: 3.838 million respectively in kickbacks from the contracting company.

The inquiry also directed departmental action besides recovery of Rs: 2.53 million of tax evasion against seven other officers including one Maj Basir Ali Sadiq but the matter was kept shelved deliberately. The court of inquiry and AGP had also recommended GHQ to initiate disciplinary action against the culprits besides recovering the embezzled money but the GHQ expressed its inability stating that since the officers had been retired from the army service, it could not take any action against them; reasons unknown whatsoever.

Nayyar Bokhari once concluded his letter to the CJP with the words:

'Dear Chief Justice, I hope you will look into the matter with a view to provide relief to the Pakistani people from injustice, corruption and abuse of office by those who claim to be defenders of the law and the state; the superior courts remained mum.'

Eight years after, when PPP came in government, the situation was seen in a different way. He remained silent when on 16th September 2010, President Zardari issued a secret NAB Ordinance and placed before both the houses of parliament in a sudden gesture, forcing an opposition walkout from the Senate and splitting the PPP, with Senator Raza Rabbani joining the opposition walkout. Nayyar Bokhari was the leader of the House in Senate then. The ordinance was kept hidden for two weeks and was suddenly placed before the Parliament on the last day of that session; a very calculated move it was.

Enraged members of both the houses blamed the government for playing tricks with parliament and PM Gilani was *'caught unaware'* though was sent to the president for promulgation under his own signatures two weeks' back. He was confused and rattled by the unexpected manipulation by his Law Ministry and promised to rectify any wrong done. PM's Advisor Senator Mian Raza Rabbani had joined the opposition benches and walked out without uttering a word on the secret NAB law amendment to take away the powers of the NAB chairman.

PM Gilani had rightly mentioned then that under the law, the president had to consult leaders of the House and the opposition for appointment of chairman NAB and he had proposed two names of Mukhtar Junejo and Syed Deedar Ali Shah for this post to the opposition leader, who did not agree on any of them. However, Minister for Law, Justice and Parliamentary Affairs Babar Awan said neither the powers of the NAB chairman were being curtailed nor the Law Ministry would get the powers to shift cases to any accountability court.

Mr Babar Awan further told that:

> 'We are not bringing a NAB chairman like Saifur Rehman to target a particular party like the PPP and create a jail for Asif Zardari and other leaders at the Attock Fort.'

Without naming the Sharif brothers, he said the National Accountability (Amendment) Ordinance was not a document like the one which facilitated leadership of a political party to leave the country along with seven boxes. He admitted that some amendments had been made in the National Accountability Ordinance 2010, which would allow transfer of cases to new accountability courts and protection to the prosecutors and judges of the Accountability courts.

On 14th February 2011, the Lahore High Court (LHC) was moved to take notice of closure of 60 corruption cases against various politicians by the Chairman NAB. The writ petition was filed by Advocate Rana Ilamudin Ghazi who contended that the NAB Chairman had no power to close a reference on his own.

It was alleged that many references involving serious allegations were filed against different political figures and other bigwigs but the bureau's chairman ordered closure of 60 cases without any lawful authority. The petitioner had pleaded that only the Accountability Courts had the power to close such references.

In our country all *Ehtesabs*, accountabilities, sanctions and law enforcements are for the poor people and middle order civil servants who do not belong to an in-government political stalwart like PM Gilani or Ch Shuja'at or a Marshall raced army General or a senior bureaucrat like Afzal Kahut.

Scenario 27

MILITARY COUP AGAIN UPHELD 2000:

On 25th January 2000 Gen Musharraf, in the capacity of Army Chief and the Chief Executive of Pakistan, issued the Oath of Office (Judges) Order 2000. The main features of the text were:

- In pursuance of the Proclamation of Emergency of 14th October 1999 declared by Gen Musharraf, the Constitution of Pakistan was declared as 'held in abeyance'.

- Pakistan would be governed 'as nearly as may be in accordance with the Constitution' and the Chief Executive 'shall be deemed always to have the power to amend it'.

- All courts in existence were allowed to continue to function and to exercise their respective powers and jurisdiction, (but) subject to the Provisional Constitution Order (PCO) No.1 of 1999 as amended and the Chief Justices and judges of Superior Courts, would be able to discharge their functions only after taking fresh oath of their office.

- For the said oath, the Judges were asked to administer it within certain time schedule determined by the Chief Executive.

Reproduction of the relevant provisions of this order would make it clearer how a policy to weed out undesirable judges was set in place by the military government in vogue:

3. Oath of Judges — (1) A person holding office immediately before the commencement of this Order as a Judge of the superior Court shall not continue to hold that office if he is not given, or does not make, oath in the form set out in the Schedule, before the expiration of such time from such commencement as the Chief Executive may determine or within such further time as may be allowed by the Chief Executive [Gen Musharraf].

(2) A Judge of the Superior Court appointed after the commencement of the order shall, before entering upon office, make oath in the form set out in the Schedule.

(3) A person referred to in clause (1) and (2) who has made oath as required by these clauses shall be bound by the provision of this Order,

the Proclamation of Emergency of the fourteenth day of October, 1999 and the Provisional Constitution Order No. 1 of 1999 as amended and, notwithstanding any judgement of any Court, shall not call in question or permit to be called in question the validity of any of the provisions thereof.

The new official form set out for the oath of office was of course framed for obedience and allegiance to the instruments referred to in clause 3 above. Many members of the judiciary naturally became apprehensive about the designs of the new rulers. The result was a sudden revolt and mass departure of judges, especially from the Supreme Court. Six of its judges, including the Chief Justice, refused to take the oath. Some of the Judges of the high courts also did not make the oath, notably those of the LHC, Sindh HC and Peshawar HC.

The outgoing CJP Saeeduzzaman Siddiqui told that when, during a meeting on 25th January 2000, Gen Musharraf told him that they are feeling difficulties in running the state business so they had decided to go for a new oath. Justice Siddiqui told the General that on 12th October 1999's meeting we had worked out a mutual understanding with each other that judiciary would continue working as such.

Gen Musharraf told about some of his apprehensions which were not based on facts. When he insisted on the new oath and fresh PCO then Justice Siddiqui flatly declined to take fresh oath. Justice Siddiqui told:

'Three serving Generals came to my residence at 9PM, continued with their arguments and requests for my oath till 1.30 that night but I did not agree'. [Rumour was that he was not called for]

The advice of fresh PCO was probably given by Sharifuddin Pirzada because hearing of the petitions against coup was coming up.

Later the uneasiness of military government surfaced that perhaps the SC was going to give verdict against the coup. There were also rumours that PML had again sent 'briefcases' for some of the judges like in 1997 but Justice Siddiqui had expelled the fears saying that up till that moment there was no such development nor had he personally thought over that possibility because the proceedings had not yet started for the petitions.

Justice Malik Qayyum, in an interview published in daily *'Jang' dated 5th February 2006*, opined that:

'I had taken oath under the said PCO after considering that one could fight with opposing winds in a better way while remaining in the system. There are judgments available from the superior courts that 'an oath under PCO does not detract you from your original commitments under your oath taken under the constitutional provisions.' [But who honoured his original commitment]

The tragedy of 2000's Pakistan was that the nicest lot of judiciary then available went home while declining to take oath under the PCO. CJP Saeeduzzaman Siddiqui should have taken oath under the PCO but then opted the way what he liked in the best interests of justice. Had the judges like him and Justice Wajeehuddin Ahmed been there in judiciary, the judgment regarding Gen Musharraf's take over would have been entirely different.'

In a way Justice Malik Qayyum was right to opine so. If the subsequent decision of Gen Musharraf's take over had to be there in place, the order could be conveyed to hold elections within 90 days. Giving three years to a military ruler was neither asked for in the petition nor was it mandated through any provision of the constitution. This time there was not any Martial Law in vogue then why the then sitting judiciary was feeling pressure in giving such decision.

The matter itself came before the Supreme Court in Zafar Ali Shah's Case, by which time the judges in question had left from office. The apex court had refused to consider the specific cases, declaring the matter closed, and stated that:

'Clearly, the Judges of the Superior Judiciary enjoy constitutional guarantee against arbitrary removal. They can be removed only by following the procedure laid down in Article 209 of the Pakistan's Constitution by filing an appropriate reference before the Supreme Judicial Council and not otherwise [save military ruler's PCOs].

The validity of the action of the Chief Executive was open to question on the touchstone of Article 209 of the Constitution. But none of the Judges took any remedial steps and accepted pension as also the right to practice law and thereby acquiesced in action.

Furthermore, the appropriate course of action for Supreme Court in these proceedings would be to declare the law to avoid the recurrence in future, but not to upset earlier actions or decisions taken in this behalf by the Chief Executive, these being past and closed transactions.'

Unquestionably, the superior judiciary of the country was in this instance intimidated and ridiculed by the military. Those who refused to succumb to the pressure from the military regime acted courageously and bravely.

At least 13 judges of the superior judiciary either refused to take a fresh oath under the PCO or they were not called up to take oath. Justice Peter Cory of the Supreme Court of Canada explains 'Oath' in one of his judgments given in 1997:

> *"Often the most significant occasion in the career of a judge is the swearing of the oath of office. It is a moment of pride and joy coupled with a realization of the onerous responsibility that goes with the office. The taking of the oath is solemn and a defining moment etched forever in the memory of the judge.*
>
> *The oath requires a judge to render justice impartially. To take that oath is the fulfilment of a life's dreams. It is never taken lightly. Throughout their careers, the Canadian judges strive to overcome the personal biases that are common to all humanity in order to provide and clearly appear to provide a fair trial for all who come before them. Their rate of success in this difficult venture is high and always goes appreciable [in most situations]."*

However, Pakistan's superior courts have been reluctant to challenge the executive to enforce fundamental rights, and have not invalidated any major legislation on account of inconformity with these rights provisions. Rather, some of the foundational principles of the 1973 Constitution, including federalism and judicial independence, have been compromised by the weakness of the judiciary, the primacy of federal law over provincial legislation, the dominance of rural and urban elites in political parties, and the subservience of political parties to their leading figures like chairmen and the presidents etc.

After a decision by the Supreme Court challenging the jurisdiction of military courts, Gen Ziaul Haq also sought to undermine the independence of the judiciary by requiring judges to take a fresh oath under the PCO on 24th March 1981. In practice, these dynamics have led to numerous amendments to the 1973 Constitution and the oscillation between parliamentary and presidential models of government.

At this moment, one should not forget the judicial heroes of Pakistan like Justice Dorab Patel, who had refused to take a fresh oath under the

Provisional Constitutional Order (PCO) promulgated by Gen Ziaul Haq. As a signatory to the judgment against the army General and following the voice of his strict conscience, no body could expect such a derogatory oath from a high esteemed judge like Dorab Patel.

> 'A lesser man might have succumbed. The temptation certainly would have been great; for due to seniority, he was set to become the chief justice of Pakistan as soon as the incumbent retired the following year and would have headed the apex court for seven years.'

Justice Dorab Patel did not think twice about rejecting [maliciously sincere] offer of Gen Ziaul Haq.

As was the custom, the then chief justice had asked the question first to the most junior judge, which at that time was Justice Ebrahim.

'Not without apprehension, he said, 'Sir, I am going home.'

The same question was put to other colleagues in the reverse order of seniority, and most of them were willing to take the oath.

"I walked up to Dorab Patel, who was seated close to me, and asked him in Gujrati, *'What is your decision?' Promptly and without the least hesitation, he said, 'How can I take such an oath!'* the then Chief Justice Anwarul Haq told with pride.

The CJP Anwarul Haq then went to the next seniors. J Shafiur Rehman and J Molvi Mushtaq both said they would take oath. When the CJP was moving to the next J Dr Javed Iqbal, he received a phone call on hot line. The CJP attended the call; straightaway came to J Molvi Mushtaq and told him with sorrow that he had been dropped from the list.

Of course, J Molvi Mushtaq had felt embarrassed before the whole team of 14 judges. In the President House next day, J Molvi Mushtaq's chair was removed at the last moment because it was unexpected news for the Presidency staff even.

Just to pay a tribute to those Honourable Judges like Ebrahim and Dorab Patel, their characters can be assessed in a significant case to quote. It was that of *Yusuf Ali Khan* in which Justice Patel liberalized the law of Contempt of Court and departed from several precedents, including judgments of the House of Lords, to hold that:

'An allegation of bias against a judge, if expressed in temperate language and without attempting to scandalize him or alleging ulterior motives, does not constitute contempt.'

Justice Dorab Patel was a judge, the nation wait for generations to rise up. He was one of the three Supreme Court judges, out of seven, who had not agreed with that controversial decision of LHC, written by Justice Molvi Mushtaq Hussain, to hang Bhutto in 1979. He did not become a party to that 'judicial murder'.

The taking over of Nawaz Sharif's government by Gen Musharraf on 12th October 1999, Proclamation of Emergency of the 14th October and Provisional Constitution Order No. 1 of 1999 as amended, were challenged before the Supreme Court under Article 184 (3) of the Constitution through several petitions, which were disposed of by means of a Short Order in the case reported as: *Zafar Ali Shah vs Gen Musharraf* **(PLD 2000 SC 869).**

After that fourth military coup, the intelligentsia of Pakistan again started looking towards the Supreme Court of Pakistan for remedy. In the first week of March 2000, the then CJP, Justice Irshad Hassan Khan asked the then Attorney General, Aziz A Munshi, to provide a list of those suspended parliamentarians against whom corruption cases were initiated by the National Accountability Bureau (NAB).

The CJP had also asked him to place the report of the State Bank on the court's record. He had observed that when the politicians are in power, they try to become dictators but when they are out of power, they become champions of the rule of law.

The Chief Justice Irshad Hasan Khan issued these orders when the advocate Zafar Ali Shah and Chaudhry Farooq claimed that there was no charge against their client. It was prayed before the apex court that:

- Send the military back to the barracks as the concept of military government was alien to the civilized world.

- The army should not be allowed to take over power after every 10 years and start blaming the politicians for all crimes (quoting that the military takeover could be compared to the situation when a hired bodyguard would enter the house of his employer, occupy it and justify his entry on the grounds that he was not treating his family well).

- The Prime Minister should not be held for removing the Army Chief as he was empowered by the Constitution to do so.

It is said that the former CAOS Gen Jehangir Karamat was rightly shown the outer door (claiming that he did not know why it was done by his client Nawaz Sharif), but the Prime Minister was justified in doing so.

12th May 2000: Presiding over a 12-member bench seized of the seven petitions challenging the military takeover, the chief justice of Pakistan directed the Attorney General to provide details of the expenditure on holding elections, including the expenses made by the candidates on their election campaigns. The Court announced to decide the issue of maintainability and merits of the case simultaneously and finally, on 12th May 2000, validated the military take over by Gen Musharraf while again putting their guns on the shoulders of 'doctrine of necessity', like his first champion Justice M Munir of 1955-58.

[The honourable bench, which had given approval of military action consisted of 12 judges; the Chief Justice Irshad Hasan Khan, Justice Mohammad Bashir Jehangiri, Justice Sheikh Ijaz Nisar, Justice Abdur Rehman Khan, Justice Sheikh Riaz Ahmad, Justice Chaudhry Mohammad Arif, Justice Munir A. Sheikh, Justice Rashid Aziz Khan, Justice Nazim Hussain Siddiqui, Justice Iftikhar Mohammad Chaudhry, Justice Qazi Mohammad Farooq and Justice Rana Bhagwandas; hats off to all of them.]

It was held by the Supreme Court that on 12th October 1999 a situation arose for which the Constitution provided no solution and intervention by the Armed Forces through an extra-Constitutional measure became inevitable and the said act was validated on the basis of the doctrine of state necessity and the principle *salus populi suprema lex* as embodied in <u>*Begum Nusrat Bhutto's case*</u> *(PLD 1977 SC 657)*.

It was further held that the 1973 Constitution would remain supreme law of the land subject to the condition that certain parts thereof would be held in abeyance on account of state necessity. The operative part of the Short Order given in *PLD 2000 SC 869* was:

'We accordingly hold as under:-

"6. (i) That Gen Musharraf, Chairman, Joint Chiefs of Staff Committee and Chief of Army Staff through Proclamation of Emergency dated the 14th October, 1999, followed by PCO 1 of

289

1999, whereby he has been described as Chief Executive, having validly assumed power by means of an extra-Constitutional step, in the interest of the State and for the welfare of the people, is entitled to perform all such acts and promulgate all legislative measures as enumerated hereinafter, namely:

All acts or legislative measures which are in accordance with, or could have been made under the 1973 Constitution, including the power to amend it;

All acts which tend to advance or promote the good of the people;

All acts required to be done for the ordinary orderly running of the State;

And all such measures as would establish or lead to the establishment of the declared objectives of the Chief Executive of Pakistan.

(ii)That constitutional amendments by the Chief Executive can be resorted to only if the Constitution fails to provide a solution for attainment of his declared objectives and further that the power to amend the Constitution by virtue of clause 6 sub-clause (i) (a) ibid is controlled by sub-clauses (b)(c) and (d) in the same clause.

(iii)   That no amendment shall be made in the salient features of the Constitution i.e. independence of Judiciary, federalism, parliamentary form of government blended with Islamic provisions.

iv)   That Fundamental Rights provided in Part II, Chapter I of the Constitution shall continue to hold the field but the State will be authorized to make any law or take any executive action in deviation of Articles 15, 16, 17, 18, 19 and 24 as contemplated by Article 233 (1) of the Constitution, keeping in view the language of Articles 10, 23 and 25 thereof.

(v)   That these acts, or any of them, may be performed or carried out by means of orders issued by the Chief Executive or through Ordinances on his advice;

(vi)   That the Superior Courts continue to have the power of judicial review to judge the validity of any act or action of the Armed Forces, if challenged, in the light of the principles underlying the law of State necessity as stated above. Their powers under Article 199 of the Constitution thus remain available to their full extent, and may be

exercised as heretofore, notwithstanding anything to the contrary contained in any legislative instrument enacted by the Chief Executive and/or any order issued by the Chief Executive or by any person or authority acting on his behalf.

(vii) That the courts are not merely to determine whether there exists any nexus between the orders made, proceedings taken and acts done by the Chief Executive or by any authority or person acting on his behalf, and his declared objectives as spelt out from his speeches dated 13th and 17th October 1999, on the touchstone of State necessity but such orders made, proceedings taken and acts done including the legislative measures, shall also be subject to judicial review by the superior courts [of Pakistan]."

The Court went on to describe the military take over as an extra-constitutional step taken by the Armed Forces for a transitional period to prevent any further destabilisation, to create a corruption-free atmosphere at the national level through transparent accountability and to revive the economy before the restoration of democratic institutions under the Constitutional provisions.

Upholding the Military Government's legitimization arguments, the Supreme Court added that as the Constitution did not offer any solution for the political crisis under the previous regime, the military intervention was quite inevitable.

Further, the apex Court ignored the Oath of Office Judges' Order 2000 and the March 2000 ban on public rallies in concluding that there was "an implied consent of the governed". Thus, the people of Pakistan in general, including politicians and parliamentarians, were deemed to have consented to the coup, as no protests had been launched against the army take-over.

In addition to endorsing the coup, *the Supreme Court granted extensive powers to the new Government, empowering it to unilaterally amend the 1973 Constitution and enact new laws without the approval of Parliament. Gen Musharraf was also allowed to hold his chair for three years and this was a gift of the Superior Judiciary for the military dictator because this facility was never prayed* by the government representatives during the whole hearing.

In nut shell, the CJ Irshad Hassan Khan in his judgment of 12th May 2000 had declared Gen Musharraf's dismissal as void and of no legal effect but gave him three more years to rule Pakistan. Besides, the court also announced for the military ruler that he would have powers to amend the constitution of Pakistan. It was amazing on two counts:

- Firstly, the judgment was being given on the constitutional petitions emanated from Nawaz Sharif's party against reaction of 12th Oct 1999's episode in which it was prayed to declare the military coup void. The judgment was required only to set aside and reject the said petitions and nothing more activism was required.

  Giving Gen Musharraf three more years to rule and powers to amend the constitution were extra facilities the bench announced. These facilities were not demanded by the respondent party nor were the subject of discussion which reflected utter cowardice of the bench and speaking for their corrupt minds.

- Secondly, while doing so the judges sitting in the bench had purposefully ignored the fact that they were giving such powers to amend the Constitution to a single handed military ruler which mandate even the the superior courts do not possess to exercise.

But it has been happening in Pakistan since its early age.

Justice Cornelius had once said that:

> 'The justice should be done at all costs and upheld even if heavens fall, let them fall [showing utter respect for justice].'

With the passage of time the values changed. In May 1993, while writing judgment in Nawaz Sharif's case, the Chief Justice Nasim Hasan Shah held that:

> 'Justice should be done in a manner that heavens should not be allowed to fall [showing a compromising attitude in justice].'

Feel the difference. True that when the judiciary would resort to deliver justice in an arena of political compromises or general public's will, the decline occurs and the history starts going distorted.

Coming back; when the Supreme Court again resorted to this *Doctrine*, contrary to the last ruling (of 1972) of Chief Justice Yaqoob Ali Khan on the subject and legitimized the illegal takeover, it became a partner of the military regime enjoying a *quid pro quo*, including the controversial three years' extension in the judges' retirement age.

In this litmus test when the military takeover by Gen Musharraf was challenged, the Supreme Court not only justified it but also granted three years to the military regime to implement its program, in addition to granting the right to make amendments to the Constitution, a right the Court did not possess itself.

It is noteworthy that though the Court did not stipulate the removal of the then President Rafiq Tarrar in its judgment, but the latter was removed and Gen Musharraf was administered oath as President by the CJP. The act was considered by many jurists as patently unconstitutional.

Most observers noticed that the then Chief Justice Irshad Hasan Khan was rewarded for this big-heartedness and generosity by Gen Musharraf when he made him Chief Election Commissioner after his retirement. Since this came up partially through concerted efforts of the then Federal Law Secretary Mr Khokhar, who was also given an out-of-turn appointment as a Supreme Court judge, even though he was a junior judge of the Lahore High Court.

This was in clear violation of the principle laid down in the 1996 Judges' Case which stipulated the seniority rule in the matter of appointment of judges. This and other appointments of junior judges were challenged but were turned down by a special bench presided over by Chief Justice Sh Riaz Ahmed.

By granting extension, Gen Musharraf violated his commitment to the nation that no amendment in the Constitution would be introduced unless it was circulated in advance for soliciting public comments. Interestingly, the extension period corresponds with the period granted by the judges to Gen Musharraf as the Chief Executive. It was not the extension granted by the military but the manner and method in which it was granted.

This was so because it clearly smacked of a bribe for 'services' rendered by judges. If this was not the case why was the extension granted in such a hushed manner in the stealth of a night as if it was a commando action? Similarly, why was the bar and parliament not involved in the process.

Other important events of that year can be summarized that on **13th February 2000:** National Accountability Bureau (NAB) filed reference No. 7/2000 against Faisal Saleh Hayat a PPP politician from Jhang and on **6th April 2000,** former Prime Minister Nawaz Sharif was sentenced to two life terms, 25 years imprisonment each.

On 20th September 2000 Aftab Ahmad Sherpao, a politician of NWFP was convicted by Accountability Court No.3. On 18th November 2000 Nusrat Bhutto was convicted in absentia. On 30th November 2000: Anwar Saifullah, a politician of NWFP was convicted in an Accountability (Ehtesab) reference. On 10th December 2000: Nawaz Sharif left Pakistan under a clandestine deal with Gen Musharraf and no court was seriously agitated over the scamp negotiations.

Afterwards, the 17th Constitutional Amendment, which later conferred absolute power in Gen Musharraf, was opposed to the spirit of parliamentary governance enshrined in the constitution. Gen Musharraf vigorously presented his case inside and outside Pakistan, asserting that he was indispensable for the state and the people on the premises of security and for the reforms he had brought about for the good of the country; but he was not believed by anyone.

The irony of fate was that when Gen Musharraf was dethroned and pushed out from Pakistan, he started canvassing his 'would be' political party in Pakistan, moved some of his old political buddies to prepare ground for his landing. But alas! He could not move forward because the PML(N) and one sizable faction of PPP cogently surfaced up with charges of murders of Nawab Bughti and then of Benazir Bhutto. More issues like Lal Mosques are still haunting him and would continue to make him restless.

Scenario 28

MILITARY GIMMICKS IN 2000:

Nawaz Sharif Convicted:

On **6th April 2000,** Pakistan's deposed Prime Minister Nawaz Sharif was awarded two sentences of life imprisonment, 25 years each starting concurrently, by an Anti Terrorist Court at Karachi for 'plotting with criminal intent' against Gen Musharraf. Nawaz Sharif was found guilty of hijacking and terrorism, but cleared of attempted murder and kidnapping. He was spared the death penalty. His brother Shahbaz and five former senior government officials were acquitted. The defendants had denied all charges levelled upon them by the military regime..

Sharif's lawyers immediately announced that they would appeal against the verdict; they ought to do so to save political career of a man twice elected as Prime Minister. But on the government side, the prosecution had also announced they would appeal against Sharif's sentence and demand the death penalty. In 1979, Zulfikar Ali Bhutto, Pakistan's first elected prime minister, was also executed by the military after a coup. Speaking outside court, Javed Jabbar, Gen Musharraf's national adviser on media and publicity, had said that:

> 'We want Nawaz Sharif to be subject to the same law he formulated and promulgated for others; his political opponents'.

The above phrase was referred to the draconian anti-terrorism laws Nawaz Sharif as Prime Minister introduced after assuming power in February 1997 keeping aside all cannons of justice.

His wife, Kulsoom Sharif had said he was the victim of a 'personal vendetta' by Gen Musharraf and accused the judge of delivering a verdict written by someone else. History is cruel to remember all the odds though the leaders are not able to see beyond the wall. Just two years back, Sharif's slave judge Malik Qayyum used to read the judgments in Lahore High Court which were sent to him by Ehtesab Chief Saif ur Rehman. One such judgment against Ms Bhutto was read over to media on 14th of a month by the then Law Minister Khalid Anwar, whereas the decision was actually signed by Justice Malik Qayyum on 15th.

Coming back; Kulsoom Sharif continued to say that:

'My husband is innocent. He has done nothing wrong. This is a politically motivated judgment under pressure. Only my husband was targeted. That is what they wanted. Such a judgment will make the nation hang its head in shame.'

During the two-month trial, the prosecutors had claimed Nawaz Sharif tried to stop a commercial aircraft with Gen Musharraf on board from landing in Pakistan, risking the lives of 197 other passengers too. Gen Musharraf's plane could land only after the army took control of Karachi airport, staging a coup hours later on 12th October 1999.

During hearing a defence lawyer, Iqbal Raad, was shot dead on 10th March in his Karachi office. Pakistan's judges were also called to swear an oath of allegiance to Gen Musharraf under a PCO arrangement. Those who refused, including the chief justice, were sent home. Giving judgment in a courtroom at Karachi, the presiding Judge Rehmat Hussain Jafri had categorically explained that:

'Nawaz Sharif had ordered three fire engines to block the runway [on 12th October 1999 at Karachi Airport] and had the landing lights switched off. If the plane had landed in presence of these things it would have crashed. The effect of the hijack was to create terror and insecurity in people and the passengers on board.'

Maryam Nawaz, daughter of the convicted PM was upset but maintained that *'we were born in Pakistan and we will die in Pakistan'*. Nawaz Sharif was facing two outstanding corruption charges and investigators were collecting documents for sixteen (16) other cases against him but he ran away to Saudia.

In nut shell, it was the end of that story which had started on **8th October 1999,** when relations had gone worsened between PM Nawaz Sharif and his army Generals. Three had resigned, criticising the government for the economic crisis and religious killings. On **12th October 1999** Nawaz Sharif sacked his Army Chief Gen Musharraf, and prevented the plane carrying the General back from Sri Lanka from landing in Pakistan.

Gen Musharraf's colleague Generals staged military coup, facilitated the PIA flight to land at Karachi and arrested Nawaz Sharif from the PM House in Islamabad. On **20th January 2000** Nawaz Sharif formally charged with terrorism, hijacking and conspiracy to murder, offences which carry the death penalty and a week after the trial opened which ended on **6th April 2000** when Nawaz Sharif was sentenced to life imprisonment twice after being found guilty of terrorism and hijacking.

In October 2000, another odd situation developed for Gen Musharraf. All the harassed and struggling politicians from all parties joined together to form a grand alliance against the military government. Gen Musharraf's opponents like Benazir Bhutto of PPP and Kulsoom Nawaz of the PML had agreed to forget past differences, including trying to avail court verdicts against each other.

The only one point agenda of the 17-party coalition was to show an exit to Gen Musharraf. Late Nawabzada Nasrullah, known in history as *Baba e Jamhooriat,* was made convener of the Grand Democratic Alliance (GDA) who was a known alliance maker. He was instrumental in forming earlier alliances such as one which led to the dismissal of Prime Minister Zulfikar Ali Bhutto in 1977 and another which had challenged the dictatorship of Gen Ziaul Haq in the 1980s to bring democracy back [*but alas! Nawabzada died earlier*].

Divisions within the alliance had already caused the going away of one Imran Khan's Justice Party when other members refused to agree to a commitment that politicians accused of corruption should be held accountable for their actions before being allowed to participate in any future elections; many alliance members dissented.

Half heartedly, the GDA had agreed to start with mobilisation of public opinion against the military regime before going for street protests. Not all Pakistanis had welcomed the GDA so Gen Musharraf was not taking them seriously because they had lost their credibility in the near past. The General kept the PPP and PML alive with their corrupt leaders declaring that: *'the voters are OK but their heads are rotten'.*

The daily *'Telegraph' dated 13th October 2000* had told that Human Rights Watch, based in New York, condemned Pakistan's military leadership for attacking civil liberties and not moving for democratic elections. Gen Musharraf was accused of committing widespread abuses in the name of political reform. In their opinion:

> *'Gen Musharraf follows a long line of generals in Pakistan who have claimed that a period of military rule is the path to true democracy. In fact, he is systematically destroying civil liberties.'*

Javed Jabbar, the Information Minister, had denied accusations saying:

> 'The report was an imbalanced, one-sided and imperfect evaluation.
> Ours is an independent, self-respecting and sovereign state. We do not
> need any sort of lecturing.'

However, general public mood was showing a vigorous change because there was seen an enormous outflow of capital and professional people from Pakistan. Benazir Bhutto, then in exile in Britain, had said that:

> 'She believed that up to £2.8 billion had been taken out of the country
> since the coup.'

Whereas Gen Musharraf had vowed that:

> 'Pakistan's survival lies in revival of the economy and good governance;
> nothing else matters as much. We have stopped the downslide; certainly
> we have turned the economic tide towards improvements.'

Despite all, throughout the year 2000, the army government had bravely faced the foreign pressure by refusing to sign the Comprehensive Test Ban Treaty and had allegedly stepped up military support to the Taliban regime in Afghanistan. Gen Musharraf was always found ready to talk to India over Kashmir, anywhere and anytime, but New Delhi kept on refusing to talk to a military regime. The army, however, failed to prevent bomb blasts and suicidal attacks which continued to shake the major cities & towns throughout the country.

As **Christina Lamb** had noted in a British newspaper **'Telegraph' dated 29th October 2000,** Gen Musharraf was determined to keep all corrupt politicians away from power. Gen Musharraf had succeeded in getting an announcement from NAB that Benazir Bhutto had misused her position as Prime Minister to accumulate £1 billion in assets including a country estate in Surrey (known as Surrey Palace), a stud farm in Texas, six homes in Florida, and two homes in France.

It had also documented at least 26 separate foreign bank accounts held by her in Switzerland, France, Britain, the United States and the United Arab Emirates. Nawaz Sharif, sentenced to life imprisonment, was also facing numerous charges of corruption and the state was moving the appellant court to convert his sentence to the death penalty.

A Prime Minister Fleds away to Saudia:

On **10th December 2000**, the former Prime Minister Nawaz Sharif opted to go in exile in Saudi Arabia after being released from Attock Fort Prison by Gen Musharraf's military regime. He left Pakistan after Gen Musharraf's government unexpectedly announced that his life sentence had been commuted but without divulging the basis for that release.

Nawaz Sharif was in military custody since the coup of 12th October 1999; subsequently convicted of kidnapping, hijacking and corruption by the same special courts which he had constituted defying the then prevailing rules, without consent of the superior judiciary and empowering them to punish his political rivals. He landed in Jeddah in a private jet belonging to the Saudi royal family. He was accompanied by 18 members of his family, including his wife Kulsoom, his three children and his elderly parents.

An official press note from the Pakistan government was:

> 'Nawaz Sharif and his family have been exiled to Saudi Arabia. The decision has been taken in the best interest of the country and the people of Pakistan,'

Later it surfaced that Nawaz Sharif and his family had appealed for clemency from Gen Musharraf several times over the past few months. They said he was suffering from high blood pressure and heart problems, therefore, be allowed to travel abroad for medical treatment. The army said it had pardoned Ex PM Nawaz Sharif, who had been given a double life sentence. They all were granted Saudi visas as a special case causing rumours that Sharif brothers were to be released on immediate basis as per Saudi ruler's wish.

The *Guardian of 11th December 2000* had categorically stated that:

> 'As a condition of his exile, Mr Sharif has agreed not to take part in politics in Pakistan for 21 years [subsequently authenticated as 10 years]. He has also forfeited property worth $8.3m (£5.7m) and agreed to pay a fine of $500,000. His brothers Abbas and Shahbaz, who were [also] serving jail sentences for corruption, were also freed and allowed to leavewith their families.'

Pakistani intelligence sources had told that Nawaz Sharif, whose two terms in office were marked by acute corruption while his family assets were estimated to be worth several hundred million dollars.

The PML had revealed then that an unnamed member of the Saudi royal family had negotiated his release. A Saudi official had confirmed it and told the media that:

'This is purely a humanitarian gesture by the kingdom and has nothing to do with politics. Mr Sharif has pledged not to undertake any political activity while in Saudi Arabia.'

The deal was an embarrassing, humiliating and shameful end to Mr Sharif's political career: he was the first Prime Minister of Pakistan to be exiled while his predecessor Benazir Bhutto was living in self-imposed exile in London. Astonishingly, when the Sharifs family left Islamabad, his wife Kulsoom Nawaz had said that:

'We are not running away in the darkness of night. We are being expelled from this country. My husband is suffering from a heart condition and high blood pressure. Pakistan will never be far from our hearts. We pray that our countrymen will be prosperous and whenever Nawaz Sharif's health is better, we will come back.'

Mr Sharif was taken to the airport from the Attock Fort where he was serving his sentence. His deal with the government had dismayed many of his political allies, who only a week ago joined other parties in an alliance with the sole goal of ending military rule in Pakistan and restoring democracy. Gen Musharraf had launched a high-profile drive to punish those guilty of corruption but his subsequent steps proved that it was a selective move aimed at those politicians who were not inclined to join his militarized way of governance.

There was intense media speculation that Sharifs would also return to the government several hundred million pounds which he had allegedly acquired through corruption while he was prime minister from February 1997 to October 1999. The Saudi royal family, which brokered the deal, had guaranteed that Sharifs would make no political statements against the military regime.

In Pakistan, there was widespread public criticism of the deal, as the army had always insisted that it would punish all corrupt politicians. Most of the people held that:

'The army has lost all its credibility by acting in such an underhand way.'

At that particular moment, three of Pakistan's leading politicians were then in exile: Nawaz Sharif of PML, Benazir Bhutto of PPP and Altaf

Hussain of MQM. Ms Bhutto's husband, Asif Ali Zardari, had been in jail on corruption charges since 1996 but neither the Saudis nor the army were interested in his release. The PPP's cry was justified when Mr Farhatullah Babar of the PPP said:

> 'We are really shocked to know that. We were not informed or taken into confidence. What does this say about the regime and our judicial system that Nawaz Sharif, who was sentenced, can be allowed to leave the country through a clandestine deal?'

Mr Babar said that Benazir Bhutto never opted to negotiate with the military regime for her husband's release.

Nawaz Sharif Deported Again (2007):

Once on 10th September 2007, Nawaz Sharif caught a sudden flight from London and travelled back to Pakistan without informing his Saudi guarantors. Probably he had made that 'come back plan' after having discussions with late Benazir Bhutto.

> [In a meeting of 27th July 2007 at Dubai, Gen Musharraf and Ms Bhutto had chalked out a program to bring back democracy in Pakistan and the latter had announced her arrival in Karachi on 18th October 2007. She had demanded Gen Musharraf would quit as Army Chief before the presidential election and give up his powers of Article 58(2)(b) to sack the government.]

Nawaz Sharif landed at Islamabad/Rawalpindi Airport but was not allowed to move away from the passenger's lounge. He had actually tried to end his exile to lead a campaign against Gen Musharraf, but was taken into custody on the basis of old corruption charges after his landing and deported back to Saudi Arabia by a special plane after three hours stay amidst clashes between PML(N) supporters and the security police on duty.

The deportation of Nawaz Sharif was challenged in the Supreme Court. Under an agreement in 2000 between Sharifs and Gen Musharraf, the exiled politicians were banned from returning for 10 years. The apex court had earlier ordered that the former PM and his brother Shahbaz Sharif, must not be stopped from returning from exile. However, as Nawaz Sharif was detained on the basis of three corruption cases pending against him in courts, he was given the option of going into exile; to Saudi Arabia again or being formally arrested and face normal trials in the Accountability courts.

301

Gen Musharraf's government had maintained that Nawaz Sharif was not 'deported back' and the media should not use this term for his going back. He had to leave the country under his agreement of 2000 and was allowed to go to Saudi Arabia as part of a moral obligation.

As narrated above in detail, Gen Musharraf had pardoned him in December 2000 under an exile agreement in which Sharifs had gone to Saudi Arabia; however, Nawaz Sharif said that:

He had agreed to live in exile for five years.'

Prince Muqrin bin Abdul Aziz, the Chief of Saudi Arabia's intelligence service, and Sa'ad Hariri, son of former Lebanese Prime Minister Rafiq Hariri, told a news conference in Rawalpindi on 8th September 2007 that:

'Nawaz Sharif should abide by the 10-year agreement'.

Worth noting that Rafiq Hariri, who was killed in a bomb blast in 2005, had mediated between Gen Musharraf and Nawaz Sharif on behalf of the Saudi government. The Saudi prince had agreed to receive Nawaz Sharif on behalf of his government if he was deported back by Gen Musharraf's military government.

'The custodian of Harmain Sharif had helped the Sharif family to get out of imprisonment under an agreement,' Hariri said, referring to Saudi Arabia's King Abdullah. The Saudi king *'hopes for the sake of the national interest of Pakistan that all parties concerned with the agreement will honour and adhere to the terms of the agreement.'* Nawaz Sharif and his younger brother Shahbaz Sharif had left Saudi Arabia for London in year 2006, of course, with Saudi Royal family's consent.

Why to London, they had never been there before; but one can see that in those days Nawaz Sharif's estate in London, as reflected in the **Daily Times dated 24th December 2009**, was as under:

[The Sharifs own property worth more than 20 million pounds (Rs 2.7 billion) in and around Central London. Of these, the Sharif family residence, three flats at 17 Avenfield House, 118 Park Lane alone are worth around 12 million pounds (Rs 1.6 billion). Flagship Investments Limited, one of the companies run by the Sharif family in London, owns property worth around 10 million pounds in Central London. This does not include the value of the company's offices. Hasan Nawaz Sharif, son of PML(N)'s Chief Nawaz Sharif, is officially listed as the director of company.

The company's listed address was Stanhope House, Stanhope Place, Marble Arch – one of the city's priciest neighbourhoods, subsequently moved to Tower Bridge House on St Katherine's Way in November 2007 – a much more upscale property located at River Thame's bank.

Known and declared properties included Flat 8 Burwood Place London W2 worth £700,000 (Rs 96.6 million); Flat 9 Burwood Place London W2 worth £900,000 (Rs 124.2 million); 10 Duke Mansions, Duke Street London W1 worth £1,495,000 (Rs 206.31 million); Flat 12a, 118 Park Lane Mayfair London SW1 worth £475,000 (Rs 65.55 million); Flat 2, 36 Green Street London W1 worth £800,000 (Rs 110.4 million); and, 117 Gloucester Place London W1 (value not yet listed); a piece of real estate near the Buckingham Palace valued at £ 4,450,000.]

Unknown, hidden or 'benami' properties might be worth millions of pounds or billions of rupees more but the only director of the company which held these assets was the son of Nawaz Sharif who had given Rs 5000 as tax in Pakistan during the same corresponding period. In UK a single person cannot own or hold so much wealth but could our beloved judiciary of Pakistan know that how much bank loans were got written off by the Sharifs throughout his power play during 1985-1999; most of the Chief Justices like Nasim H Shah, Saeeduzzaman Siddiqui and Iftikhar Chaudhry can be seen in their pockets.

Coming back, the PML(N) won a Supreme Court battle in August 2007 against ban of Sharifs. They announced their come back home on 10th September to challenge Gen Musharraf. Hariri said they would like to see Nawaz Sharif honour his exile commitment. Gen Musharraf had also conveyed Sharifs through Pakistan's Consulates in Saudi Arabia, to abide by the agreement as his return would destabilize the political environment ahead of general elections expected in next five months.

Gen Musharraf's government held the stance that:

'They should honour their commitment. Their commitment was with the leadership of a third country which has very close ties with Pakistan. If Nawaz Sharif breaks this commitment he will create a bad perception about Pakistan in the Middle East.'

In the meantime the Army regime had also manoeuvred to get from a concerned anti-terrorism court at Lahore, arrest warrants of Shahbaz Sharif in a murder case which was then lying there pending trial. The military government had also pleaded for Nawaz Sharif's arrest warrants on corruption charges before another accountability court. Therefore, the military government, NAB, FIA and the police were fully 'equipped' to deal with untimely arrival of Sharifs.

On an earlier occasion, Prime Minister Shaukat Aziz of PML(Q) had vowed in an interview dated 2nd September 2007 at Islamabad that:

> 'Benazir Bhutto and Nawaz Sharif may be constitutionally barred from contesting elections and should only return after the ballot.'

Benazir Bhutto was living in self- exile in Dubai and London since 1998.

Coming back; as per ARY One World's TV news, an officer of National Accountability Bureau (NAB) had read out the corruption charges to Nawaz Sharif in the airport lounge. The former PM heard the charges with patience but gone a little pale, felt embarrassed, tried to argue with the NAB team which mainly smiled but remaining silent. Nawaz Sharif thought for a while and gave consent to fly back to Saudia instead of going to Adyala jail or the Attock Fort again.

Earlier in May 2004, Shahbaz Sharif had also tried once to land at Lahore Airport but was forcibly deported back immediately after. At that time he was shown, by a senior ISI officer, the purported written agreement which had allowed the Sharif family to secure their exile to Saudi Arabia. To subdue much trumpeted public debate on whether such an agreement actually did exist or not, the ISI officer had also shown that agreement to a number of influential journalists then present at the Lahore Airport.

The **Times of India dated 20th November 2010** had also confirmed that an agreement was in place. The paper published the news as:

> 'An unpublicised agreement between Nawaz Sharif and the Saudi Arabian government that provided for the former Pakistani premier to stay away from active politics in return for the dropping of criminal charges against him is set to expire in next 12 days. The country is agog with speculation as to what steps the PML(N) strongman will take once his commitment is over. The agreement, signed by Sharif and the Saudi royal family, was valid for 10 years and barred him from taking part in active politics during this period.'

What really happened was that when Nawaz Sharif was found guilty of charges placed on him and on 6th April 2000 he was sentenced for life imprisonment twice, the government prosecutors vowed to launch an appeal in the higher court urging that *'why Nawaz Sharif should not be given death penalty'*. His friends and mentors in the Saudi royal family became perturbed when they learnt about the perspective appeal.

Worried, the Saudis wanted to be reassured by Gen Musharraf that the deposed prime minister would not meet the same fate as had his predecessor Z A Bhutto in April 1979.

The Saudis resolved the issue by pressurising Gen Musharraf into accepting a deal whereby Nawaz Sharif would be released by him on the condition that he and his family would live in exile in Saudi Arabia for 10 years. And so on the 10th December 2000, Nawaz Sharif along with his 18 family members, truckload of suitcases full of jewellery & dollars and tens rolls of Persian carpets left for Jeddah on a Royal Saudi plane.

From all accounts it appears that the deal between Gen Musharraf and the Saudis had initially been a verbal one. However, later when Gen Musharraf came under local media pressure to explain the deal he took the precautionary measures of requesting the Saudis to confirm the deal in writing. Thus a document was prepared & delivered to the General.

The journalists who had seen the documents confirmed that:

> *'It consisted of a few papers on the Saudi Arabian Interior Ministry's letterhead listing out a number of conditions which were signed by Nawaz Sharif and countersigned by Prince Nayef bin Abdul Aziz, the Saudi Minister of the Interior.'*

Having given hope of preventing Nawaz Sharif and Shahbaz Sharif from returning to Pakistan on the basis of the Saudi agreement, Gen Musharraf's government petitioned the NAB Court at Rawalpindi on 3rd August 2007 to reopen three cases against the two Sharif brothers and other members of their family, which had been filed with the court in 2000, but were shelved in record room after the Sharif family's departure to Saudi Arabia. The cases were related to:

• Hudaibiya Paper Mill

• Ittefaque Foundries

• The Sharif family's 50 acre real estate in Raiwind

According to the prosecution these cases involved charges of *'wilful* 'default and fake documentation against Sharif and his family members.

The fact remains that though the Supreme Court had given verdict in favour of Nawaz Sharif and his family members in 2007 on the basis that a citizen could not be barred to come in his own country, Pakistan, but the historians would also raise the following questions:

- When Nawaz Sharif left the country on 10th December 2000, he was undergoing two sentences each of life imprisonment, then under what law that punishment could be overlooked. Where were the superior courts then to take notice of it.

- If Nawaz Sharif was given the facility of 'sentences taken back' under a Saudi sponsored deal, then why the same facility was not extended to all the prisoners of Pakistan. Had the courts ever pondered then that the rich were getting relaxations whereas the poor were left in prisons to decay. Was the principles of 'rule of law' and 'equality for all' were considered by the superior courts.

- Had any superior court taken *suo moto* notice of the issue then written extensively in newspapers with respect to the Saudi Contract of remaining away for ten years.

- Had the judiciary then taken notice of their 'punishment system' which was selective for some one amounting to twisting the law as the Army Generals wanted?

The societies are bound to perish when there are such glaring examples of 'selective justice' available abundantly on record and the judiciary ignores them.

(Part of this essay published at www.Pakspectator.com
on 10th September 2011)

Scenario 29

GEN MUSHARRAF TRAPPED IN 9/11 EVENT (2001):

Unlike Gen Ziaul Haq, who used to speak very often that:

'After 90 days he would hold general elections and quit'.

Gen Musharraf usually proclaimed, referring to his televised speech of October 1999, saying that:

'I am a soldier, I don't believe in sharing power. I believe in the unity of command'.

He had rarely disguised his desire to exercise absolute control over state power. In August 2001, he had named himself President in 'the national interest'. Episode of 'Nine Eleven' in America provided him an opportunity to strengthen his grip over political affairs in Pakistan. Gen Musharraf, sensing an opportunity to secure international acceptance for his coup (of October 1999), quickly agreed to place Pakistan in the lap of American sponsored 'war on terror' coalition.

The US Congress waived democracy sanctions imposed under Section 508 of the US Foreign Operations Appropriations Act after the military coup of 12th October 1999 as well as those which were thrust upon Pakistan after its nuclear tests of 28th May 1998.

Japan and European donors followed America, rescheduling loans and extending grants in aid. International support boosted Gen Musharraf's domestic standing, providing him the chance to win confidence of the general populace within the country. He gained more strength; thus on 6th October 2001, the day America launched its first military attack on Afghanistan, Gen Musharraf extended his tenure as Chief of the Army Staff (COAS) for an indefinite period pushing aside all the prevailing rules, norms and traditions of army.

In Pakistan military interventions have usually been undertaken in response to notions of perceived national crises, therefore, to overcome the problems associated with legitimacy the military rulers *'tend to look for institutional mechanisms that can prolong their rule and give it a stable and permanent legitimate foundation'*. The constitutional manipulators and twisters like Sharifuddin Pirzada were always available to them suggesting legal and constitutional instruments for *'neutralization of [existing] political arena and subordination of the state to the military hierarchy'.*

For Gen Musharraf, the judiciary functioned as a subsumed institution for military; it was a general perception available on record.

The judiciary, instead of dragging those so called legal experts associated with proactive Generals to face treason charges under Article 6 of the Constitution, used to seek 'guidance' from them in issuing legitimacy in favour of their own manufactured charters of coercion like Legal Framework Order (LFO). By putting guns on the shoulders of such legal 'Mir Jaffers' and their brother judges sitting on rostrums to approve their suggestions, the military rulers like Gen Musharraf used to feel honour to dismiss the elected government, dissolve the national assembly, appoint military services chiefs and approve appointments to the judiciary.

On 20th June 2001, Irshad Hassan Khan, Chief Justice of Pakistan, the principal keeper of law and the supreme provider of justice in the country, administered the oath of office swearing in Gen Musharraf as President of Pakistan while he was in the uniform of an Army Chief. Both had walked over the Constitutional provisions.

General Justice is now a sixty-two years story where the legislative pillar of the state has been a consistent looser. Justice Muhammad Munir decided in favour of a General. Justice Anwarul Haq decided in favour of a General and Justice Irshad Hassan Khan decided in favour of a General and more to come perhaps.

After 9/11, Gen Musharraf was conveyed a threat that:

'*If you want to live in 21st century come with America otherwise you would be pushed into the stone age.*'

Those were all threats. The discussion broke down in media that what was the other option available. The subsequent events proved that the whole game was fabricated to target and take control of the Islamic world through Iraq and Pakistan. The attack on Twin Towers was the starting point of the wholesome game. Pakistan had faced such situations before but handled in a fine way conveying correct message for its enemies of international stature.

Compare that threat with that similar kind of situation which Pakistan had faced earlier. In mid 1980s Pakistan got information that certain

Israeli pilots were performing rehearsals in remote areas of Rajasthan (India) using Indian Air Force planes probably aiming at Kahuta Nuclear Plant. Pakistan had to convey very clear messages to both India and Israel to correct their thinking and wind up all such practices otherwise 'would be dealt with relentlessly'.

Though Pakistan was not a proclaimed nuclear power then but a lucid communication was made that:

> *'Pakistan keeps **that thing** and we would not hesitate to use it wherever needed'.*

Rajiv Ghandhi, the Indian Prime Minister then, went so embarrassed that he not only called off the Rajasthan exercises and despatched the Israeli pilots back immediately but during the next SAARC Conference himself offered Gen Ziaul Haq to mutually sign a bilateral agreement for not attacking each other's nuclear arsenals.

Similarly Israel was loudly told that:

> *'Pakistan would not bother that from which side planes are coming, from east or west, but we'll teach you a lesson **lest Pakistan should do that job for first and last time but we'll do**. Pakistan should not be taken as Iraq. We have enough material to destroy your whole country at least.'*

It was an excessively harsh message for a country which itself had surfaced on globe as a result of 'terror' phenomenon but their Indian friends had read in between the lines.

The nations have to take such ultimate decisions at times to keep its survival intact. There are no two opinions that Gen Musharraf had to take that decision to neutralize the threats after 9/11 episode and to divert the first possible American attack on Pakistan but should not have taken it as a permanent policy for all times to come. Otherwise, in army there exists a standing rule that while formulating a policy or plan an operation, the commander has to mark a line which is not to be crossed at any cost. If you cross that line or limit you sometimes go 180 angles opposite to the determined goals and objectives.

The same happened with Pakistan in the contemporary Afghan War on Terror (WOT) in which due to Gen Musharraf's short sightedness, we lost every thing. It was not our war and there were no soviets in Afghanistan to be expelled away.

Gen Musharraf in fact could not understand the hidden American plans behind the WOT slogans through which the US wanted to swallow Iraq and Pakistan; nothing doing with Afghanistan. We went too far against the normal terms of relationship between two independent states.

There was no logic in obeying any American order blindly which was not implemented in their own states. We handed them over Yousaf Ramzi, Amil Kansi, Eqbal Beg, Ayub Afridi and Anwar Khatak like people for what; just to get few thousand dollars that too through recommendations of Rehman Malik, the CIA's paid and planted person in Pakistan's bureaucracy since 1995. The said acts were not done through any acceptable rule, law or procedure of Pakistan nor of America even.

We imported every kind of terrorism, bomb blasts, suicidal bombers and terrorists in our country amidst loss of lives and economy for nothing. What kind of decisions we had made and what commitments we are sticking to, that too with historical liars.

Exactly a decade back, on **19th September 2001**, Gen Musharraf addressed the nation, acknowledging that many Pakistanis were bitterly opposed to his policy of support for the US in its efforts to track down Osama Bin Laden and dealing with his Al-Qaeda. He made it clear that:

'The US plans are not an attack on Afghanistan or Islam'.

In fact it was an attack on both.

Gen Musharraf had told the utter lies in his televised address that:

"Thousands of lives have been lost in the wake of terrorism in America on which I, my government, and the whole Pakistani nation are deeply grieved. This terrorist incident has sent a wave of profound grief, indignation and a sense of revenge in the United States. Their target is Osama, the al-Qaeda and the Taliban. They also intend to launch a prolonged war against international terrorism.

There are three important things in which the United States is seeking our support. First, the exchange of intelligence and information; second, the use of our airspace; and third, they are asking for logistic support from us. I want to apprise you of our internal situation. In my opinion, it is the most delicate phase since 1971 and God forbid, [any miscalculation] may endanger our territorial integrity and our survival. Our nuclear strength and our Kashmir cause may be harmed. This is the worst case scenario.

The better side of it would be that we could emerge as a responsible and honourable nation and all our problems could diminish.

Our neighbouring country India has readily offered all their bases, facilities, and logistic support to the US and in turn wants from US to declare Pakistan a terrorist state. I only want to tell them in English: Lay off. Now in my view there are four critical concerns: Firstly, ensuring the country's security and stability from external threat; secondly our economy; thirdly our nuclear assets and fourthly the Kashmir cause. Pakistan comes first, everything else is secondary.

On this occasion, we have to make a strategic decision. Leaving aside questions of weakness of faith or cowardice, we should not invite trouble for nothing. The future of 140 million people cannot be jeopardized. What have I not done for Afghanistan and Taliban? Even now, we are trying our best to hold negotiations with them; I sent DG ISI with my personal letter to Mullah Omar. We are also telling the US to show restraint and balance in their intentions. We can influence decisions of the world community by standing with them.

I am only concerned about Pakistan but some people; some elements are trying to take advantage of this occasion to carry forward their personal agenda, their parties' agenda. I appeal to all the Pakistanis to show unity and solidarity and to protect the interests of the country. In conclusion, I would like to take leave after quoting this prayer of Moses as cited in the Taha chapter of the Holy Kora'an:

> *'My Lord! Expand my chest, make my work easy, and open the knot of my tongue, so that the people can understand what I say.' Long live Pakistan!"*

The government of Pakistan faced intense American pressure, while being threatened by a potentially violent domestic backlash from Islamic groups which opposed any form of assistance to US military retaliation against neighbouring Afghanistan's ruling Taliban militia and Osama who was taken as the prime suspect for terrorist attacks on New York and Washington on 11th September 2001.

Gen Musharraf in the 35-minute televised address to the nation also said that America had not completed its operational plan for a proposed attack on Afghanistan till then. To this extent the General was true because the first US attack on Afghanistan was launched on 6th October after full assurance of our ISI.

The world media forums had noted that most Pakistanis were deeply uncomfortable with the idea of allowing American forces on to their soil. Gen Musharraf also said he was asking America to provide evidence against Osama but admitted that Washington had not provided any detailed evidence of his involvement in the attack.

Here comes two versions: The western media (referring to daily *'the Telegraph' dated 20th September 2001*) had held that Osama had denied responsibility and the Taliban government of Afghanistan had stripped him of all communications equipment necessary to organise complex terrorist activities after America blamed him for the destruction of two American embassies in Africa three years ago.

The spokesmen of the Islamic groups in Pakistan had told the media that:

'The Taliban government in Afghanistan had held Osama with them but urged that the US authorities should convince them through international jurists that why Osama be handed over to America just against an allegation. The Taliban wanted cogent proof of Osama's involvement in 9/11 affairs. Osama was Taliban's guest; by virtue of Afghan traditions dear to them.' What was the actual truth, still unknown'. (Ref: **Jernailon Ki Syasat by Sohail Warroich P-182**)

Gen Musharraf received only muted support from Pakistan's mainstream politicians, intellectuals, editors and the armed forces but one Islamic group had vowed 'holy war' if Pakistan aided America. Gen Musharraf was in hot waters even before that crisis of 9/11. He had seized power in a bloodless coup two years ago, with the pledge that he would end Pakistan's endemic and crippling corruption but, instead of holding elections, he transformed himself from the 'Chief Executive' to a President in June 2001. However, the American President Bush had welcomed Gen Musharraf's speech, saying:

'It was an indication of the strong relationship between the United States and Pakistan to counter terrorism'.

Though there have been tens of movies, documentaries and books written in this context that the 9/11 event was not an actual tragedy; it was a fabricated act allegedly of some keenly fundamentalist Jews which did not even form a part of mainstream American stake holders in politics or economy. No concerted investigation has surfaced yet nor have the American governments ever seriously tried to answer hundreds of simple questions from the American intelligentsia.

Lt Gen Hamid Gul, once added some more points in that long list during an interview published in *'Jang' of 19th November 2001,* urging:

- When the first plane collided with Twin towers, why the US Air Force could not get alert through its own 'watch system'?

- Why the world's best Air Force could only move after 75 minutes of getting 'Alert Signal' despite the fact on record that President Bush had issued that signal for American Forces just ten minutes after the first attack on Twin Towers [it was not lazyness].

- Despite such a grave failure, President Bush went to CIA HQ to pat 'certain people'[who were they actually].

- For complete one hour, three planes were changing directions in air, why the Air Traffic Control Tower could not take notice of it.

- During routine enquiries of 9/11 episode, what explanation came from Air Traffic Control people in this respect; were they thoroughly examined.

- Still there is no enquiry on record that why the 'Warning Switch' of Pentagon was turned off and who had done so and for what purpose and on whose ultimate instructions.

- Who got benefited from the 9/11 episode; Muslims or Jews or Afghanis or Al-Qaeda or America itself?

- What conclusive evidence had come up that the Muslims were responsible for it and if so, the Pakistanis or Afghanis.

- The named culprits were from Middle Eastern origin then why Afghanistan and Pakistan were selected for punishment.

- Where lies that Air Training School in the world where a pilot of Boeing 757 becomes so expert within six months that he could fly so accurately through sky-high buildings of New York and collides with Twin Towers such precisely without Air Traffic Control's guidance as per practice.

The above observations and many more had come on media record during the first week of 9/11 event. Gen Musharraf had also realised that and that was why he had conveyed through his speech of 19th September that Pakistan would not follow the US blindly. Later he swirled away from his promise with the nation and fell in America's lap like a broken feather. In those moments of distress he should have behaved like a statesman and:

- Gen Musharraf should have pressed Americans through diplomatic means to forward proof of involvement of Osama or Taliban in 9/11 disaster.

- Gen Musharraf should have called the expert jurists to guide him under international obligations to counteract or deal with those baseless accusations whatsoever.

- Gen Musharraf should have consulted China first for having their confidence to counter the American pressure on issues in which Pakistan was not directly involved.

[Pakistan approached China but much after making commitment with America. Then the Chinese government had refused to give consent for Pakistan Delegation's visit to Beijing. They politely told Gen Musharraf to see the Chinese Ambassador in Islamabad.]

- Gen Musharraf could also request the international Jurist's body at Geneva for opinion and guidance amidst such allegations for which Pakistan was not a party.

- Gen Musharraf should have called a meeting of OIC (organisation of Islamic Countries) to agitate them in the name of Islam which was being targeted then.

[The tragedy: that there was an OIC meeting in routine those days but, instead of asking for their diplomatic help, Gen Musharraf's delegation conveyed them, just 36 hours before meeting, that Pakistan had got enough evidence of Osama & Taliban's involvement.]

Instead of raising hue & cry that some people are with me and some against me in Pakistan, Gen Musharraf should have sent a delegation to pope for want of interference. He should have told Americans bluntly that he was not even an elected representative of the nation; so if the people came out in streets against his un-realistic decisions, he would not find a place to hide [rather take him to gallows].

Referring to [Washington Blogs borrowed by] *'A True Pakistani' placed at www.Pakspectator.com dated 21st September 2011*; it is the truth that 'war on terrorism' produced more terrorists. Intelligent persons could think that American treatment of the Muslim world could have produced violent and vengeful anti-Americanism.

For over 50 years the successive American administrations, for the sake of geopolitical hegemony and preferential access to resources, have backed brutal dictators, subverted governments, and invaded and occupied countries as it suited their agenda of 'world leadership'. Power and oil were the major reasons [rather goals].

The 9/11 event was also a step towards intensifying of American lust for more, but the facts ultimately surfaced with odd stories. 1500 Architects and Engineers have already disproved US official claims. 48% of Americans want a fresh investigation and they do not buy their own government's state lies at all. See some glimpses what the Americans themselves believe:

- The 9/11 Commission's Co-Chairs said: *'they knew that military officials misrepresented the facts to the Commission, and the Commission considered recommending criminal charges for such false statements'.*

- The 9/11 Commission's Co-Chair Lee Hamilton said: *'I don't believe for a minute we got everything right; the people should keep asking questions about 9/11, and that the debate should continue'.*

- The 9/11 Commission's Member Timothy Roemer said: *'we were extremely frustrated with the false statements we were getting'.*

- The 9/11 Commission's Member Max Cleland resigned from the Commission, stating: *'It is a national scandal; this investigation is now compromised; and one of these days we will have to get the full story because the 9/11 issue is so important to America. But this White House wants to cover it up'.*

- The 9/11 Commission's Member Bob Kerrey said: *'there are ample reasons to suspect that there may be some alternative to what we outlined in our version; we didn't have access; the investigation depended too heavily on the accounts of Al Qaeda detainees who were physically coerced into talking and making false admissions'.*

- The Senior Counsel to the 9/11 Commission, John Farmer, said:

  'At some level of the government, at some point in time…there was an agreement not to tell the truth about what happened.

I was shocked at how different the truth was from the way it was described .... The tapes told a radically different story from what had been told to us and the public for two years....

This is not spin. This is not true. It's almost a culture of concealment, for lack of a better word. There were interviews made at the FAA's New York Centre the night of 9/11 and those tapes were destroyed; CIA tapes of the interrogations were destroyed.

The story of 9/11 itself, to put it mildly, was distorted and was completely different from the way things happened'.

- Former military analyst Daniel Ellsberg said:

'The case of a certain 9/11 whistleblower is far more explosive than the Pentagon Papers. The government is ordering the media to cover up her allegations about 9/11.

Some of the claims concerning government involvement in 9/11 are credible, that very serious questions have been raised about what they [US government officials] knew beforehand and how much involvement there might have been, that engineering 9/11 would not be humanly or psychologically beyond the scope of the current administration, and that there's enough evidence to justify a new, 'hard-hitting' investigation into 9/11 with testimony taken under oath.'

- A 27-year CIA veteran, Raymond McGovern, who chaired National Intelligence Estimates and personally delivered intelligence briefings to Presidents Reagan and George Bush, their Vice Presidents, Secretaries of State, the Joint Chiefs of Staff, and many other senior government officials said: *'I think at simplest terms, there's a cover-up. The 9/11 Report is a joke'.* Mostly Americans believed him.

- A 29-year CIA veteran, former National Intelligence Officer (NIO) and former Director of the CIA's Office of Regional and Political Analysis, William Bill Christison said: *'I now think there is persuasive evidence that the events of September did not unfold as the Bush administration and 9/11 Commission would have us believe.'*

- A number of intelligence officials, including a CIA Operations Officer who co-chaired a CIA multi-agency task force, named Lynne Larkin, sent a joint letter to Congress expressing their concerns about *'serious shortcomings, omissions and major flaws'* in the 9/11 Commission

Report and offering their services for a new investigation; however, ignored.

- A decorated 20-year CIA veteran and prize winning investigative reporter Seymour Hersh, called the best on-ground field officer in the Middle East and whose astounding career formed the script for the Academy Award winning motion picture Syriana, Robert Baer said: *'the evidence points at 9/11 having had aspects of being an inside job'*.

- The Division Chief of the CIA's Office of Soviet Affairs, who served as Senior Analyst from 1966 – 1990, served as Professor of International Security at the National War College from 1986 – 2004, Melvin Goodman said: *'the final [9/11 Commission] report is ultimately a cover-up'*.

- The Co-Chair of the Congressional Inquiry into 9/11 event and former Head of the Senate Intelligence Committee, Bob Graham, told: *'an FBI informant had hosted and rented a room to two hijackers in 2000 and that, when the Inquiry sought to interview the informant, the FBI refused outright, and then sent him to an unknown location, and that a high-level FBI official stated these blocking manoeuvres were undertaken under orders from the White House'*.

- Democratic US Senator Patrick Leahy said: *'the two questions that the congress will not ask . . . is why 9/11 happened on George Bush's watch when he had clear warnings that it was going to happen? Why did they allow it to happen?'*

- Republican Congressman Ron Paul called for a new 9/11 investigation stating: *'we see the [9/11] investigations that have been done so far as more or less cover-up and no real explanation of what went on'*.

- Democratic Congressman Dennis Kucinich hinted: *'we aren't being told the truth about 9/11'*.

- Republican Congressman Jason Chafetz said: *'we need to be vigilant and continue to investigate 9/11'*.

- Democratic Senator Mike Gravel stated: *'he supports a new 9/11 investigation and that we don't know the truth about 9/11'*.

- Republican Senator Lincoln Chaffee endorsed a new 9/11 investigation.

- Democratic Congressman Dan Hamburg did not believe the official version of events.

- Republican Congressman and senior member of the House Armed Services Committee, who had also served for six years as the Chairman of the Military Research and Development Subcommittee, Curt Weldon, had explicitly shown that:

  'The US tracked hijackers before 9/11, is open to hearing information about explosives in the Twin Towers, and is open to the possibility that 9/11 was an inside job.'

- The Commanding General of US European Command and Supreme Allied Commander Europe, decorated with the Bronze Star, Silver Star and Purple Heart, General Wesley Clark, said:

  'We've never finished the investigation of 9/11 and whether the administration actually misused the intelligence information it had. The evidence seems pretty clear to me. I've seen that for a long time'.

- Former Deputy Secretary for Intelligence and Warning under Presidents Nixon, Ford, and Carter, Morton Goulder; the former Deputy Director to the White House Task Force on Terrorism, Edward L. Peck and former US Department of State Foreign Service Officer, J. Michael Springmann, had jointly called for a new investigation into 9/11.

- Former Federal Prosecutor, Office of Special Investigations, US Department of Justice under Presidents Jimmy Carter and Ronald Reagan; former US Army Intelligence officer and celebrated media commentator on terrorism and intelligence services, John Loftus said:

  'The information provided by European intelligence services prior to 9/11 was so extensive that it is no longer possible for either the CIA or FBI to assert a defence of incompetence'.

- The Group Director on matters of the national security in the US Government Accountability Office said that President Bush did not respond to unprecedented warnings of the 9/11 disaster and conducted a massive cover-up instead of accepting responsibility.

- Deputy Assistant Secretary of Defence under President Ronald Reagan, Col. Ronald D. Ray, said: 'the official story of 9/11 is of the dog that doesn't hunt'.

- Several key employees for the Defence Department said that the government covered up their testimony about tracking Mohammed Atta before 9/11.

- The former director of the FBI, Louis Freeh, said: *'there was a cover up by the 9/11 Commission'*.

Numerous other politicians, judges, legal scholars, and attorneys also question at least some aspects of the government's version of 9/11. *'It was all drama and will remain a drama';* Beyond doubt! Gen Musharraf was trapped in 9/11 accusation knowingly or due to his in-built cowardice for which the whole nation suffered.

It was all drama and will remain a drama, no difference if America replays a tape of it every year at Zero Point New York or through media campaigns.

[Part of this essay was published at www.Pakspectator.com
dated 21st September 2011]

Scenario 30

MUSHARRAF – THE 'BRUTUS' OF 2000-01:

Gen Musharraf brought key changes in his army set-up to prolong his stay in power, moved certain known figures from strategic seats to comparatively ineffective places to demonstrate strength to be seen and realized by his American masters and to be felt by the intelligentsia in the country as well. These changes were done at senior levels of the army leadership and the most significant was of 31st August 2000. It was the transfer of Lt Gen Mohammad Aziz from the post of Chief of the General Staff (CGS) in the GHQ Rawalpindi to that of Commander 4 Corps Lahore. Lt Gen Mohammad Yusaf Khan, Commander 2 Corps Multan, was moved to GHQ as the new CGS.

The changes, which were made a few days before the departure of Gen Musharraf to New York in 2000 to attend the UN Millennium summit, had three connotations:

- The shifting of Lt Gen Aziz was a pre-emptive move by Gen Musharraf to prevent any possible threat to his position from him.
- It was a conciliatory move to dispel US concerns over his role in assisting the Islamic extremist organizations.

  [*The Pentagon had viewed Lt Gen M Aziz as the evil genius of the military regime and as a godfather of the Taliban of Afghanistan and the 300,000-strong armed jehadist militants of Pakistan belonging to different Islamic schools of thought*]
- Gen Musharraf knew that in the backdrop of US disliking for Lt Gen Aziz it might be difficult for him to secure US support for resumption of the IMF assistance and re-scheduling of Pakistan's external debts.

An apparent impression conveyed to the media was that it was a normal transfer to give Lt Gen Aziz an experience as a Corps Commander without which he would be ineligible for consideration as the next COAS, which was a fact otherwise. The fact remains that no Pakistani army chief can seize and sustain himself in power without the support of the CGS who controls the Directorates-General of Military Intelligence and Military Operations, and the GOC 10 Corps, Rawalpindi.

In 2001, another development took place. Promoted to the ranks of four star Generals, Lt Gen M Yusaf, Chief of the General Staff (CGS), was appointed Vice Chief of Army Staff and Lt Gen M Aziz Khan, Commander 4 Corps at Lahore was elevated to the post of Chairman Joint Chiefs of Staff Committee (JCSC) on 7th October 2001. Gen Musharraf's tenure as COAS had expired the same day but his retirement as COAS could not take effect due to the Supreme Court's Judgement mandating him to complete his 'reforms' and to stay for three years till 12th October 2002.

[*It was a historical blunder on the part of the Supreme Court of Pakistan (J Irshad Hasan Khan was the Chief Justice) that the court, while writing judgment of Zafar Ali Shah Case on 12th May 2000, had given three years stay to Gen Musharraf in the name of 'eradicating corruption' which relief was not even asked for. Perhaps it was a secret deal between the two top maligned minds because after retirement Chief Justice Irshad Hasan Khan was made the Chief Election Commissioner of Pakistan; a constitutional post.*]

The most significant change appeared with the un-ceremonial exit of Lt Gen Mahmud Ahmed, the chief of the ISI, who (allegedly forced to get) resigned on 8th October 2001 because of differences over the reshuffling in the military high command.

[*Gen Mahmud was known to visit the United States regularly during his time as the head of ISI consulting senior officials in the US administration in the weeks before 9/11. In fact, he was with a Congressman Porter Goss and Democratic Senator Bob Graham in Washington, discussing Osama over breakfast, when the attacks of 11th September 2001 happened. He was immediately called into meetings with American officials where demands of Pakistani cooperation were made and he was told to convey this to the Pakistani government.*]

One could see the dreadful advice of the US bosses and their immense pressure behind Lt Gen Mahmud's quit in the backdrop of America's first attack launched on Afghanistan on 6th October 2001. A highly ambitious officer, Pakistan's chief spymaster, virtually ran Pakistan's Afghan policy, though had been supporting the Taliban regime but later he withdrew him back in the light of Gen Musharraf's obligations towards US after 9/11 episode of attack on Twin Towers.

In dirty power play, even then Lt Gen Mahmud could not earn trust of his army chief. Considered the second most powerful member of the military junta, he was a key player in the military coup of 12th October

1999 that had brought Gen Musharraf to power. As the then Corps Commander Rawalpindi, he was one of the two Generals who ordered the troops to move into the PM's official residence and arrest Nawaz Sharif, the Prime Minister. His loyalty was above board but not believed and depended by Gen Musharraf.

In the monthly *'Newsline Karachi' of October 2001*, Zahid Hussain had expressed his views as:

> *'Despite his hardline views on other issues, Lt Gen Mahmud went along with Gen Musharraf on withdrawing support from the then Taliban regime. The former ISI chief who was in America during the days of 11th September terrorist attack, led talks with senior US officials on Pakistan's cooperation with the US anti-terrorism campaign. He also went to Afghanistan twice before his departure (to Washington) to persuade the Taliban government to accede to international demands to surrender Osama bin Laden.'*

Gen Musharraf had consolidated his power base as he kicked out his three top Generals known for their hard-line Islamic views and the changes were rightly made to coincide with American and British attack on Afghanistan. It was seen as a part of Gen Musharraf's plan to bring a fresh team of liberal loyalists, who could support his pro-west policy, into key positions of army at whatever price.

The shake-up of 2001 in the army high command had changed the entire composition of the Pakistan army which had ruled the country since seizing power in October 1999. The re-assignment of Lt Gen Aziz to a weak, feeble and largely ceremonial post of Chairman, Joint Chiefs of Staff Committee, had consolidated Gen Musharraf's position that had emerged as the sole power centre.

The bearded Lt Gen Aziz was also the main player in the 1999 military coup and was corps commander Lahore before being elevated to his new position which kept him out of the decision-making process.

A firm conservative, Lt Gen Aziz had significant influence in determining Pakistan's policy on Kashmir. There had been a sharp divergence of views particularly on Kashmir, Afghanistan, signing of the Comprehensive Test Ban Treaty (CTBT) and some other issues among the then Generals of Pakistan Army. The hardliner Generals were alleged to likely block Gen Musharraf's more liberal and pragmatic policies, with LT Gen M Aziz and some other Generals suspecting to:

'Prevent Pakistan from showing any flexibility in its policy of supporting Islamic militancy in Kashmir, the then Taliban regime in Afghanistan and Afghan fighting factions.'

It was not surprising that some of the Islamic political parties had publicly aligned themselves with Lt Gen Aziz and some other hardliners whom they described as 'pro-jihad' Generals. This trio formed the nucleus of the ruling junta which also included Lt Gen Muzaffar Usmani, then Deputy Chief of the Army Staff, yet another bearded General known for his more Islamic fundamentalist views who had also been retired in the reshuffle. Every decision taken by Gen Musharraf's Cabinet and the National Security Council (NSC) once had to be stamped by these Generals; they were so in.

Gen Musharraf had felt bound to consult the above Generals in all policies and military decisions before according approval for implementation. He, however, went successful in countering the challenges from the then allegedly pro-Taliban Islamic fundamentalists and Kashmiri fighters, while the army appeared to be stood united behind him.

Looking back a bit earlier, one of the first acts of Gen Musharraf, after his appointment as the COAS by the then Prime Minister Mr Nawaz Sharif in October 1998, was to move Lt Gen Aziz from the post of Deputy Director-General ISI dealing with Kashmir and Afghanistan, to the GHQ as the CGS. He then shifted Lt Gen Mahmood Ahmed (the then Commandant National Defense College) to command GOC 10 Corps, the most trusted one in army.

However, Gen Musharraf could not succeed in having his nominee selected as Director General of the ISI. The then PM Nawaz Sharif instead had appointed Lt Gen Ziauddin, belonging to a family of PML(N)'s loyalists, as the DG ISI, the most vulnerable slot.

Gen Musharraf did not want Lt Gen Ziauddin, an engineer by profession, to handle Kashmir and Afghanistan affairs as an ISI Chief. He disliked the later immensely and distrusted him as Mr Sharif's mole in the Pakistan Army. Gen Musharraf, therefore, transferred the Kashmir and Afghanistan operations of ISI to the DG MI and made Lt Gen Aziz as the CGS to deal with these sensitive affairs. The entire Kargil operation of 1999 was handled by Lt Gen Aziz and Lt Gen Ziauddin was not capable enough to have an air of its implementation.

The insiders also held that with the posting of Gen Ziauddin as DG ISI, the COAS, Gen Musharraf had immediately withdrawn the whole wing of internal/political affairs from ISI HQ and placed it with MI wing in the GHQ. The surveillance of political people, serving and otherwise, has been the main source of tension between the rulers and COAS since the last three decades. Nawaz Sharif had nothing to do much with Kashmir or Afghanistan affairs. The only strength of ISI near a political ruler is the department's role in political coercion.

The appointment of Lt Gen Aziz as the CGS had attracted considerable murmuring in ranks because he was the junior-most Lt General that time. It was a reflection of Gen Musharraf's trust in him. Previously, the tradition in the Pakistan army had been to appoint one of the seniors, if not the senior-most, Lt Generals as the CGS. Lt Gen Aziz's friendship with Gen Musharraf dated back to the days of Gen Ziaul-Haq in 1980s, when the two along with Maj Gen Mehmood Durrani, afterwards a dearest adviser of Gen Musharraf and his number one person in the United States, played an active role in training and arming of the Afghan Mujahideen in Afghanistan where they were blocking way of Russians.

Lt Gen Aziz was Gen Ziaul Haq's Deputy Military Secretary and, like Gen Musharraf, had also served in the Special Services Group (SSG), a commando force. The friendship between Gen Musharraf and Lt Gen Mahmood Ahmed dated back to the days of their career as young officers of an Artillery Regiment. All of them were close protégés of Lt Gen Hamid Gul, the then DG ISI, under Ms Benazir Bhutto during her first tenure as the Prime Minister during 1988-1990.

The idea of keeping the Indian security forces bleeding on Azad Jammu & Kashmir borders by employing strategic military tactics was their brain-child. This working relationship brought them close to the Islamic political parties and soon they were labelled as 'Mulla' Generals by the army contingents under their command.

It was Lt Gen M Aziz, Lt Gen Mahmud Ahmed and Lt Gen Usmani, who three had refused to accept Lt Gen Ziauddin as the COAS and staged a coup against Nawaz Sharif and seized power much before Gen Musharraf's plane landed at Karachi on 12th October 1999.

[On 12th day of October 1999, Lt Gen Mahmud had led 10 Corps troops (111 Brigade) into the PM House, after moving in SSG troops, which were hastily lifted by a helicopter earlier from Mangla Cantonment on orders of the CGS Lt Gen Aziz. It was Lt Gen Muzzafar Usmani as Commander 5 Corps Karachi, who took over the Airport to allow landing of the PIA aircraft in which the COAS was

travelling along with tens of other passengers, and which was dangerously low on fuel then.

Lt Gen M Aziz Khan as the CGS had masterminded the counter-coup which brought Gen Musharraf back as COAS. But when the moment of replacing Lt Gen Aziz cropped up, Gen Musharraf had selected Lt Gen Yusaf as CGS. The CGS slot is considered to be the most powerful in the Pakistan Army after that of the COAS, particularly because the elite SSG Brigade plus is under his direct control. Lt Gen Aziz was the one who had denied control of GHQ to the new team of Lt Gen Ziauddin Butt, the newly appointed Army Chief by the then PM Nawaz Sharif.]

The other Lt Generals ex-post facto approved the action of the three above mentioned Generals. Lt Gen Mahmud Ahmed and Lt Gen M Aziz Khan continued to enjoy the confidence of Gen Musharraf till the visit of President Clinton to Pakistan in March 2000. There were persistent reports of differences with Lt Gen Aziz, who strongly opposed any pressure on the then Taliban regime or Osama issue and any action against the Pakistan-based activities of organizations such as *Harkat ul Mujahideen*, the *Lashkar-e-Toiba* and the *Al Badr* etc.

Despite all, Gen Musharraf continued to enjoy the support of Lt Gens Yusaf and Usmani. There had been a speculation in high circles that Gen Musharraf wanted to displace Lt Gen Mahmud Ahmed from ISI and wanted to adjust Lt Gen Usmani as the DG ISI. This proposed move was perhaps based on the fact that when Gen Musharraf went to New York, he had asked Lt Gen Usmani to look after routine work of the COAS in the GHQ, indicating his confidence in the officer.

The critical moment in Gen Musharraf's presidency was 9/11 of 2001, when Washington suddenly and direly needed his support in the international anti-terrorism campaign and to crush the Taliban in Afghanistan. Thus he became a pivotal player on the world stage and a close ally, welcomed in Washington and London alike, as a statesman of international status and standing.

Getting benefit of this 9/11 situation and in the backdrop of American support Gen Musharraf had also played some of his hidden cards at home front. What he did with his closest companion Generals who brought him in power on 12th October 1999 can be judged from an article captioned as: *'Pakistani leader's attempt to rein in militants is met with defiance'*, by **Rory McCarthy** appeared in **The Guardian of 25th May 2002**:

'Hours after the September 11 attacks Washington had **ordered Islamabad** [one may ponder over the language] to halt unconditionally its long-criticised support for the Taliban regime in Afghanistan. Within days General Pervez Musharraf, Pakistan's straight-talking military dictator, called together his 12 or 13 most senior officers. Although he expects his Generals to speak freely at these meetings they rarely oppose the army chief's decisions.

This time the atmosphere was cold. Gen Musharraf laid out his proposal to support America in the imminent war against the Taliban and Osama bin Laden. There was, he told them, simply no other choice. Officially the public was told the officers supported Gen Musharraf unanimously. But now it has emerged that four of his most senior generals opposed him outright. ...... the four openly challenged the president's pro-US stance. In military terms it was a stunning display of disloyalty.

.... the angriest among the four that night was Lieutenant General Mehmood Ahmed, the religious hardliner who headed the ISI and was once Gen Musharraf's closest ally.

Three other Lieutenant Generals had joined his protest: Muzaffar Usmani, a corps commander (at Karachi) who was instrumental in orchestrating the coup of October 1999 that brought the army back to power; Jamshaid Gulzar Kiani, Commander the 10 Corps Rawalpindi; and Mohammad Aziz Khan, the Kashmir-born Lahore corps commander and a former ISI deputy chief.

Within a month the dissenters were silenced. Gen Ahmed and Gen Usmani were sacked. Gen Kiani lost his corps to become Adjutant-General (quite an unattractive post after corps job) while Gen Khan was promoted to the only theoretically powerful, but largely ceremonial, position of Chairman Joint Chiefs of Staff committee.

It was exactly what Washington wanted; firm leadership against the militant wing of the army.'

This event was better described by Eric Margolis, a famous defence analyst and columnist, in his communication that:

'I've felt certain sympathy for Gen. Musharraf, who overthrew .... Then came 9/11; the Bush Administration put a gun to Musharraf's head, ordering him to ditch Pakistan's Afghan ally, Taliban, open Pak *bases to US forces, arrest anti-American militants, and fire the capable nationalist officers - and close friends - who put him into power, Generals Aziz and Mahmoud.*

Obey, Washington warned Islamabad, or we will foreclose your loans, impose trade sanctions, cut off spare parts, and give India a green light to go after you. Tough Ziaul Haq, Pakistan's last military ruler would have stood up to American bullying.

Former Prime Minister Benazir Bhutto would have cleverly managed to somehow finesse Washington's threats. But Musharraf, with a near-bankrupt nation, and faced with what he viewed as a Hobson's choice between obedience and ruin, caved in to Washington's demands and became, overnight, its compliant servitor.' (Ref: Soldier of the RAJ by **Eric Margolis appeared on 30th June 2003** in www.EricMargolis.com)

Days and nights passed, the decisions were taken as per speculations but went un-implemented. Gen Musharraf continued to hold strength in the close army circles and had secretly opted to change his team one by one so that the stake-holders of politics would remain satisfied. General elections of 2002 were announced but under strict supervision and control of military sponsored teams.

Scenario 31

TWO MILITARY RULERS AT 180 ANGLES APART:

Gen Musharraf vs Gen Ziaul Haq:

In the last quarter of 2001, Gen Musharraf had consolidated his power base as he kicked out three top generals, Lt Gen Aziz, Lt Gen Mahmud Ahmed and Lt Gen Usmani, known for their hard-line Islamic views in a major shake up in the army top brass. The changes, which coincided with attack against Afghanistan by the American and NATO forces, was seen as a part of Gen Musharraf's plan to bring liberal loyalist Generals into key positions of the Pakistan's army set up.

The said lot of newly appointed senior officers were known for their thinking favouring pro-west policies. Gen Musharraf had gone too far to please the US President Mr Bush and his team in the name of participation in 'War on Terror'. His cooperation with the Americans were applauded and thus the *'TIME' magazine of 29th April 2006* included his name in 'top 100 personalities' of the world along with those who had influenced the world opinion most.

One can recall the history when Gen Ziaul Haq had managed to hang Z A Bhutto through judicial gimmicks, the Americans were quite happy over that 'act of bravery'. The Americans had declared Gen Ziaul Haq as their right hand statesman though the Russian threats to Afghanistan were not 'fully cleared' then. But what were their inner feelings about the General, following lines from a CIA report of 1982 (since declassified) would make it clear, and though may appeal someone as a balanced report:

- [*Pakistan's President Ziaul-Haq faces growing domestic problems but no immediate threat to his rule. Gen Ziaul Haq lacks an organized constituency outside the Army; however, he could find his hold on power challenged should an opposition emerge.*

- *Gen Ziaul Haq's visit to Washington will be paralleled by the arrival in Pakistan of the most visible symbol of the new US relationship; the first six of 40 F-16 fighter aircrafts.*

  Islamabad is aware that only the United States can offset Soviet pressures and provide Pakistan with the sophisticated weapons it needs. The US-Pakistan deal on economic aid and weapons sales undoubtedly has strengthened Pakistan's international position and restored some of its self-confidence.

- *Gen Ziaul Haq's hold on power remains firm for now, but his failure to fashion acceptable political institutions and win broad popular backing leave him vulnerable should he blunder, the economy stagnate, or a popular leader from masses suddenly emerge to unite the opposition.*

Although the opposition parties so far remain ineffective, there are signs of increased impatience with martial law and stronger calls for return to civilian government through elections. When change comes, it is likely to be abrupt and violent.

- *Ethnic tensions, especially in Balochistan, will continue to be an irritant, but do not threaten Pakistan's national integrity. Random terrorist actions are unlikely to bring about the downfall of the government. Terrorism weakens Gen Ziaul Haq's government to the extent that it undermines public confidence in the regime's ability to maintain public order.*

- *Gen Ziaul Haq is generally respected or at least tolerated, in Pakistan, but he arouses no strong enthusiasm. The political parties are in disarray and unable to muster any significant opposition.*

There is diffused dissatisfaction, however, with martial law, which has continued uninterrupted for over five years. Gen Ziaul Haq thus finds himself with no direct challengers, but without any broad based popular support to protect him if unrest develops.

- *Gen Ziaul haq does have the support of Pakistan's strongest institution, the Army. He has skilfully manipulated senior officer appointments to ensure a loyal senior officers corps to ensure his smooth running.*

The Pak-Army's influence now extends into almost all areas of the society, as serving and retired Army officers have been appointed to fill positions in the bureaucracy and state-run industries. The bureaucracy has vehemently opposed this activism.

That occasions some resentment, particularly among line officers, about the Army's continued martial law responsibilities and the abundant corruption. But the military men and commanders realize that their interests are bound up with Gen Ziaul Haq and chances that a sudden coup will depose him, are minimal.

- *Barring an assassin's bullet, President Gen Ziaul Haq probably will maintain his hold on government over the next year. We believe, however, that increasingly open public dissatisfaction with martial law and an uncertain economic climate could - over the next one to three years - confront Gen Ziaul Haq with the choice of facing serious unrest or opting for a civilian regime under Army tutelage. Although such a regime would lack a popular consensus, it might attract enough of the moderate opposition to give Gen Ziaul Haq more time to govern Pakistan.*

- *Nevertheless, recently there have been some signs of increased impatience within key pro-Zia constituencies over the continuation of martial law and stronger calls in the country for a return to civilian government through general elections (if held).*

  (Censored) the major opposition leaders are convinced the time is ripe to move against Gen Ziaul Haq. Some senior security officials believe the tide of public opinion is running against him and are increasingly sceptical about the regime's ability to contain possible internal disorders. Should the economy falter and affect the interests of the urban middle classes and their allies, opposition to Gen Ziaul Haq could increase rapidly.]

Just for a moment, if one inserts the name of Gen Musharraf where Gen Ziaul Haq's name is placed, the above statement of 1982 was holding well during 2001-2008. The CIA had not opted for a re-writing on Pakistan, they preferred to use a 'cut & paste' mechanism. The above excerpts clearly reflected that during Gen Musharraf's rule we had not moved ahead from 1982 situation. A well versed saying: **'A nation which lives through 'cut and paste' mode of history can't break the trajectory of its past.'** It mostly fits on Pakistan for all times.

Military, during Gen Musharraf's era, which was holding both power and guns, was not able to play a key role in shaping the future course of events. It should have proactively taken that its continued interference in politics and economy had weakened the Federation and its institutions as World Economic Forum's Global Competitiveness Report 2005 had (once more) indicated by rating quality of Pakistan's public institutions at 102 out of 104 countries.

Coming back to our original topic, in Pakistan, Lt Generals retire at the age of 57 or on completion of four years as Lt Generals, whichever is earlier. Gen Musharraf granted himself an extension in October 2001 when he was due for retirement as the COAS and was supposed to hand over power to an elected political leadership before 12th October 2002 (hats off to some corrupt minds of our superior judiciary), in accordance with a judgment of the Supreme Court. That day had never seen dawn, Gen Musharraf was there as COAS (+ President) while all threatening Lt Generals were sent home.

One shouldn't be surprised, if concerned over this prospect, the US had planned so. It made no difference to the US if Gen Musharraf had been continuing in power as the President in uniform or a non-political civilian, elected in a sham election, functioning as the Prime Minister so long as the things were delivered. This is what Gen Ziaul Haq did and that is what the present PPP regime is doing in association with the incumbent COAS Gen Kiyani.

For thirty six of its 63 year's existence Pakistan has been under military rule. The military has been responsible to a great extent for Pakistan's present impasse, though the politicians were also to be blamed for the similar follies. Throughout his rule of eight years, Gen Musharraf stressed his commitment to human rights, religious tolerance and a free press. But the time proved that all his steps moved to concentrate power in his own hands, and while he talked largely of accountability he had allowed no space for holding the army or any of his corrupt army officers accountable and all the superior judiciary remained silent indirectly providing strength to the illegal and illogical military rule.

During the two Afghan Wars, one fought by Gen Ziaul Haq in 1980s and the other handled by Gen Musharraf and PPP in 2000s, Pakistan's army and their commanders played two different roles, quite opposing and at 180 angles in their objectives. Both wars were fought on Afghan soil; the previous one was for helping Afghanis whereas the later was fought against them.

Keeping the political interpretations aside, one can say that the 1980's Afghan *Jihadi* war was planned and fought for the sake of Pakistan's self interests. Pakistan's intelligence had utilised his resources and men in the battle fields in a manner that ISI had surfaced as a powerful intelligence agency in the world. It is said that to curtail its power and to contain Pakistan's army to its size, the crash of August 1988 was planned and launched but still the people are astray that who was the beneficiary.

331

Ikram Sehgal had differentiated between the two army dictators [but then Gen Musharraf had just started his governance] in daily *'the News' dated 9th October 2001* saying that:

> 'Continuity demands that Gen Musharaf see out his full term as President starting from the day he leaves his office of COAS. As President he still remains the Supreme Commander of the Armed Forces. Unlike Gen Ziaul Haq who manipulated his subordinate appointments to remain in power, Gen Musharraf seems to be a self-confident product of his colleague's aspirations for a better Pakistan, as it appears.
>
> Does he need to hang onto various jobs out of a prime motivation of his own security? If I am not mistaken about the man's character he will not allow his colleagues and so-called friends to influence him to manipulate things very much as the late Gen Ziaul Haq did, instead he will boldly follow the full transparent route in processing the sanctity of appointments and tenures thereof in the Armed Forces.'

But, Mr Sehgal, Gen Musharraf did not allow his *'friends to manipulate things'*; however, he had simply preferred to lie down before the American President, CIA and Pentagon.

Referring to Irfan Siddiqui in daily *'Jang' dated 18th August 2011:*

- In the Afghan War of 1980s, Gen Ziaul Haq had opted to help the oppressed ones and to stand in front of a super power whereas in the second Afghan war, Gen Musharraf & PPP regimes exactly did the same but in reverse order.

- Gen Ziaul Haq was fighting against an aggressor then super power [Russia] whereas Gen Musharraf & PPP regimes preferred to stand by the assailant super power [America].

- Gen Ziaul Haq had taken decision for the sake of Islamic brotherhood keeping Afghanistan's geo political position in mind whereas Gen Musharraf & PPP governments took decisions for the sake of strengthening their own rule keeping America's obedience in sight.

- Gen Ziaul Haq had kept America at a distance despite utilizing their military and financial aid. No American military or political person was allowed to keep direct contact with Afghan Mujahideen. All ammunition or other aid was distributed through Pakistan's ISI and no US official could interfere in Pakistan's war policy or strategy.

Contrarily Gen Musharraf & PPP regimes placed Pakistan's military air bases, air space, naval coasts, road infrastructure, army and the ISI at the disposal of Americans.

- Gen Ziaul Haq and the then ISI had taken all the strategic decisions at their own to achieve their targets whereas Gen Musharraf and his subsequent PPP regime passed on their powers and prerogatives to Washington and the Americans made decisions to be acted upon by us.

- Gen Ziaul Haq remained involved in Afghan war for nine years but Pakistan was not converted into a battlefield whereas Gen Musharraf brought war into Pakistan and innocent blood of thousands of civilians and army men was visibly seen on our soils throughout seven years of war for his part and ensuing years of the PPP's rule.

- Gen Ziaul Haq ended all training camps in Afghanistan which were known as hostile to Pakistan but Gen Musharraf and the PPP regimes themselves aided Indian, Israeli, American and Afghan antagonistic groups to develop their anti-Pakistan training sites in both countries.

- Gen Ziaul Haq had continued developing Pakistan's nuclear program during his nine years of Afghan war whereas Gen Musharraf disgraced Dr Qadeer Khan, kept him in home custody. During his tenure and succeeding PPP's regime allowed Americans to speak almost daily that *'Pakistan's nuclear arsenal are not safe'*.

- Gen Ziaul Haq kept the whole nation involved in Afghan war whereas Gen Musharraf could not take the nation into confidence for a day even in connection with American crusade. During latter's eight years war followed by PPP's rule, hatred for Americans, as per various survey reports of 2010, had touched a level of 84% once, the all times low.

Furthermore, Gen Ziaul Haq had snubbed all those separatist movements which were being nurtured in Afghanistan with the help of Indian RAW but during Gen Musharraf's & PPP regimes all those nurseries of autonomist and nationalist groups got a new life again. The spill of hard luck for general populace of Pakistan continues as since the end of latest saga of military rule in 2008, the succeeding PPP regime proved that political leadership is equally awful, terrible, dreadful, appalling and horrific.

It is for the historians and students of current affairs to ascertain that how the two military rulers had behaved in our recent past.

www.ingramcontent.com/pod-product-compliance
Lightning Source LLC
Chambersburg PA
CBHW031145270326
41931CB00006B/147